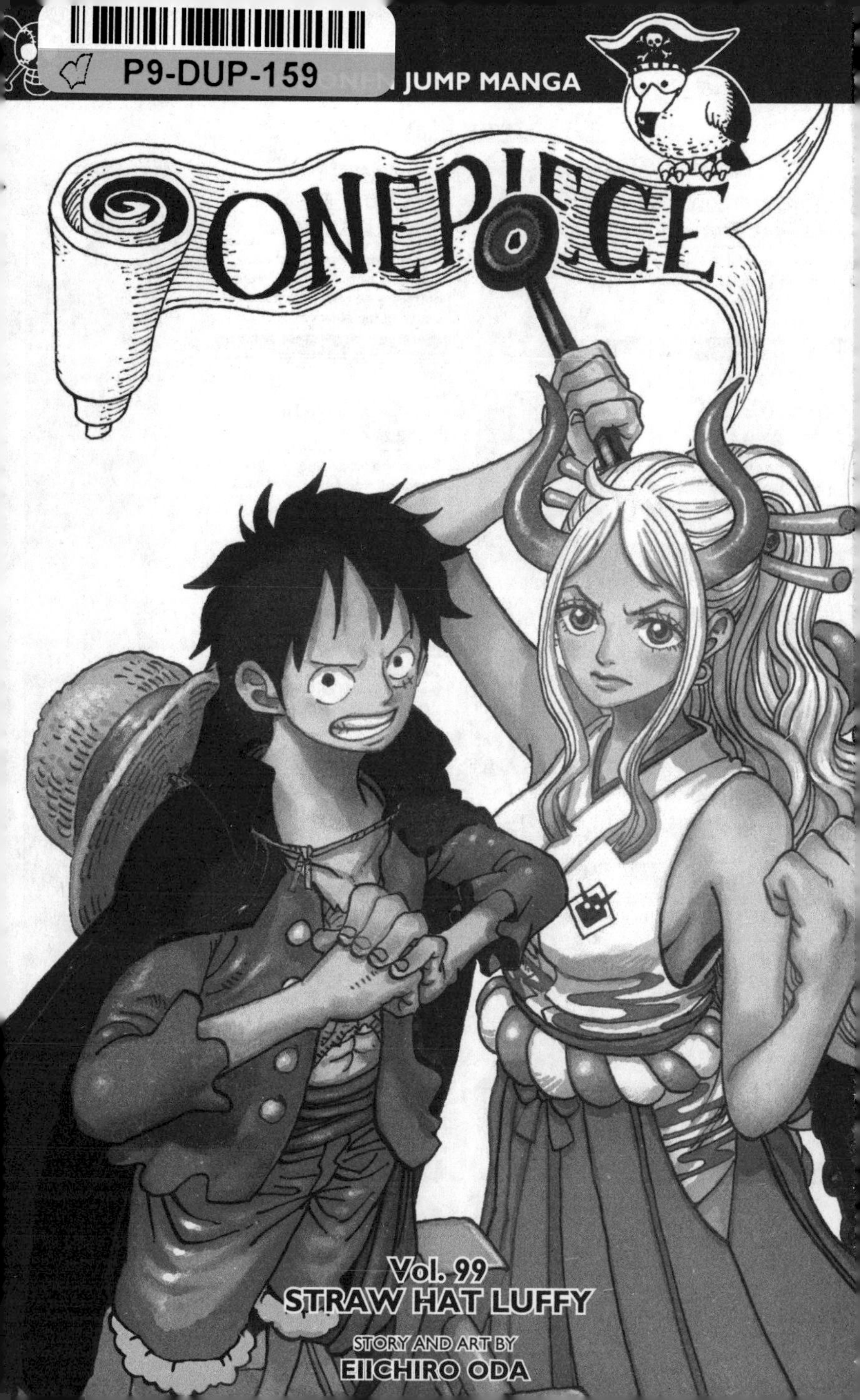

JUMP MANGA
ONE PIECE
Vol. 99
STRAW HAT LUFFY
STORY AND ART BY
EIICHIRO ODA

The Straw Hat Crew

Chopperemon [Ninja]
Tony Tony Chopper

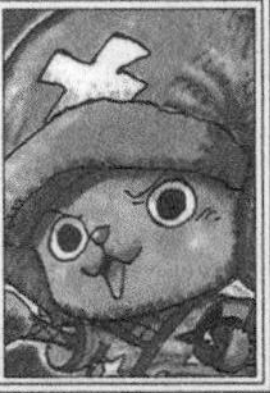

Studied powerful medicines in the Birdie Kingdom as he waited to rejoin the crew.

Ship's Doctor, Bounty: 100 berries

Luffytaro [Ronin]
Monkey D. Luffy

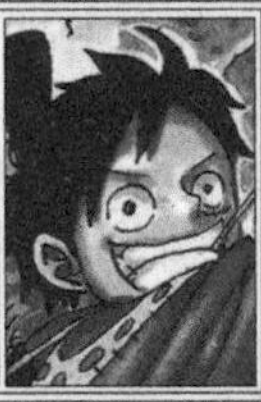

A young man dreaming of being the Pirate King. After two years of training he rejoins his friends in search of the New World!

Captain, Bounty: 1.5 billion berries

Orobi [Geisha]
Nico Robin

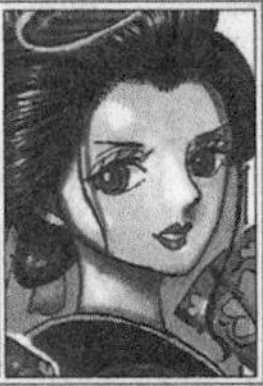

Spent time on the island of Baltigo with Dragon, Luffy's father and leader of the Revolutionary Army.

Archeologist, Bounty: 130 million berries

Zolojuro [Ronin]
Roronoa Zolo

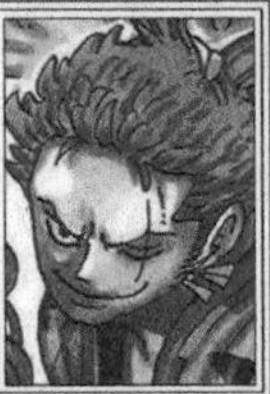

Swallowed his pride on Gloom Island and trained under Mihawk before rejoining Luffy.

Fighter, Bounty: 320 million berries

Franosuke [Carpenter]
Franky

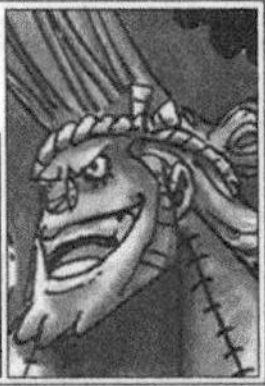

Upgraded himself into "Armored Franky" in the Future Land, Baldimore.

Shipwright, Bounty: 94 million berries

Onami [Kunoichi]
Nami

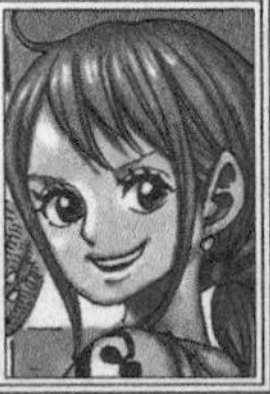

Learned about the climates of the New World on Weatheria, a Sky Island that studies the atmosphere.

Navigator, Bounty: 66 million berries

Bonekichi [Ghost]
Brook

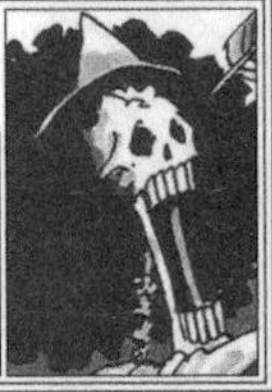

Originally captured by Long-Arm bandits for a freak show, he is now the mega-star "Soul King" Brook.

Musician, Bounty: 83 million berries

Usohachi [Toad Oil Salesman]
Usopp

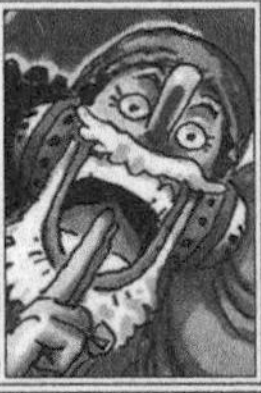

Received Heraclesun's lessons on the Bowin Islands in his quest to be the "king of the snipers."

Sniper, Bounty: 200 million berries

Jimbei, First Son of the Sea [Former Warlord]

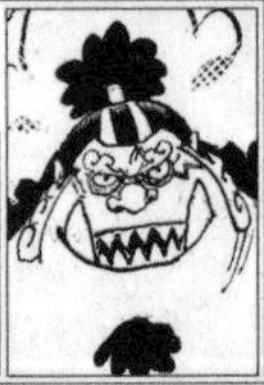

A man loyal to the code. Acted as rear guard against Big Mom to help Luffy escape, then rejoined before the raid.

Helmsman, Bounty: 438 million berries

Sangoro [Soba Cook]
Sanji

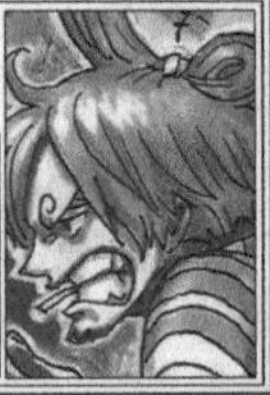

Honed his skills fighting with the masters of Newcomer Kenpo in the Kamabakka Kingdom.

Cook, Bounty: 330 million berries

Shanks

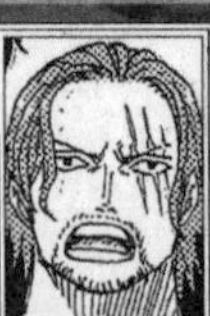

One of the Four Emperors. Waits for Luffy in the "New World," the second half of the Grand Line.

Captain of the Red-Haired Pirates

Land of Wano (Kozuki Clan)

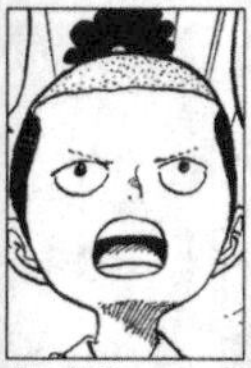
Kozuki Momonosuke
Daimyo (Heir) to Kuri in Wano

Akazaya Nine

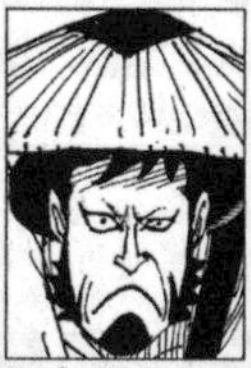
Foxfire Kin'emon
Samurai of Wano

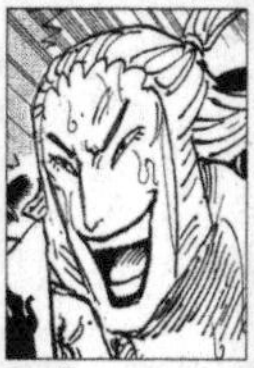
Denjiro
Formerly Kyoshiro

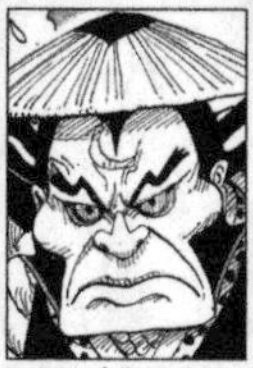
Raizo of the Mist
Ninja of Wano

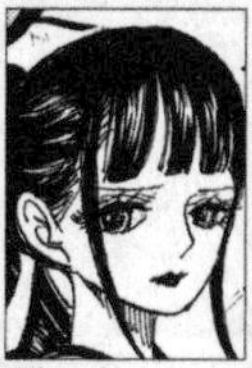
Kikunojo
Samurai of Wano

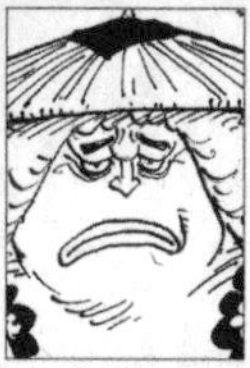
Ashura Doji (Shutenmaru)
Chief, Atamayama Thieves Brigade

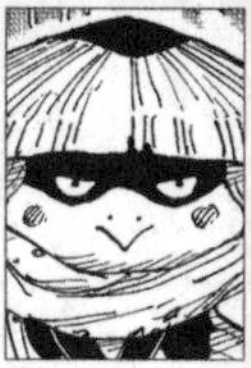
Kawamatsu
Samurai of Wano

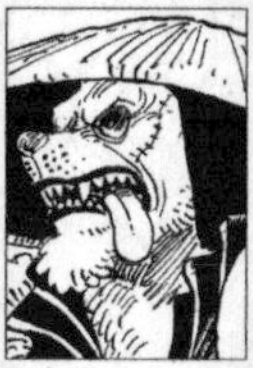
Duke Dogstorm
King of the Day, Mokomo

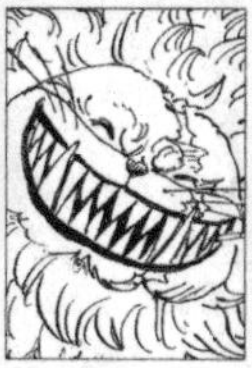
Cat Viper
King of the Night, Mokomo

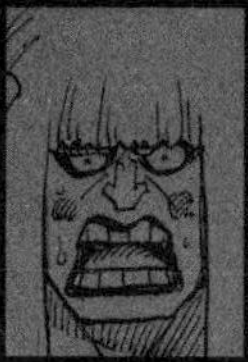
Evening Shower Kanjuro
Samurai of Wano

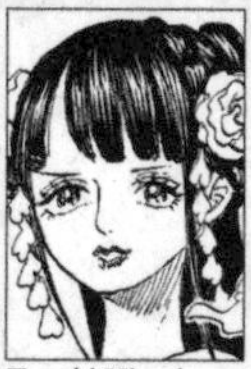
Kozuki Hiyori
Momonosuke's Little Sister

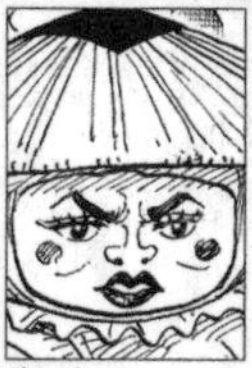
Shinobu
Veteran Kunoichi

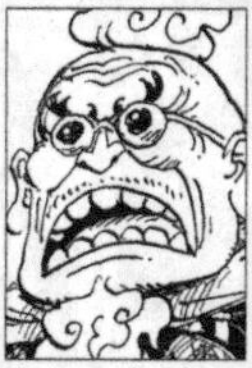
Hyogoro the Flower
Senior Yakuza Boss

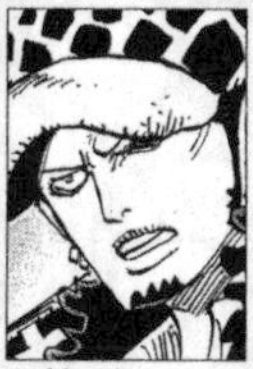
Trafalgar Law
Captain, Heart Pirates

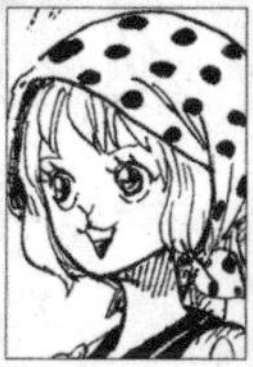
Carrot (Bunny Mink)
Battlebeast Tribe, Kingsbird

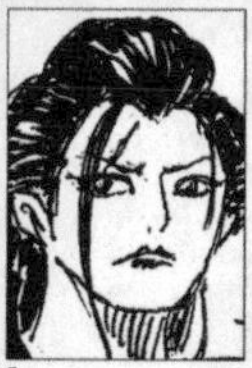
Izo
Former 16th Div. Leader, Whitebeard Pirates

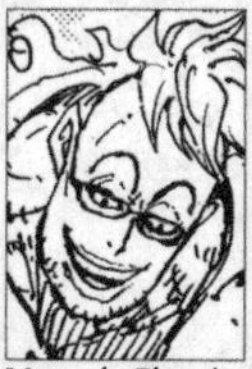
Marco the Phoenix
Former 1st Div. Leader, Whitebeard Pirates

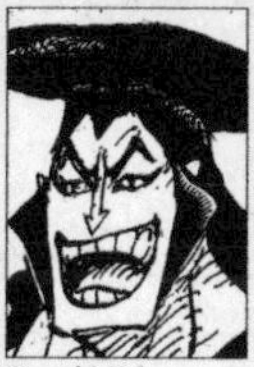
Kozuki Oden
Heir to the Shogunate of Wano

Kid Pirates

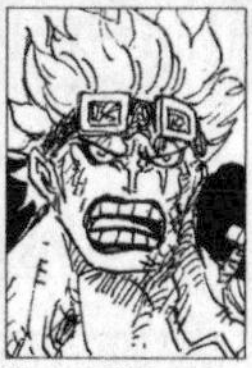
Eustass Kid
Captain, Kid Pirates

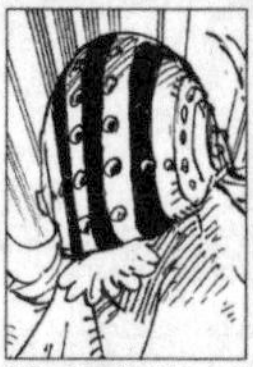
Killer (Hitokiri Kamazo)
Fighter, Kid Pirates

Animal Kingdom Pirates

Kaido, King of the Beasts (Emperor of the Sea)

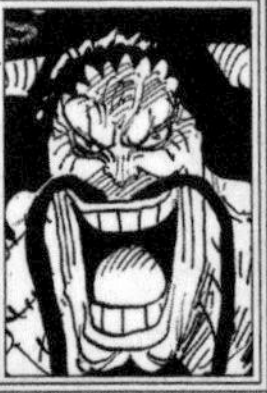

A pirate known as the "strongest creature alive." Despite numerous tortures and death sentences, none have been able to kill him.

Captain, Animal Kingdom Pirates

Lead Performers

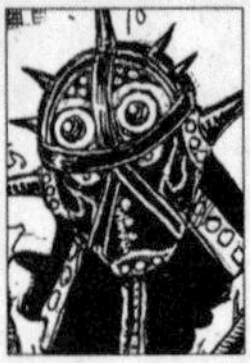
King the Wildfire

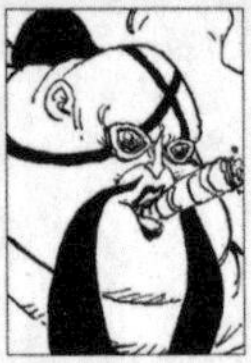
Queen the Plague

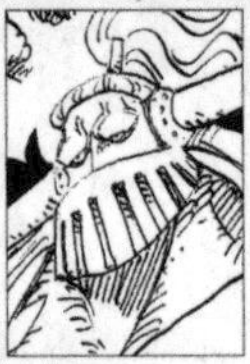
Jack the Drought

Tobi Roppo

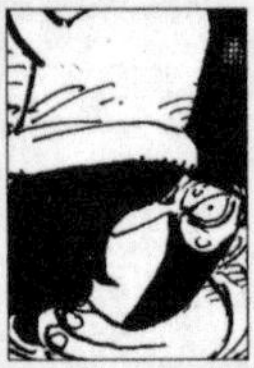
Page One

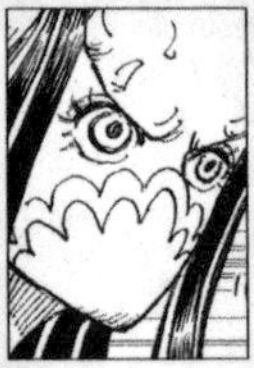
Ulti

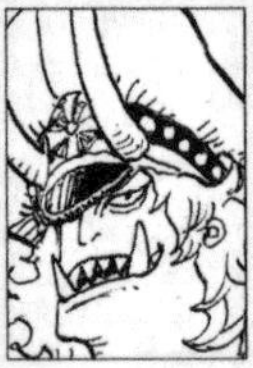
Sasaki

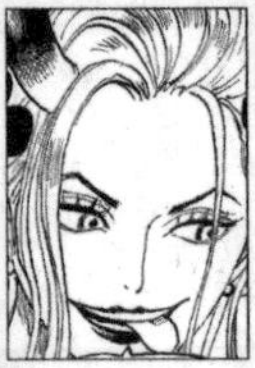
Black Maria

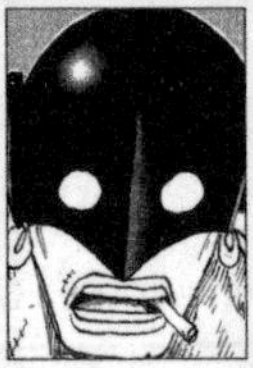
Who's-Who

Headliners

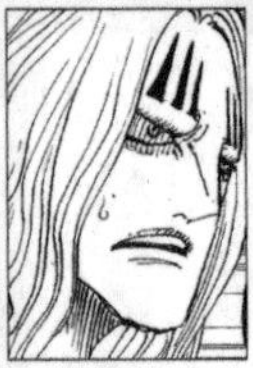
Basil Hawkins

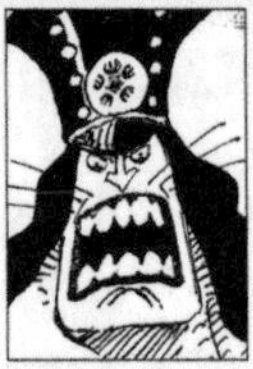
Holdem

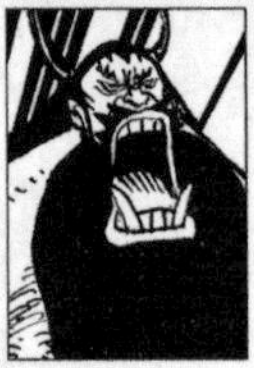
Babanuki

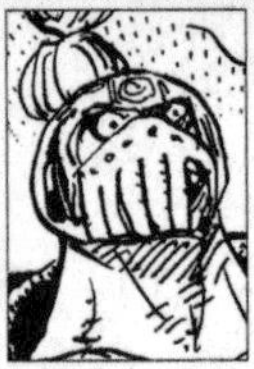
Daifugo

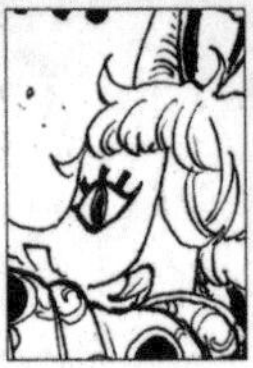
Bao Huang

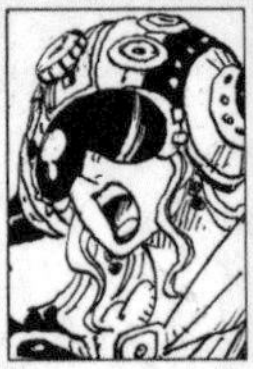
Solitaire

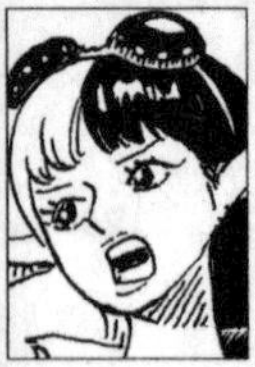
Speed

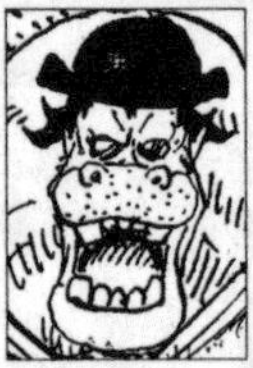
Dobon

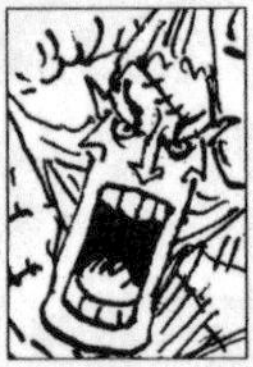
Briscola

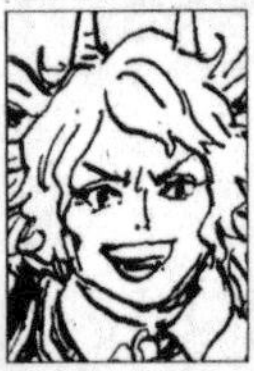
Hamlet

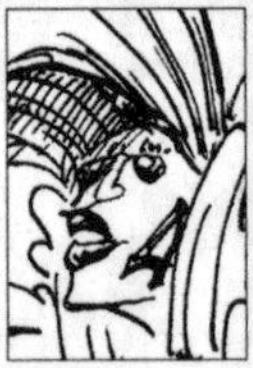
Fourtricks

and decide to launch a sneak attack. With new powerful friends in tow, the raid on Onigashima begins!! While the Emperor's followers block the way on the island, Kaido's daughter Yamato shows up and swears to fight on Luffy's side. The Akazaya samurai face off against Kaido on the roof of the castle, fighting to avenge their beloved Lord Oden. But Kaido steadily gains the upper hand... Luffy and others are heading for the roof too, but Kaido's henchmen stand in their way.

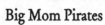

Big Mom Pirates

Big Mom
(Emperor of the Sea)

One of the Four Emperors. Uses the Soul-Soul Fruit that extracts life span from others.

Captain, Big Mom Pirates

C. Perospero

1st Son of Charlotte

Scratchmen Apoo

Captain, On-Air Pirates

Land of Wano (Kurozumi Clan)

Kurozumi Orochi

The ruler of Wano, using Kaido's help. He cunningly schemed to overthrow his archenemy, the Kozuki Clan.

Shogun of Wano

Kurozumi Kanjuro

Orochi's Spy

Left Kaido's Pirates to fight on Luffy's side!

X. (Diez) Drake

Former Tobi Roppo

Fukurokuju

Former Leader, Orochi Oniwabanshu

Hotei

Former Leader, Mimawari-gumi

Orochi Oniwabanshu

Former Private Ninja Squad of the Shogun

Yamato (Alias: Kozuki Oden)

Kaido's Daughter

Numbers

Jaki (No. 4)

Goki (No. 5)

Nangi (No. 7)

Haccha (No. 8)

Juki (No. 10)

Story

After two years of hard training, the Straw Hat pirates are back together, first at the Sabaody Archipelago and then through Fish-Man Island to their next stage: the New World!!

Luffy and crew ally with Momonosuke's faction in order to defeat Kaido, one of the Four Emperors. They overcome hurdles to recruit allies for the raid, but the spy Kanjuro reveals his treachery and kidnaps Momonosuke. The allied forces chase after him

Vol. 99
STRAW HAT LUFFY

CONTENTS

Chapter 995:
A KUNOICHI'S OATH

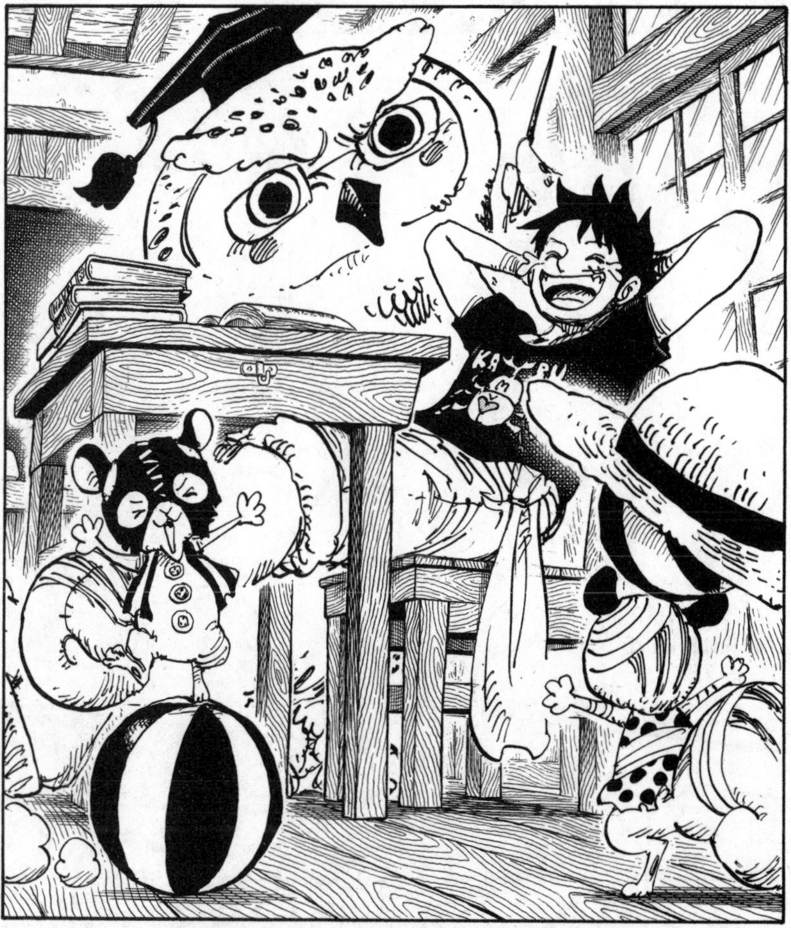

READER REQUEST: "LUFFY TRIES TO STUDY BUT GETS BORED RIGHT AWAY" BY P.N. WALKING MAMA FROM SETAGAYA WARD

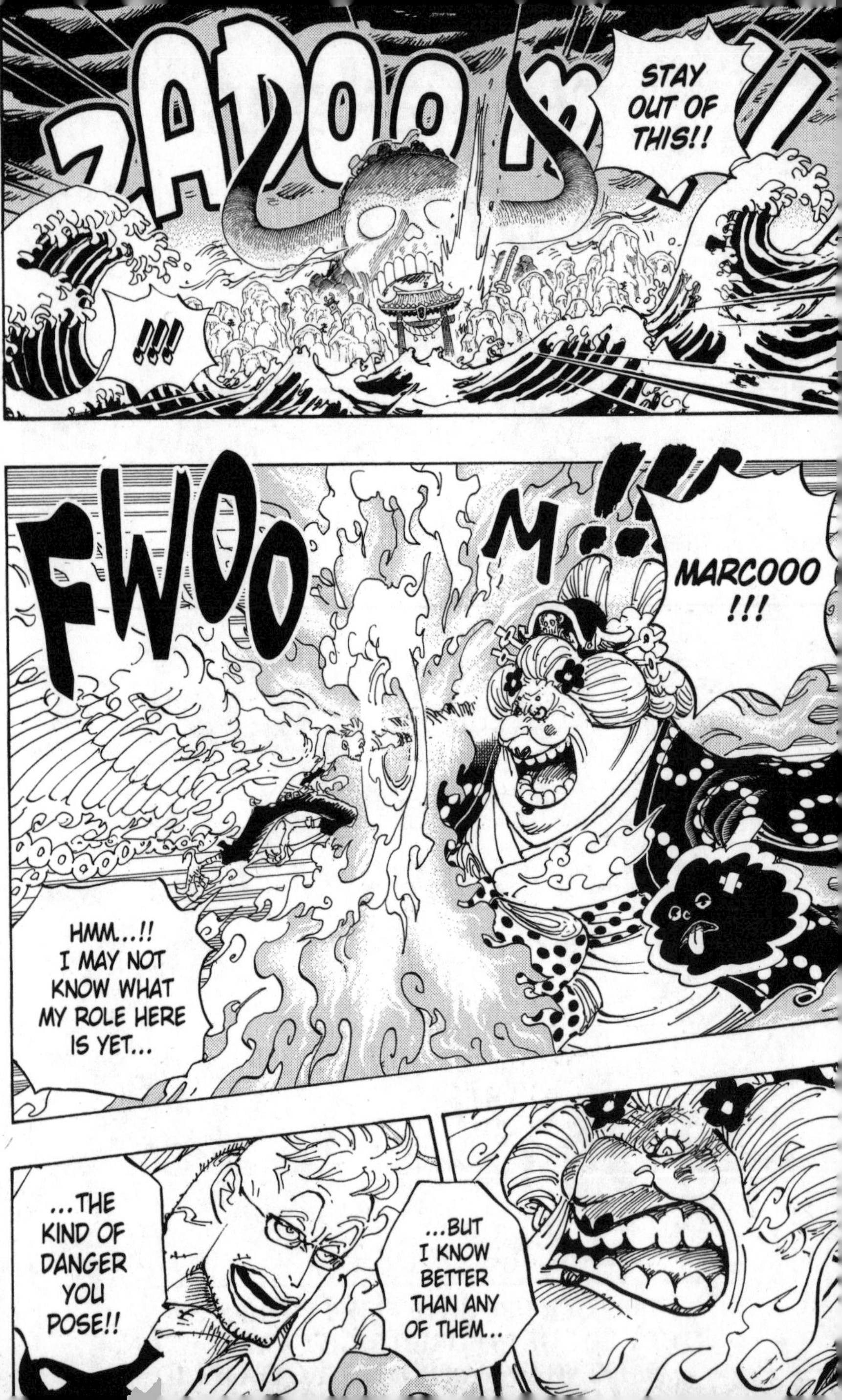
STAY OUT OF THIS!!
ZADOO
!!!
MARCOOO!!!
FWOOM!!
HMM...!! I MAY NOT KNOW WHAT MY ROLE HERE IS YET...
...BUT I KNOW BETTER THAN ANY OF THEM...
...THE KIND OF DANGER YOU POSE!!

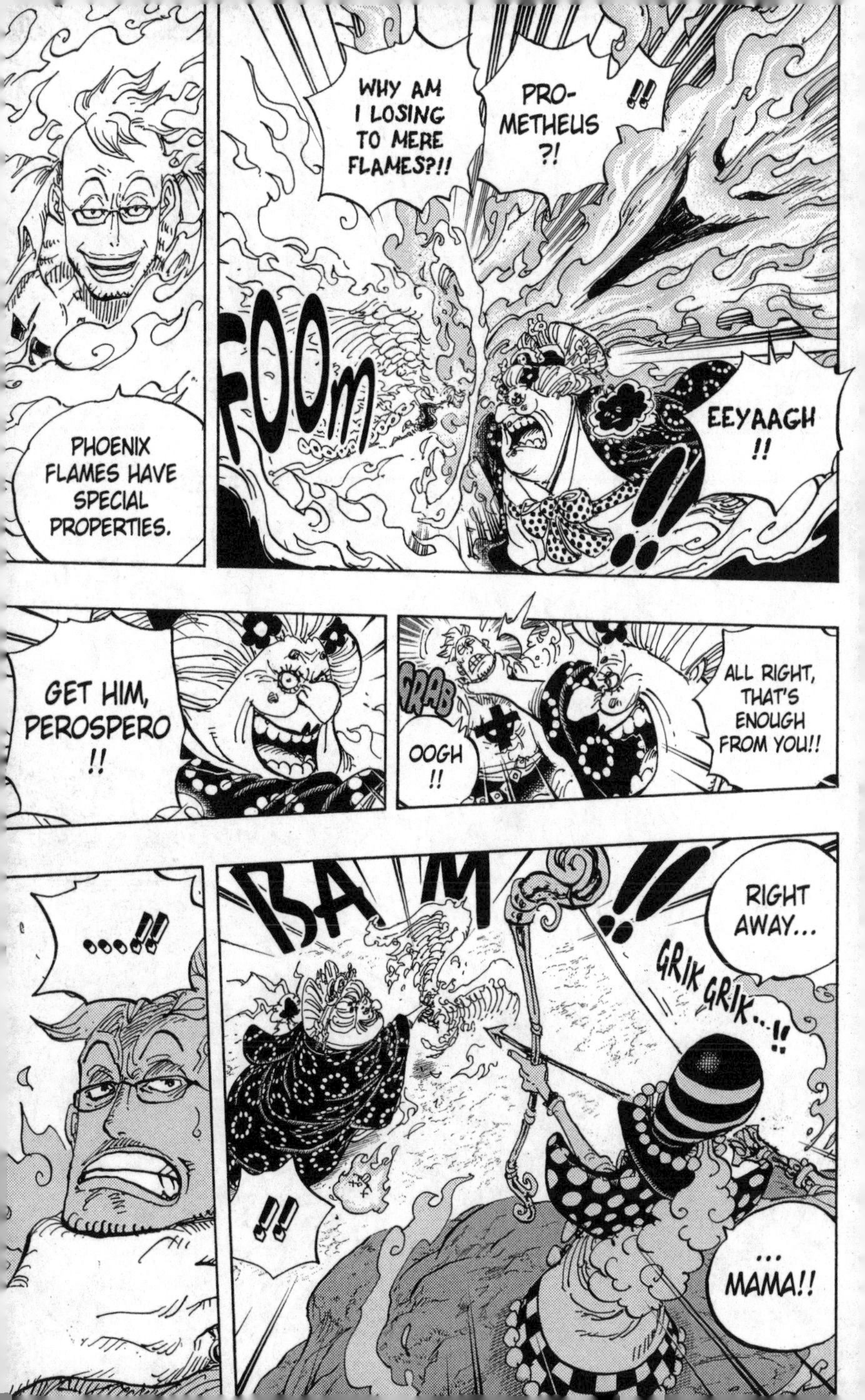
!!
PRO-METHEUS ?!
WHY AM I LOSING TO MERE FLAMES?!!
EEYAAGH !!
FOOM
PHOENIX FLAMES HAVE SPECIAL PROPERTIES.
ALL RIGHT, THAT'S ENOUGH FROM YOU!!
GRAB
OOGH !!
GET HIM, PEROSPERO !!
RIGHT AWAY...
BAM!!
GRIK GRIK...!!
!!
...MAMA!!
...!!

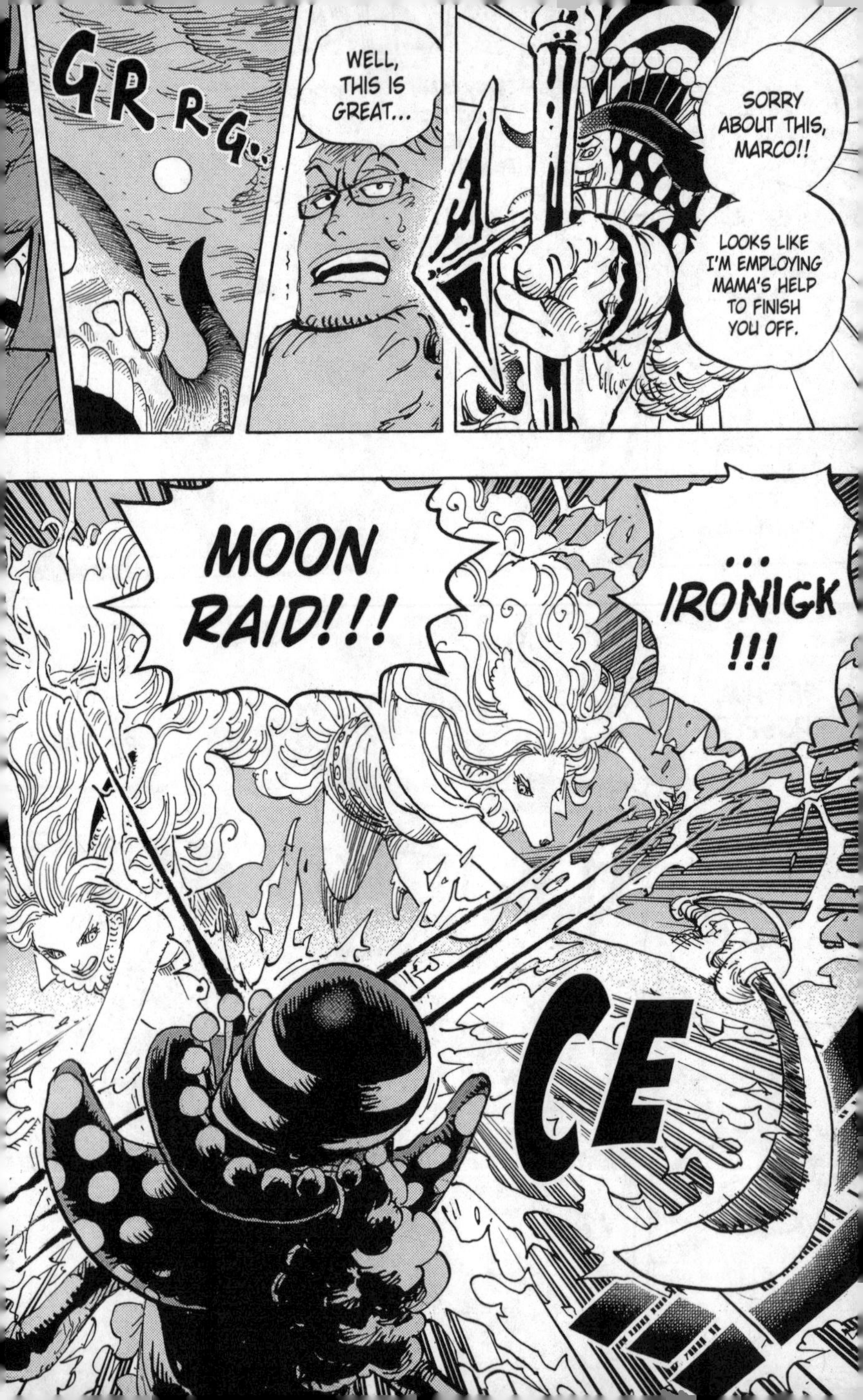
SORRY ABOUT THIS, MARCO!!
LOOKS LIKE I'M EMPLOYING MAMA'S HELP TO FINISH YOU OFF.
WELL, THIS IS GREAT...
GRRRG..
...IRONIGK!!!
MOON RAID!!!
CE

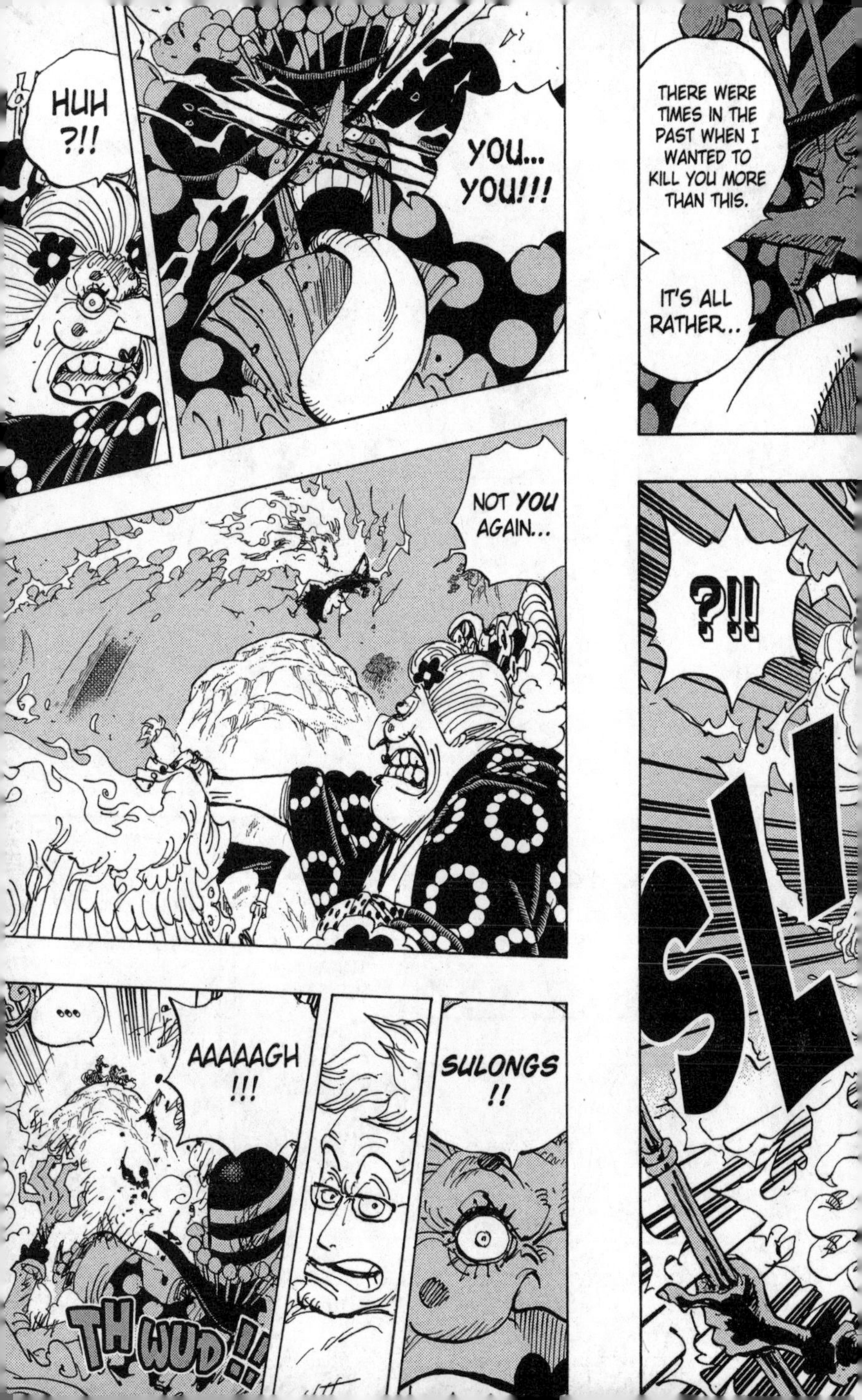
THERE WERE TIMES IN THE PAST WHEN I WANTED TO KILL YOU MORE THAN THIS.
IT'S ALL RATHER...
YOU... YOU!!!
HUH ?!!
?!!
SL
NOT *YOU* AGAIN...
SULONGS !!
AAAAAGH !!!
...
THWUD!!

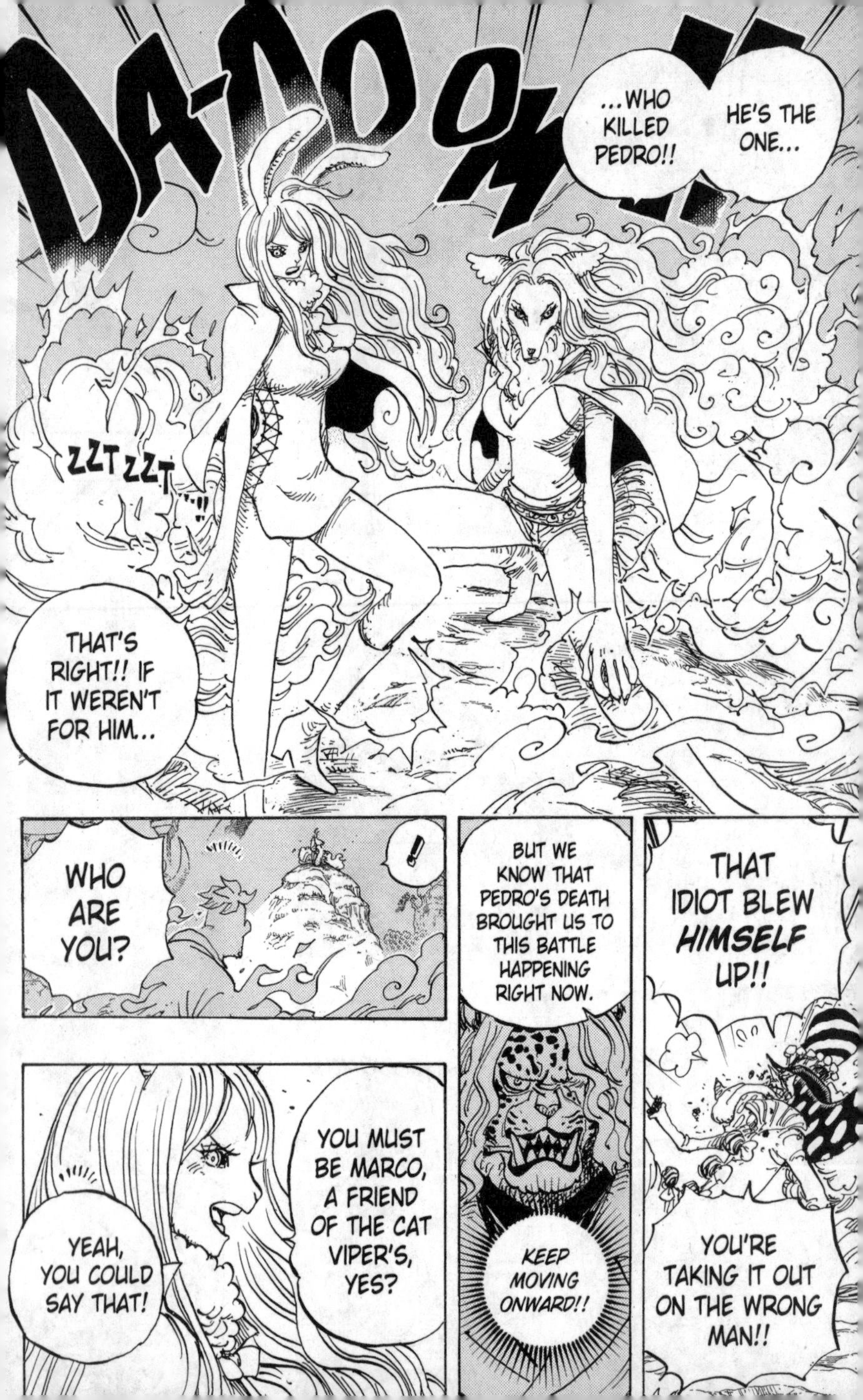
DA-DOOM
HE'S THE ONE...
...WHO KILLED PEDRO!!
ZZT ZZT
THAT'S RIGHT!! IF IT WEREN'T FOR HIM...
THAT IDIOT BLEW *HIMSELF* UP!!
YOU'RE TAKING IT OUT ON THE WRONG MAN!!
BUT WE KNOW THAT PEDRO'S DEATH BROUGHT US TO THIS BATTLE HAPPENING RIGHT NOW.
KEEP MOVING ONWARD!!
!
WHO ARE YOU?
YOU MUST BE MARCO, A FRIEND OF THE CAT VIPER'S, YES?
YEAH, YOU COULD SAY THAT!

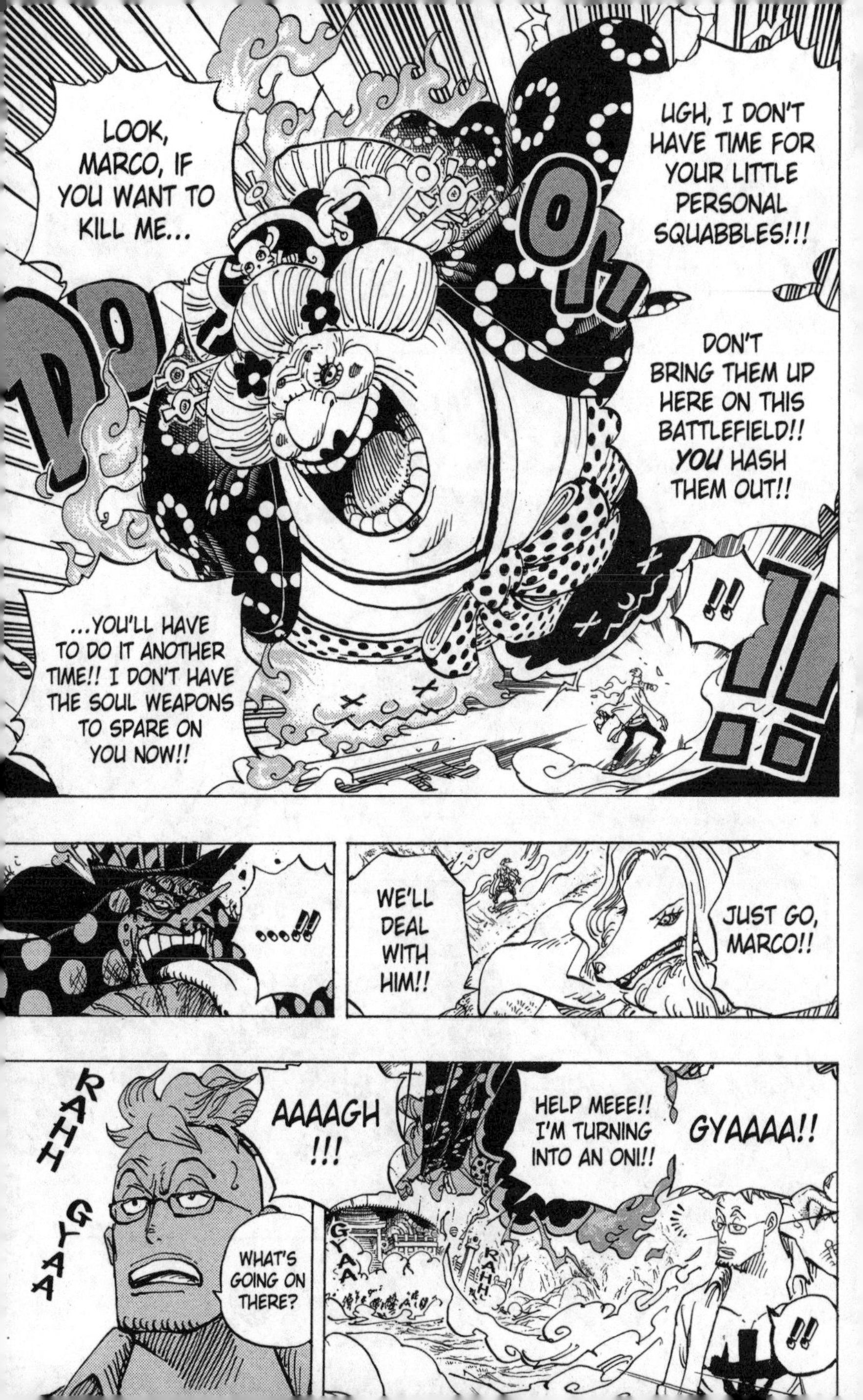

UGH, I DON'T HAVE TIME FOR YOUR LITTLE PERSONAL SQUABBLES!!!
DON'T BRING THEM UP HERE ON THIS BATTLEFIELD!! *YOU* HASH THEM OUT!!
LOOK, MARCO, IF YOU WANT TO KILL ME...
!!
...YOU'LL HAVE TO DO IT ANOTHER TIME!! I DON'T HAVE THE SOUL WEAPONS TO SPARE ON YOU NOW!!
JUST GO, MARCO!!
WE'LL DEAL WITH HIM!!
....!!
GYAAAA!!
HELP MEEE!! I'M TURNING INTO AN ONI!!
AAAAGH!!!
!!
RAHH
GYAA
WHAT'S GOING ON THERE?
RAHH GYAA

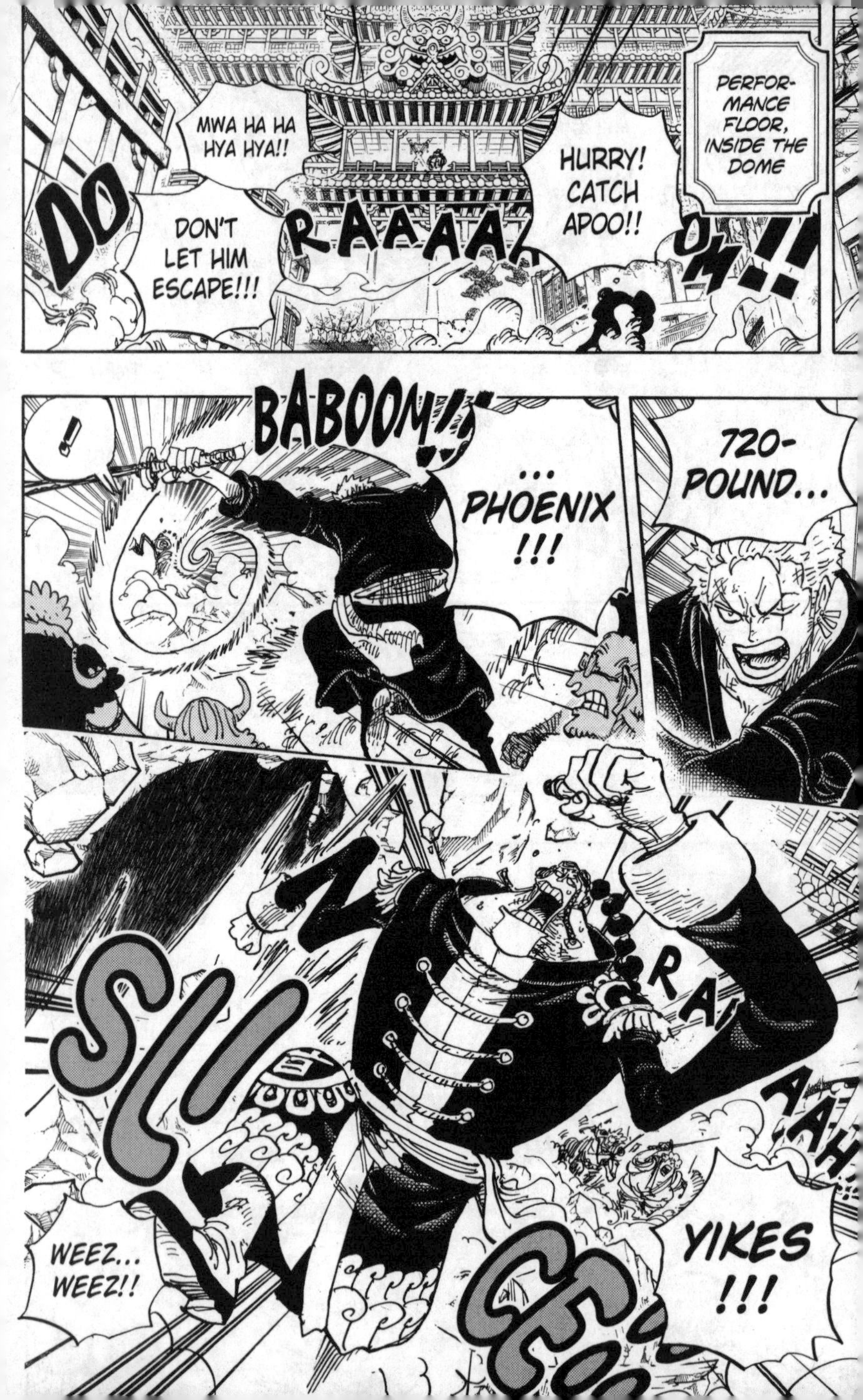
PERFORMANCE FLOOR, INSIDE THE DOME
DOOM!!
HURRY! CATCH APOO!!
RAAAA
MWA HA HA HYA HYA!!
DON'T LET HIM ESCAPE!!!
720-POUND...
...PHOENIX!!!
BABOOM!!
!
ZRAAAH!!
YIKES!!!
WEEZ... WEEZ!!
SLI
CE

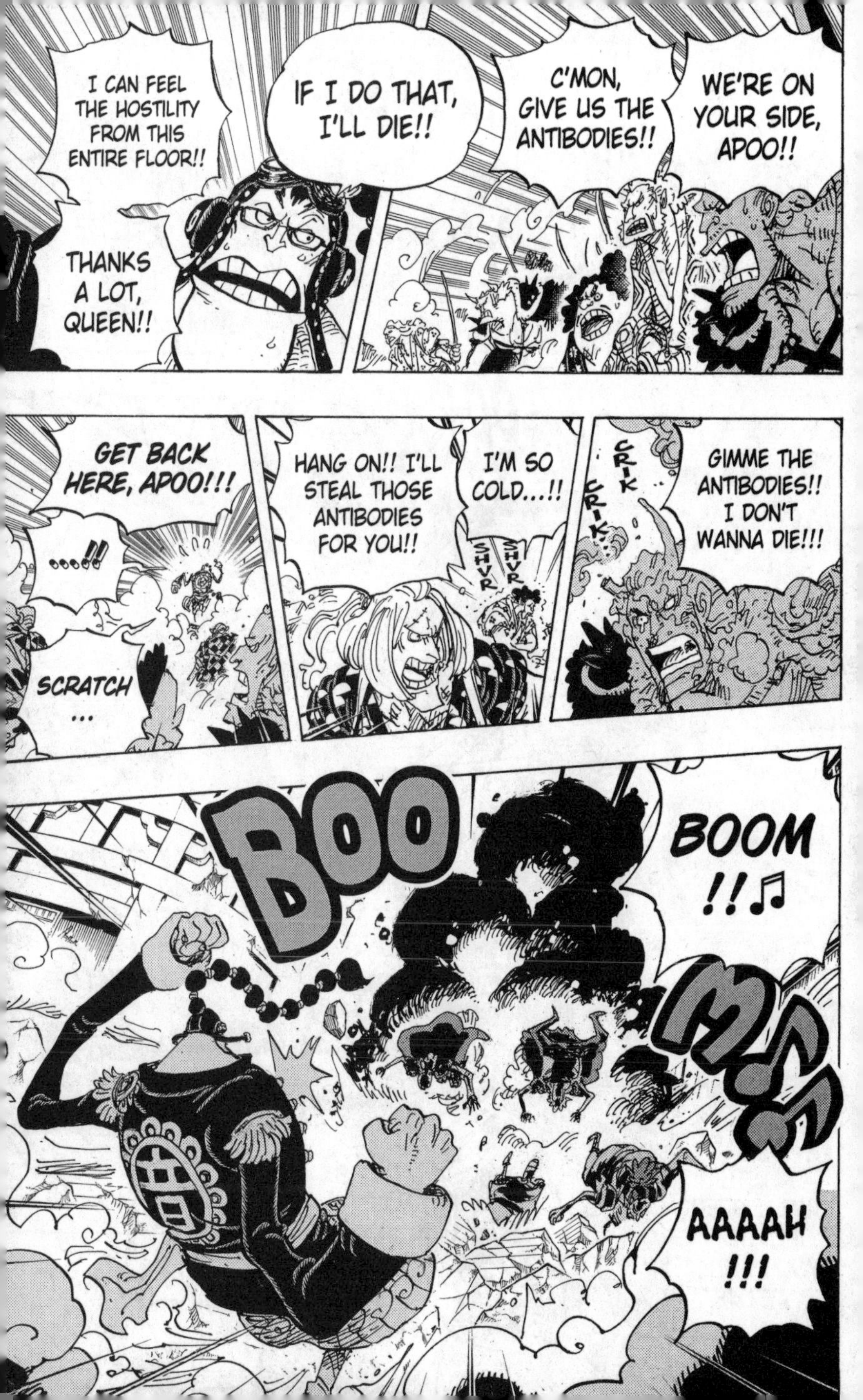
WE'RE ON YOUR SIDE, APOO!!
C'MON, GIVE US THE ANTIBODIES!!
IF I DO THAT, I'LL DIE!!
I CAN FEEL THE HOSTILITY FROM THIS ENTIRE FLOOR!!
THANKS A LOT, QUEEN!!
GIMME THE ANTIBODIES!! I DON'T WANNA DIE!!!
CRIK
CRIK
I'M SO COLD...!!
SHVR
SHVR
HANG ON!! I'LL STEAL THOSE ANTIBODIES FOR YOU!!
GET BACK HERE, APOO!!!
....!!
SCRATCH ...
BOOM !!♫
BOO
AAAAH !!!

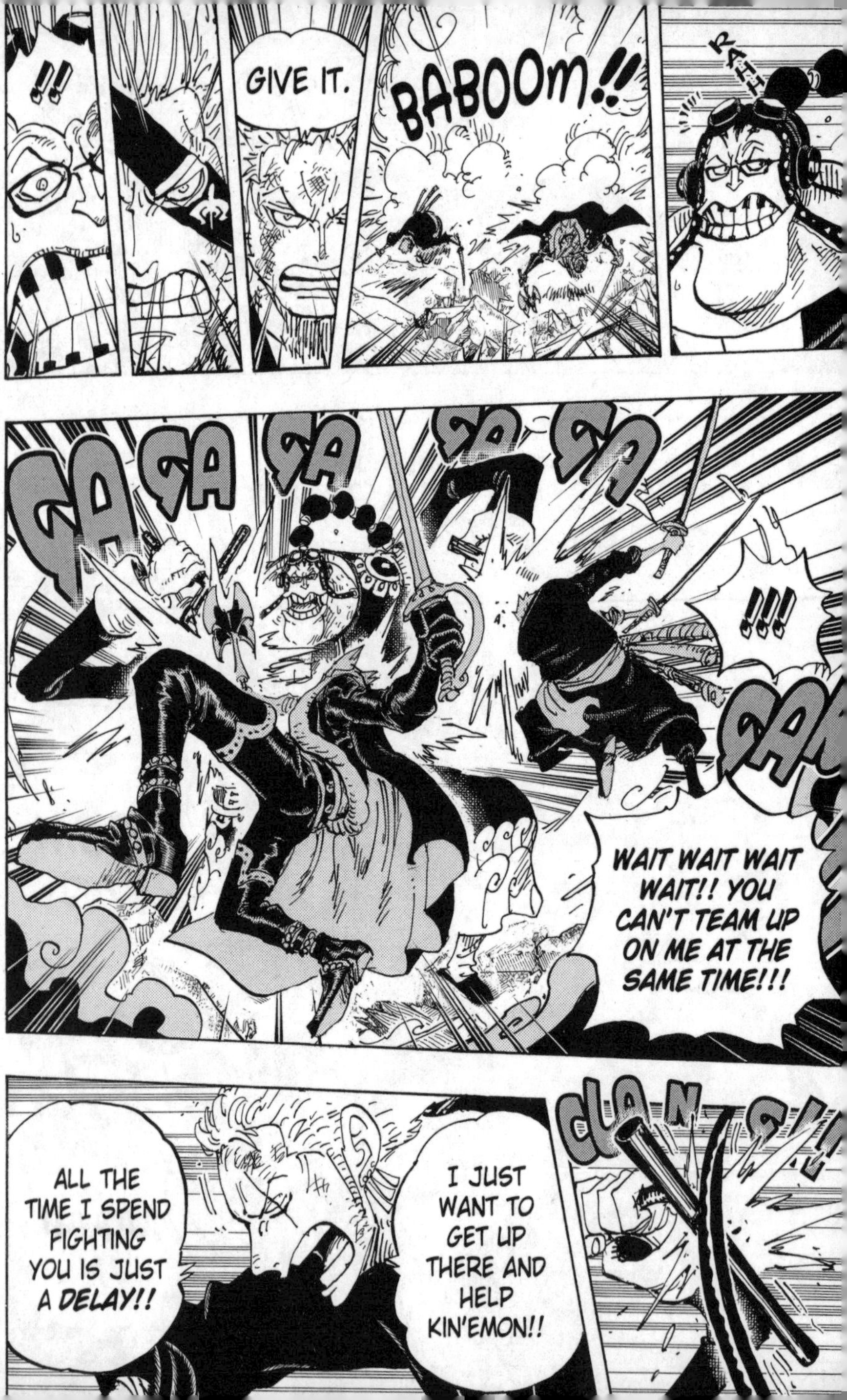
RAHH
BABOOM!!
GIVE IT.
!!
!!!
GA
WAIT WAIT WAIT WAIT!! YOU CAN'T TEAM UP ON ME AT THE SAME TIME!!!
GA GA GA GA GA
CLANG!!
I JUST WANT TO GET UP THERE AND HELP KIN'EMON!!
ALL THE TIME I SPEND FIGHTING YOU IS JUST A *DELAY!!*

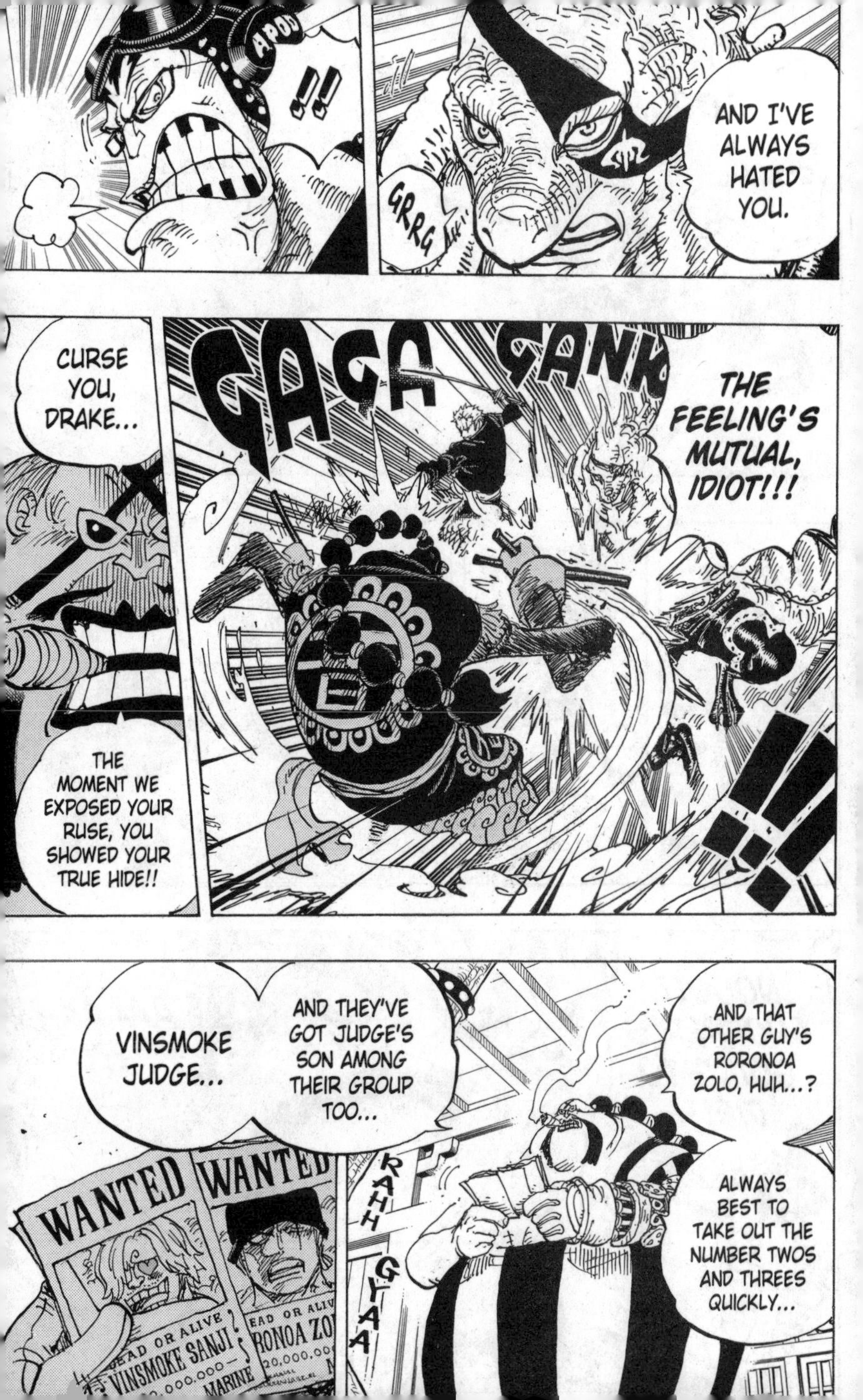
AND I'VE ALWAYS HATED YOU.
GRRG
APOO
!!
GAGA
GANK
THE FEELING'S MUTUAL, IDIOT!!!
!!
CURSE YOU, DRAKE...
THE MOMENT WE EXPOSED YOUR RUSE, YOU SHOWED YOUR TRUE HIDE!!
AND THAT OTHER GUY'S RORONOA ZOLO, HUH...?
ALWAYS BEST TO TAKE OUT THE NUMBER TWOS AND THREES QUICKLY...
RAHH
GYAA
VINSMOKE JUDGE...
AND THEY'VE GOT JUDGE'S SON AMONG THEIR GROUP TOO...
WANTED
WANTED
DEAD OR ALIVE
VINSMOKE SANJI
MARINE

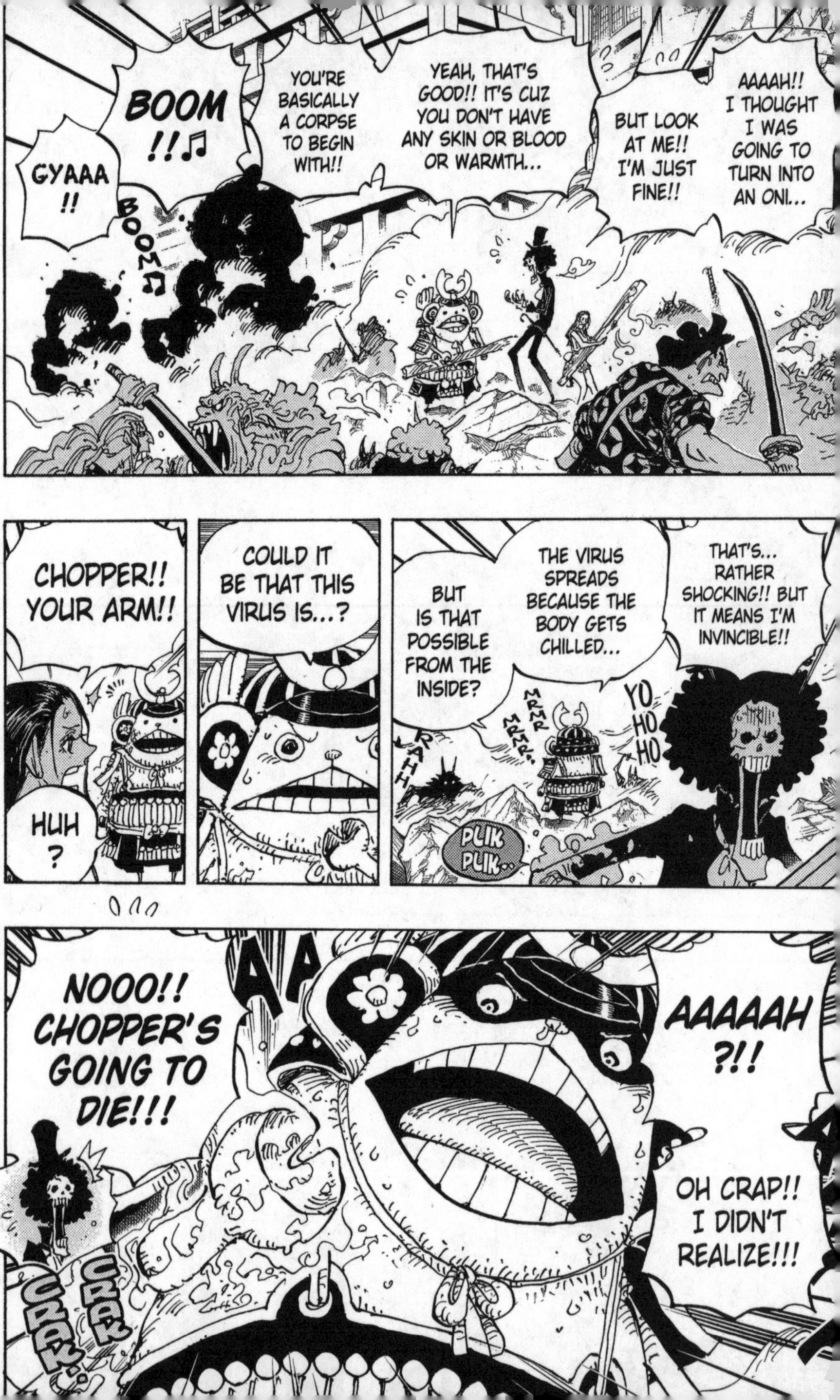
AAAAH!! I THOUGHT I WAS GOING TO TURN INTO AN ONI...
BUT LOOK AT ME!! I'M JUST FINE!!
YEAH, THAT'S GOOD!! IT'S CUZ YOU DON'T HAVE ANY SKIN OR BLOOD OR WARMTH...
YOU'RE BASICALLY A CORPSE TO BEGIN WITH!!
BOOM!!♫
GYAAA!!
BOOM♫
THAT'S... RATHER SHOCKING!! BUT IT MEANS I'M INVINCIBLE!!
YO HO HO
THE VIRUS SPREADS BECAUSE THE BODY GETS CHILLED...
BUT IS THAT POSSIBLE FROM THE INSIDE?
MRMR MRMR
RAHHH
PLIK PLIK..
COULD IT BE THAT THIS VIRUS IS...?
CHOPPER!! YOUR ARM!!
HUH?
AAAAAH?!!
OH CRAP!! I DIDN'T REALIZE!!!
AA
NOOO!! CHOPPER'S GOING TO DIE!!!
CRAK CRAK

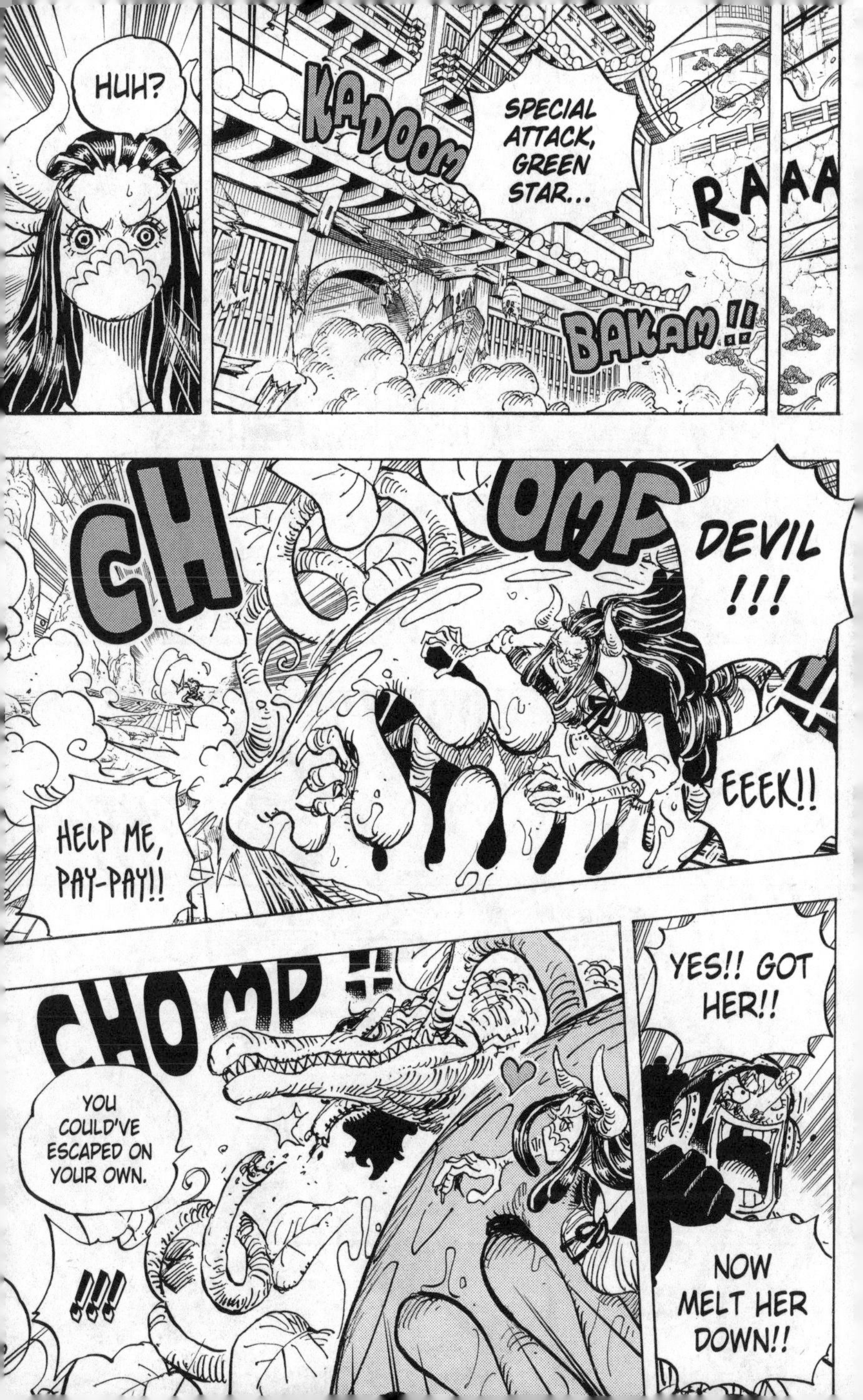
RAAA
KADOOM
SPECIAL ATTACK, GREEN STAR...
BAKAM!!
HUH?
DEVIL!!!
OMP
CH
EEEK!!
HELP ME, PAY-PAY!!
YES!! GOT HER!!
NOW MELT HER DOWN!!
CHOMP!!
YOU COULD'VE ESCAPED ON YOUR OWN.
!!!

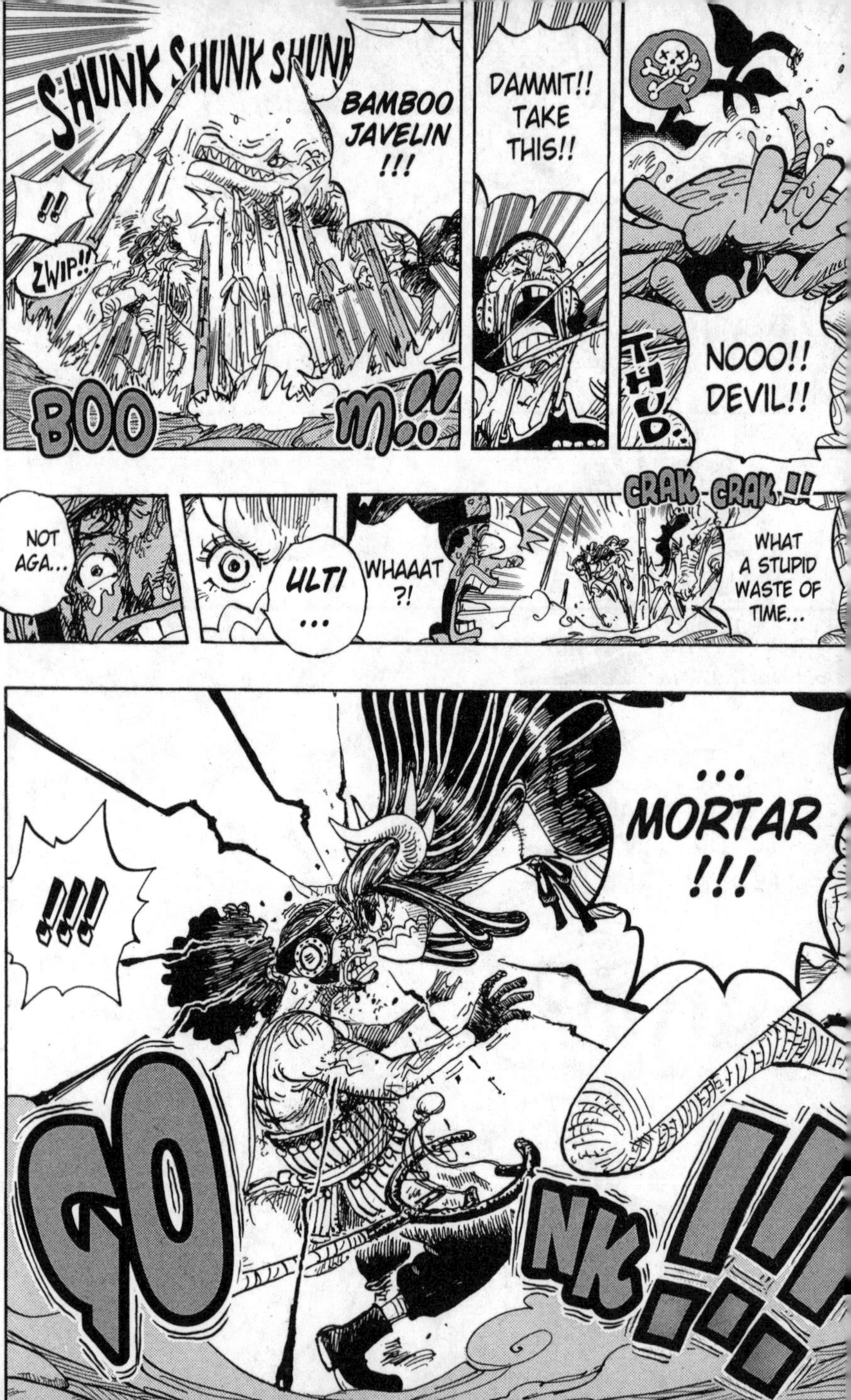
NOOO!! DEVIL!!
THUD..
DAMMIT!! TAKE THIS!!
BAMBOO JAVELIN!!!
SHUNK SHUNK SHUNK
!!
ZWIP!!
BOOM..!!
CRAK CRAK!!
WHAT A STUPID WASTE OF TIME...
WHAAAT?!
ULTI...
NOT AGA...
...MORTAR!!!
!!!
GONK...!!!

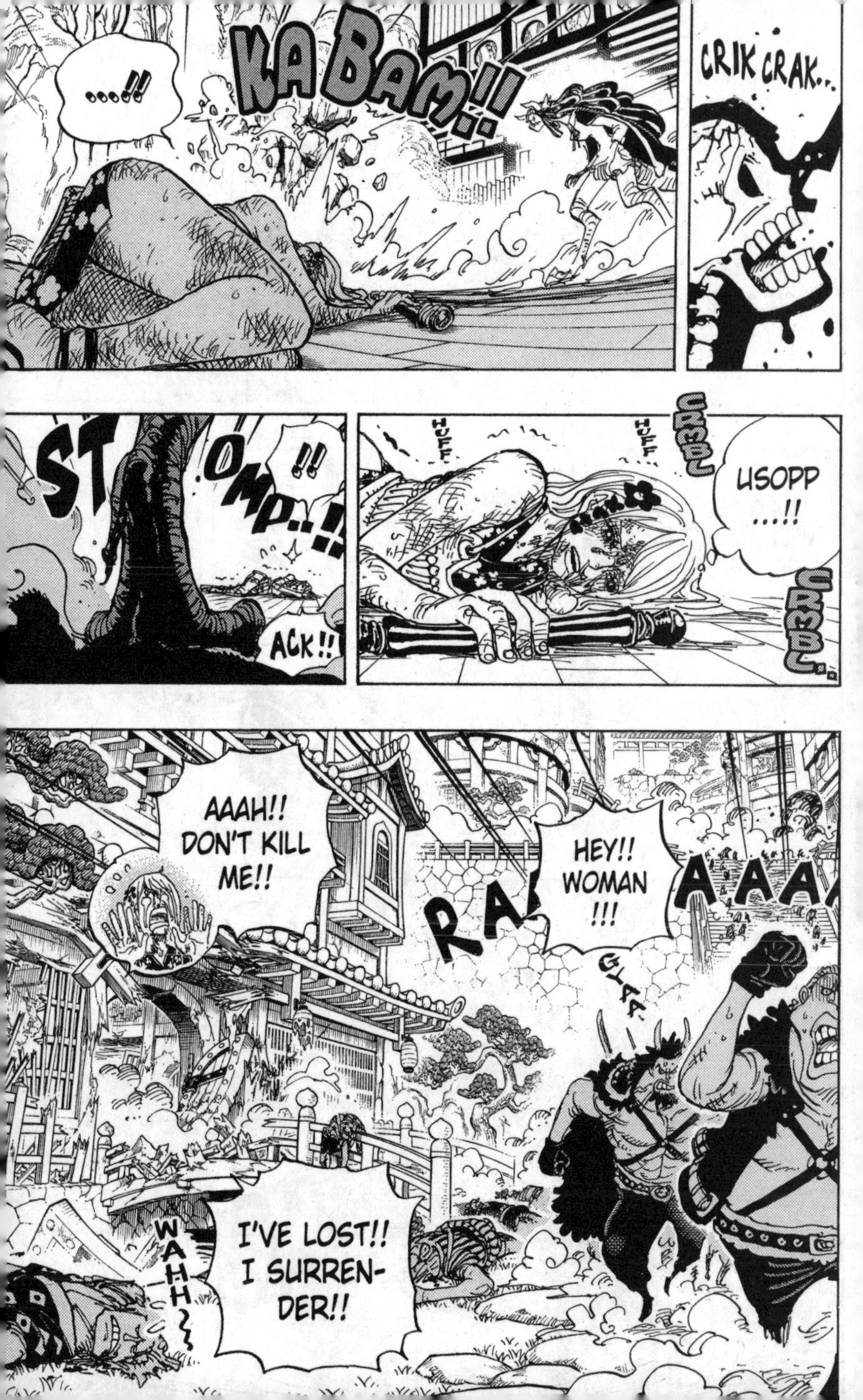
CRIK CRAK..
KA BAM!!
....!!
HUFF
HUFF
CRMBL
USOPP ...!!
CRMBL
STOMP..!!
ACK!!
AAA
HEY!! WOMAN !!!
RA
GYAA
AAAH!! DON'T KILL ME!!
I'VE LOST!! I SURREN-DER!!
WAHH~

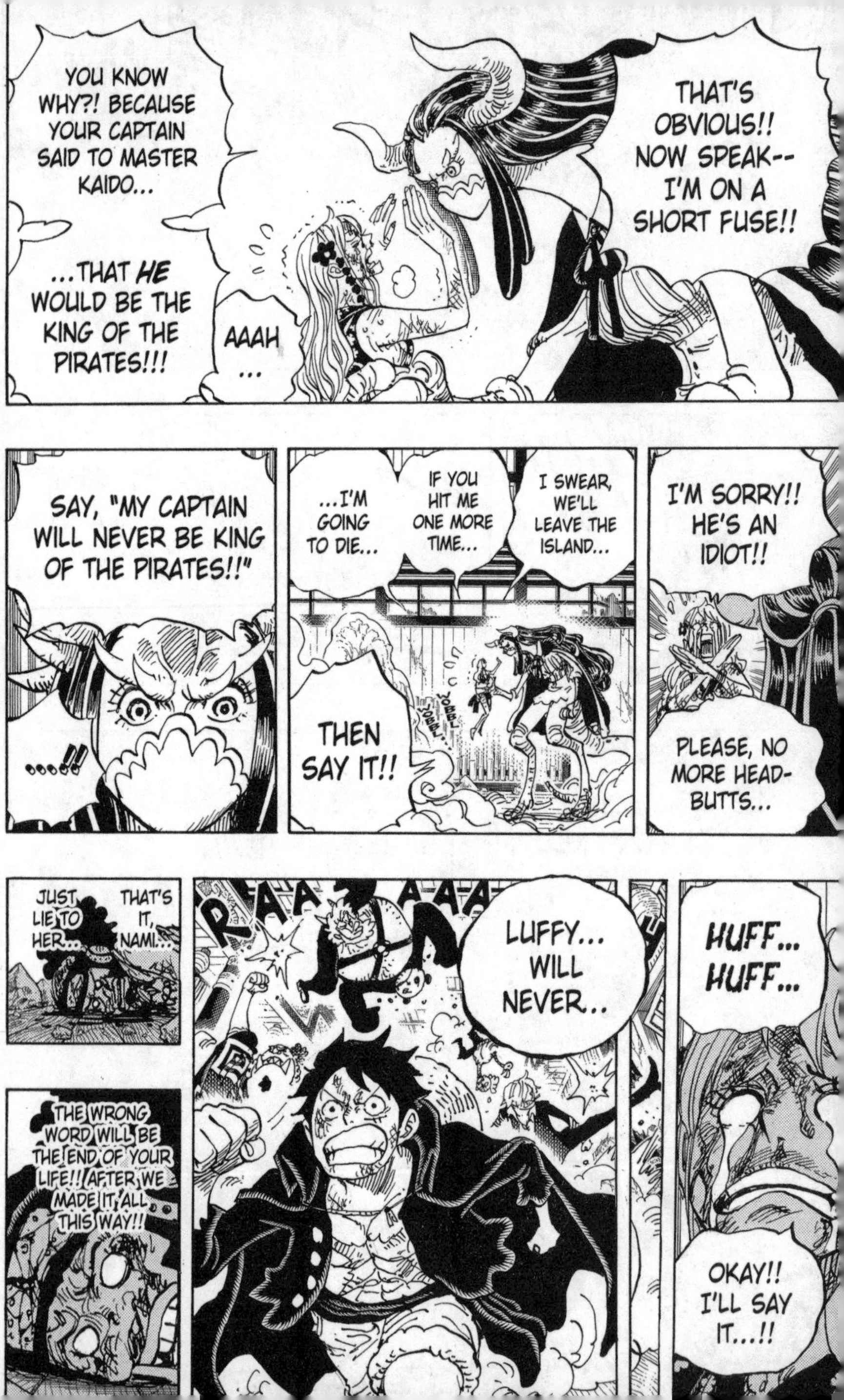
THAT'S OBVIOUS!! NOW SPEAK-- I'M ON A SHORT FUSE!!
YOU KNOW WHY?! BECAUSE YOUR CAPTAIN SAID TO MASTER KAIDO...
...THAT HE WOULD BE THE KING OF THE PIRATES!!!
AAAH ...
I'M SORRY!! HE'S AN IDIOT!!
PLEASE, NO MORE HEAD-BUTTS...
I SWEAR, WE'LL LEAVE THE ISLAND...
IF YOU HIT ME ONE MORE TIME...
...I'M GOING TO DIE...
WOBBL WOBBL
THEN SAY IT!!
SAY, "MY CAPTAIN WILL NEVER BE KING OF THE PIRATES!!"
.....!!
HUFF... HUFF...
OKAY!! I'LL SAY IT...!!
LUFFY... WILL NEVER...
THAT'S IT, NAMI...
JUST LIE TO HER...
THE WRONG WORD WILL BE THE END OF YOUR LIFE!! AFTER WE MADE IT ALL THIS WAY!!

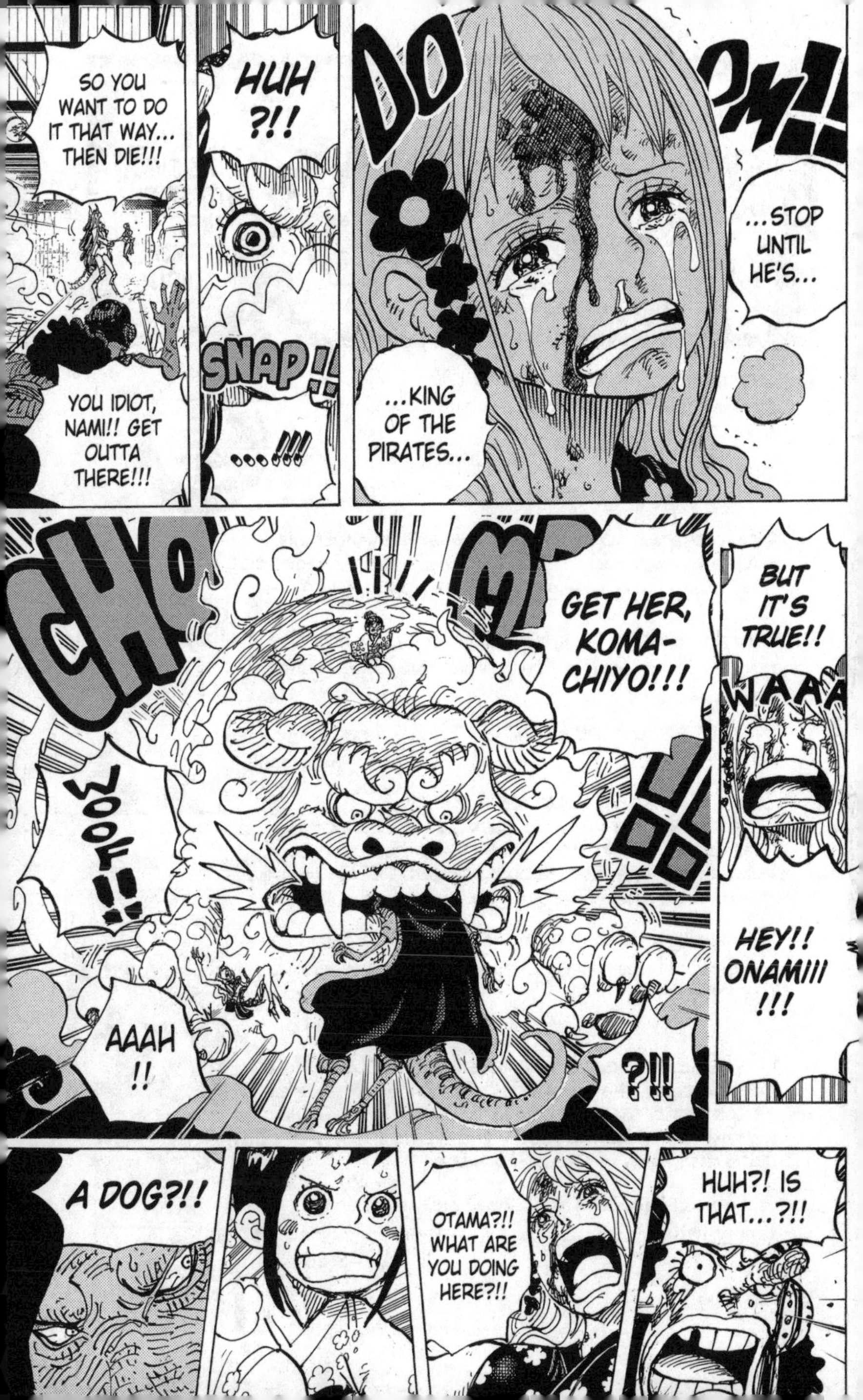
DO
OM!!
...STOP UNTIL HE'S...
...KING OF THE PIRATES...
HUH ?!!
SNAP!!
...!!!
SO YOU WANT TO DO IT THAT WAY... THEN DIE!!!
YOU IDIOT, NAMI!! GET OUTTA THERE!!!
BUT IT'S TRUE!!
WAAA
HEY!! ONAMI!!! !!!
GET HER, KOMA-CHIYO!!!
CHO
M
WOOF!!
?!!
AAAH !!
HUH?! IS THAT...?!!
OTAMA?!! WHAT ARE YOU DOING HERE?!!
A DOG?!!

SBS Question Corner

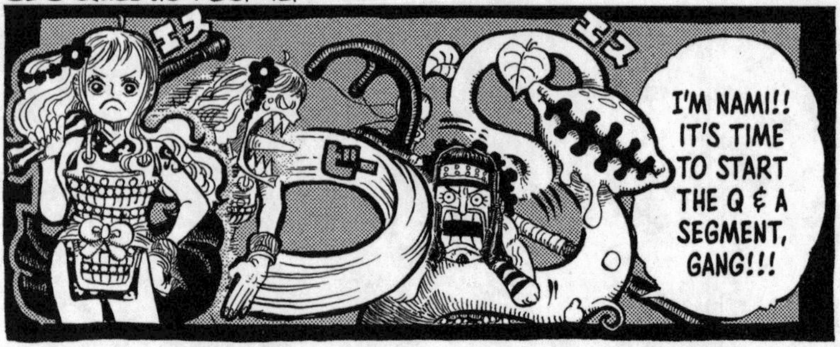
I'M NAMI!! IT'S TIME TO START THE Q & A SEGMENT, GANG!!!
(Hamane, Kanagawa)

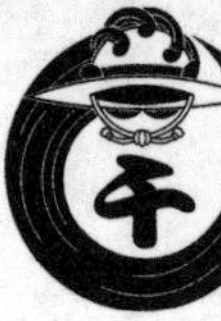

Q: Sensei, congratulations on reaching 1,000 chapters of *One Piece.* For volume 99, which I assume contains chapter 1,000, I have this message.

Start the SBS!

--Goemon

A: Gosh, thanks so much. A thousand chapters is such a milestone, so this volume is very special to... Hey, you started the segment!!

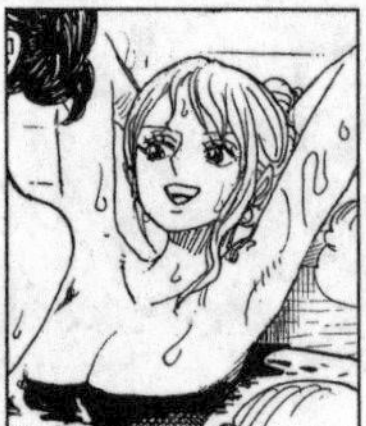

Q: Odacchi, check out this symbol: π. Do you know how to read that? It's pronounced "pi." Now please read the following statement.

Nami's ππ are the best! ("Pai-pai" means boobs.)

--Sanadacchi

A: Sanada!! Get outta here!!! Listen, this is a very special volume, it's got chapter 1,000 in it!! Talk about a rocket start into depravity!! Talk about rocket ππ!! Shut up!!! Man, I wish the PTA liked me.

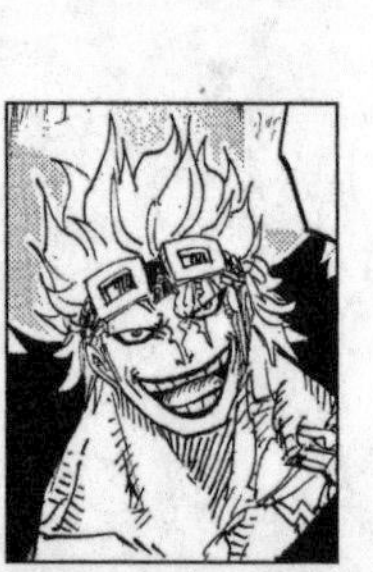

Q: You casually revealed the name of Kaido's Devil Fruit in volume 98, so now you get to casually reveal the name of Kid's Devil Fruit!

--Takumiso

A: It's the Magnet-Magnet Fruit. Huh? Did I not say that before? He can control iron at will using magnet powers. I suppose I should be saying these things in the manga. I'll make sure to bring it up somewhere.

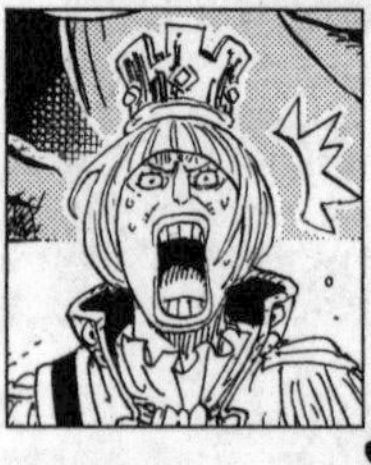

Q: I'd be grateful for life if you allowed Stelly to sit on the Empty Throne.

--Seito

A: No way.

Chapter 996:

ISLAND OF THE STRONGEST

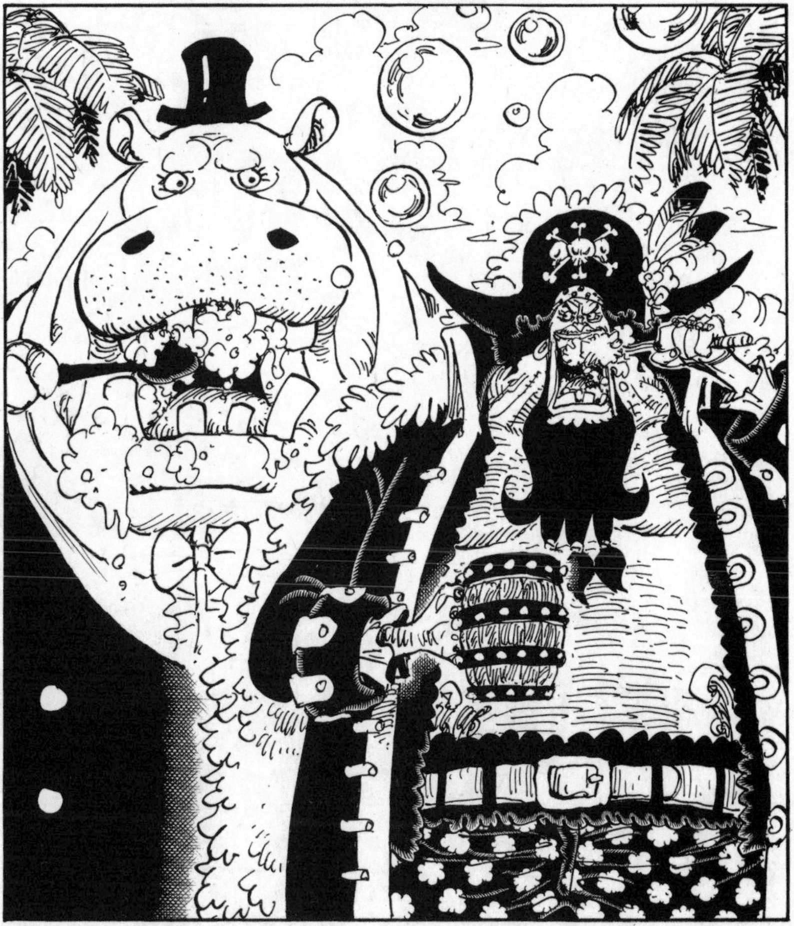

READER REQUEST: "BLACKBEARD AND A HIPPO BRUSHING THEIR TEETH" BY EBI

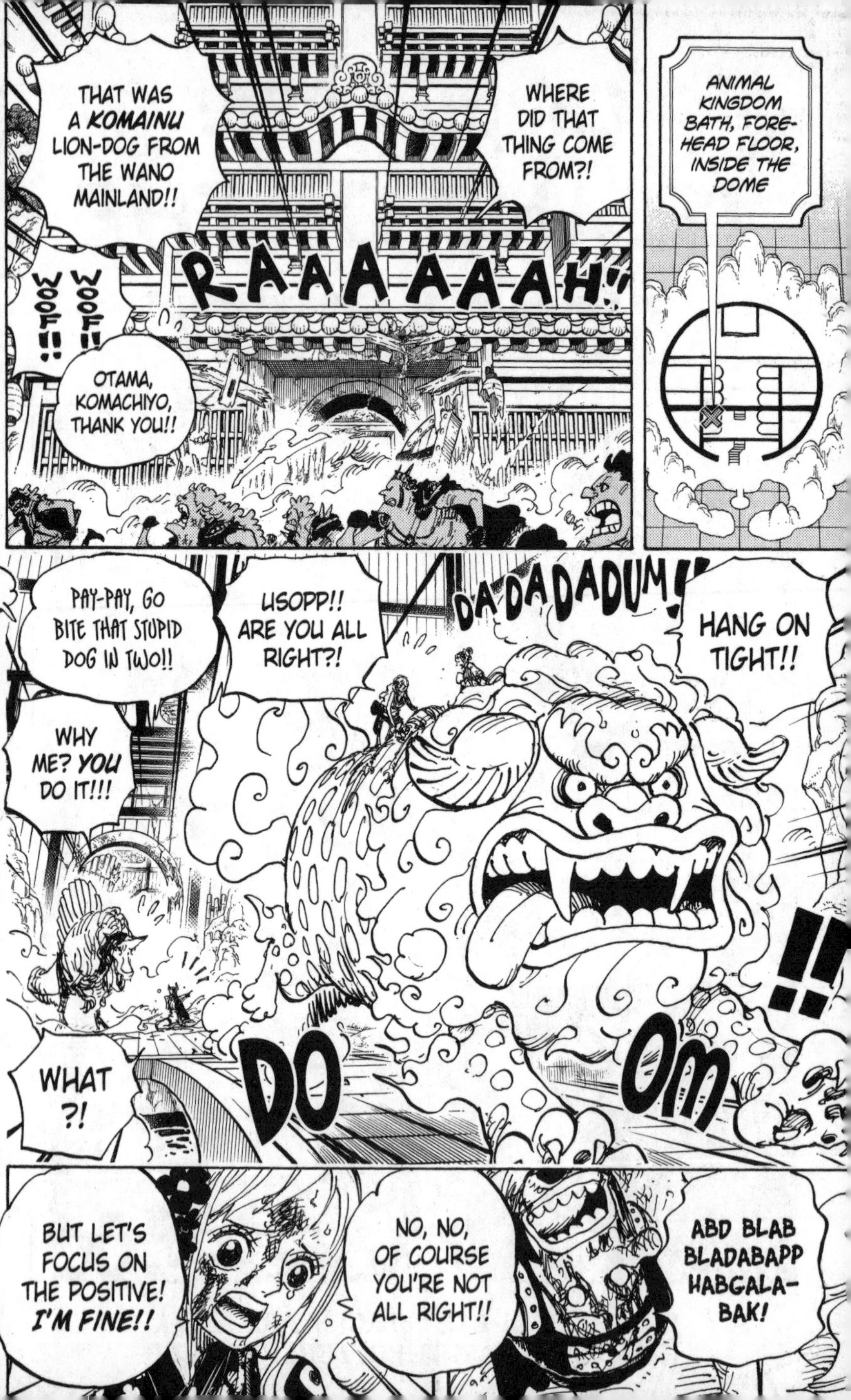
ANIMAL KINGDOM BATH, FOREHEAD FLOOR, INSIDE THE DOME
WHERE DID THAT THING COME FROM?!
THAT WAS A *KOMAINU* LION-DOG FROM THE WANO MAINLAND!!
RAAAAAAH!!
WOOF!! WOOF!!
OTAMA, KOMACHIYO, THANK YOU!!
HANG ON TIGHT!!
DA DA DADUM!!
USOPP!! ARE YOU ALL RIGHT?!
PAY-PAY, GO BITE THAT STUPID DOG IN TWO!!
WHY ME? *YOU* DO IT!!!
DOOM!!
WHAT?!
ABD BLAB BLADABAPP HABGALA-BAK!
NO, NO, OF COURSE YOU'RE NOT ALL RIGHT!!
BUT LET'S FOCUS ON THE POSITIVE! *I'M FINE!!*

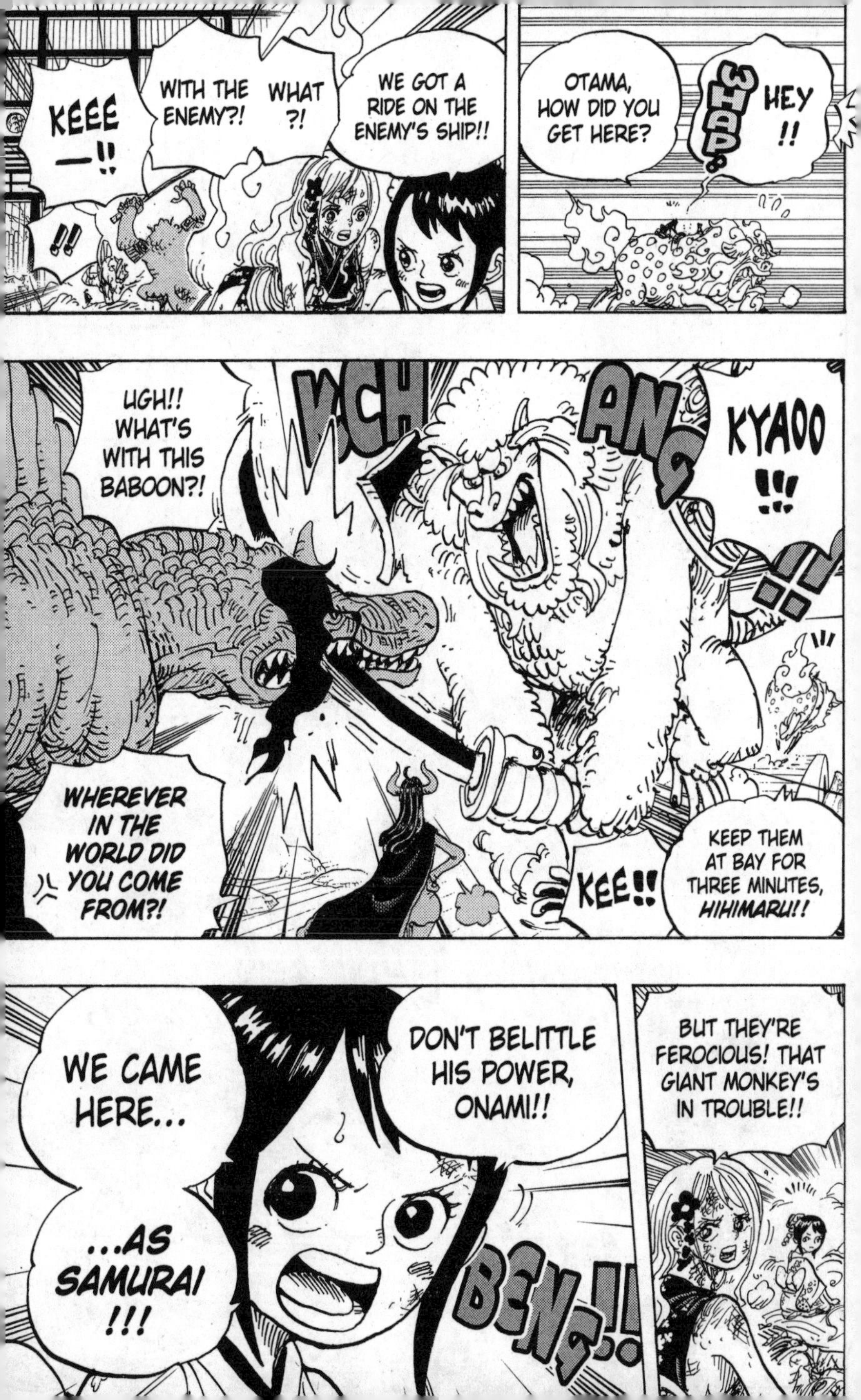
HEY !!
WHAP
OTAMA, HOW DID YOU GET HERE?
WE GOT A RIDE ON THE ENEMY'S SHIP!!
WHAT ?!
WITH THE ENEMY?!
KEEE —!!
!!
KYAOO !!!
KCH
ANG
!!
UGH!! WHAT'S WITH THIS BABOON?!
KEEP THEM AT BAY FOR THREE MINUTES, HIHIMARU!!
KEE!!
WHEREVER IN THE WORLD DID YOU COME FROM?!
BUT THEY'RE FEROCIOUS! THAT GIANT MONKEY'S IN TROUBLE!!
DON'T BELITTLE HIS POWER, ONAMI!!
WE CAME HERE...
BENG!!
...AS SAMURAI !!!

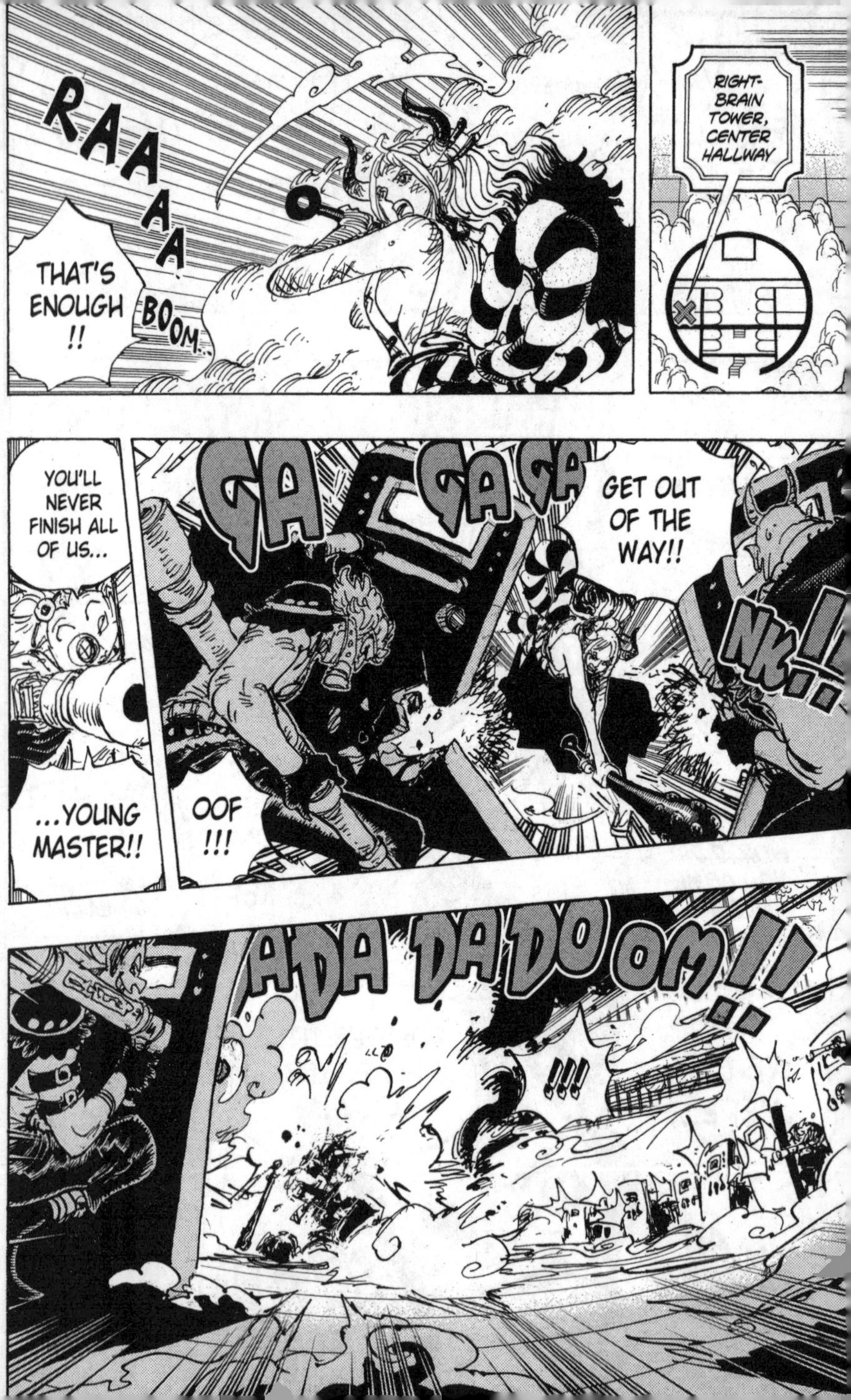

RIGHT-BRAIN TOWER, CENTER HALLWAY
RAAAAA
THAT'S ENOUGH!!
BOOM
NK..!!
GET OUT OF THE WAY!!
GA GA GA
OOF!!!
YOU'LL NEVER FINISH ALL OF US...
...YOUNG MASTER!!
DA DA DOOM!!
!!!

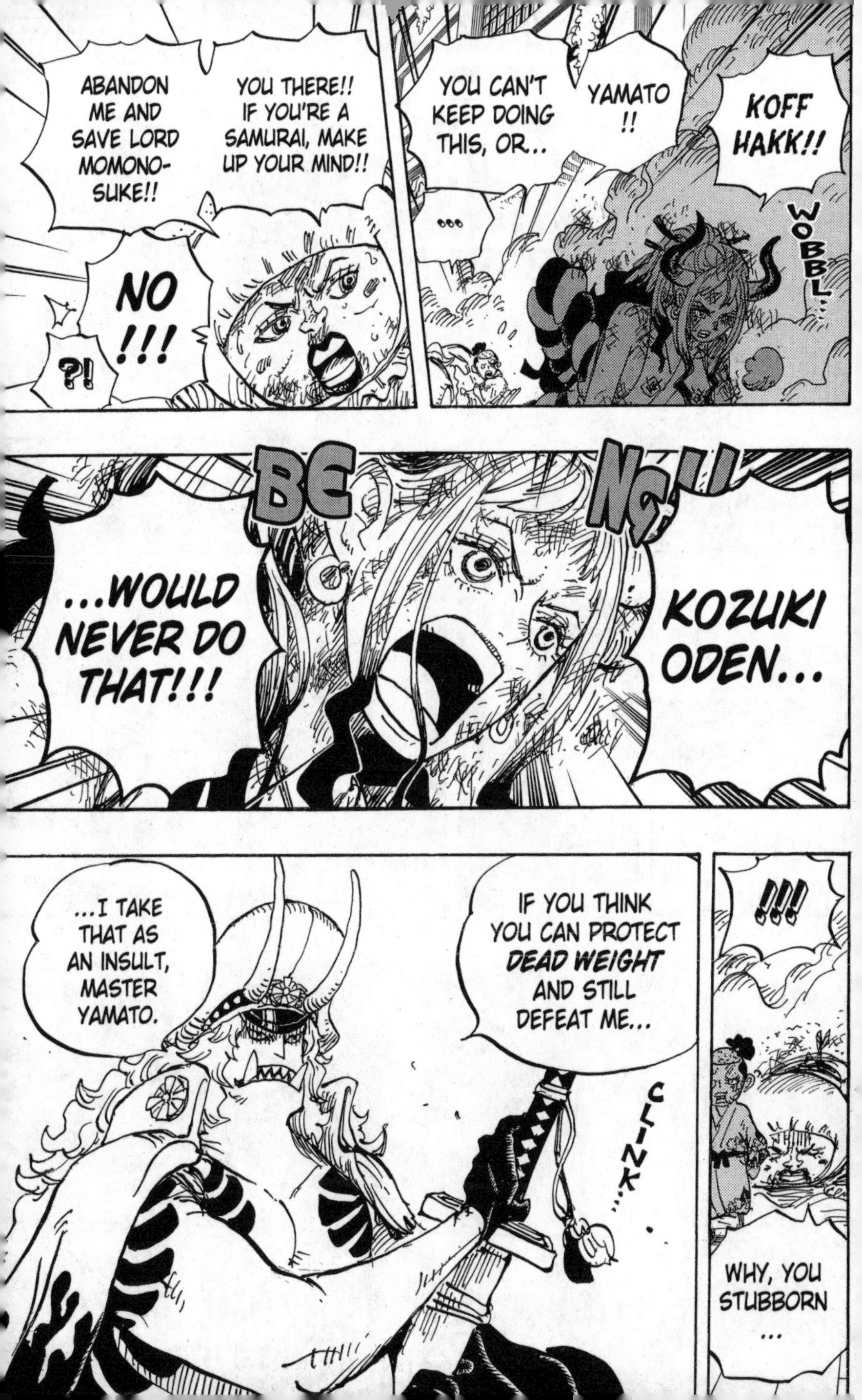
KOFF HAKK!!
YAMATO !!
YOU CAN'T KEEP DOING THIS, OR...
WOBBL...
...
YOU THERE!! IF YOU'RE A SAMURAI, MAKE UP YOUR MIND!!
ABANDON ME AND SAVE LORD MOMONOSUKE!!
NO !!!
?!
BENG!!
KOZUKI ODEN...
...WOULD NEVER DO THAT!!!
!!!
WHY, YOU STUBBORN ...
IF YOU THINK YOU CAN PROTECT DEAD WEIGHT AND STILL DEFEAT ME...
...I TAKE THAT AS AN INSULT, MASTER YAMATO.
CLINK...

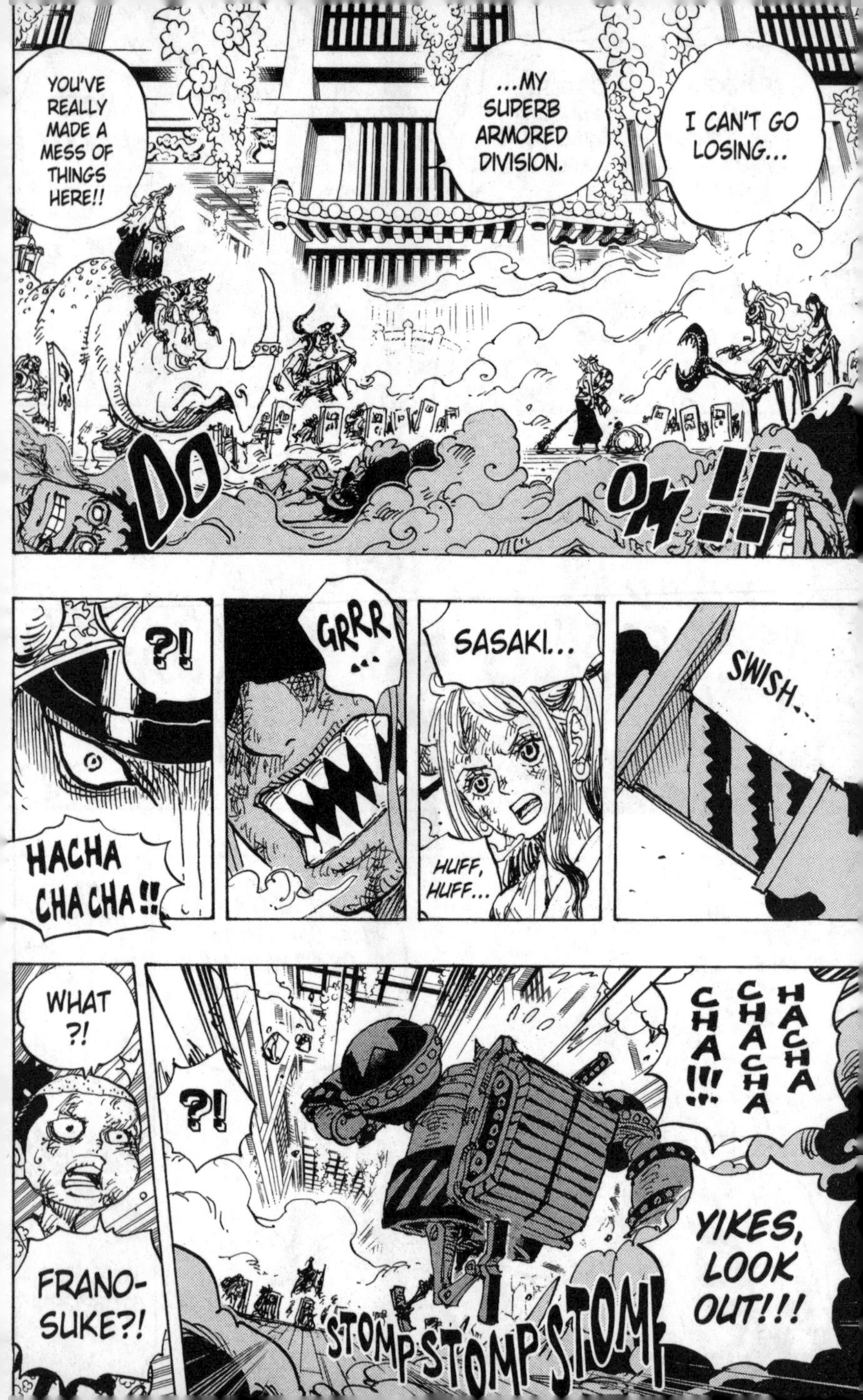
I CAN'T GO LOSING...
...MY SUPERB ARMORED DIVISION.
YOU'VE REALLY MADE A MESS OF THINGS HERE!!
DOOM!!
SWISH...
SASAKI...
HUFF, HUFF...
GRRR...
?!
HACHA CHACHA!!
HACHA CHACHA CHA!!!
?!
YIKES, LOOK OUT!!!
STOMP STOMP STOM
WHAT ?!
FRANO-SUKE?!

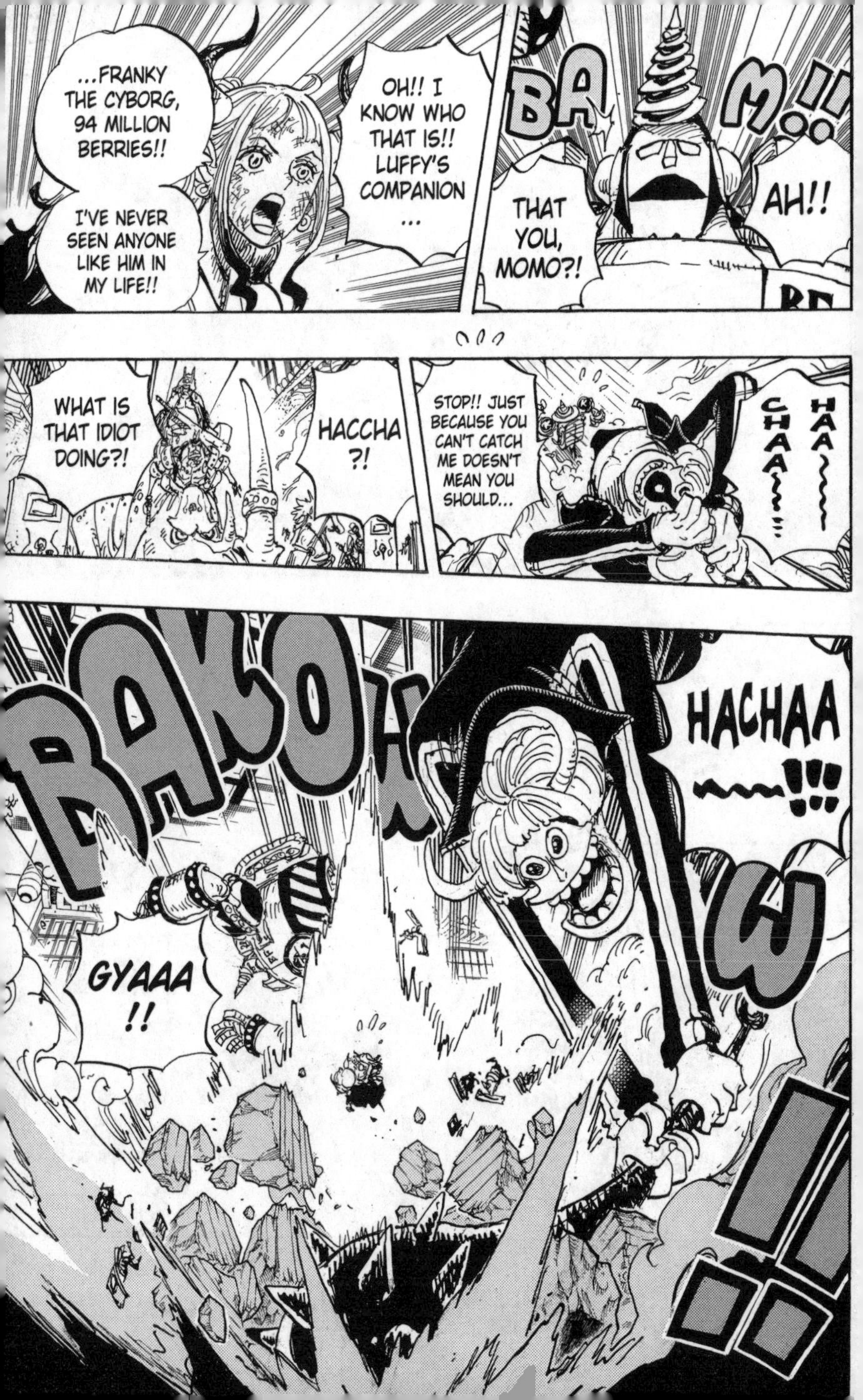
BAM!!
AH!!
THAT YOU, MOMO?!
OH!! I KNOW WHO THAT IS!! LUFFY'S COMPANION ...
...FRANKY THE CYBORG, 94 MILLION BERRIES!!
I'VE NEVER SEEN ANYONE LIKE HIM IN MY LIFE!!
HAA~~
CHAA~~!!
STOP!! JUST BECAUSE YOU CAN'T CATCH ME DOESN'T MEAN YOU SHOULD...
HACCHA ?!
WHAT IS THAT IDIOT DOING?!
HACHAA ~~!!!
GYAAA !!

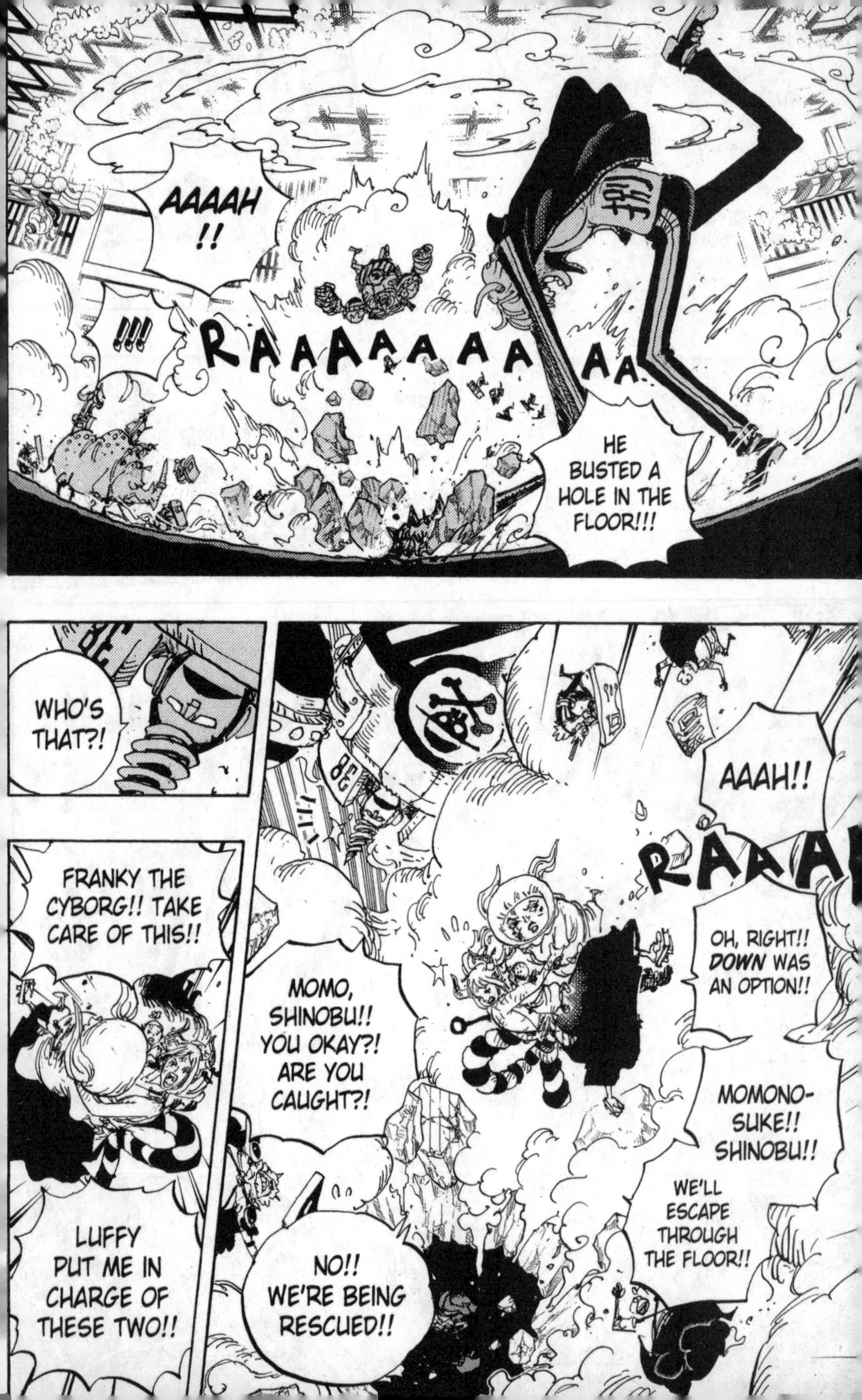
AAAAH !!
!!!
RAAAAAAAAA
HE BUSTED A HOLE IN THE FLOOR!!!
AAAH!!
RAAA
OH, RIGHT!! DOWN WAS AN OPTION!!
MOMONO-SUKE!! SHINOBU!!
MOMO, SHINOBU!! YOU OKAY?! ARE YOU CAUGHT?!
WE'LL ESCAPE THROUGH THE FLOOR!!
NO!! WE'RE BEING RESCUED!!
WHO'S THAT?!
FRANKY THE CYBORG!! TAKE CARE OF THIS!!
LUFFY PUT ME IN CHARGE OF THESE TWO!!

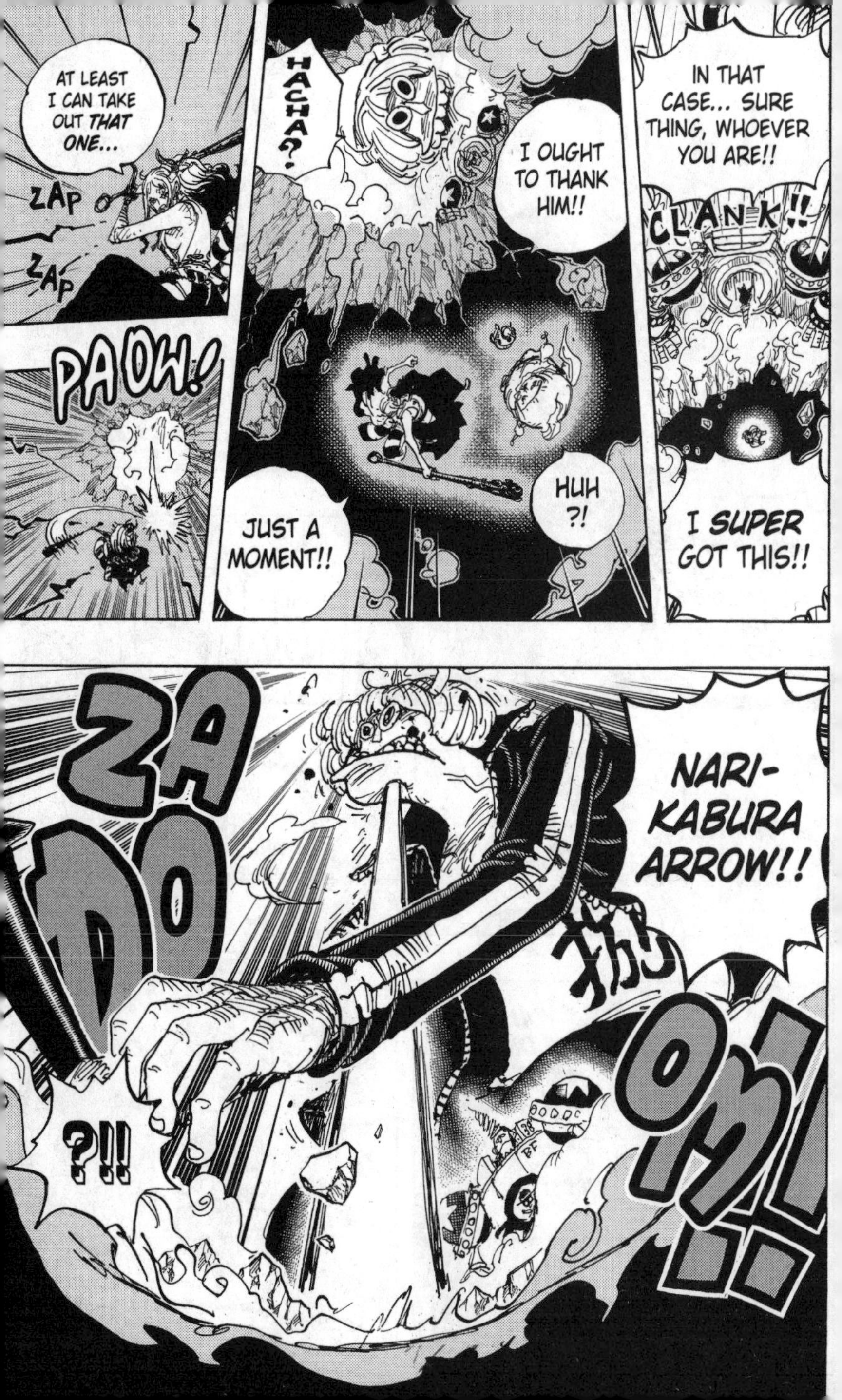
IN THAT CASE... SURE THING, WHOEVER YOU ARE!!
CLANK!!
I SUPER GOT THIS!!
HACHA?
I OUGHT TO THANK HIM!!
HUH ?!
JUST A MOMENT!!
AT LEAST I CAN TAKE OUT *THAT* ONE...
ZAP
ZAP
PAOW!
NARI-KABURA ARROW!!
ZADOOM!!
?!!

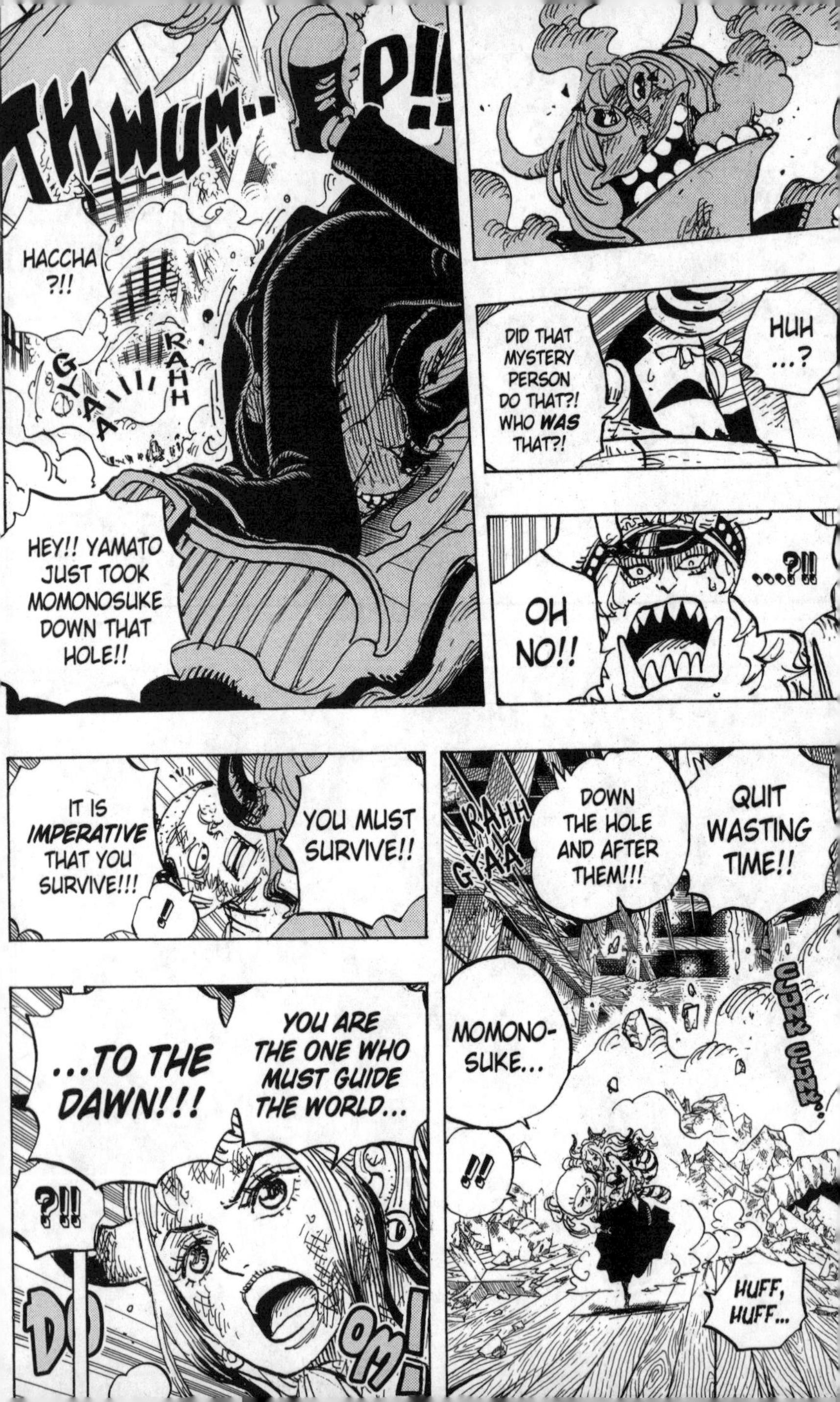
HUH ...?
DID THAT MYSTERY PERSON DO THAT?! WHO WAS THAT?!
...?!!
OH NO!!
THWUM...P!!
HACCHA ?!!
GYAA
RAHH
HEY!! YAMATO JUST TOOK MOMONOSUKE DOWN THAT HOLE!!
QUIT WASTING TIME!!
DOWN THE HOLE AND AFTER THEM!!!
RAHH
GYAA
CLINK CLINK..
MOMONO-SUKE...
!!
HUFF, HUFF...
YOU MUST SURVIVE!!
IT IS IMPERATIVE THAT YOU SURVIVE!!!
!
YOU ARE THE ONE WHO MUST GUIDE THE WORLD...
...TO THE DAWN!!!
?!!
DOOM!

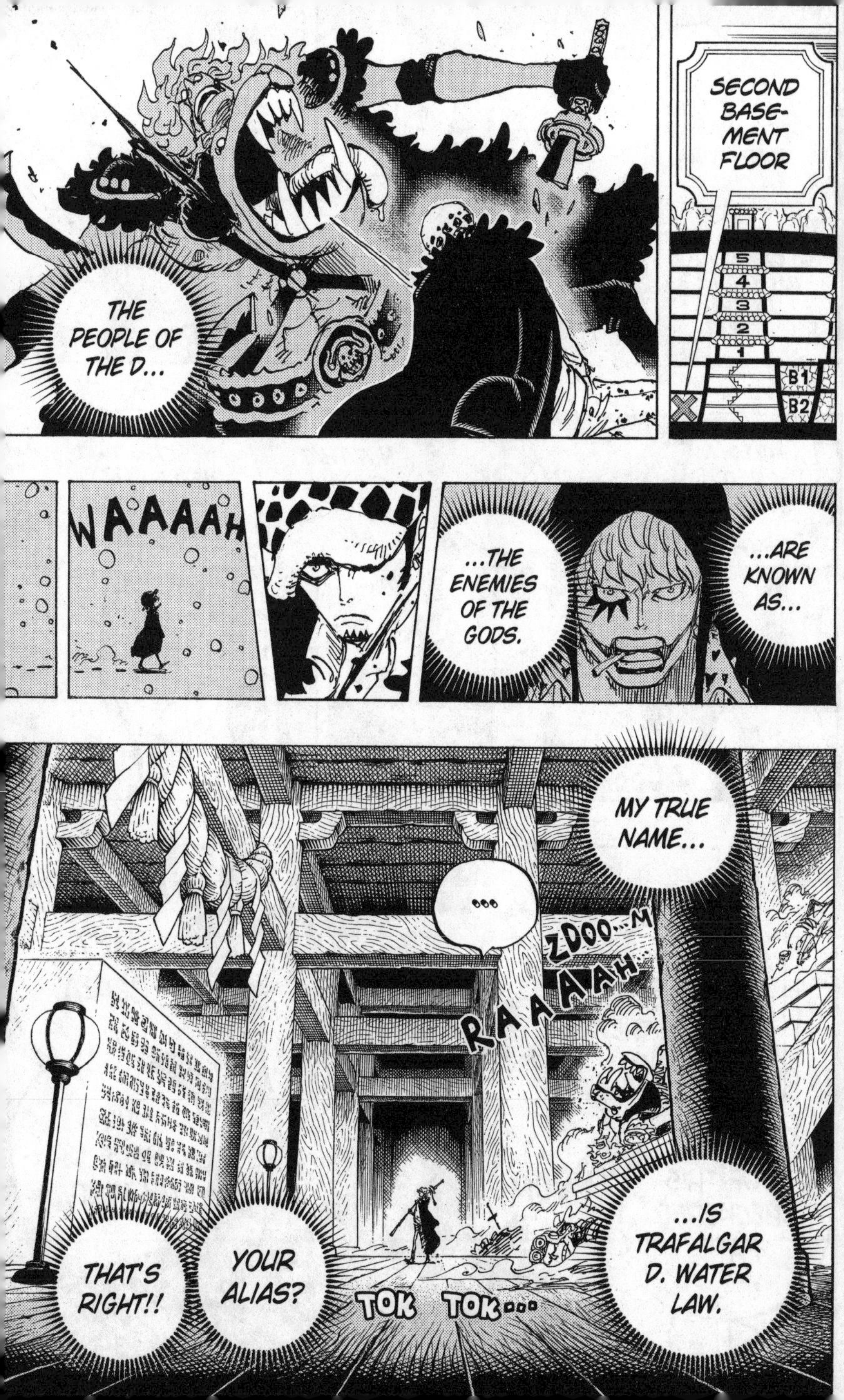
SECOND BASEMENT FLOOR
5
4
3
2
1
B1
B2
THE PEOPLE OF THE D...
...ARE KNOWN AS...
...THE ENEMIES OF THE GODS.
WAAAAH
MY TRUE NAME...
...
ZDOOOM
RAAAAH
...IS TRAFALGAR D. WATER LAW.
TOK TOK...
YOUR ALIAS?
THAT'S RIGHT!!

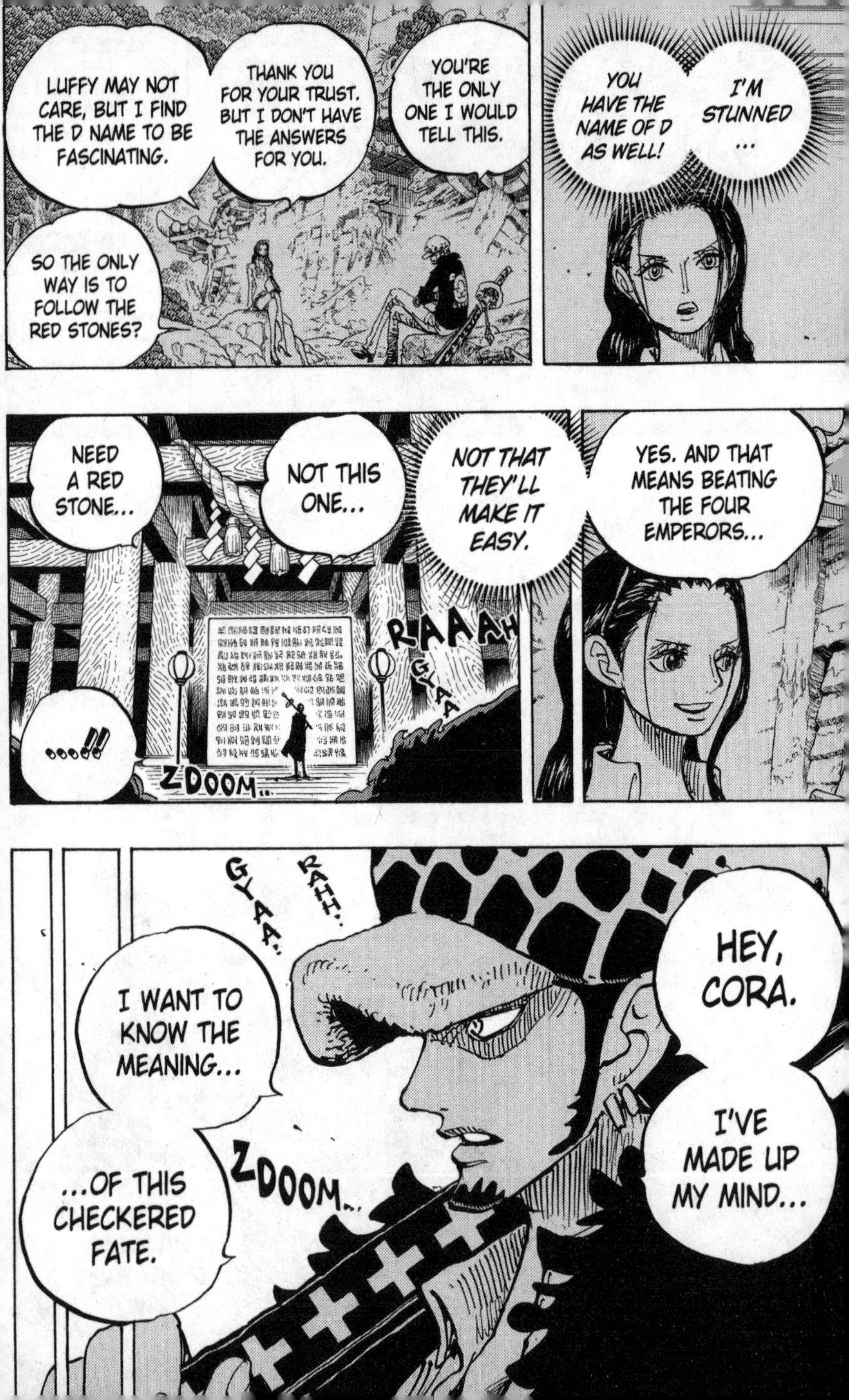
I'M STUNNED...
YOU HAVE THE NAME OF D AS WELL!
YOU'RE THE ONLY ONE I WOULD TELL THIS.
THANK YOU FOR YOUR TRUST. BUT I DON'T HAVE THE ANSWERS FOR YOU.
LUFFY MAY NOT CARE, BUT I FIND THE D NAME TO BE FASCINATING.
SO THE ONLY WAY IS TO FOLLOW THE RED STONES?
YES. AND THAT MEANS BEATING THE FOUR EMPERORS...
NOT THAT THEY'LL MAKE IT EASY.
RAAAH
GYAAA
NOT THIS ONE...
NEED A RED STONE...
......!!
ZDOOM..
HEY, CORA.
I'VE MADE UP MY MIND...
RAHH!
GYAA..
I WANT TO KNOW THE MEANING...
...OF THIS CHECKERED FATE.
ZDOOM..

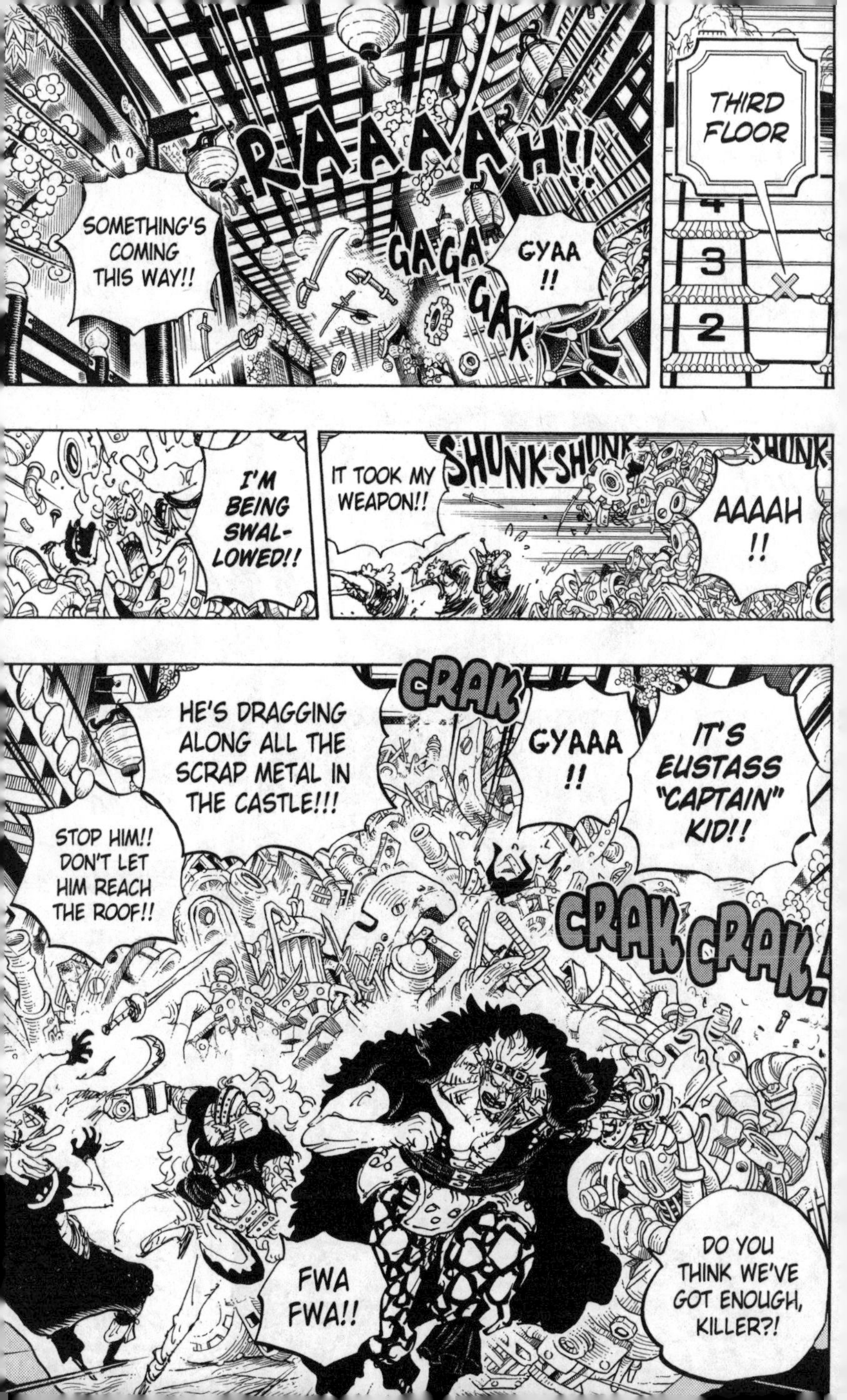
THIRD FLOOR
4
3
2
RAAAAH!!
GYAA!!
GAGAGAK
SOMETHING'S COMING THIS WAY!!
SHUNK
SHUNK-SHUNK
AAAAH!!
IT TOOK MY WEAPON!!
I'M BEING SWALLOWED!!
CRAK
IT'S EUSTASS "CAPTAIN" KID!!
GYAAA!!
HE'S DRAGGING ALONG ALL THE SCRAP METAL IN THE CASTLE!!!
CRAK CRAK
STOP HIM!! DON'T LET HIM REACH THE ROOF!!
DO YOU THINK WE'VE GOT ENOUGH, KILLER?!
FWA FWA!!

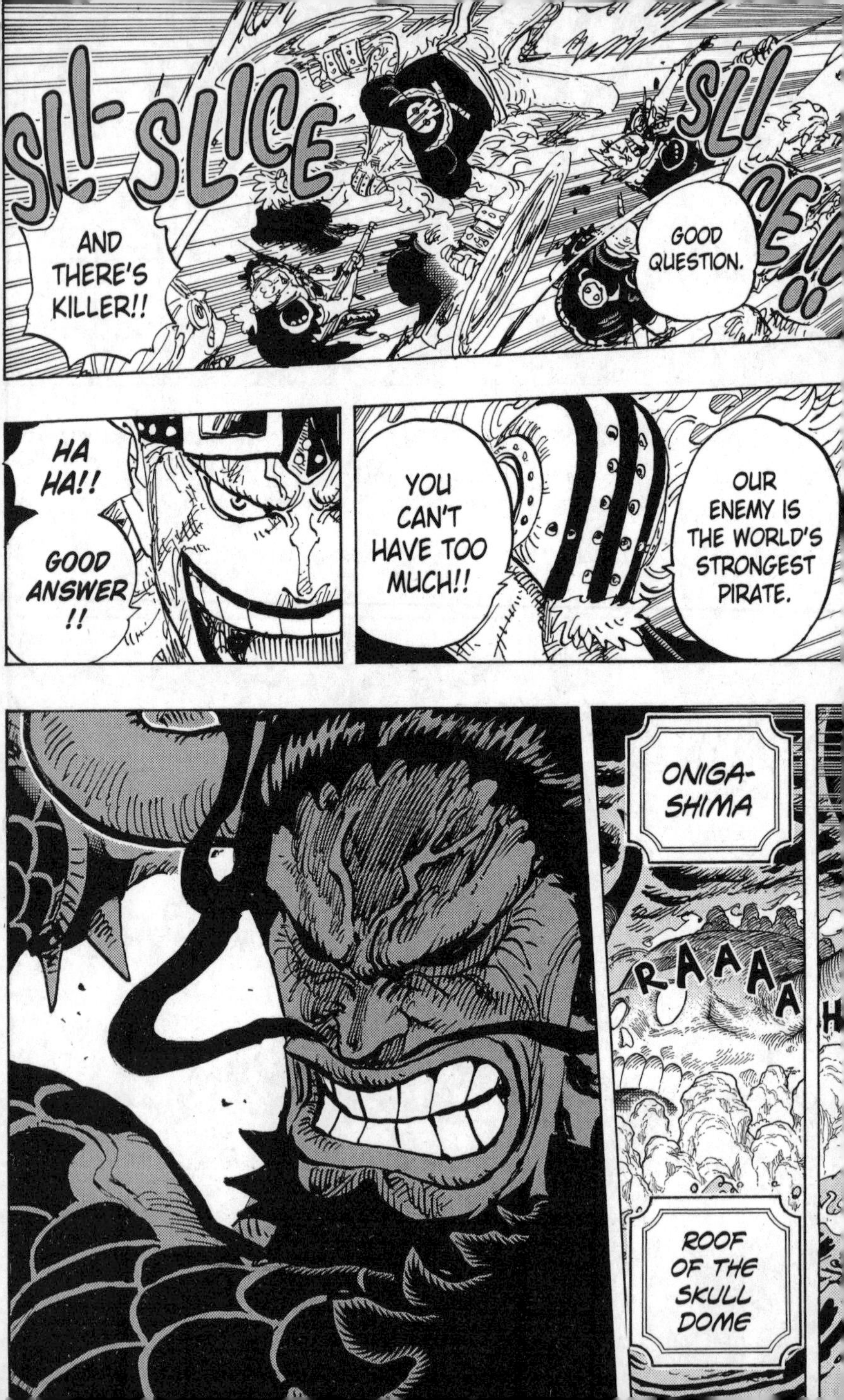
SLI-CE!!
GOOD QUESTION.
SLI-SLICE
AND THERE'S KILLER!!
OUR ENEMY IS THE WORLD'S STRONGEST PIRATE.
YOU CAN'T HAVE TOO MUCH!!
HA HA!!
GOOD ANSWER!!
ONIGA-SHIMA
RAAAAH
ROOF OF THE SKULL DOME

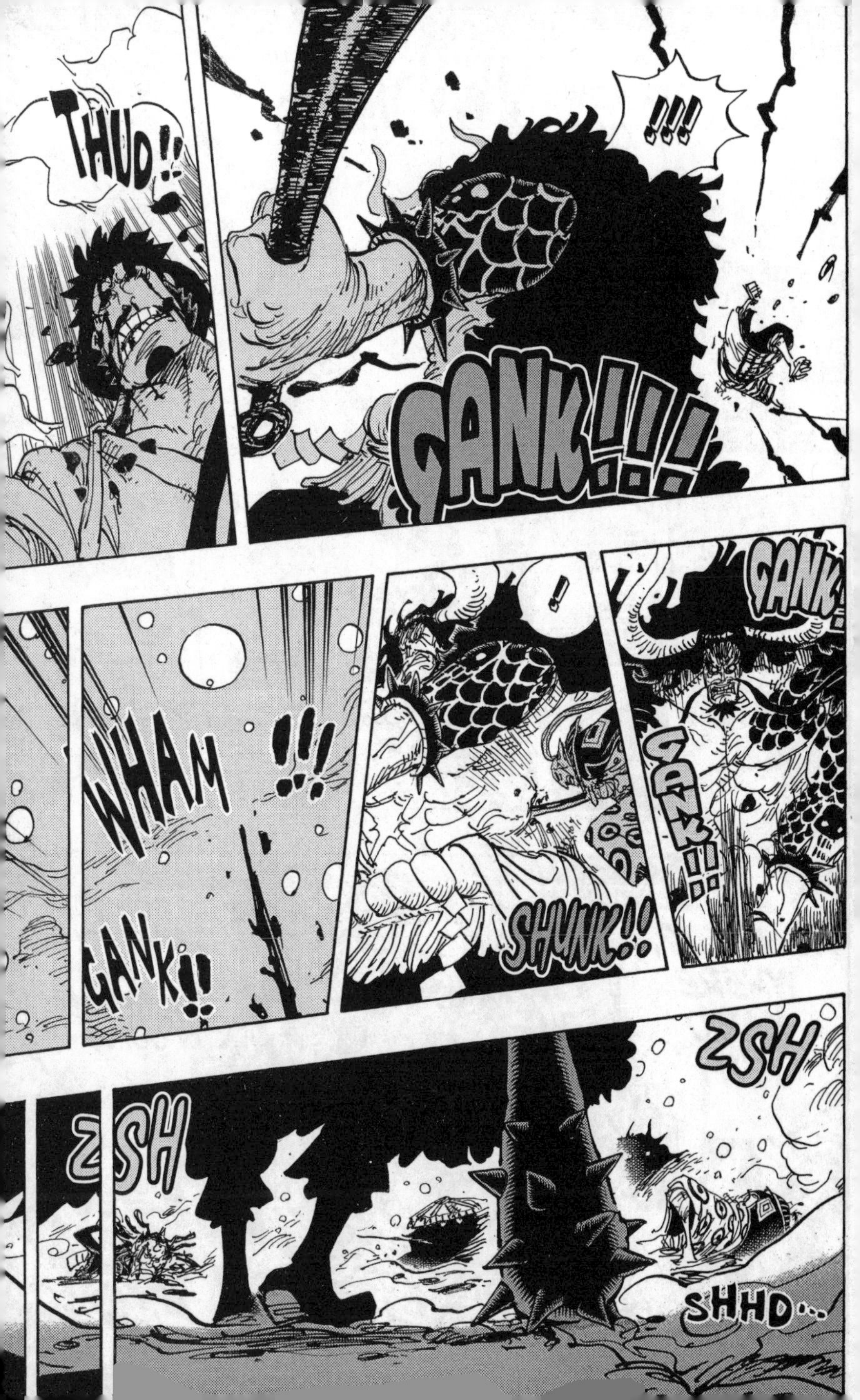
!!!
GANK!!!!
THUD!!
GANK!
GANK!!
!
SHUNK!!
WHAM!!!
GANK!!
ZSH
SHHD...
ZSH

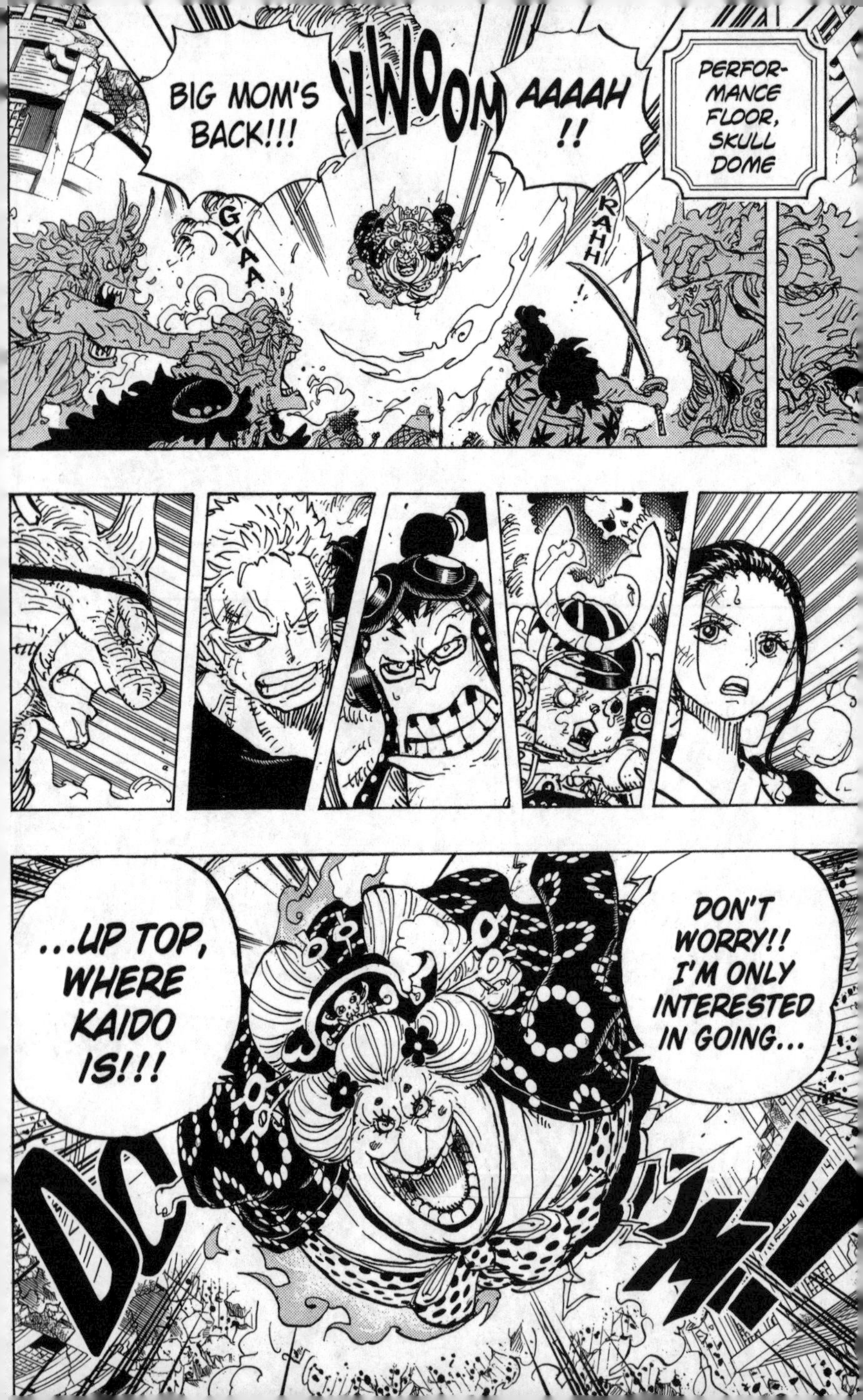
PERFOR-MANCE FLOOR, SKULL DOME
AAAAH!!
VWOOM
BIG MOM'S BACK!!!
RAHH!!
GYAA
DON'T WORRY!! I'M ONLY INTERESTED IN GOING...
...UP TOP, WHERE KAIDO IS!!!

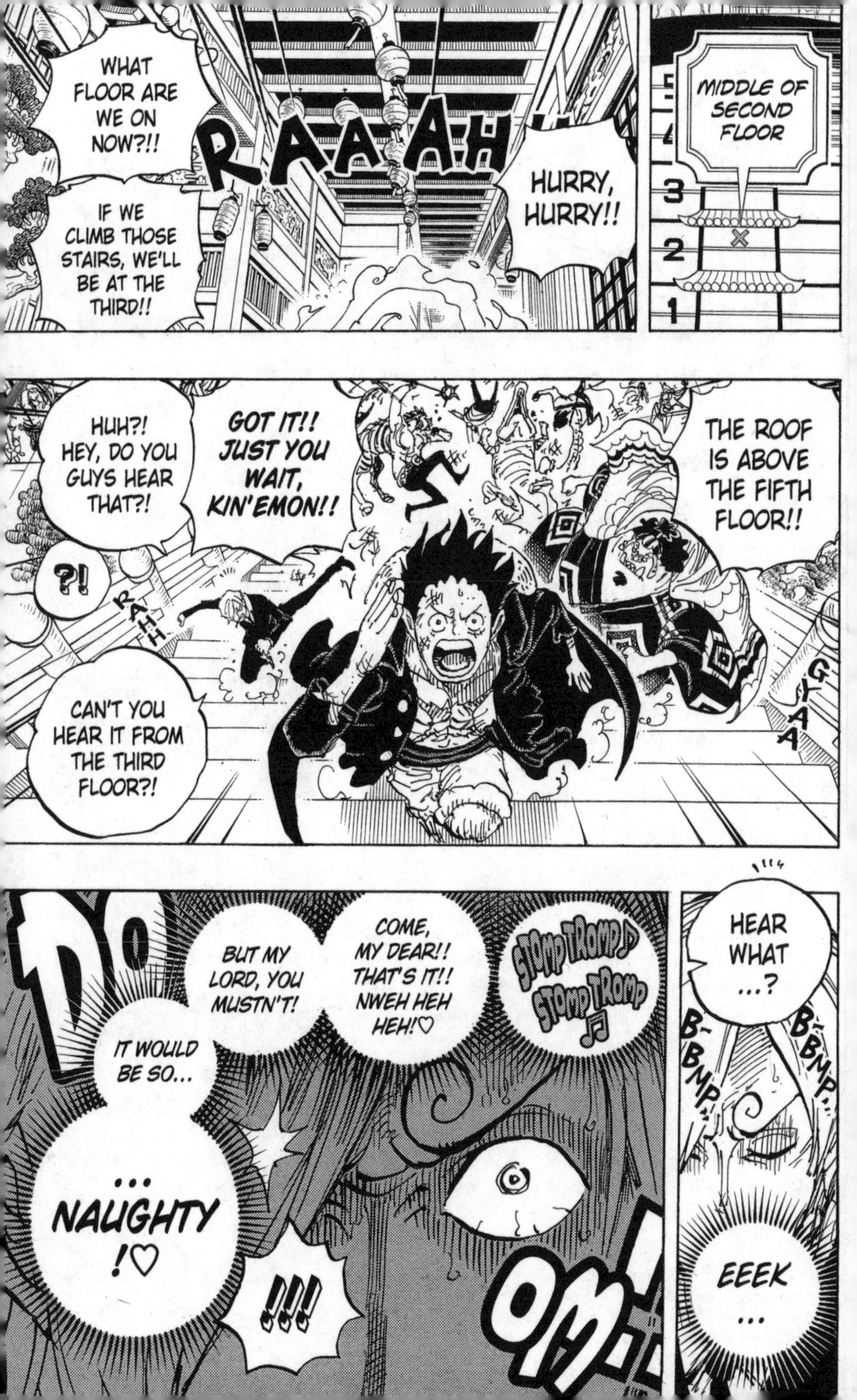
MIDDLE OF SECOND FLOOR
3
2
1
HURRY, HURRY!!
RAAAH
WHAT FLOOR ARE WE ON NOW?!!
IF WE CLIMB THOSE STAIRS, WE'LL BE AT THE THIRD!!
THE ROOF IS ABOVE THE FIFTH FLOOR!!
GYAA
GOT IT!! JUST YOU WAIT, KIN'EMON!!
HUH?! HEY, DO YOU GUYS HEAR THAT?!
?!
RAHH
CAN'T YOU HEAR IT FROM THE THIRD FLOOR?!
HEAR WHAT ...?
B-BMP...
B-BMP...
EEEK ...
STOMP TROMP♪ STOMP TROMP♫
COME, MY DEAR!! THAT'S IT!! NWEH HEH HEH!♡
BUT MY LORD, YOU MUSTN'T!
IT WOULD BE SO...
...NAUGHTY!♡
!!!

SBS Question Corner

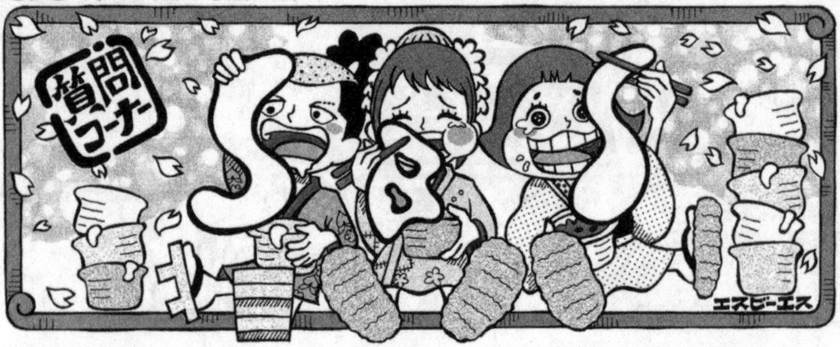
質問コーナー
エスビーエス

(Eri Kazama, Saitama)

Q: Odacchi! Heso! Please draw an anthropomorphic version of Nami's climate baton! Speaking for all Nami fans.

--Tsubocchi

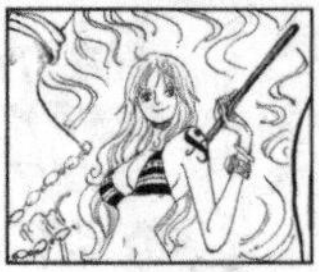

A: Okay. I'm good at this!

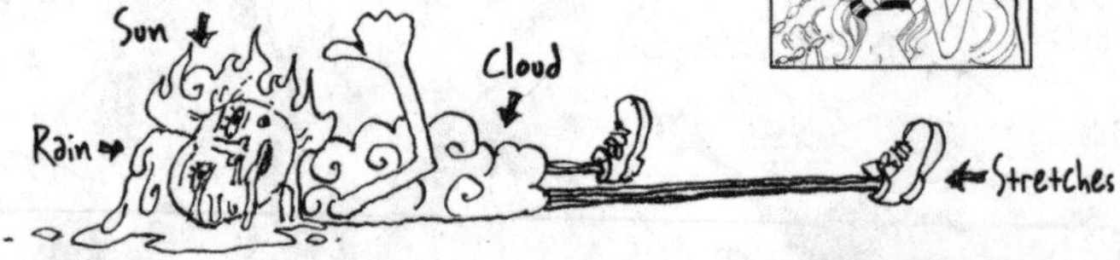
Sun
Cloud
Rain
Stretches

Q: When Komachiyo and Otama saved Usopp, he said, "Abd blab bladabapphabgalabak!" (in chapter 996). Is it possible that he's saying "Who do you think I am?!" Anyway, I'm glad that Nami's all right!!

--Yana

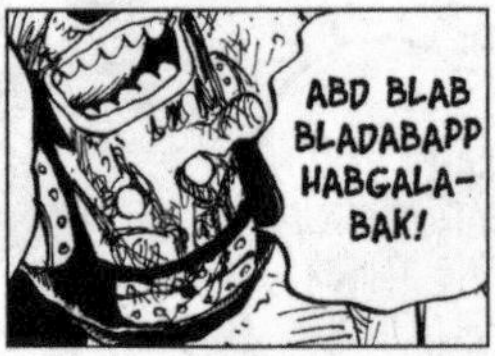
ABD BLAB BLADABAPP HABGALA-BAK!

A: Wow!! You figured it out!! Correct!! LOL.

Q: When Kaido eats fish, does he eat the skin too?

--Ebi

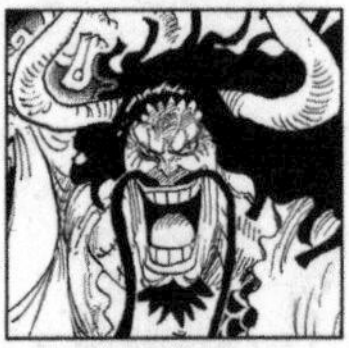

A: Actually, he loves the skin. This is how the conversation goes at the table.
"Hey...is the skin safe to eat on this fish?"
"Yes! We scraped the scales off!"
"Worororo ro."

Q: Good evening, Odacchi. When the Straw Hats' hair grows out, who cuts it?

--Pumpkin

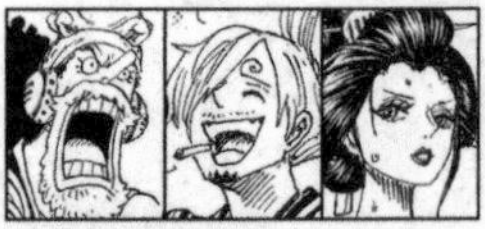

These three ↑

A: There are three people on the crew who are good at cutting hair. So when someone wants a cut, they just ask.

Q: What kind of person is Otoko's mother, meaning Yasuie's wife? Is she still alive?

--Goemon

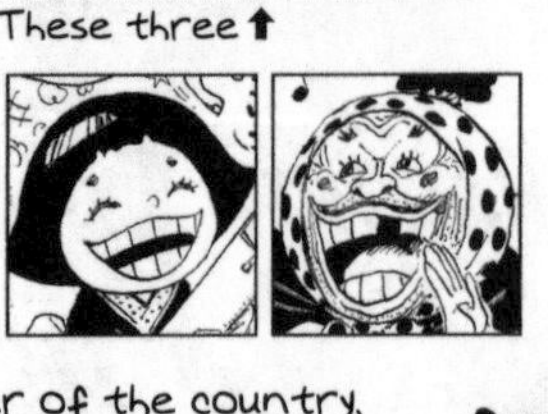

A: Yasuie was married long ago. They had no children, and he's been alone ever since his wife died. After he survived Kaido's takeover of the country, he found an orphan baby in Ebisu Town. That was Otoko. But Otoko doesn't know they aren't related by blood.

Chapter 997:
FLAME CLOUDS

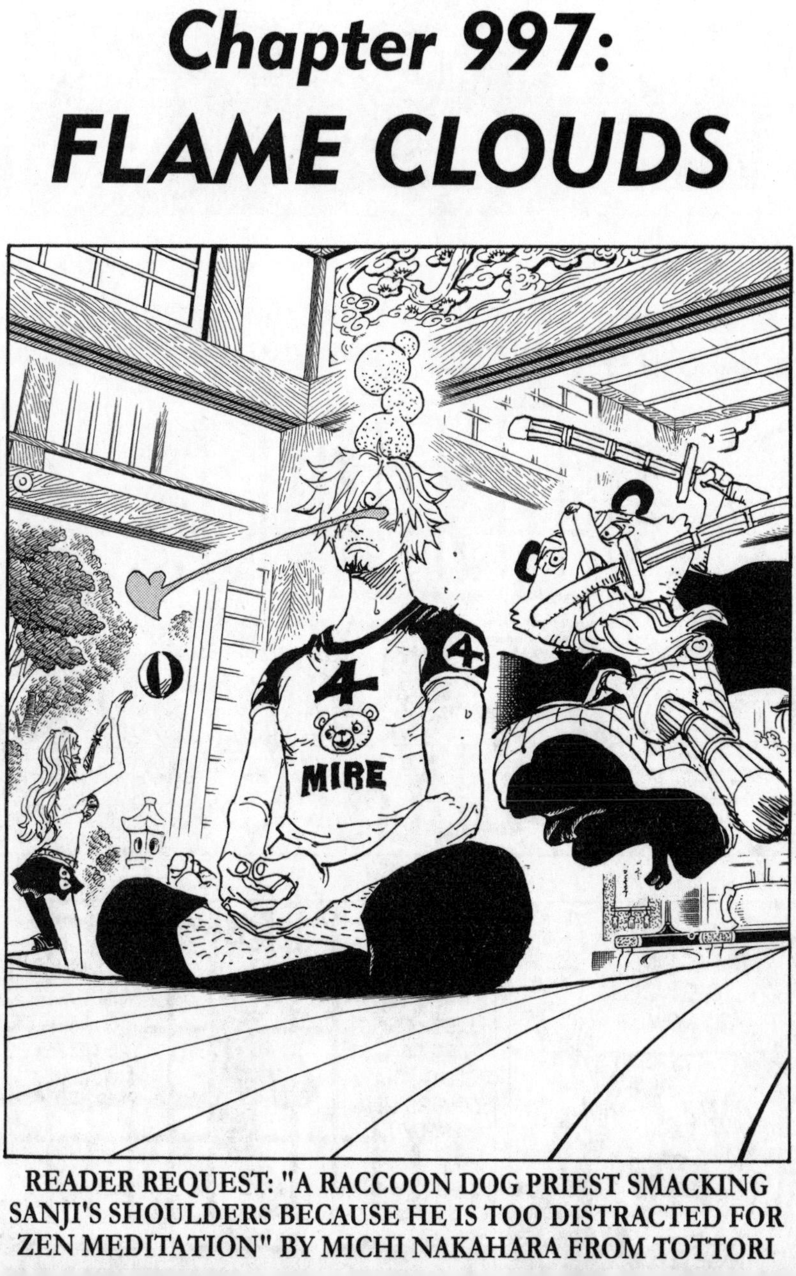
4
4
MIRE

READER REQUEST: "A RACCOON DOG PRIEST SMACKING SANJI'S SHOULDERS BECAUSE HE IS TOO DISTRACTED FOR ZEN MEDITATION" BY MICHI NAKAHARA FROM TOTTORI

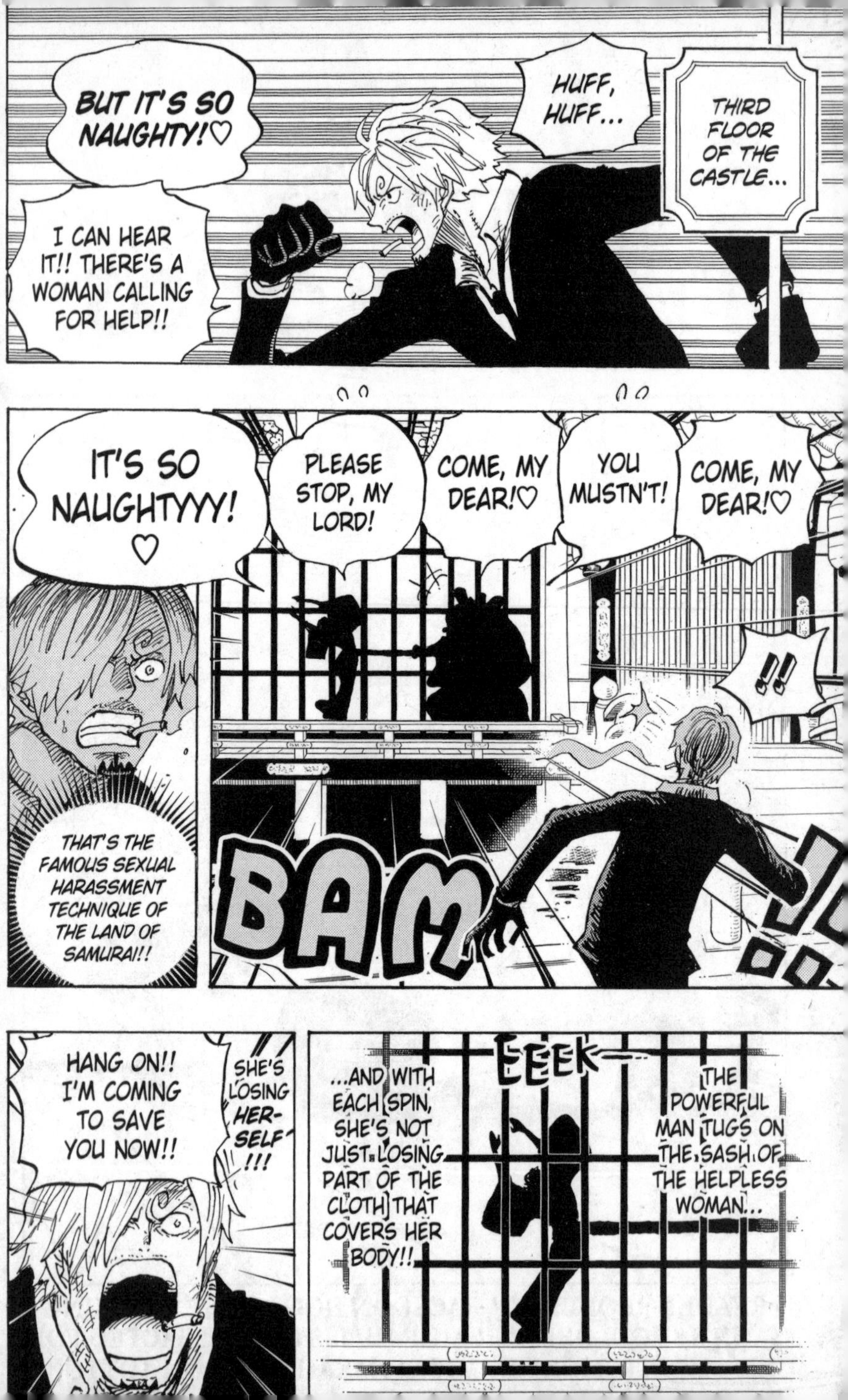
THIRD FLOOR OF THE CASTLE...
HUFF, HUFF...
BUT IT'S SO NAUGHTY!♡
I CAN HEAR IT!! THERE'S A WOMAN CALLING FOR HELP!!
COME, MY DEAR!♡
YOU MUSTN'T!
COME, MY DEAR!♡
PLEASE STOP, MY LORD!
!!
BAM
IT'S SO NAUGHTYYY! ♡
THAT'S THE FAMOUS SEXUAL HARASSMENT TECHNIQUE OF THE LAND OF SAMURAI!!
EEEK
THE POWERFUL MAN TUGS ON THE SASH OF THE HELPLESS WOMAN...
...AND WITH EACH SPIN, SHE'S NOT JUST LOSING PART OF THE CLOTH THAT COVERS HER BODY!!
SHE'S LOSING HER-SELF!!!
HANG ON!! I'M COMING TO SAVE YOU NOW!!

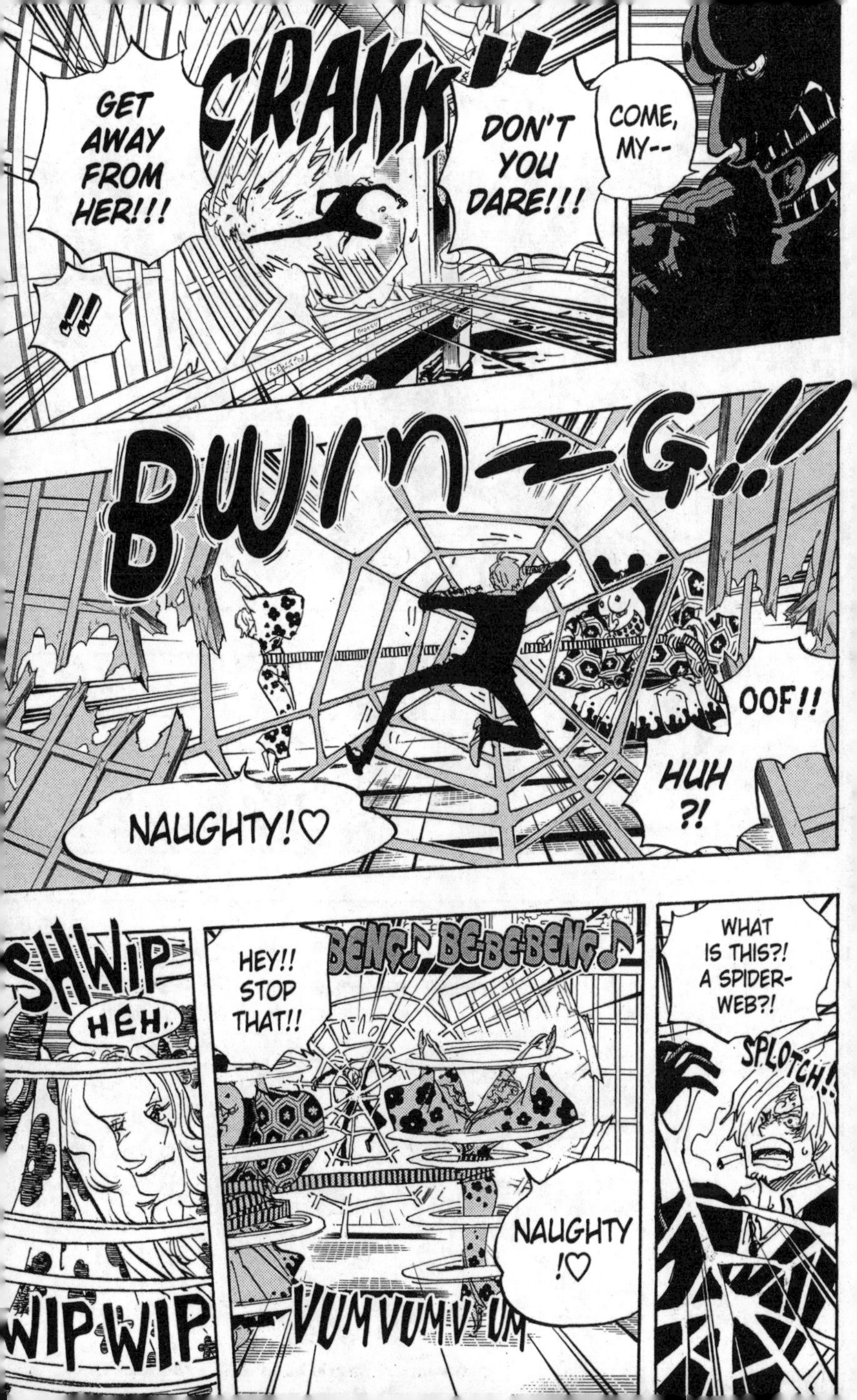
COME, MY--
DON'T YOU DARE!!!
CRAKK
GET AWAY FROM HER!!!
!!
BWINNG!!
OOF!!
HUH ?!
NAUGHTY!♡
WHAT IS THIS?! A SPIDER-WEB?!
SPLOTCH!!
BENG♪ BE-BE-BENG♪
HEY!! STOP THAT!!
NAUGHTY !♡
VUM VUM V UM
SHWIP
HEH
WIP WIP

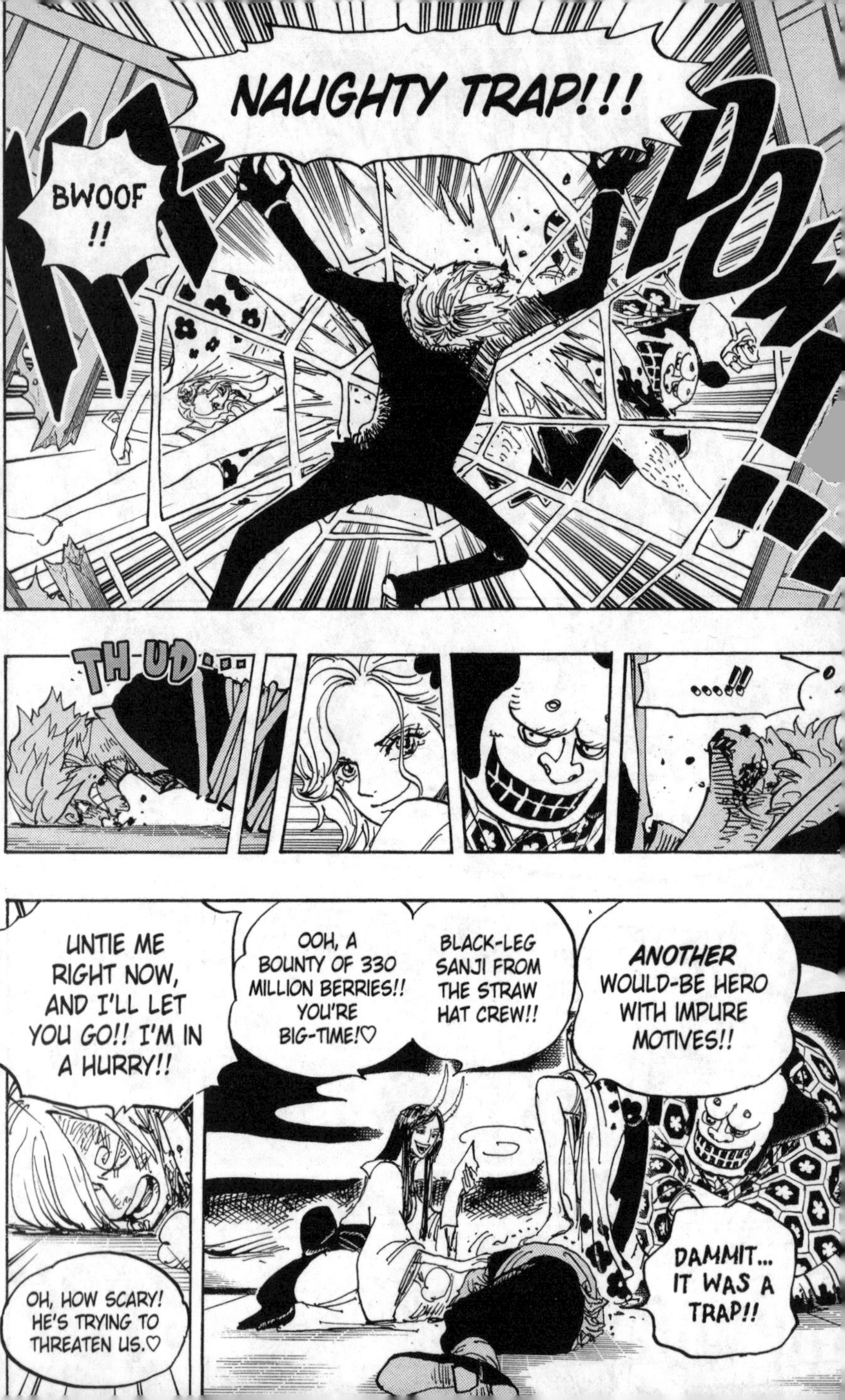
NAUGHTY TRAP!!!
BWOOF !!
...!!
THUD...
ANOTHER WOULD-BE HERO WITH IMPURE MOTIVES!!
BLACK-LEG SANJI FROM THE STRAW HAT CREW!!
OOH, A BOUNTY OF 330 MILLION BERRIES!! YOU'RE BIG-TIME!♡
DAMMIT... IT WAS A TRAP!!
UNTIE ME RIGHT NOW, AND I'LL LET YOU GO!! I'M IN A HURRY!!
OH, HOW SCARY! HE'S TRYING TO THREATEN US.♡

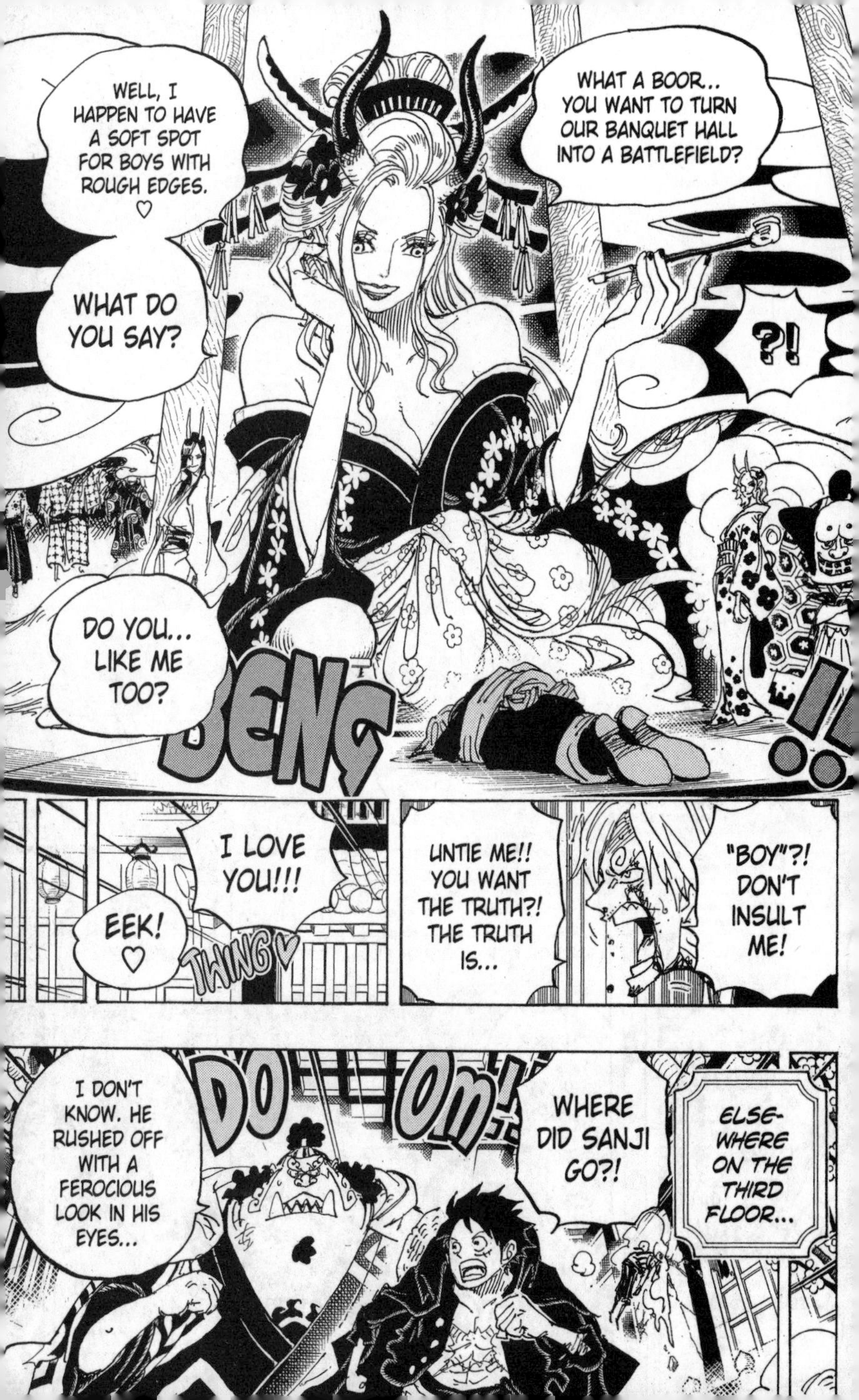
WHAT A BOOR.. YOU WANT TO TURN OUR BANQUET HALL INTO A BATTLEFIELD?
?!
!!..
WELL, I HAPPEN TO HAVE A SOFT SPOT FOR BOYS WITH ROUGH EDGES. ♡
WHAT DO YOU SAY?
DO YOU... LIKE ME TOO?
BENG
"BOY"?! DON'T INSULT ME!
UNTIE ME!! YOU WANT THE TRUTH?! THE TRUTH IS...
I LOVE YOU!!!
EEK! ♡
THING♡
ELSE-WHERE ON THE THIRD FLOOR...
WHERE DID SANJI GO?!
DO OM!
I DON'T KNOW. HE RUSHED OFF WITH A FEROCIOUS LOOK IN HIS EYES...

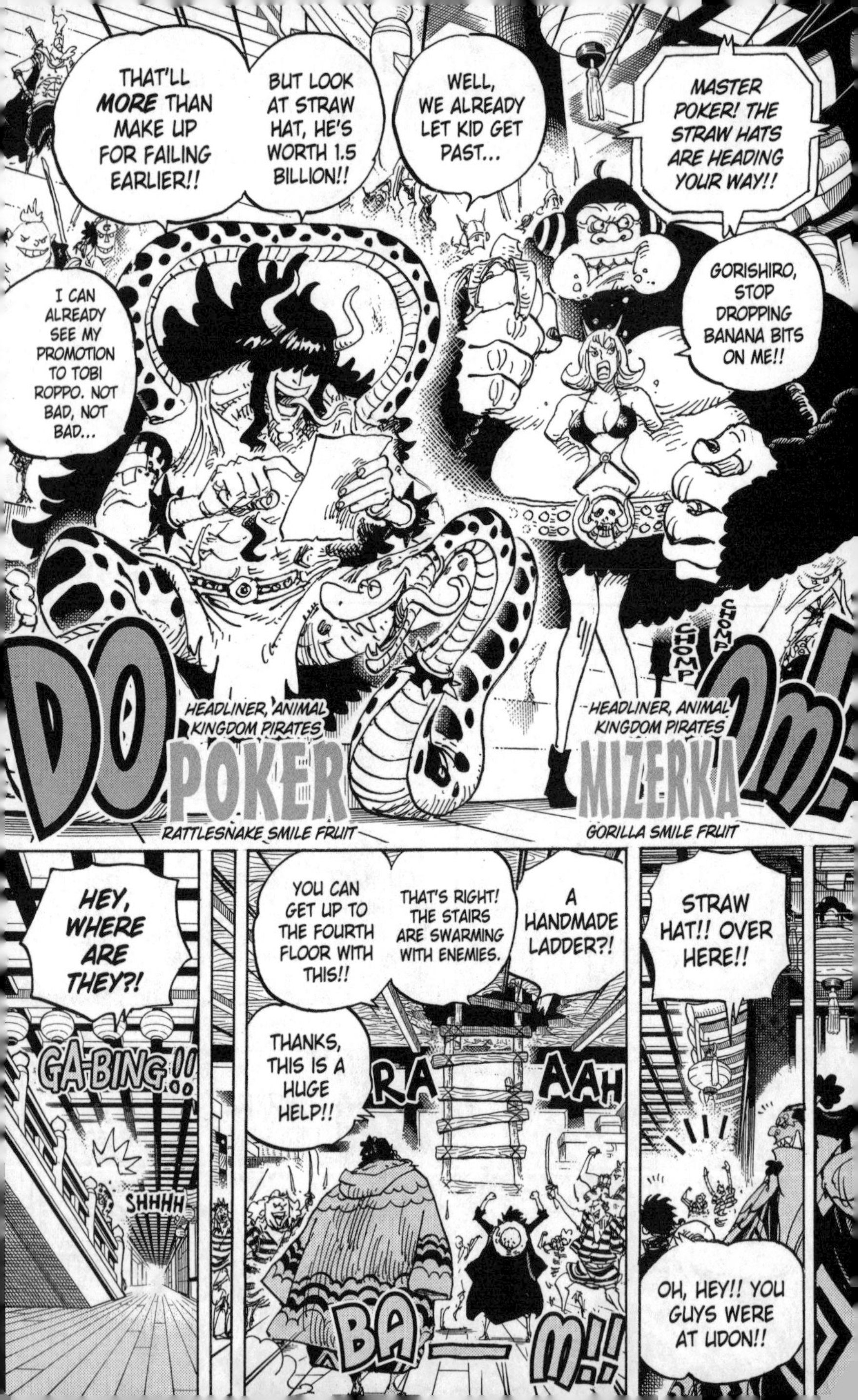
MASTER POKER! THE STRAW HATS ARE HEADING YOUR WAY!!
WELL, WE ALREADY LET KID GET PAST...
BUT LOOK AT STRAW HAT, HE'S WORTH 1.5 BILLION!!
THAT'LL MORE THAN MAKE UP FOR FAILING EARLIER!!
GORISHIRO, STOP DROPPING BANANA BITS ON ME!!
I CAN ALREADY SEE MY PROMOTION TO TOBI ROPPO. NOT BAD, NOT BAD...
CHOMP
CHOMP
DOOM!
HEADLINER, ANIMAL KINGDOM PIRATES
MIZERKA
GORILLA SMILE FRUIT
HEADLINER, ANIMAL KINGDOM PIRATES
POKER
RATTLESNAKE SMILE FRUIT
STRAW HAT!! OVER HERE!!
OH, HEY!! YOU GUYS WERE AT UDON!!
A HANDMADE LADDER?!
THAT'S RIGHT! THE STAIRS ARE SWARMING WITH ENEMIES.
YOU CAN GET UP TO THE FOURTH FLOOR WITH THIS!!
THANKS, THIS IS A HUGE HELP!!
RAAAH
BA-M!!
HEY, WHERE ARE THEY?!
GA-BING!!
SHHHH

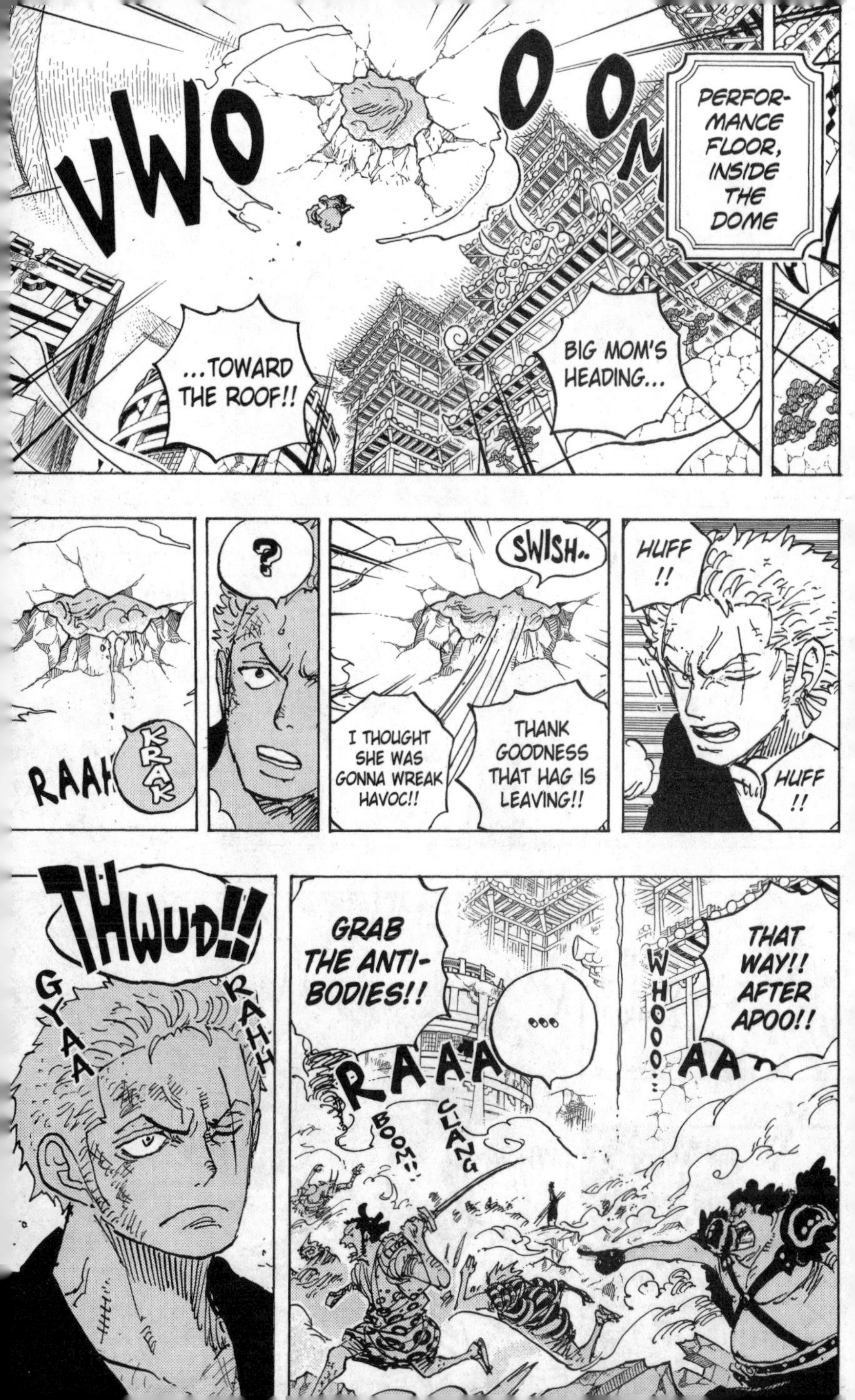
PERFORMANCE FLOOR, INSIDE THE DOME
VWOOOOM
BIG MOM'S HEADING...
...TOWARD THE ROOF!!
HUFF !!
HUFF !!
SWISH..
THANK GOODNESS THAT HAG IS LEAVING!!
I THOUGHT SHE WAS GONNA WREAK HAVOC!!
?
KRAK
RAAH
THAT WAY!! AFTER APOO!!
WHOOO..
AA
...
GRAB THE ANTI-BODIES!!
RAAA
CLANG
BOOM!!
THWUD!!
RAHH
GYAA

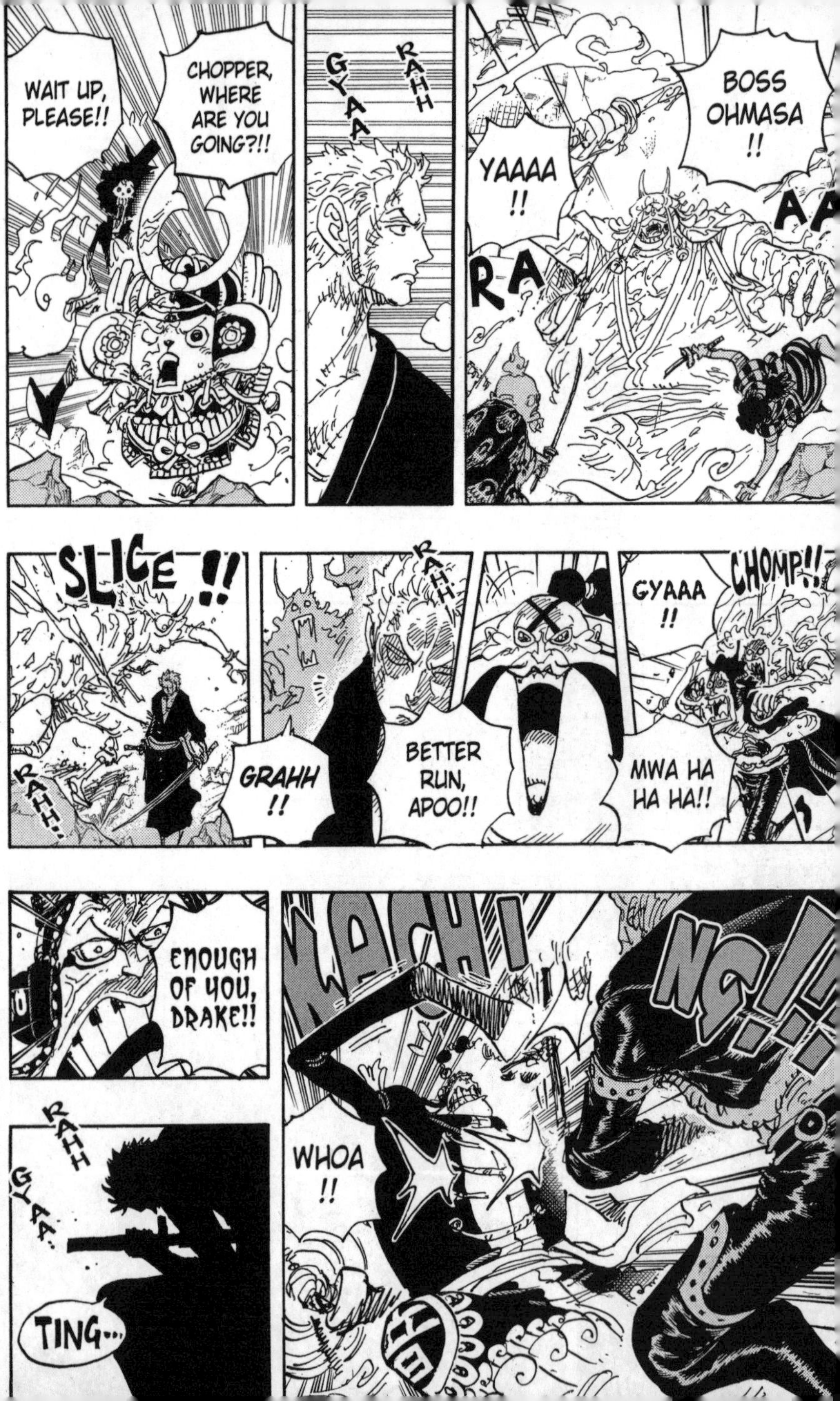
BOSS OHMASA !!
AA
YAAAA !!
RA
RAHH
GYAA
CHOPPER, WHERE ARE YOU GOING?!!
WAIT UP, PLEASE!!
CHOMP!!
GYAAA !!
MWA HA HA HA!!
BETTER RUN, APOO!!
RAHH
GRAHH !!
SLICE !!
RAHH..
KACHING!!!
WHOA !!
ENOUGH OF YOU, DRAKE!!
RAHH
GYAA..
TING...

RAAAAAH...

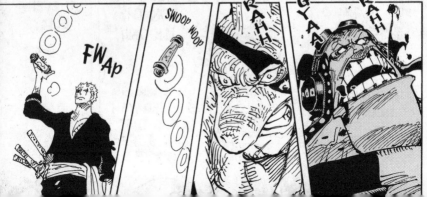

FWAP

SWOOP WOOP

RAHH

GYAA

RAHH

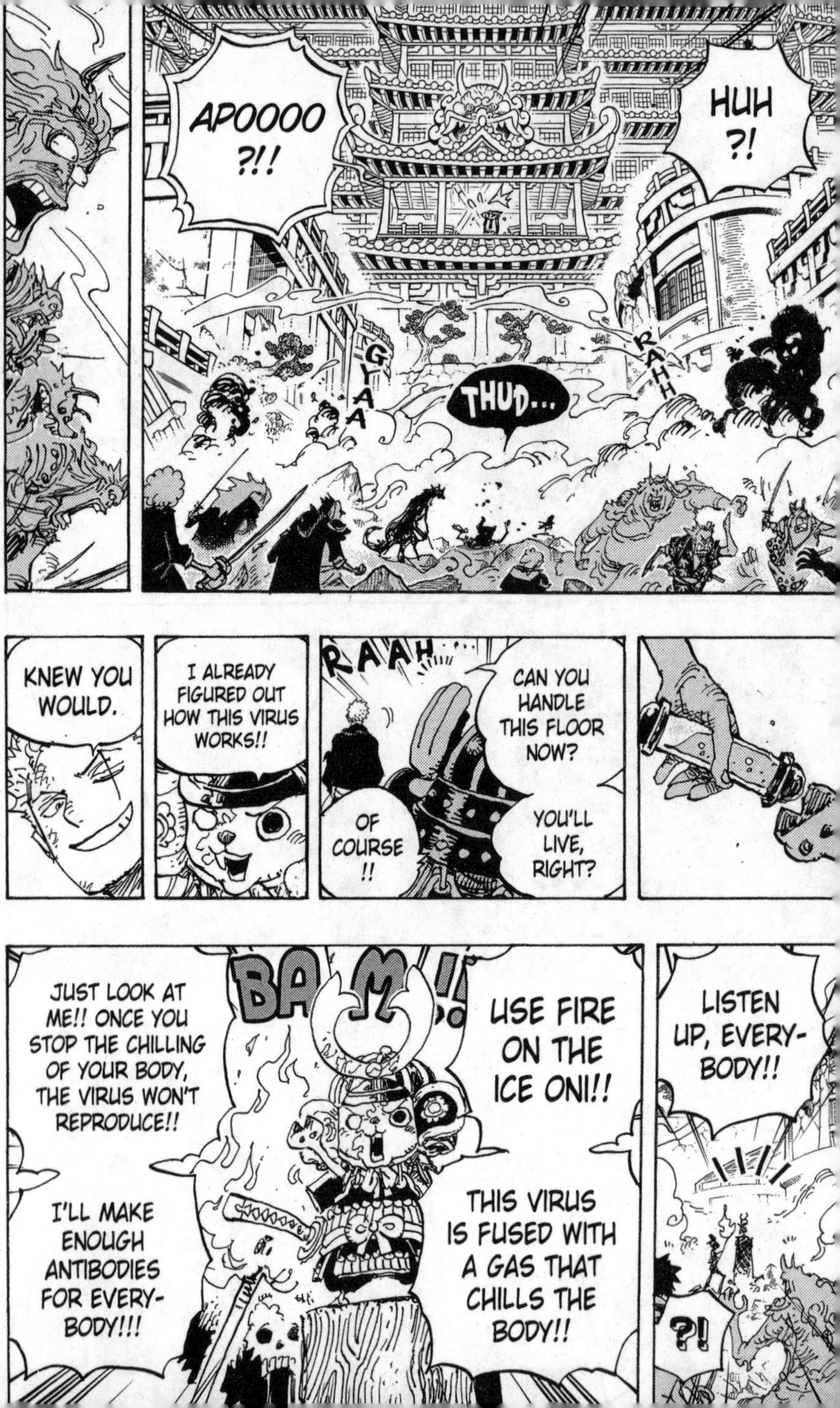
HUH ?!
APOOOO ?!!
RAHH
THUD...
GYAA
CAN YOU HANDLE THIS FLOOR NOW?
YOU'LL LIVE, RIGHT?
RAAH...
OF COURSE !!
I ALREADY FIGURED OUT HOW THIS VIRUS WORKS!!
KNEW YOU WOULD.
LISTEN UP, EVERY-BODY!!
?!
BAM!!
USE FIRE ON THE ICE ONI!!
THIS VIRUS IS FUSED WITH A GAS THAT CHILLS THE BODY!!
JUST LOOK AT ME!! ONCE YOU STOP THE CHILLING OF YOUR BODY, THE VIRUS WON'T REPRODUCE!!
I'LL MAKE ENOUGH ANTIBODIES FOR EVERY-BODY!!!

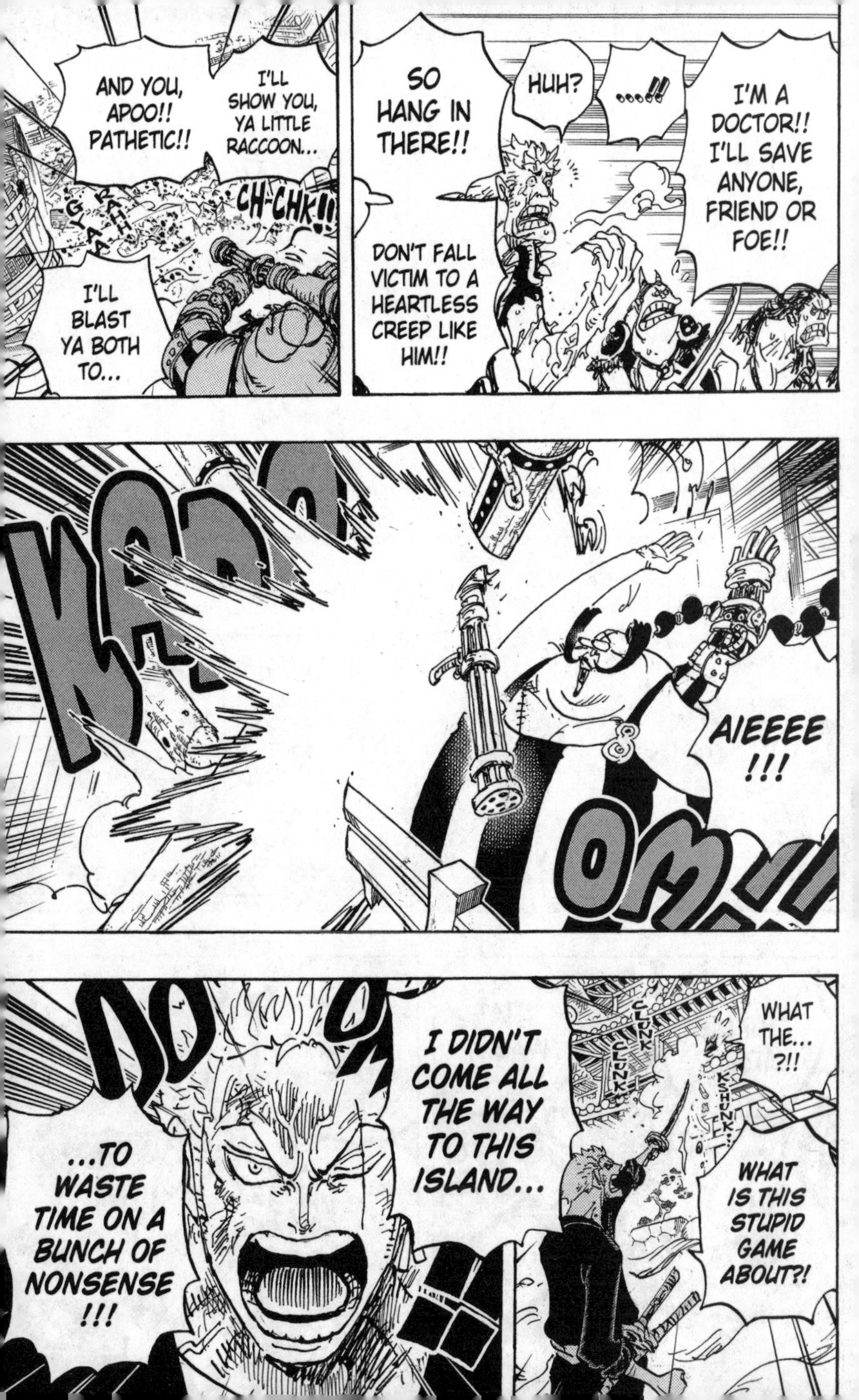
I'M A DOCTOR!! I'LL SAVE ANYONE, FRIEND OR FOE!!
....!!
HUH?
SO HANG IN THERE!!
DON'T FALL VICTIM TO A HEARTLESS CREEP LIKE HIM!!
I'LL SHOW YOU, YA LITTLE RACCOON...
CH-CHK!!!
AND YOU, APOO!! PATHETIC!!
I'LL BLAST YA BOTH TO...
AIEEEE !!!
WHAT THE... ?!!
CLUNK
CLUNK
KSHUNK
WHAT IS THIS STUPID GAME ABOUT?!
I DIDN'T COME ALL THE WAY TO THIS ISLAND...
...TO WASTE TIME ON A BUNCH OF NONSENSE !!!

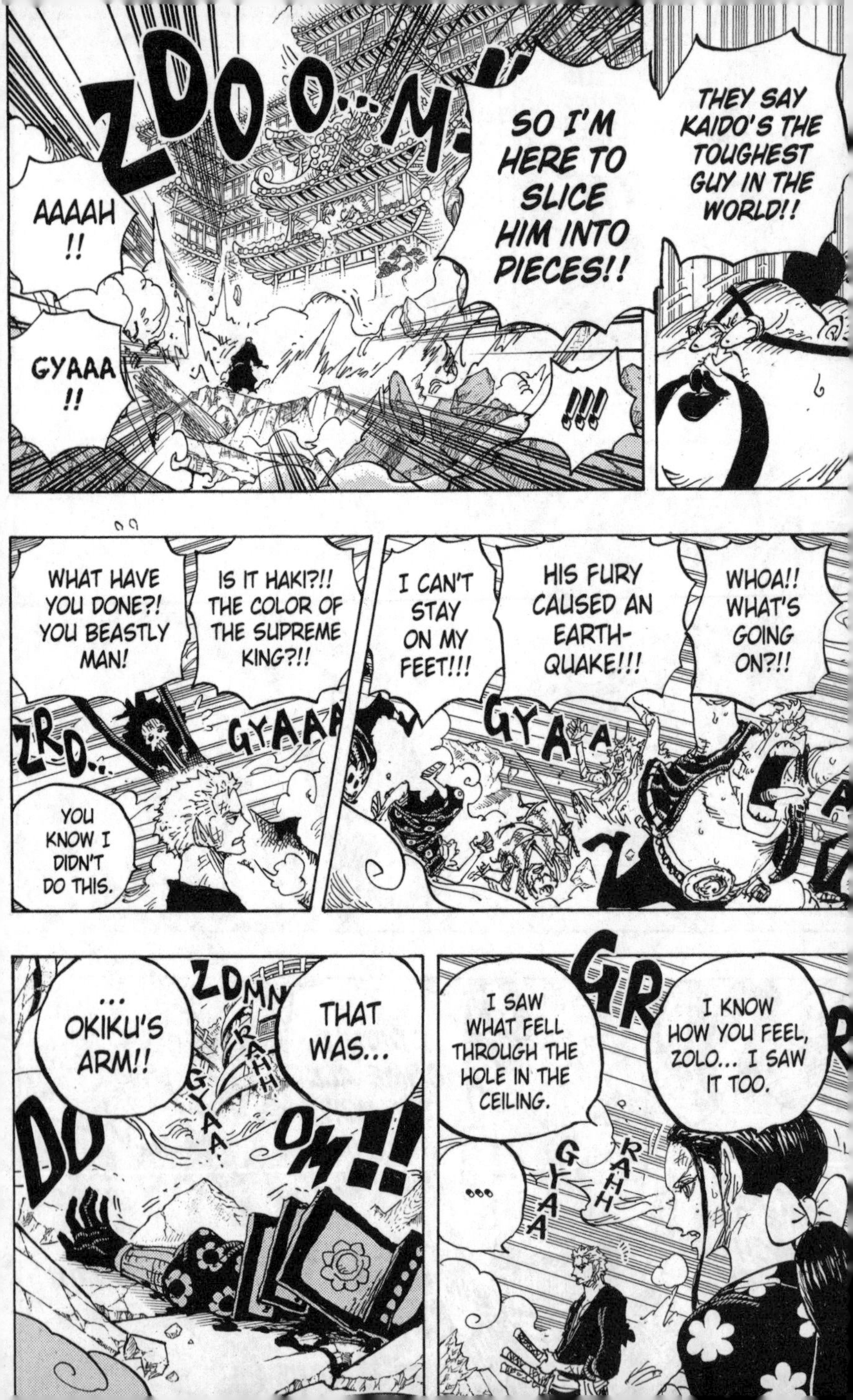

THEY SAY KAIDO'S THE TOUGHEST GUY IN THE WORLD!!
SO I'M HERE TO SLICE HIM INTO PIECES!!
ZDOO...M
!!!
AAAAH!!
GYAAA!!
WHOA!! WHAT'S GOING ON?!!
HIS FURY CAUSED AN EARTH-QUAKE!!!
I CAN'T STAY ON MY FEET!!!
GYAA A
IS IT HAKI?!! THE COLOR OF THE SUPREME KING?!!
WHAT HAVE YOU DONE?! YOU BEASTLY MAN!
GYAAA
ZRD..
YOU KNOW I DIDN'T DO THIS.
I KNOW HOW YOU FEEL, ZOLO... I SAW IT TOO.
GR
I SAW WHAT FELL THROUGH THE HOLE IN THE CEILING.
RAHH
GYAA
...
THAT WAS...
...OKIKU'S ARM!!
ZDMN
RAHH
GYAA
DOOM!!

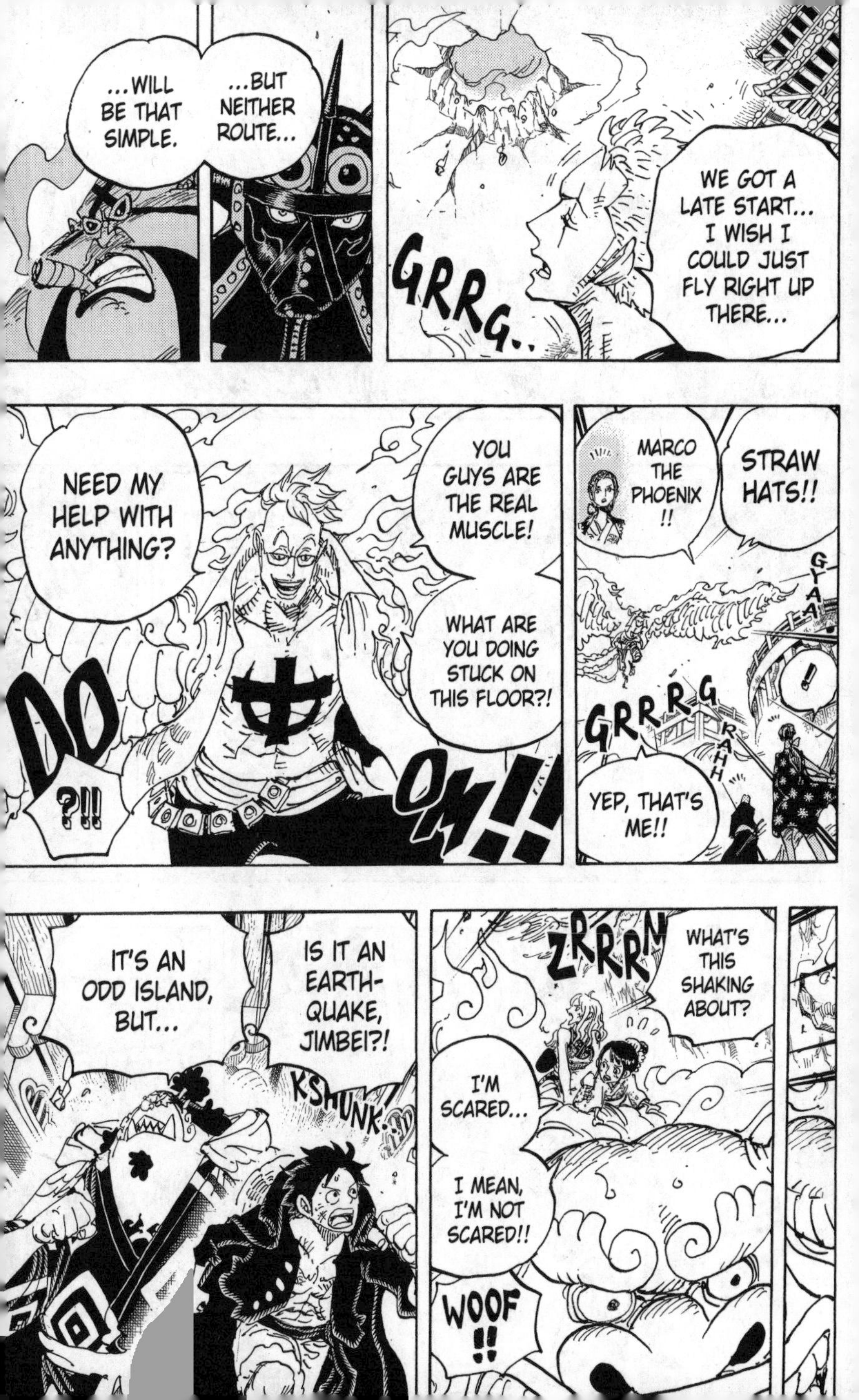
WE GOT A LATE START... I WISH I COULD JUST FLY RIGHT UP THERE...
GRRG..
...BUT NEITHER ROUTE...
...WILL BE THAT SIMPLE.
STRAW HATS!!
MARCO THE PHOENIX !!
GYAA
!
GRRRG
RAHH
YEP, THAT'S ME!!
YOU GUYS ARE THE REAL MUSCLE!
NEED MY HELP WITH ANYTHING?
WHAT ARE YOU DOING STUCK ON THIS FLOOR?!
DOOM!!
?!!
ZRRRN
WHAT'S THIS SHAKING ABOUT?
I'M SCARED...
I MEAN, I'M NOT SCARED!!
WOOF !!
IS IT AN EARTH-QUAKE, JIMBEI?!
IT'S AN ODD ISLAND, BUT...
KSHUNK

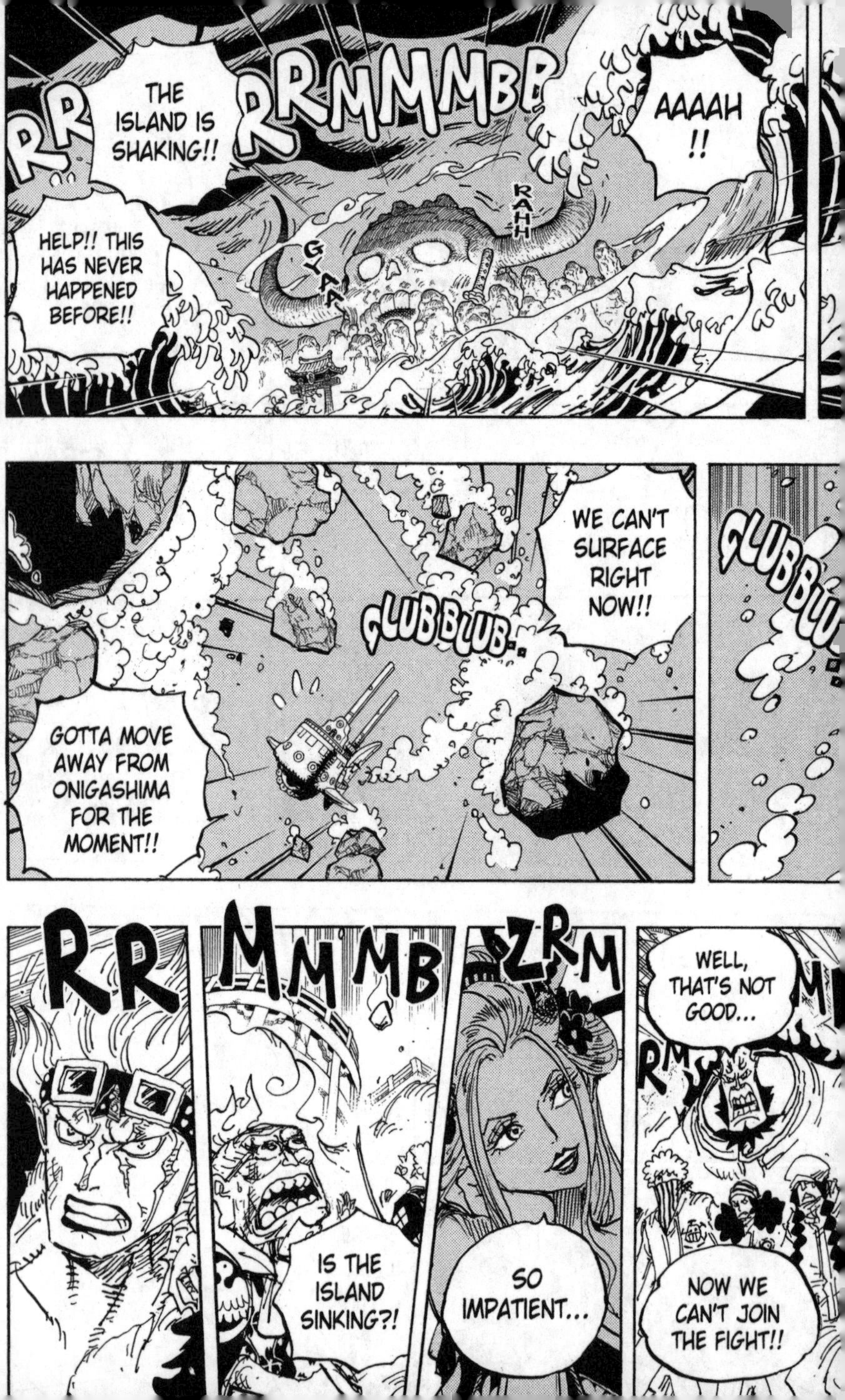
AAAAH!!
RRMMMMBB
RR
THE ISLAND IS SHAKING!!
RAHH
GYAA
HELP!! THIS HAS NEVER HAPPENED BEFORE!!
GLUB BLU
WE CAN'T SURFACE RIGHT NOW!!
GLUB BLUB
GOTTA MOVE AWAY FROM ONIGASHIMA FOR THE MOMENT!!
M
WELL, THAT'S NOT GOOD...
RM
NOW WE CAN'T JOIN THE FIGHT!!
ZRM
SO IMPATIENT...
MMMB
IS THE ISLAND SINKING?!
RR

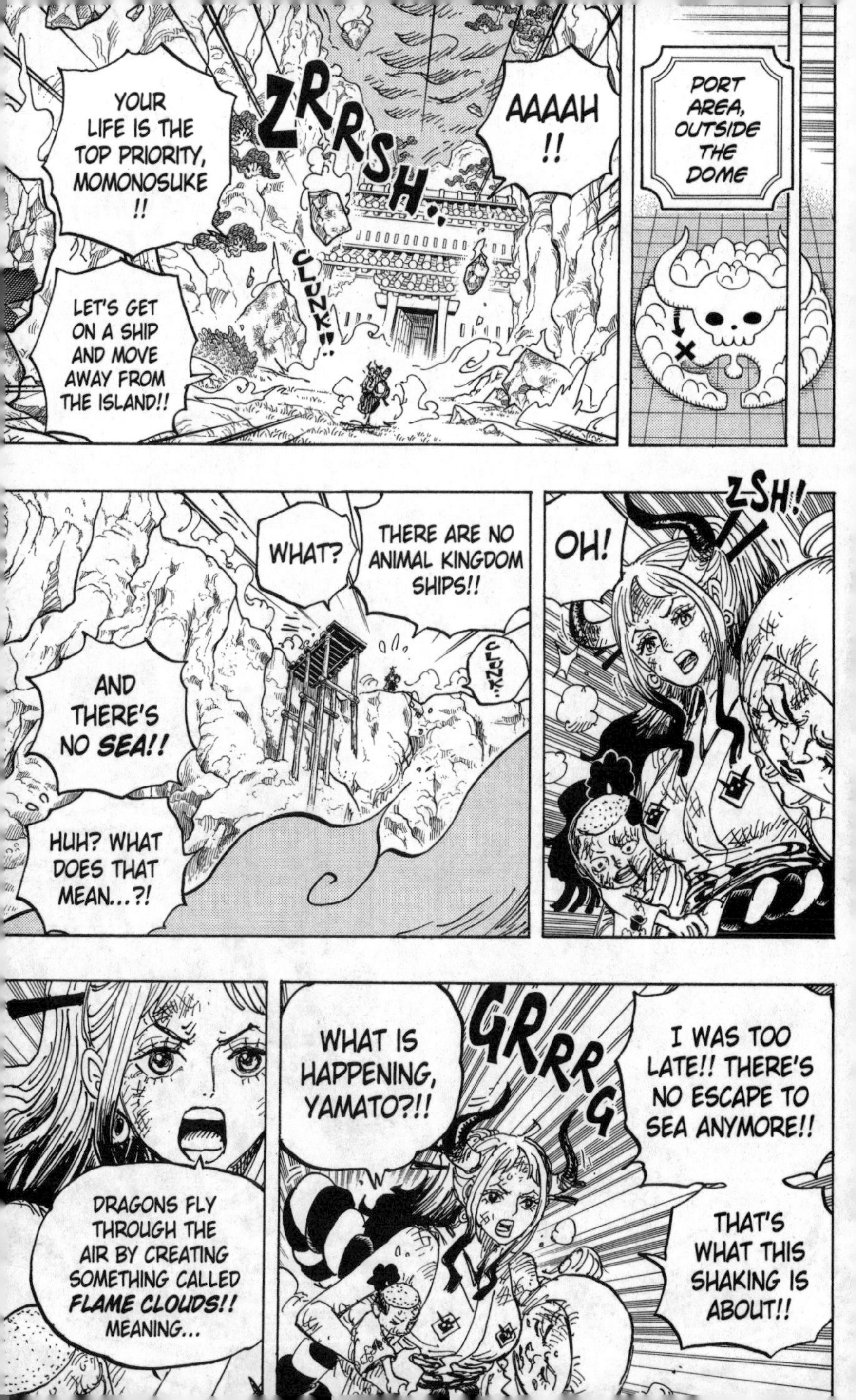
PORT AREA, OUTSIDE THE DOME
AAAAH!!
ZRRSH
CLUNK!!
YOUR LIFE IS THE TOP PRIORITY, MOMONOSUKE!!
LET'S GET ON A SHIP AND MOVE AWAY FROM THE ISLAND!!
Z-SH!
OH!
THERE ARE NO ANIMAL KINGDOM SHIPS!!
WHAT?
CLUNK.
AND THERE'S NO SEA!!
HUH? WHAT DOES THAT MEAN...?!
I WAS TOO LATE!! THERE'S NO ESCAPE TO SEA ANYMORE!!
GRRRG
WHAT IS HAPPENING, YAMATO?!!
THAT'S WHAT THIS SHAKING IS ABOUT!!
DRAGONS FLY THROUGH THE AIR BY CREATING SOMETHING CALLED FLAME CLOUDS!! MEANING...

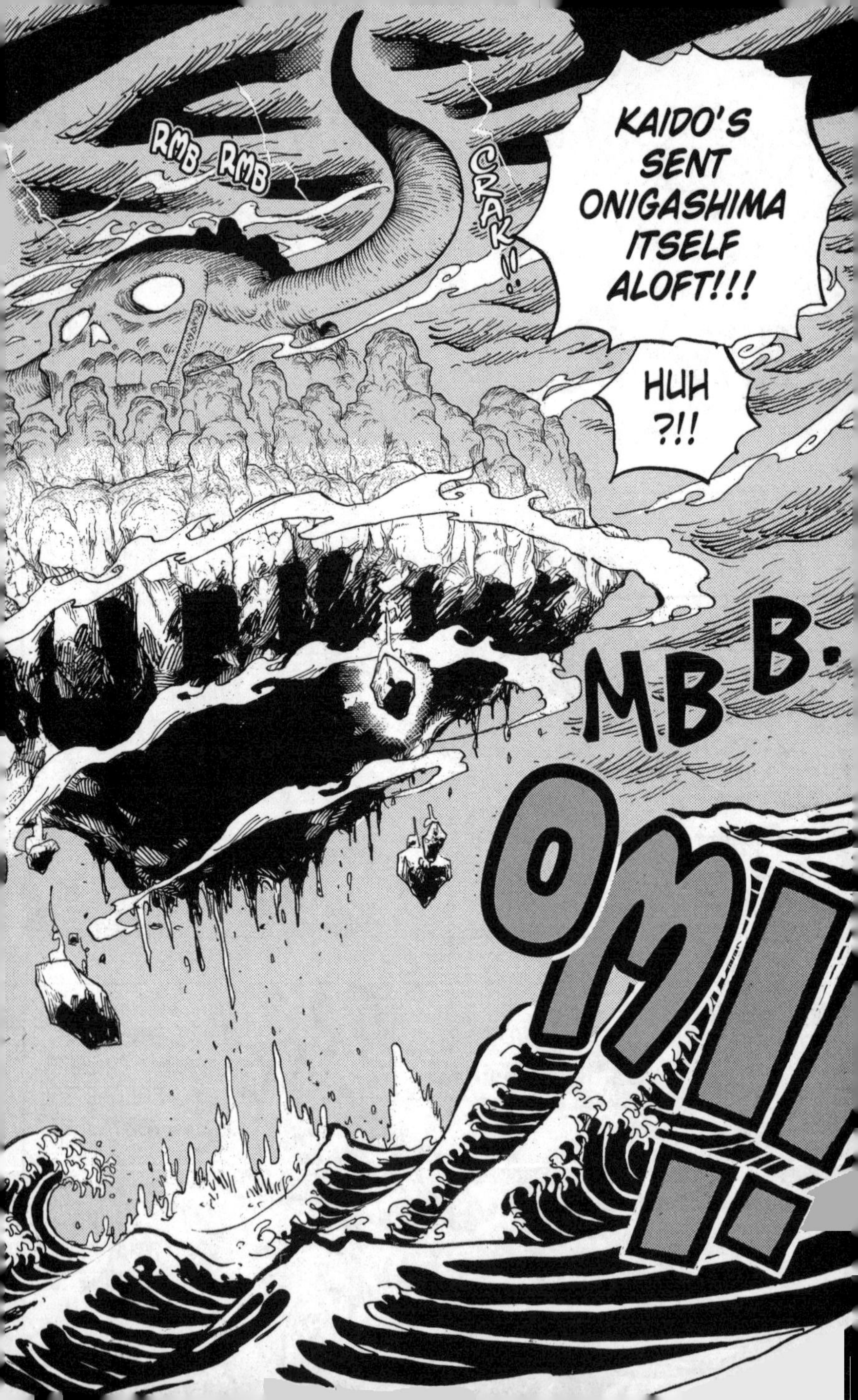
KAIDO'S SENT ONIGASHIMA ITSELF ALOFT!!!
HUH ?!!
CRAK!!
RMB RMB
B.
MB

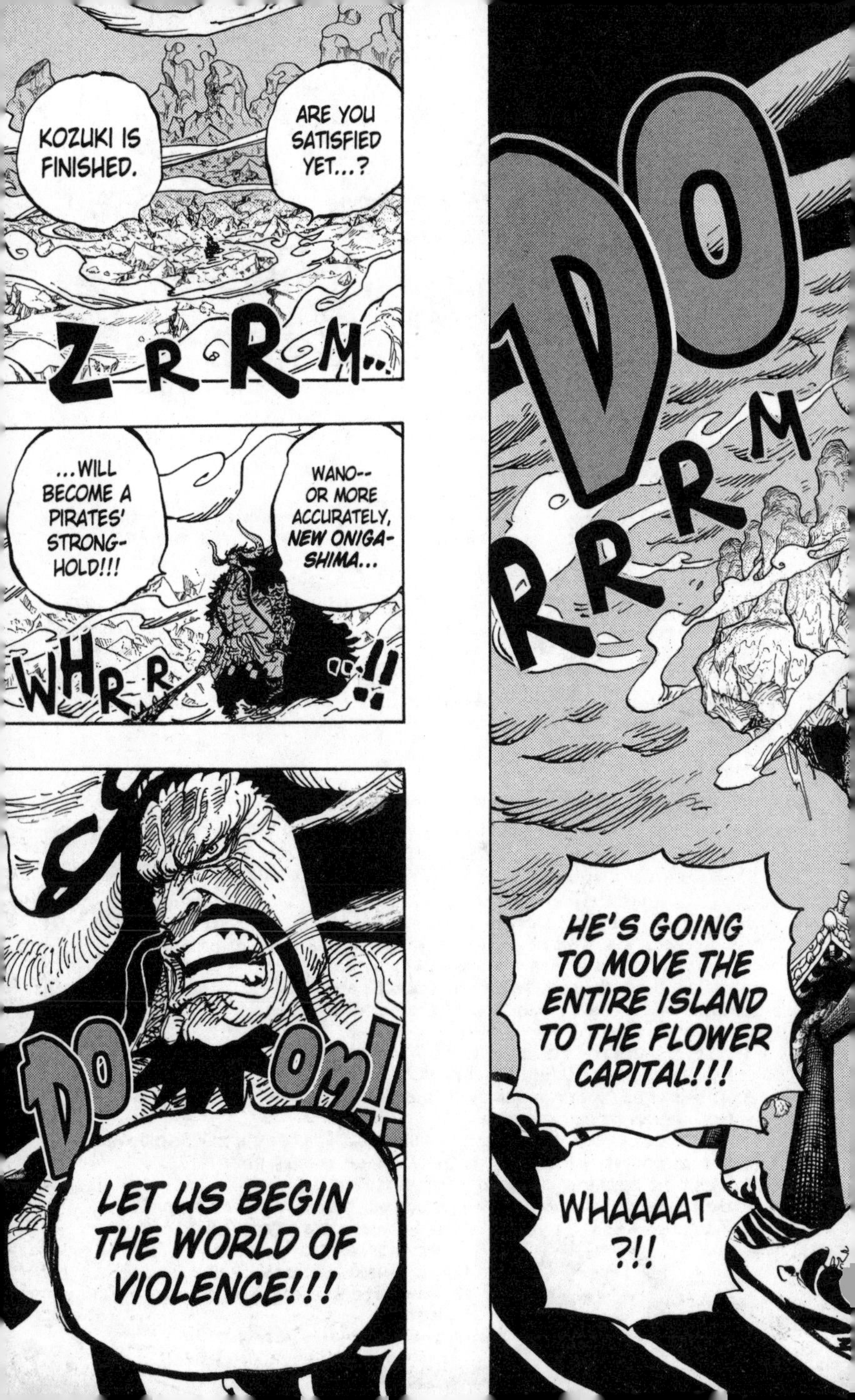
DOOO
RRRRM
HE'S GOING TO MOVE THE ENTIRE ISLAND TO THE FLOWER CAPITAL!!!
WHAAAAT ?!!
ARE YOU SATISFIED YET...?
KOZUKI IS FINISHED.
ZRRRM..
WANO-- OR MORE ACCURATELY, NEW ONIGASHIMA...
...WILL BECOME A PIRATES' STRONGHOLD!!!
WHRRR
DOOM!!
LET US BEGIN THE WORLD OF VIOLENCE!!!

SBS Question Corner

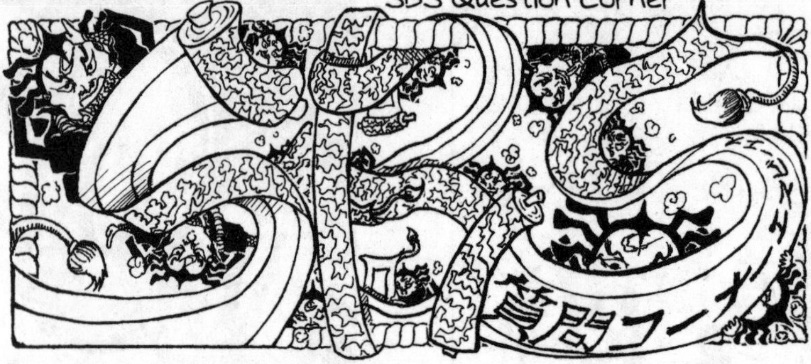
質問コーナー

(Mr. Anonymous, Tokyo)

Q: I want to know about the Straw Hats' taste in eggs sunny-side up! Who likes them soft-boiled, what do they eat them with, and so on.

--Odamania

A: Oooh, I see. This is a good question! Let's find out!

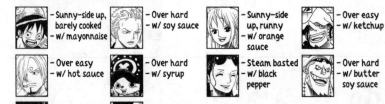

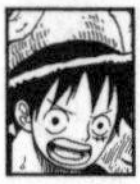
- Sunny-side up, barely cooked
- w/ mayonnaise

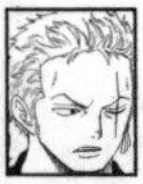
- Over hard
- w/ soy sauce

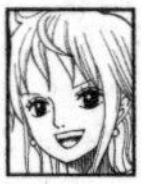
- Sunny-side up, runny
- w/ orange sauce

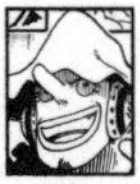
- Over easy
- w/ ketchup

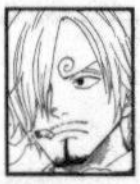
- Over easy
- w/ hot sauce

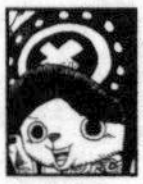
- Over hard
- w/ syrup

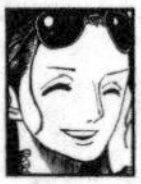
- Steam basted
- w/ black pepper

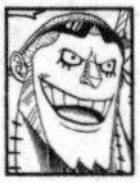
- Over hard
- w/ butter soy sauce

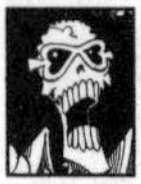
- Over easy
- w/ ketchup

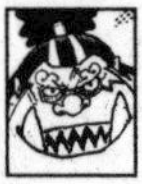
- Steam basted
- w/ salt

Q: Jimbei!! Congratulations on officially joining the Straw Hats! We've been waiting for so long!! Now you can tell us all of the profile information that's been revealed for the others in the SBS so far!!

--Yashirai

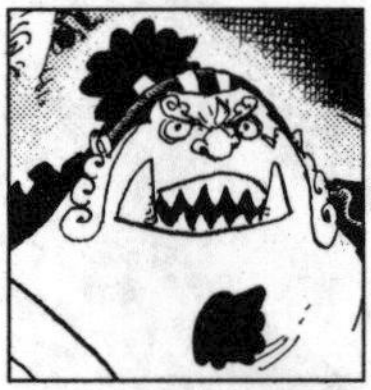

A: Okay. They were nice enough to include all of the categories. This is all of the information I've revealed for Luffy and the gang. It's already been revealed that Jimbei's favorite food is "mozuku seaweed in vinegar" and "fruit." So here are the other answers.

1. Least favorite food: parfaits (hard to eat)
2. Image color & number: ochre, 10
3. If the crew were a family: father (Franky used to be dad, is now perverted grandma)
4. Smell: smells like the ocean
5. Image prefecture: Kagoshima
6. Image country: India
7. Image animal: bear
8. Best at cooking: Seared bonito tuna
9. Bedtime and wake-up time: Sleep at 3 a.m., wake at 9 a.m.
10. Inside his head:

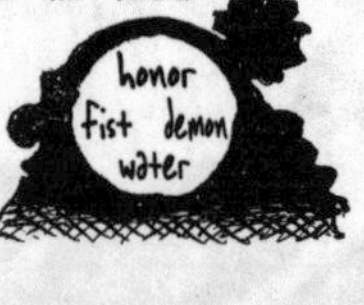
honor
fist
demon
water

11. If he wasn't a pirate he'd be a: train station employee
12. Ice: swallows, doesn't chew
13. Favorite season: autumn on a summer island
14. Image flower: peony

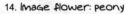

Chapter 998:
ANCIENT TYPES

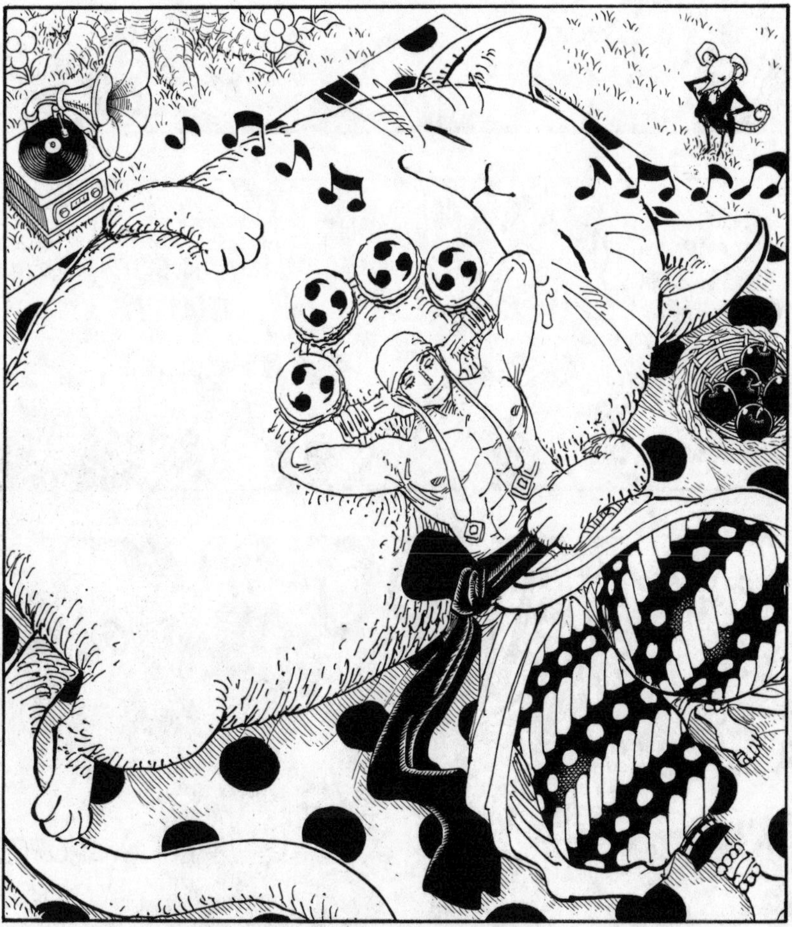

READER REQUEST: "ENERU KICKING BACK AND LISTENING TO MUSIC WITH A CAT" BY X-5GO

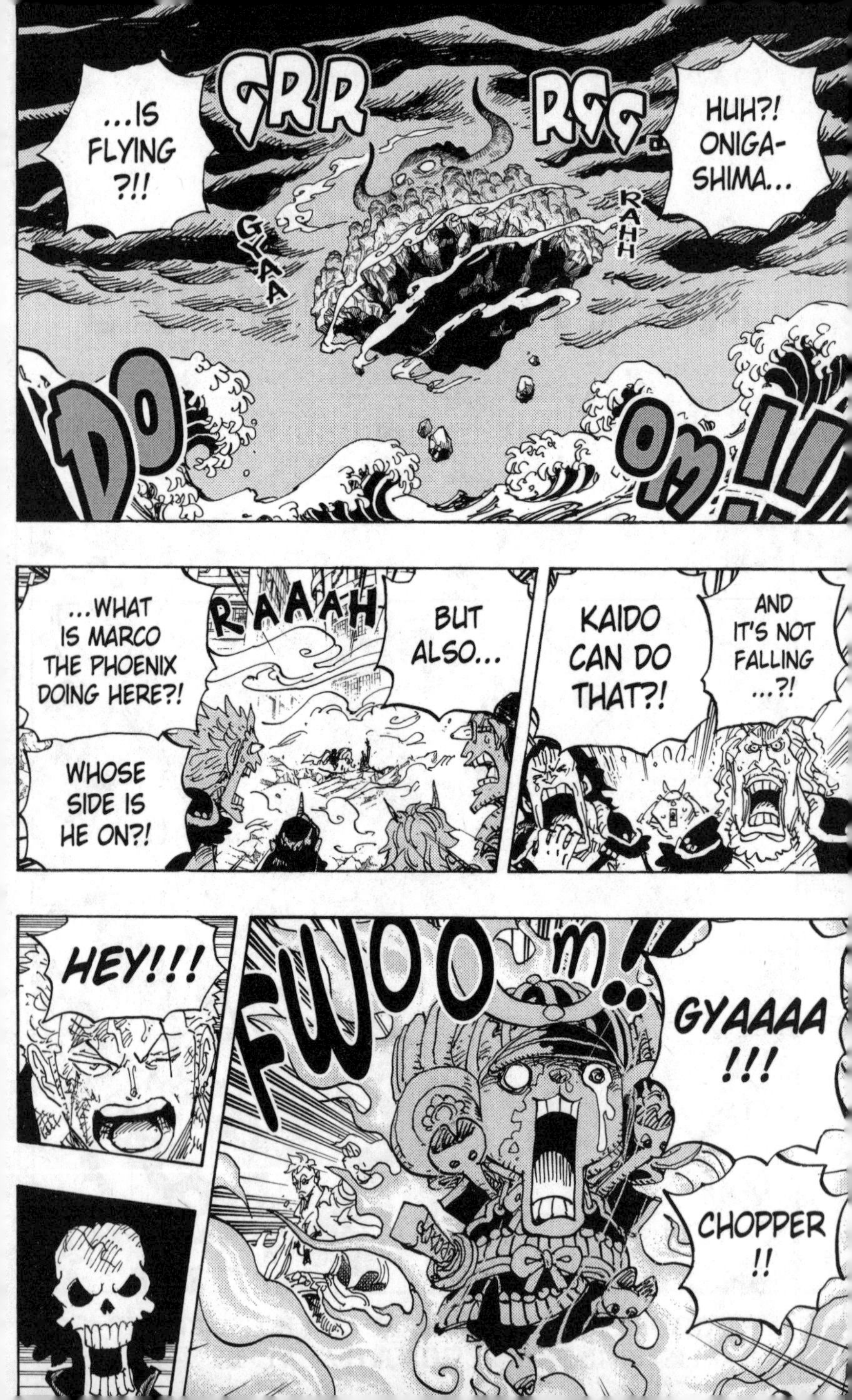
HUH?! ONIGA-SHIMA...
RGG.
RAHH
GRR
...IS FLYING ?!!
GYAA
DOOM!!
AND IT'S NOT FALLING ...?!
KAIDO CAN DO THAT?!
BUT ALSO...
RAAAH
...WHAT IS MARCO THE PHOENIX DOING HERE?!
WHOSE SIDE IS HE ON?!
FWOOOm..
GYAAAA !!!
CHOPPER !!
HEY!!!

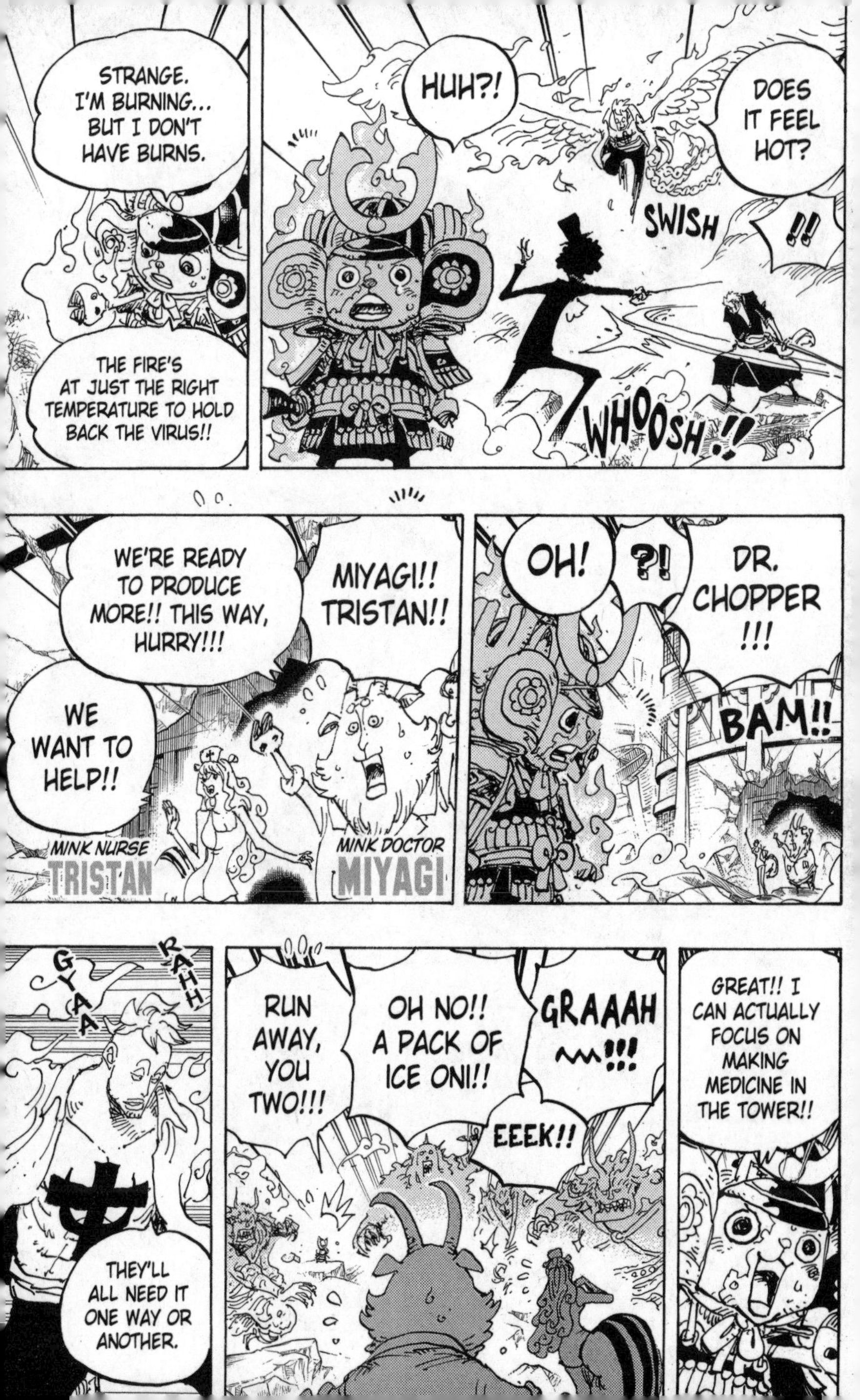
DOES IT FEEL HOT?
HUH?!
!!
SWISH
WHOOSH!!
STRANGE. I'M BURNING... BUT I DON'T HAVE BURNS.
THE FIRE'S AT JUST THE RIGHT TEMPERATURE TO HOLD BACK THE VIRUS!!
DR. CHOPPER!!!
?!
OH!
BAM!!
MIYAGI!! TRISTAN!!
WE'RE READY TO PRODUCE MORE!! THIS WAY, HURRY!!!
WE WANT TO HELP!!
MINK DOCTOR MIYAGI
MINK NURSE TRISTAN
GREAT!! I CAN ACTUALLY FOCUS ON MAKING MEDICINE IN THE TOWER!!
GRAAAH~!!!
OH NO!! A PACK OF ICE ONI!!
RUN AWAY, YOU TWO!!!
EEEK!!
RAHH
GYAA
THEY'LL ALL NEED IT ONE WAY OR ANOTHER.

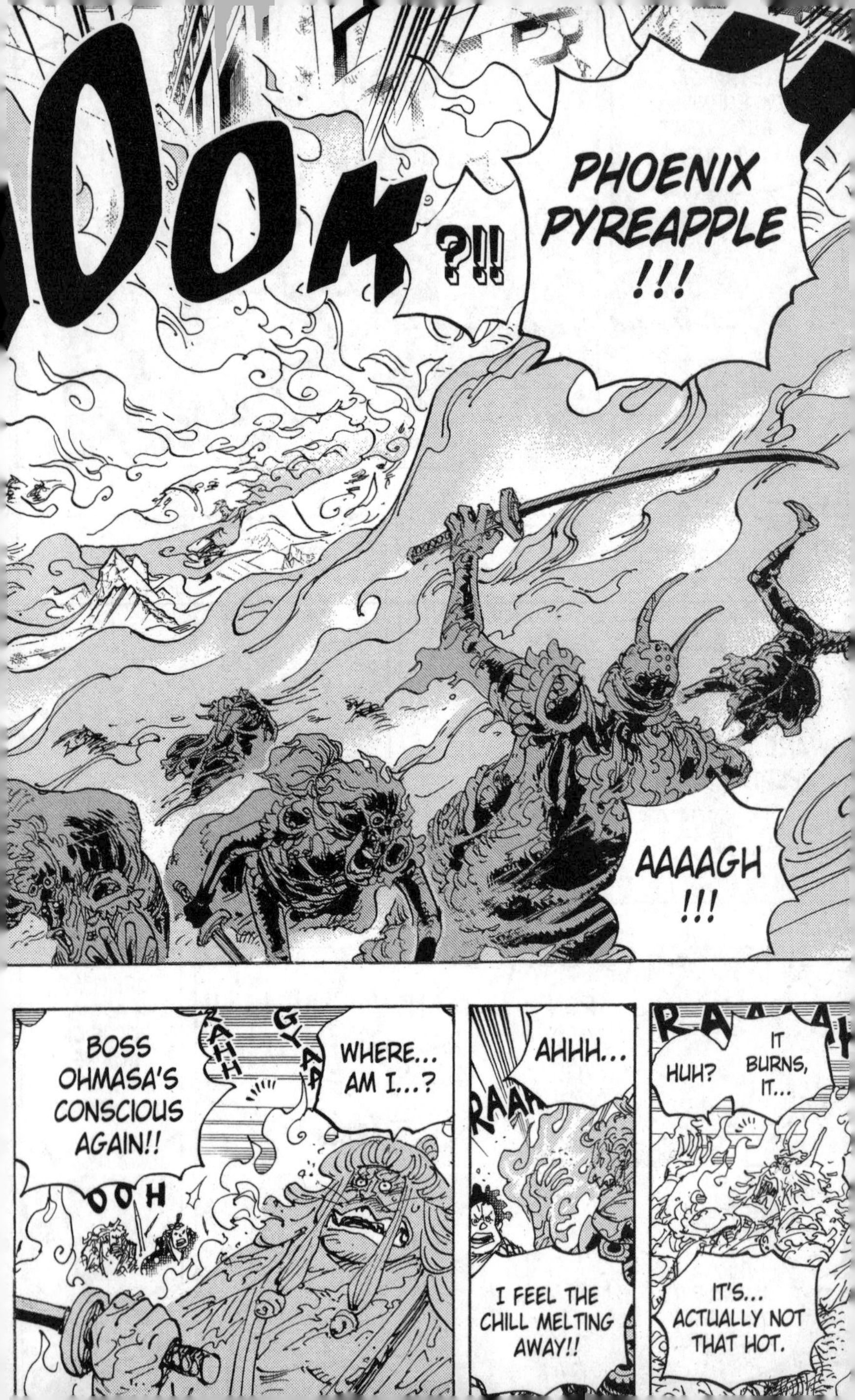
PHOENIX PYREAPPLE !!!
OOM
?!!
AAAAGH !!!
HUH?
IT BURNS, IT...
IT'S... ACTUALLY NOT THAT HOT.
AHHH...
I FEEL THE CHILL MELTING AWAY!!
WHERE... AM I...?
BOSS OHMASA'S CONSCIOUS AGAIN!!
OOH

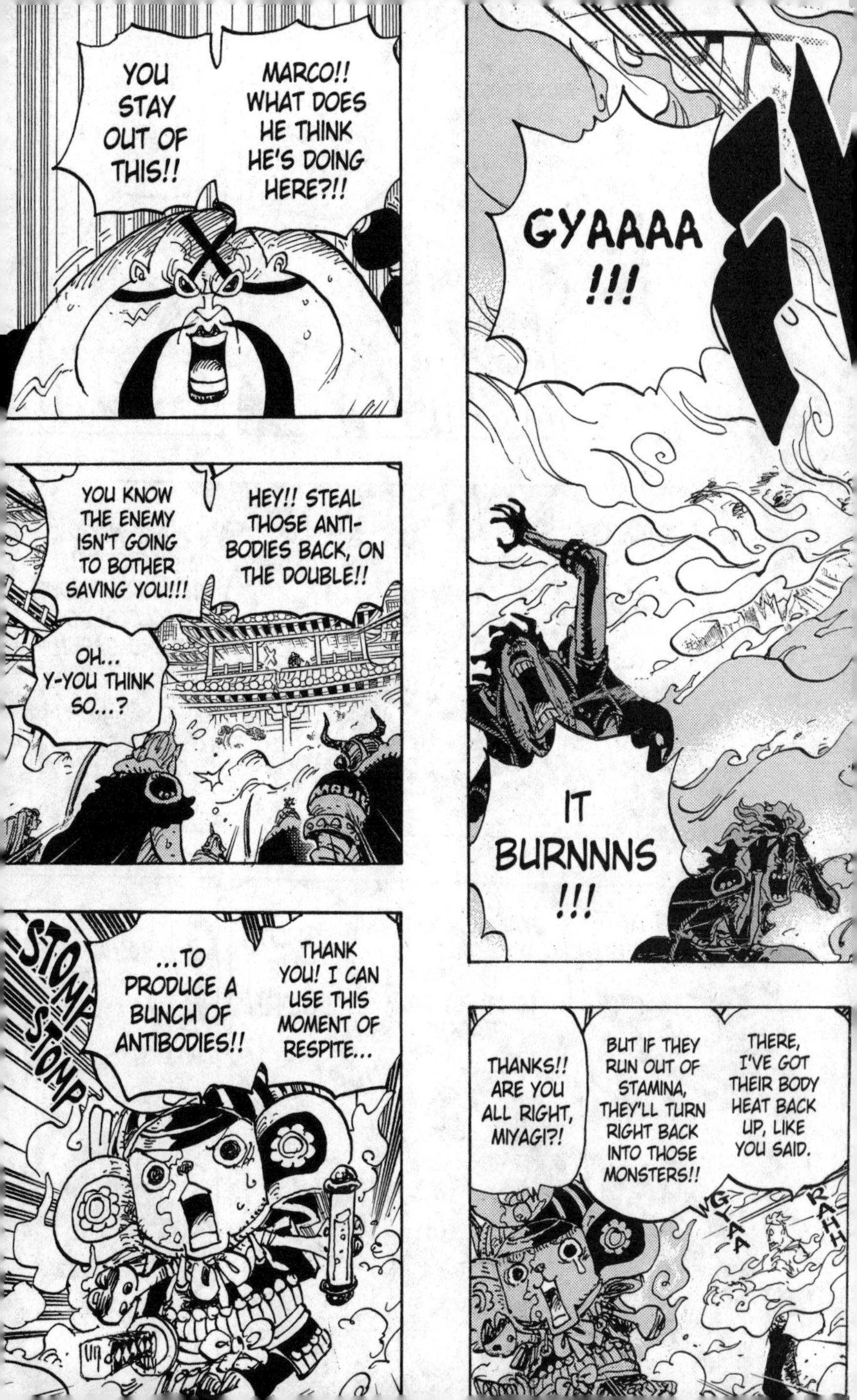
GYAAAA !!!
IT BURNNNS !!!
MARCO!! WHAT DOES HE THINK HE'S DOING HERE?!!
YOU STAY OUT OF THIS!!
HEY!! STEAL THOSE ANTI-BODIES BACK, ON THE DOUBLE!!
YOU KNOW THE ENEMY ISN'T GOING TO BOTHER SAVING YOU!!!
OH... Y-YOU THINK SO...?
THERE, I'VE GOT THEIR BODY HEAT BACK UP, LIKE YOU SAID.
BUT IF THEY RUN OUT OF STAMINA, THEY'LL TURN RIGHT BACK INTO THOSE MONSTERS!!
THANKS!! ARE YOU ALL RIGHT, MIYAGI?!
RAHH
GYAA
THANK YOU! I CAN USE THIS MOMENT OF RESPITE...
...TO PRODUCE A BUNCH OF ANTIBODIES!!
STOMP STOMP

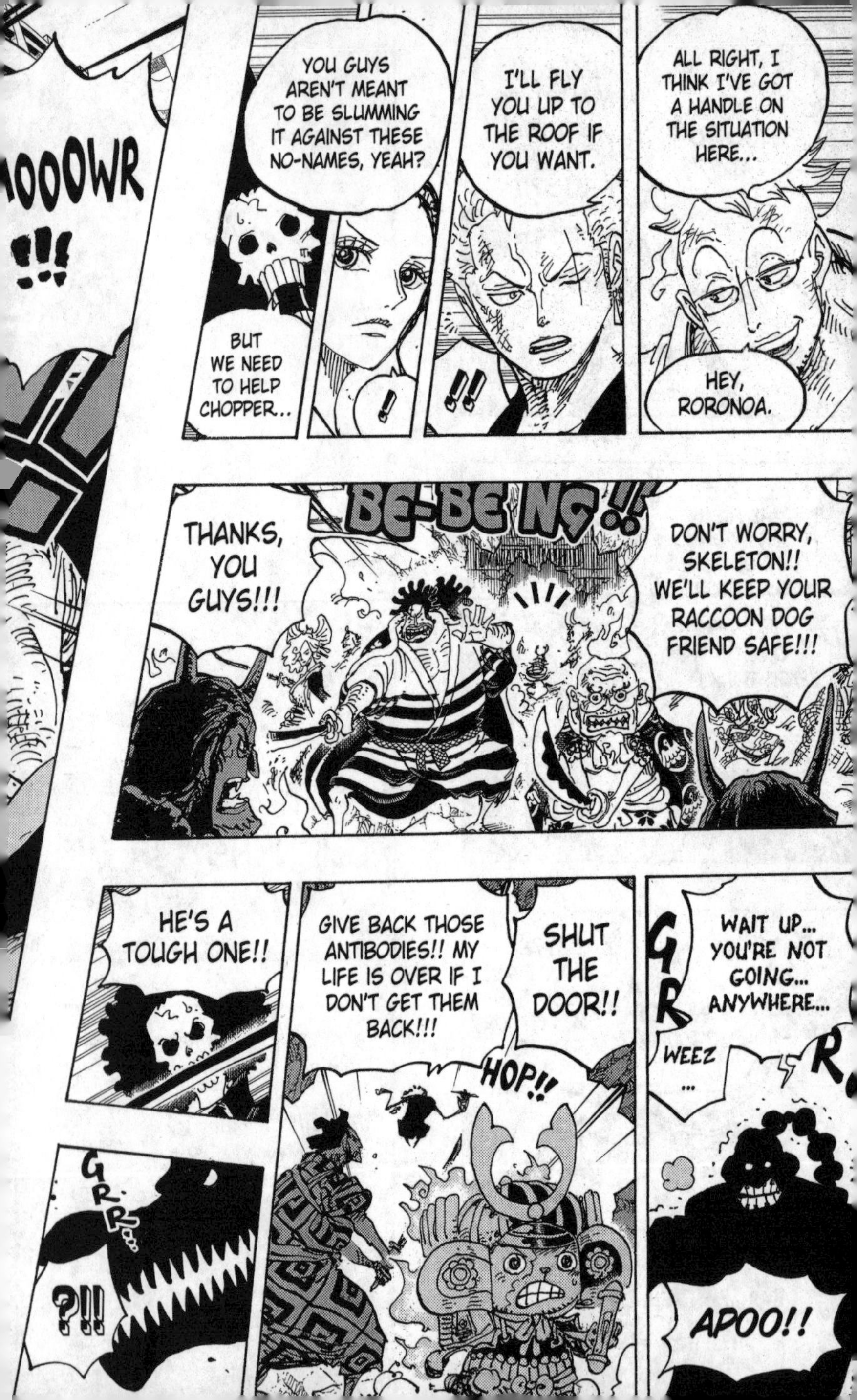
ALL RIGHT, I THINK I'VE GOT A HANDLE ON THE SITUATION HERE...
HEY, RORONOA.
I'LL FLY YOU UP TO THE ROOF IF YOU WANT.
!!
YOU GUYS AREN'T MEANT TO BE SLUMMING IT AGAINST THESE NO-NAMES, YEAH?
!
BUT WE NEED TO HELP CHOPPER...
OOOWR
!!!
DON'T WORRY, SKELETON!! WE'LL KEEP YOUR RACCOON DOG FRIEND SAFE!!!
BE-BE NG!!
THANKS, YOU GUYS!!!
WAIT UP... YOU'RE NOT GOING... ANYWHERE...
GR
R
WEEZ ...
APOO!!
SHUT THE DOOR!!
GIVE BACK THOSE ANTIBODIES!! MY LIFE IS OVER IF I DON'T GET THEM BACK!!!
HOP!!
HE'S A TOUGH ONE!!
GRR
?!!

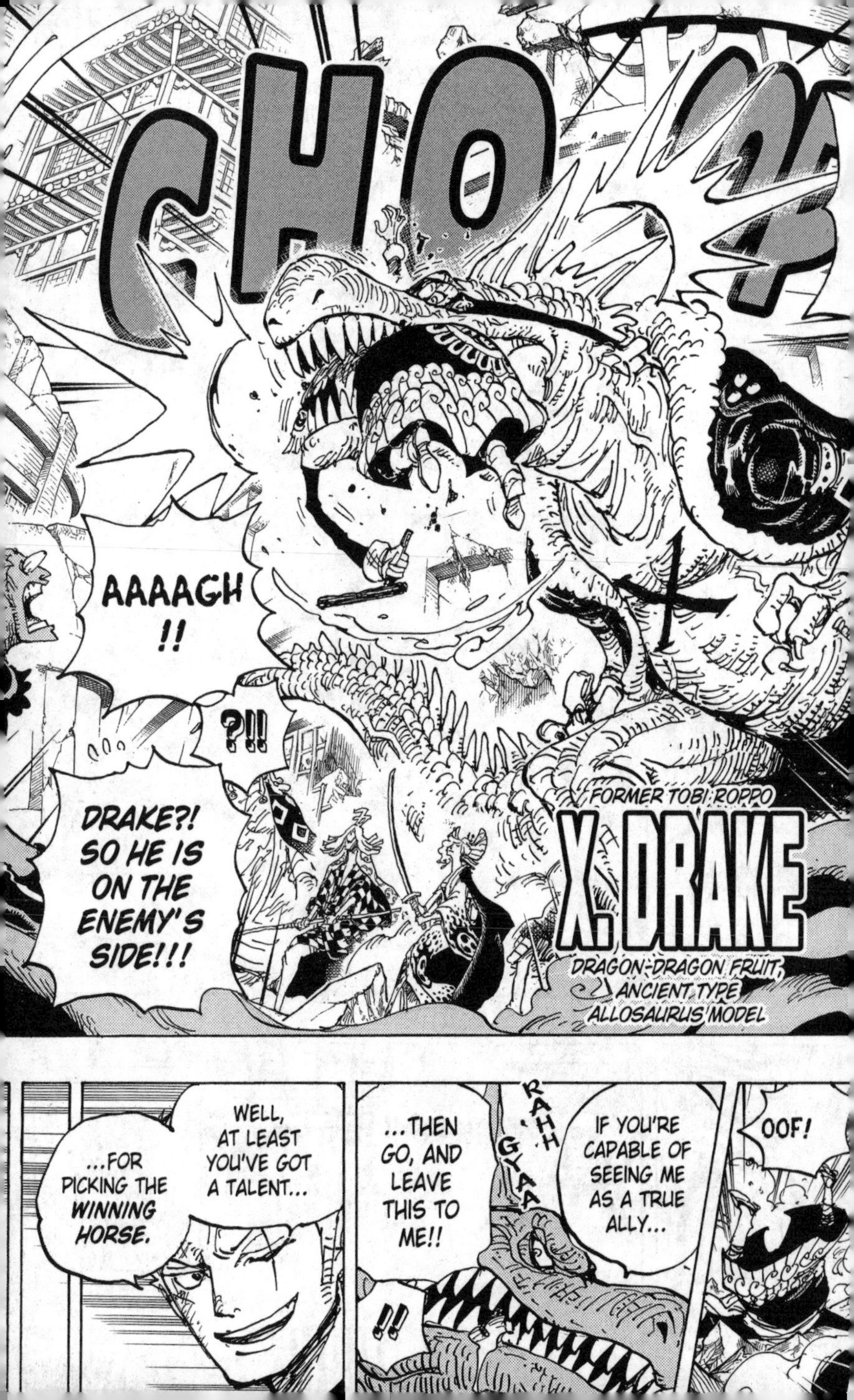

CHO
AAAAGH!!
?!!
FORMER TOBI ROPPO
X. DRAKE
DRAGON-DRAGON FRUIT, ANCIENT TYPE ALLOSAURUS MODEL
DRAKE?! SO HE IS ON THE ENEMY'S SIDE!!!
OOF!
IF YOU'RE CAPABLE OF SEEING ME AS A TRUE ALLY...
RAHH
GYAA
...THEN GO, AND LEAVE THIS TO ME!!
!!
WELL, AT LEAST YOU'VE GOT A TALENT...
...FOR PICKING THE WINNING HORSE.

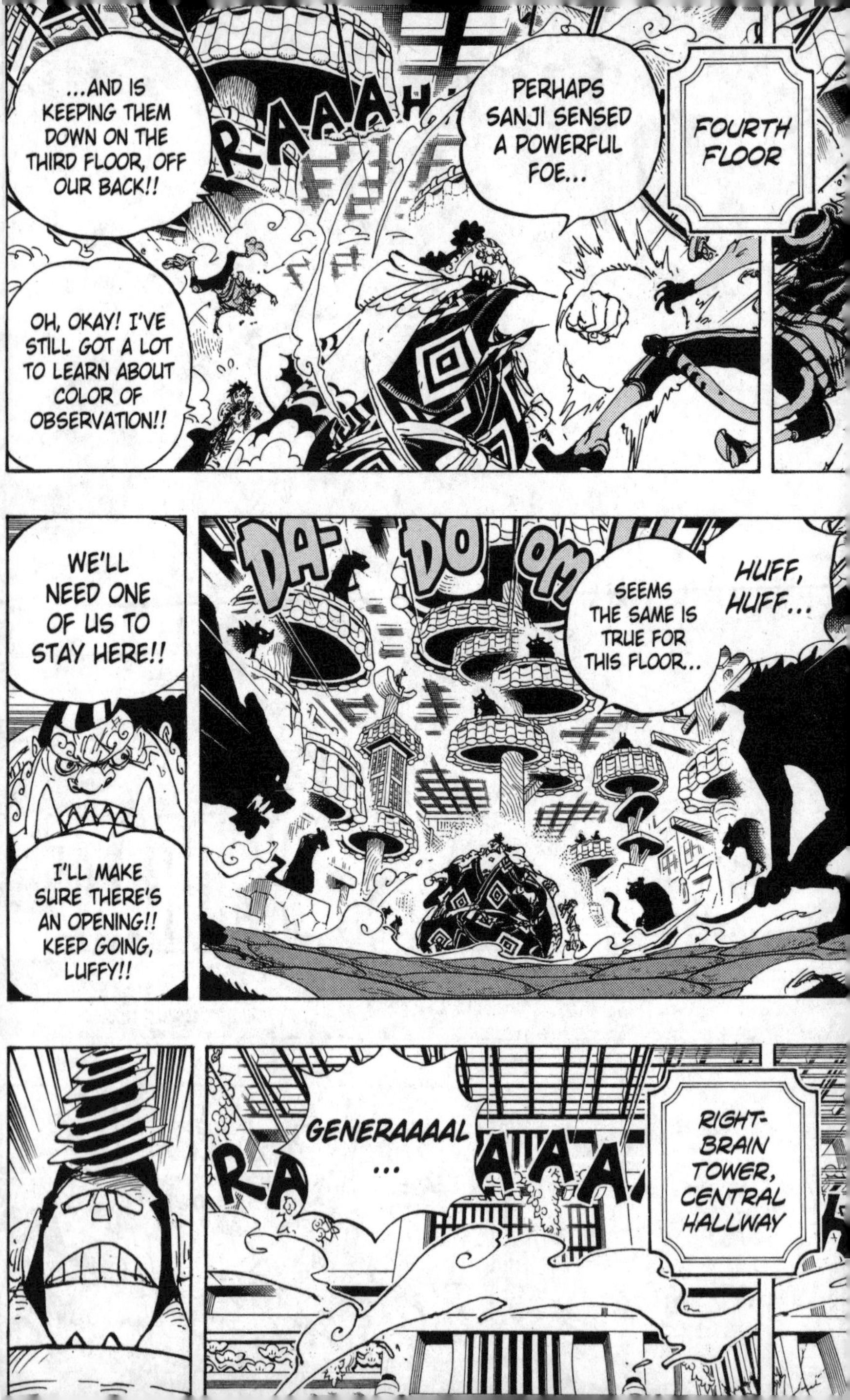
FOURTH FLOOR
PERHAPS SANJI SENSED A POWERFUL FOE...
RAAAH
...AND IS KEEPING THEM DOWN ON THE THIRD FLOOR, OFF OUR BACK!!
OH, OKAY! I'VE STILL GOT A LOT TO LEARN ABOUT COLOR OF OBSERVATION!!
HUFF, HUFF...
SEEMS THE SAME IS TRUE FOR THIS FLOOR...
DA-DO-OM
WE'LL NEED ONE OF US TO STAY HERE!!
I'LL MAKE SURE THERE'S AN OPENING!! KEEP GOING, LUFFY!!
RIGHT-BRAIN TOWER, CENTRAL HALLWAY
RAAAAA
GENERAAAAL ...

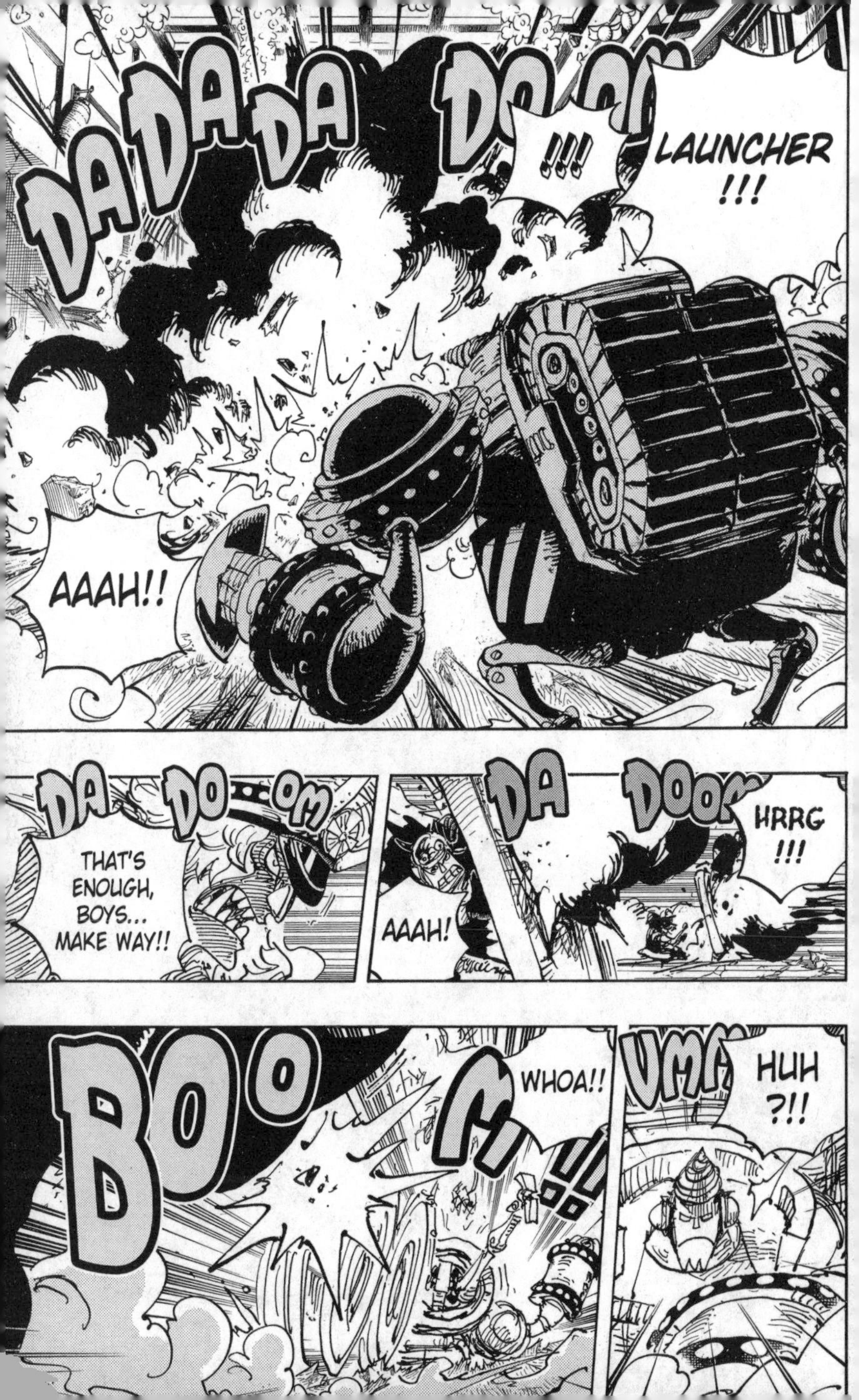
LAUNCHER !!!
!!!
DADADADA DOO
AAAH!!
HRRG !!!
DA DOO
AAAH!
DA DO-OM
THAT'S ENOUGH, BOYS... MAKE WAY!!
HUH ?!!
BOOO
WHOA!!

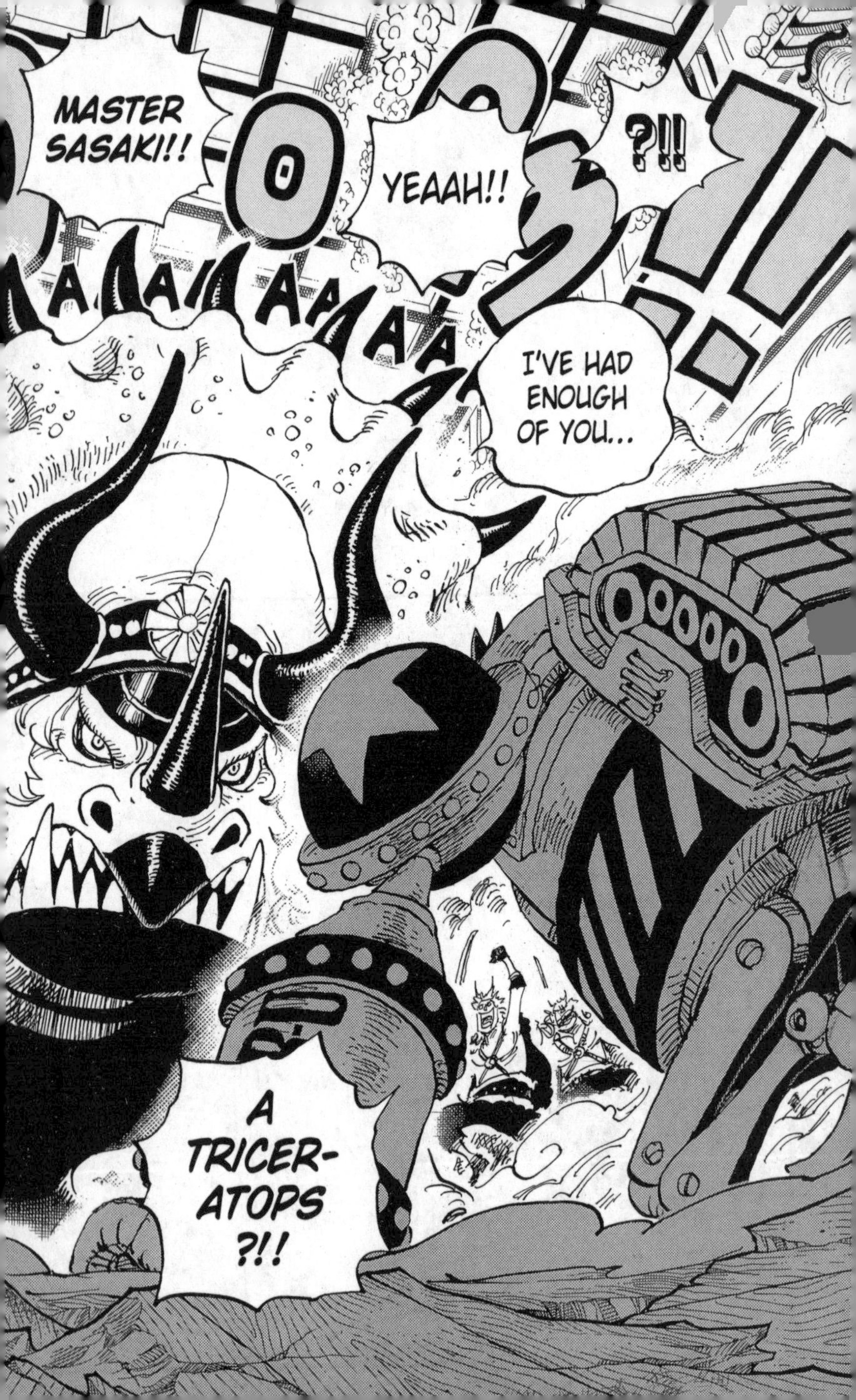
?!!
YEAAH!!
MASTER SASAKI!!
I'VE HAD ENOUGH OF YOU...
A TRICER-ATOPS ?!!

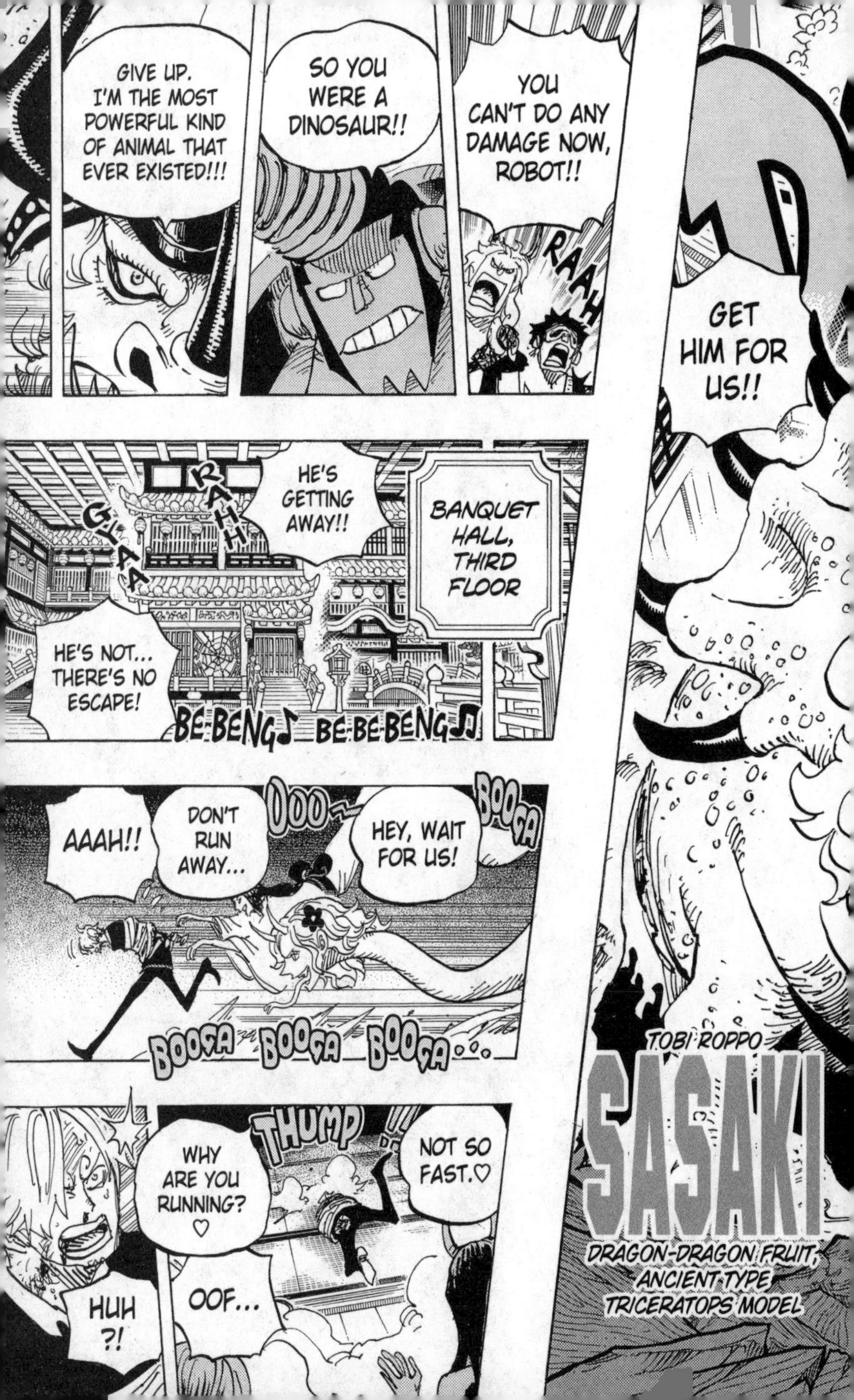
GET HIM FOR US!!
TOBI ROPPO
SASAKI
DRAGON-DRAGON FRUIT, ANCIENT TYPE TRICERATOPS MODEL
YOU CAN'T DO ANY DAMAGE NOW, ROBOT!!
RAAAH
SO YOU WERE A DINOSAUR!!
GIVE UP. I'M THE MOST POWERFUL KIND OF ANIMAL THAT EVER EXISTED!!!
BANQUET HALL, THIRD FLOOR
HE'S GETTING AWAY!!
RAHH
GYAA
HE'S NOT... THERE'S NO ESCAPE!
BE-BENG♪ BE-BE-BENG♫
BOOGA
HEY, WAIT FOR US!
OOO~
DON'T RUN AWAY...
AAAH!!
BOOGA BOOGA BOOGA...
NOT SO FAST.♡
THUMP
WHY ARE YOU RUNNING? ♡
OOF...
HUH?!

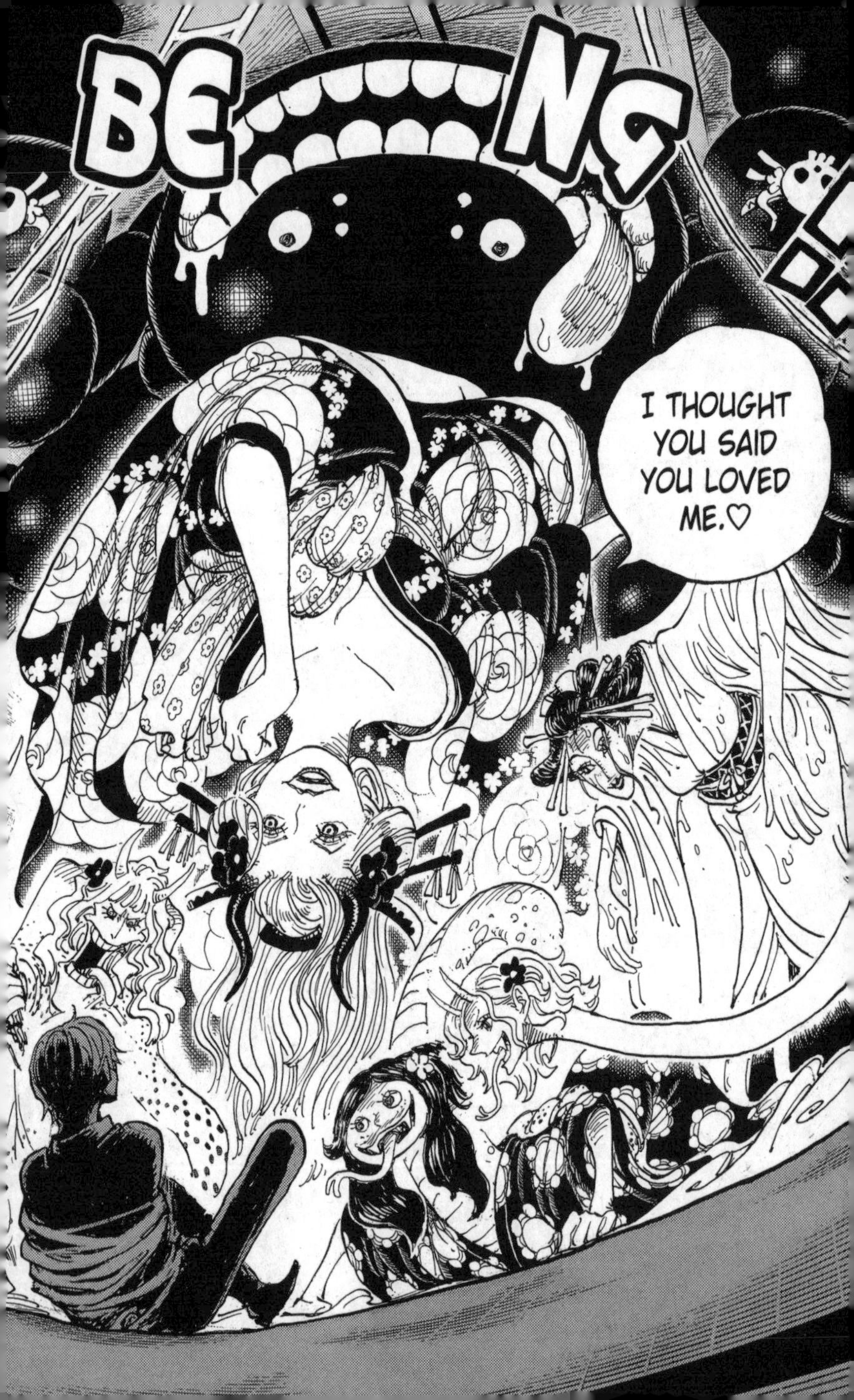
BE NG
I THOUGHT YOU SAID YOU LOVED ME.♡

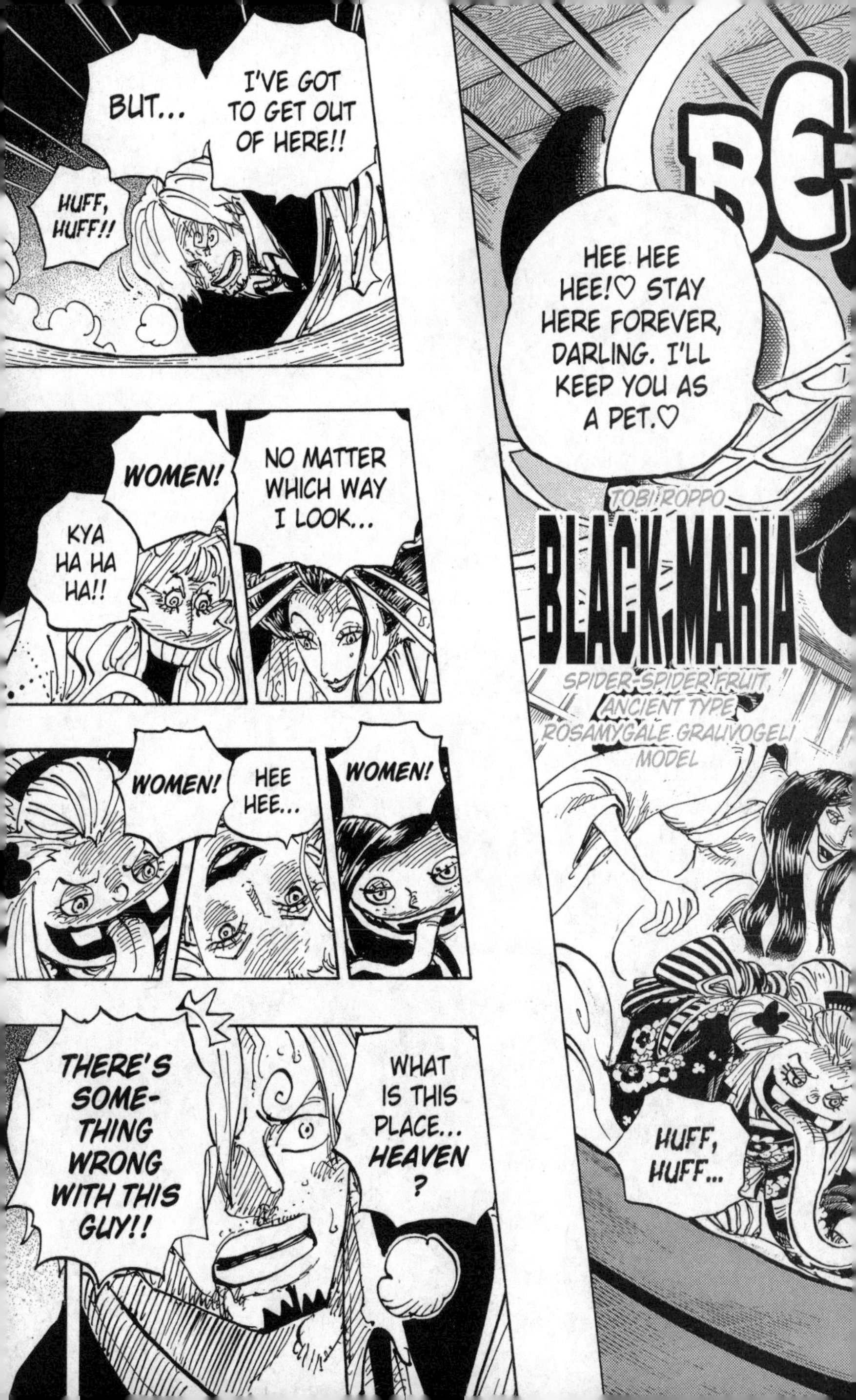
HEE HEE HEE!♡ STAY HERE FOREVER, DARLING. I'LL KEEP YOU AS A PET.♡
TOBI ROPPO
BLACK MARIA
SPIDER-SPIDER FRUIT, ANCIENT TYPE ROSAMYGALE GRAUVOGELI MODEL
HUFF, HUFF...
I'VE GOT TO GET OUT OF HERE!!
BUT...
HUFF, HUFF!!
NO MATTER WHICH WAY I LOOK...
WOMEN!
KYA HA HA HA!!
WOMEN!
HEE HEE...
WOMEN!
WHAT IS THIS PLACE... HEAVEN?
THERE'S SOME-THING WRONG WITH THIS GUY!!

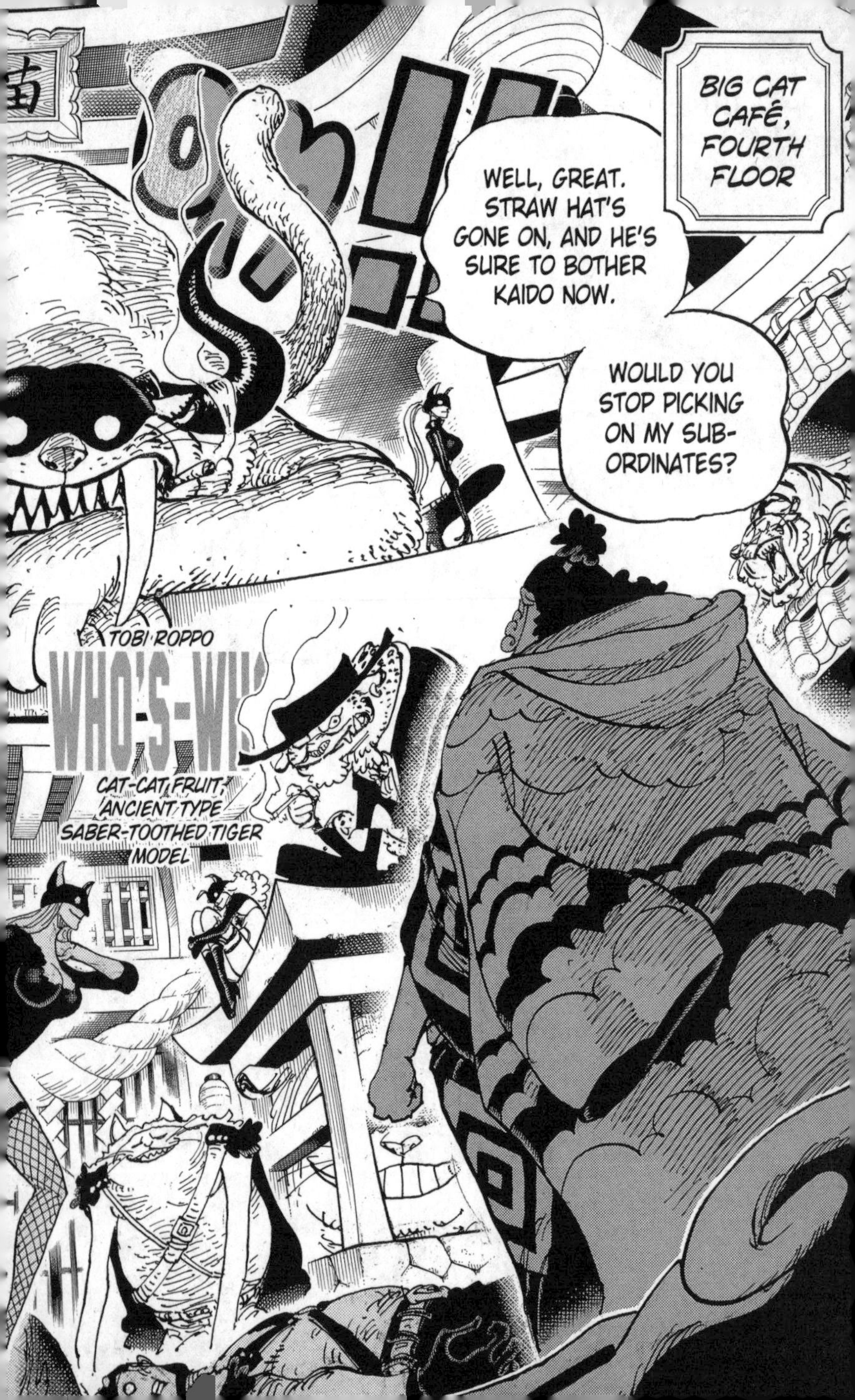
BIG CAT CAFÉ, FOURTH FLOOR
WELL, GREAT. STRAW HAT'S GONE ON, AND HE'S SURE TO BOTHER KAIDO NOW.
WOULD YOU STOP PICKING ON MY SUB-ORDINATES?
TOBI ROPPO
WHO'S-WH
CAT-CAT FRUIT, ANCIENT TYPE SABER-TOOTHED TIGER MODEL

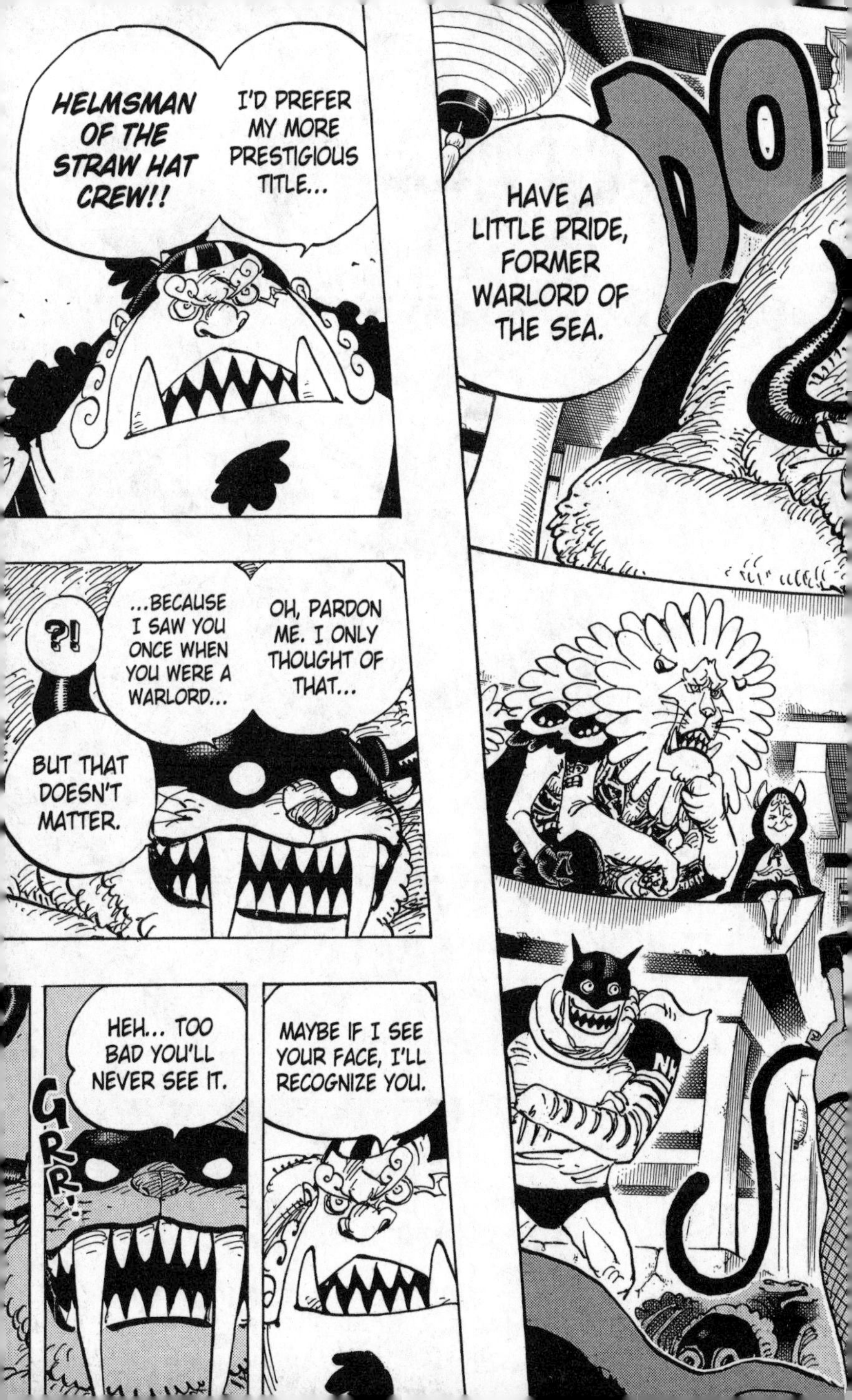
DOO
HAVE A LITTLE PRIDE, FORMER WARLORD OF THE SEA.
I'D PREFER MY MORE PRESTIGIOUS TITLE...
HELMSMAN OF THE STRAW HAT CREW!!
OH, PARDON ME. I ONLY THOUGHT OF THAT...
...BECAUSE I SAW YOU ONCE WHEN YOU WERE A WARLORD...
?!
BUT THAT DOESN'T MATTER.
MAYBE IF I SEE YOUR FACE, I'LL RECOGNIZE YOU.
HEH... TOO BAD YOU'LL NEVER SEE IT.
GRR!

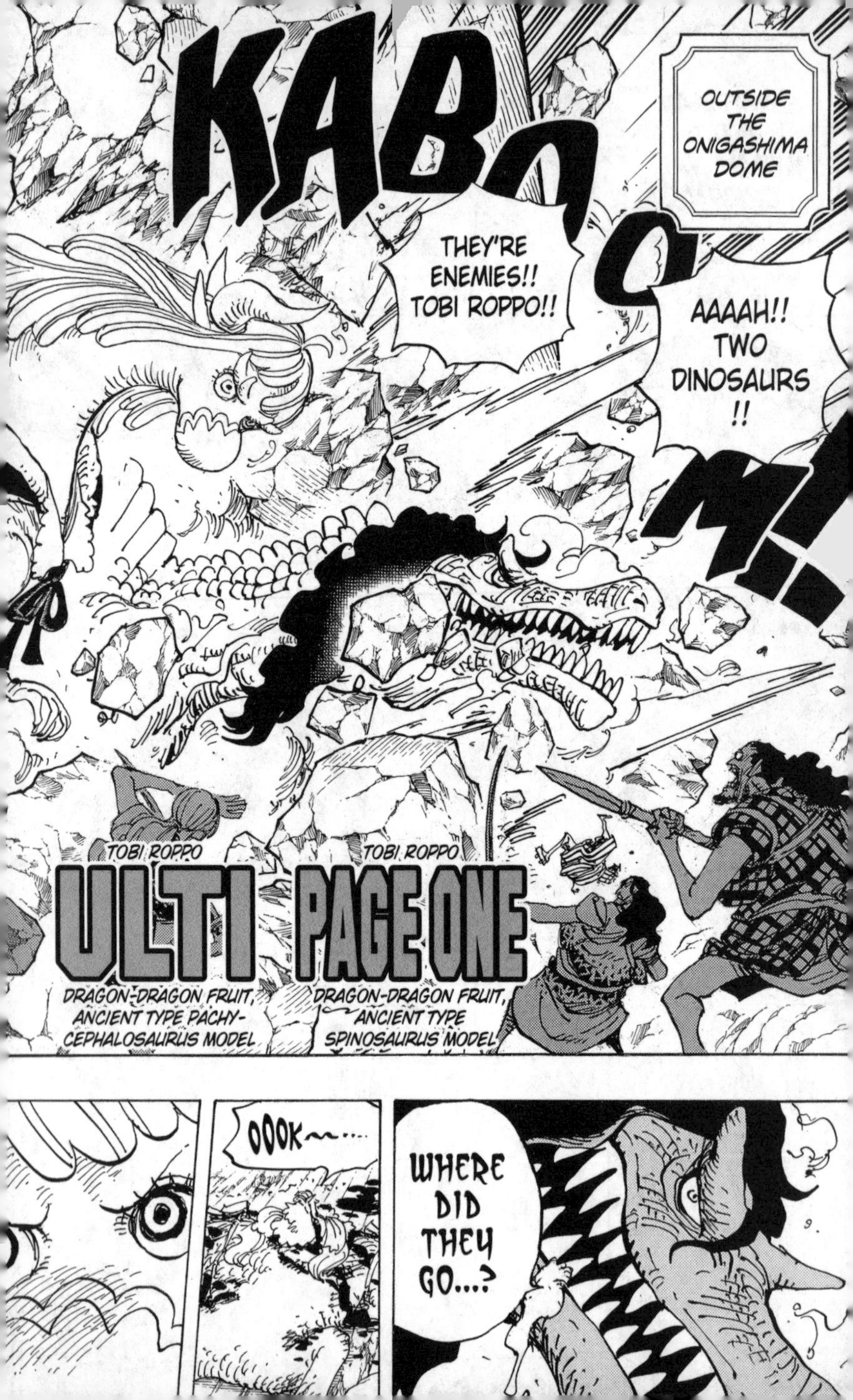

OUTSIDE THE ONIGASHIMA DOME
AAAAH!! TWO DINOSAURS !!
KABOOM!!
THEY'RE ENEMIES!! TOBI ROPPO!!
TOBI ROPPO
PAGE ONE
DRAGON-DRAGON FRUIT, ANCIENT TYPE SPINOSAURUS MODEL
TOBI ROPPO
ULTI
DRAGON-DRAGON FRUIT, ANCIENT TYPE PACHY-CEPHALOSAURUS MODEL
WHERE DID THEY GO...?
OOOK~....

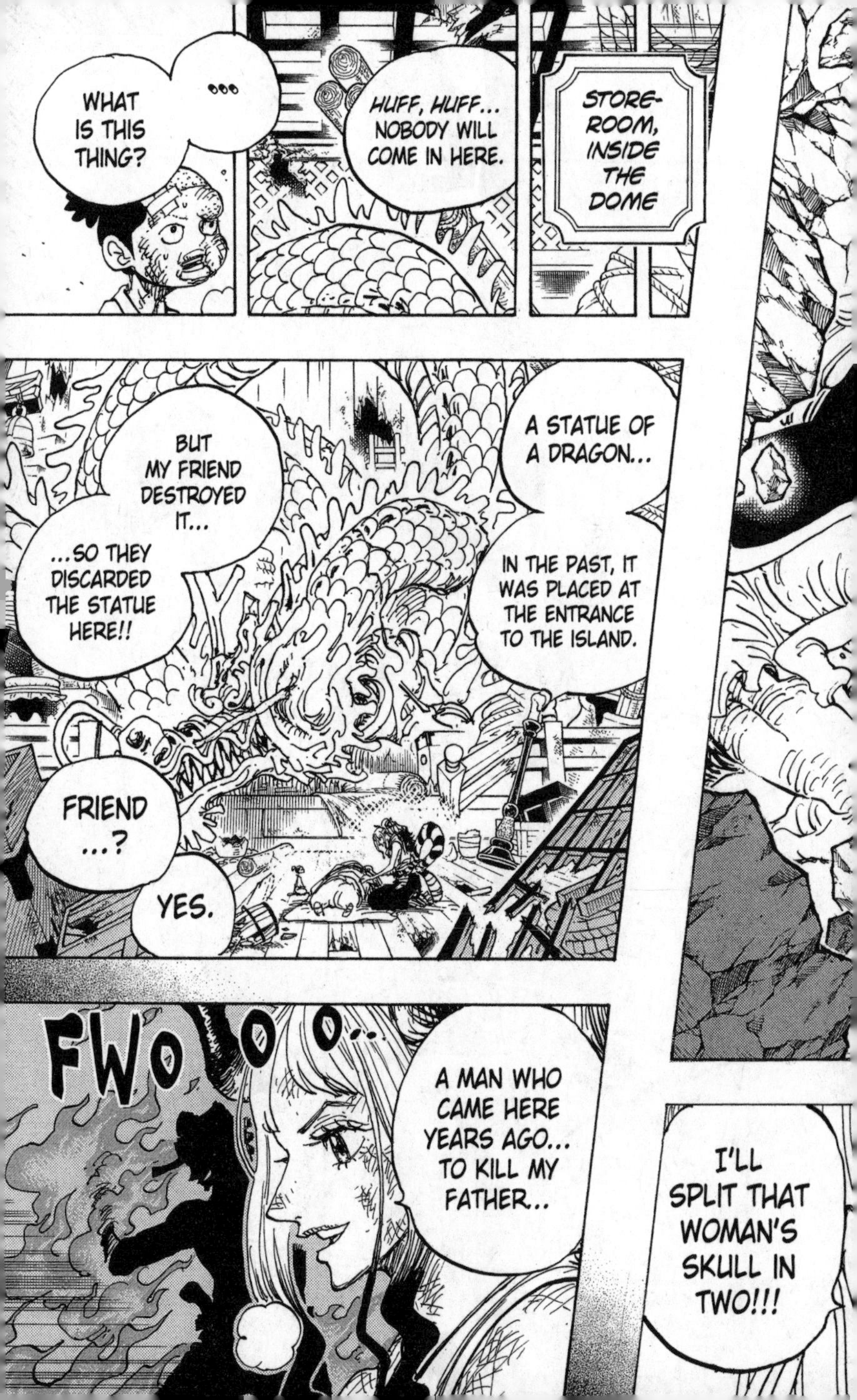
STORE-ROOM, INSIDE THE DOME
HUFF, HUFF... NOBODY WILL COME IN HERE.
...
WHAT IS THIS THING?
A STATUE OF A DRAGON...
IN THE PAST, IT WAS PLACED AT THE ENTRANCE TO THE ISLAND.
BUT MY FRIEND DESTROYED IT...
...SO THEY DISCARDED THE STATUE HERE!!
FRIEND ...?
YES.
I'LL SPLIT THAT WOMAN'S SKULL IN TWO!!!
A MAN WHO CAME HERE YEARS AGO... TO KILL MY FATHER...
FWOOO...

COLORING CORNER

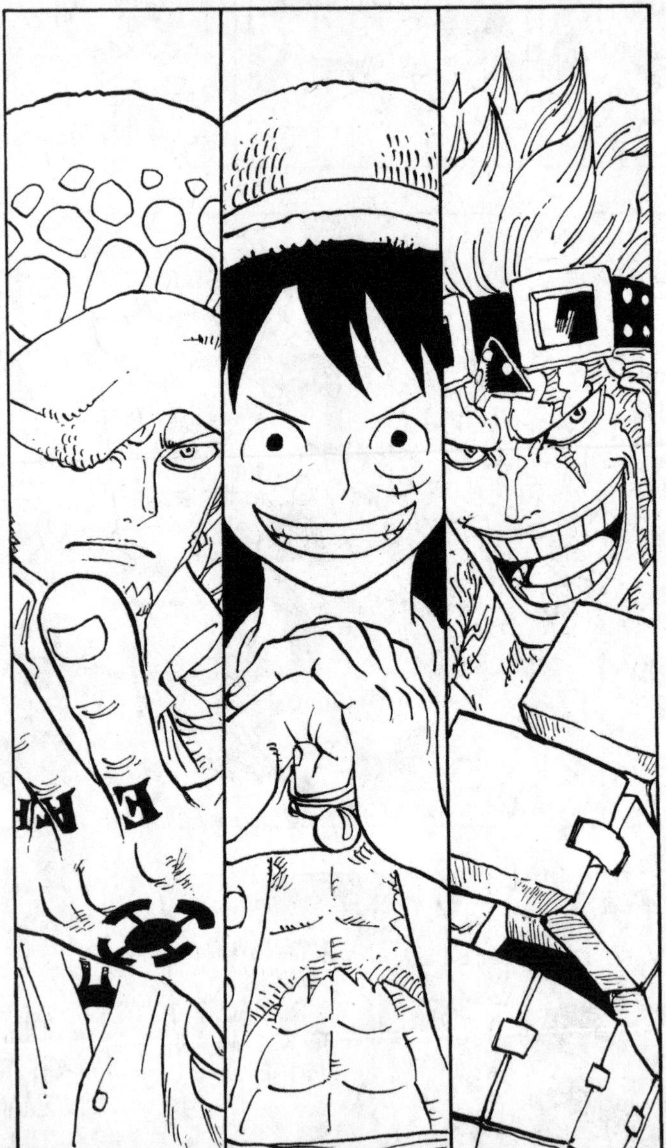

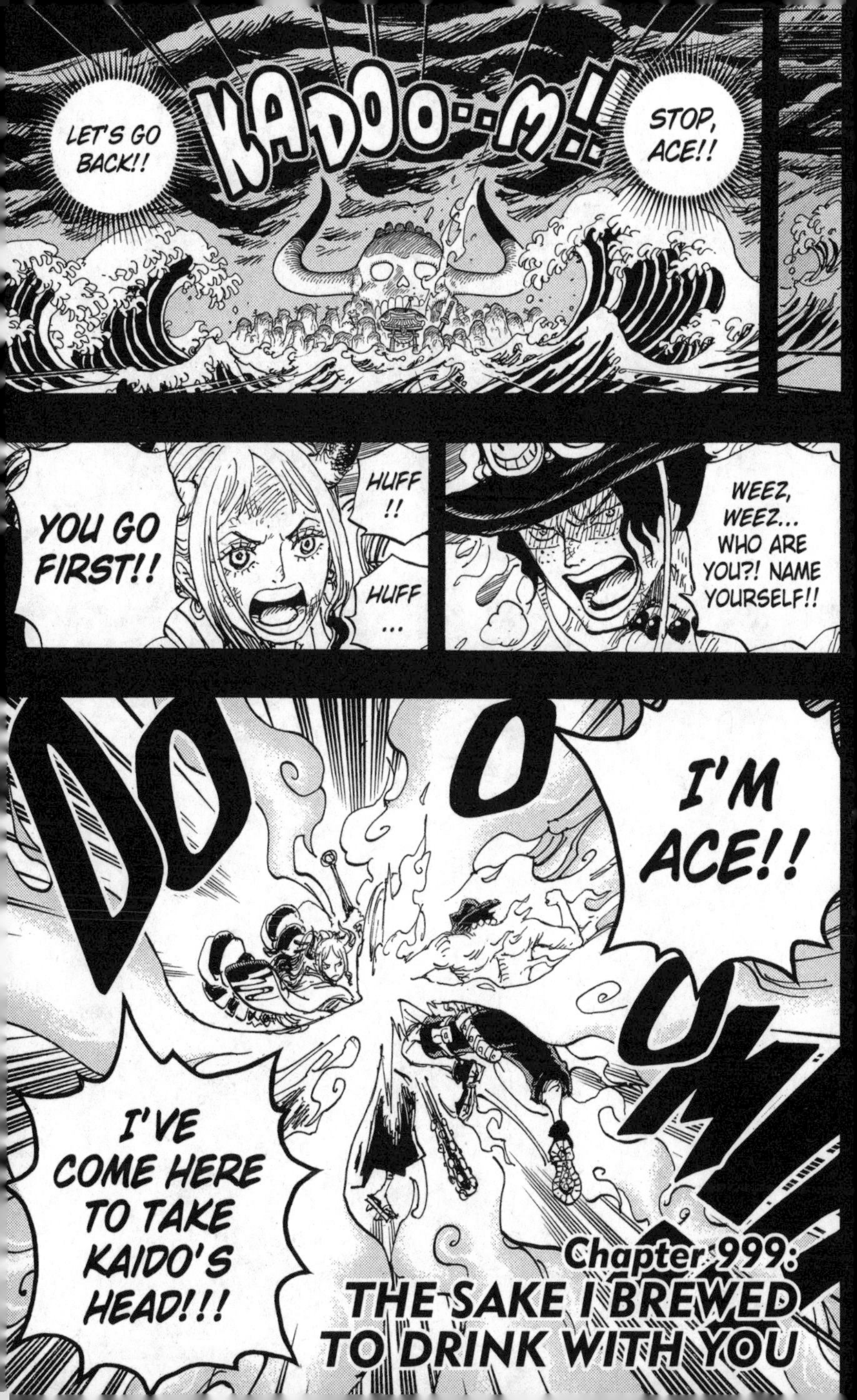
STOP, ACE!!
KADOO..M!!
LET'S GO BACK!!
WEEZ, WEEZ... WHO ARE YOU?! NAME YOURSELF!!
HUFF!!
HUFF...
YOU GO FIRST!!
I'M ACE!!
DOOOM
I'VE COME HERE TO TAKE KAIDO'S HEAD!!!

Chapter 999: THE SAKE I BREWED TO DRINK WITH YOU

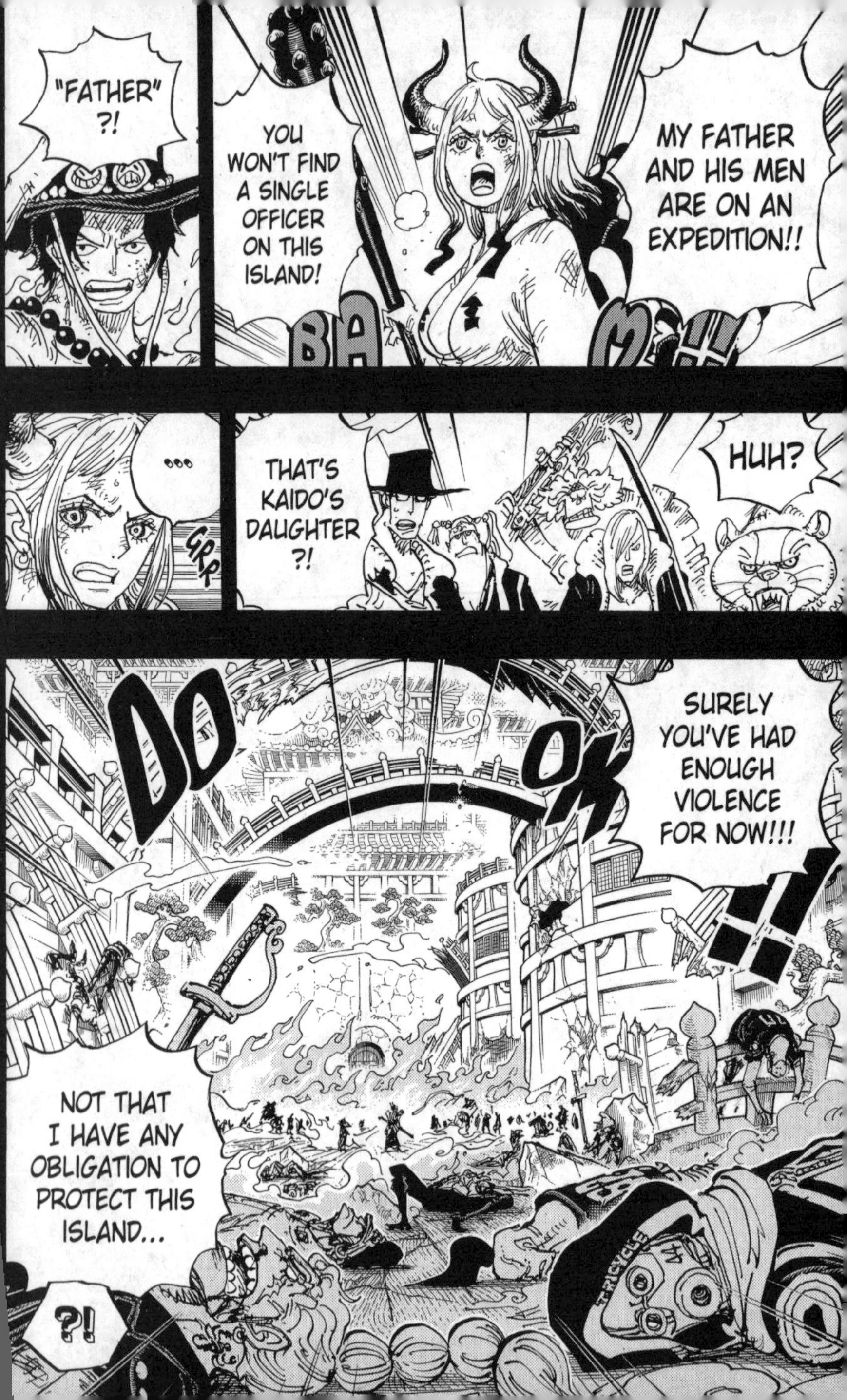
MY FATHER AND HIS MEN ARE ON AN EXPEDITION!!
YOU WON'T FIND A SINGLE OFFICER ON THIS ISLAND!
BA
M
"FATHER" ?!
HUH?
THAT'S KAIDO'S DAUGHTER ?!
...
GRR
SURELY YOU'VE HAD ENOUGH VIOLENCE FOR NOW!!!
DO
OM
!!
NOT THAT I HAVE ANY OBLIGATION TO PROTECT THIS ISLAND...
?!

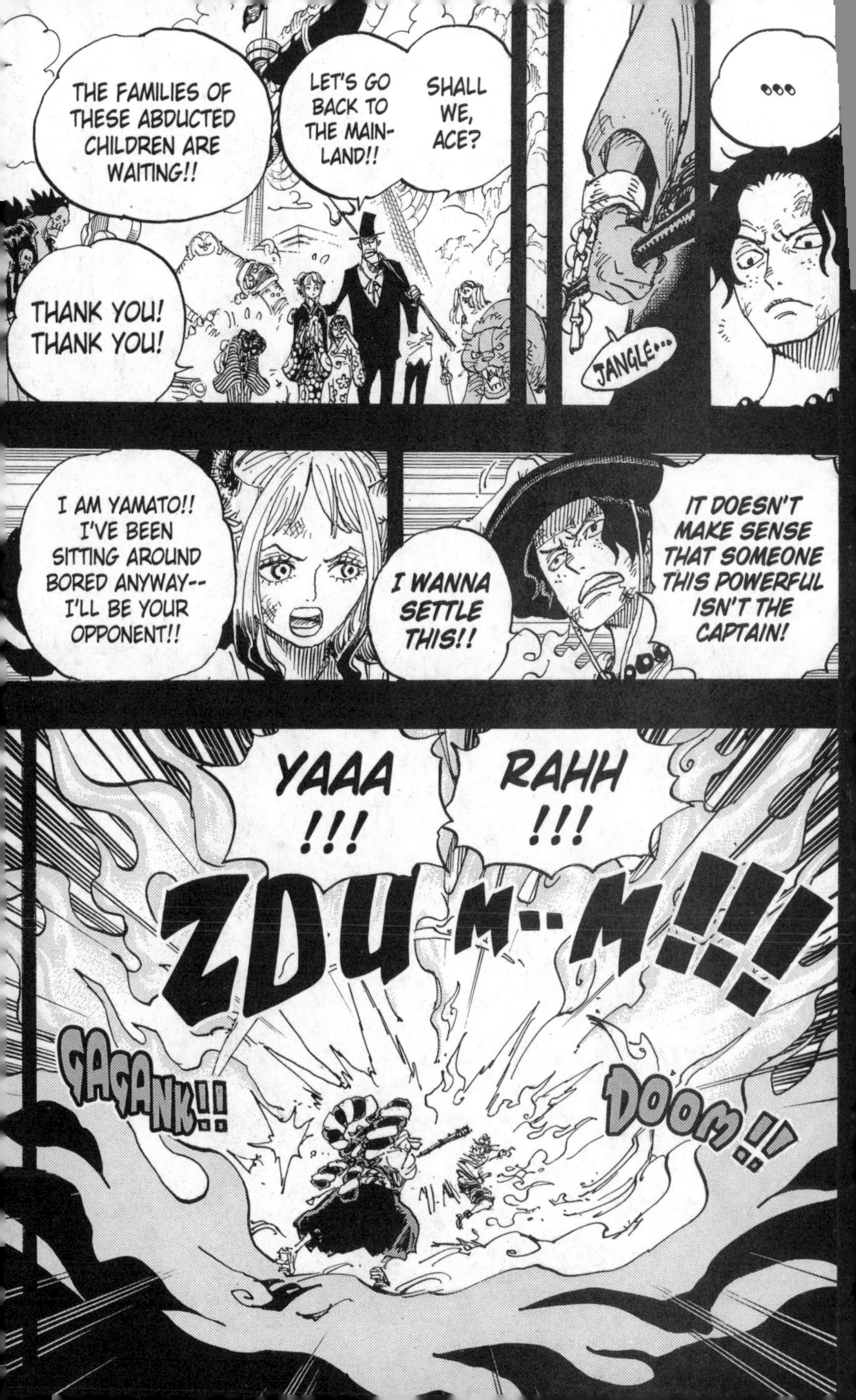
...
JANGLE...
SHALL WE, ACE?
LET'S GO BACK TO THE MAIN-LAND!!
THE FAMILIES OF THESE ABDUCTED CHILDREN ARE WAITING!!
THANK YOU! THANK YOU!
IT DOESN'T MAKE SENSE THAT SOMEONE THIS POWERFUL ISN'T THE CAPTAIN!
I WANNA SETTLE THIS!!
I AM YAMATO!! I'VE BEEN SITTING AROUND BORED ANYWAY-- I'LL BE YOUR OPPONENT!!
YAAA!!!
RAHH!!!
ZDUM--M!!!
DOOM!!
GAGANK!!

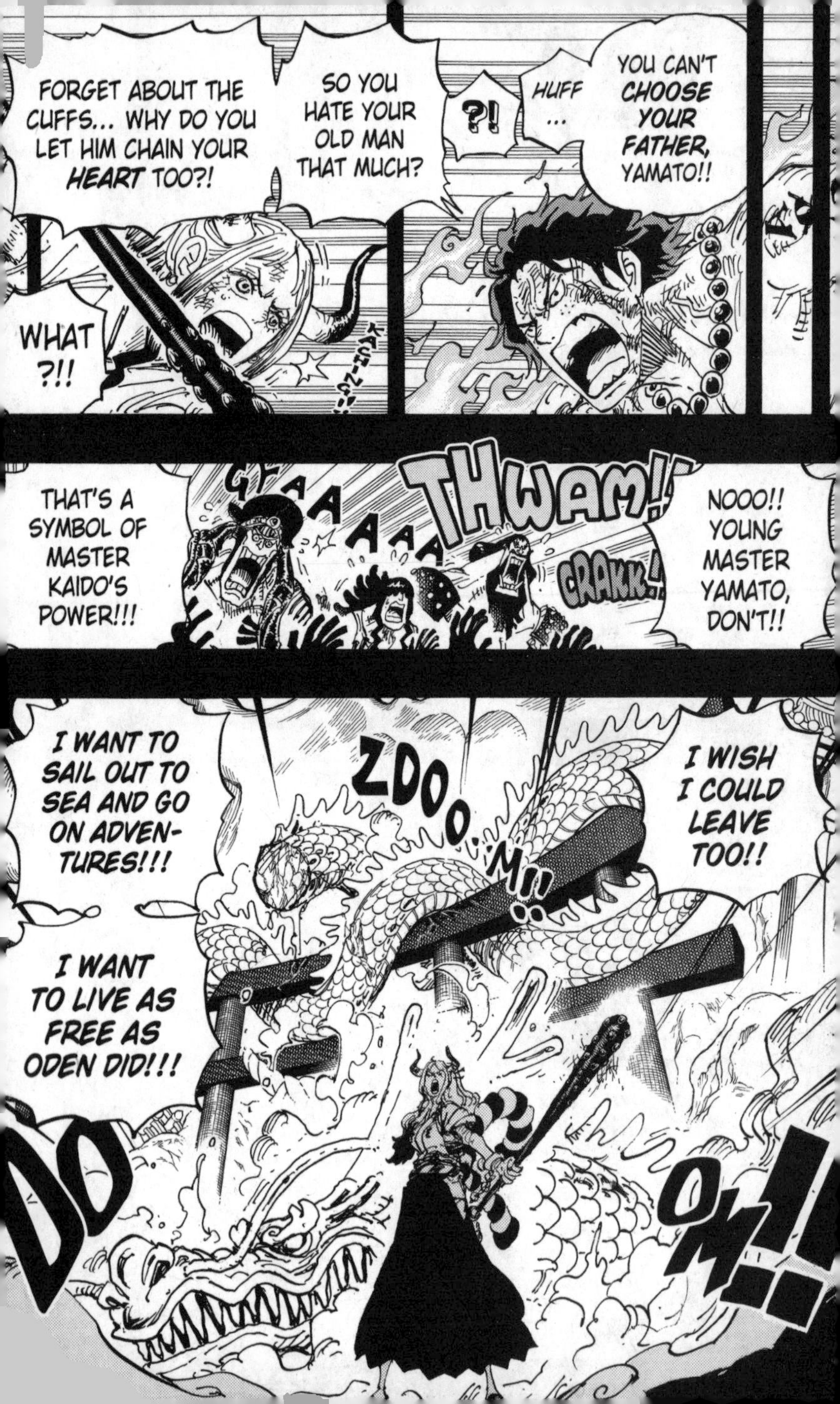
YOU CAN'T CHOOSE YOUR FATHER, YAMATO!!
HUFF ...
?!
SO YOU HATE YOUR OLD MAN THAT MUCH?
FORGET ABOUT THE CUFFS... WHY DO YOU LET HIM CHAIN YOUR HEART TOO?!
WHAT ?!!
KACHING!!
NOOO!! YOUNG MASTER YAMATO, DON'T!!
THWAM!!
CRAKK!!
GYAAAAAA
THAT'S A SYMBOL OF MASTER KAIDO'S POWER!!!
I WISH I COULD LEAVE TOO!!
ZDOOOM!!
I WANT TO SAIL OUT TO SEA AND GO ON ADVEN-TURES!!!
I WANT TO LIVE AS FREE AS ODEN DID!!!
OM!!
DO

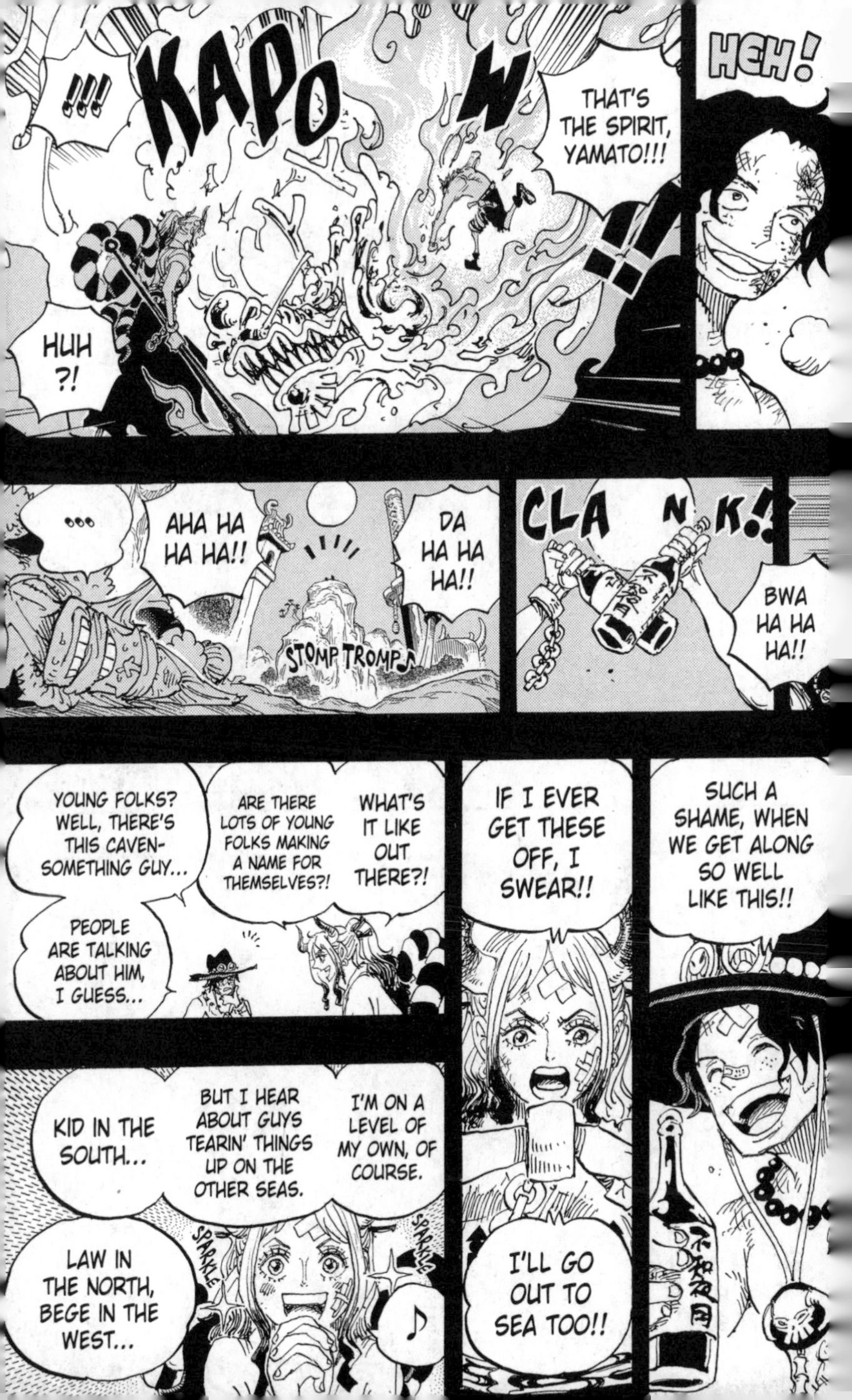
HEH!
THAT'S THE SPIRIT, YAMATO!!!
!!
KAPOW
!!!
HUH ?!
CLANK!!
BWA HA HA HA!!
DA HA HA HA!!
AHA HA HA HA!!
...
STOMP TROMP♪
SUCH A SHAME, WHEN WE GET ALONG SO WELL LIKE THIS!!
IF I EVER GET THESE OFF, I SWEAR!!
I'LL GO OUT TO SEA TOO!!
WHAT'S IT LIKE OUT THERE?!
ARE THERE LOTS OF YOUNG FOLKS MAKING A NAME FOR THEMSELVES?!
YOUNG FOLKS? WELL, THERE'S THIS CAVEN-SOMETHING GUY...
PEOPLE ARE TALKING ABOUT HIM, I GUESS...
I'M ON A LEVEL OF MY OWN, OF COURSE.
BUT I HEAR ABOUT GUYS TEARIN' THINGS UP ON THE OTHER SEAS.
KID IN THE SOUTH...
LAW IN THE NORTH, BEGE IN THE WEST...
SPARKLE
SPARKLE
♪

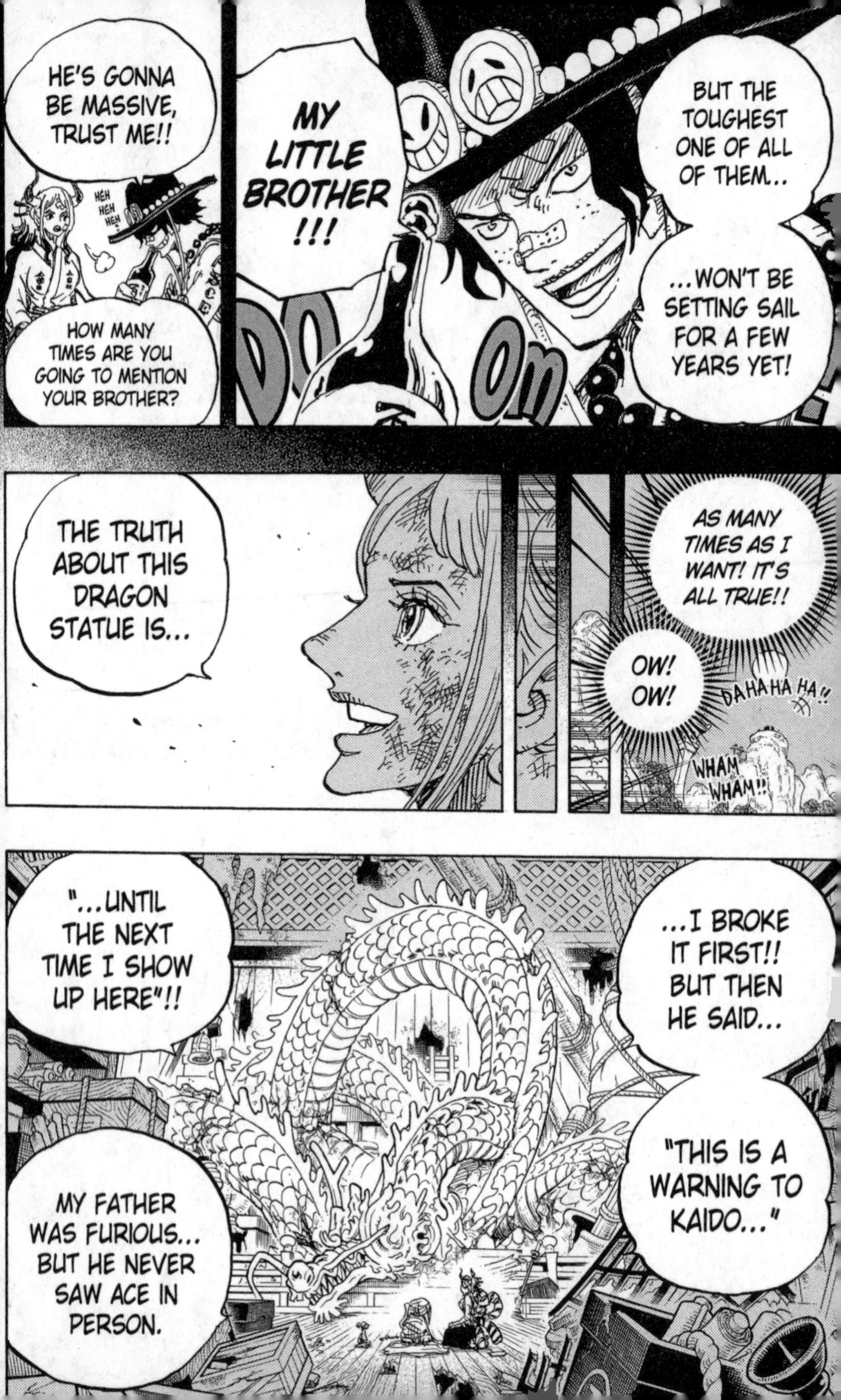
BUT THE TOUGHEST ONE OF ALL OF THEM...
...WON'T BE SETTING SAIL FOR A FEW YEARS YET!
MY LITTLE BROTHER!!!
HE'S GONNA BE MASSIVE, TRUST ME!!
HEH HEH HEH
HOW MANY TIMES ARE YOU GOING TO MENTION YOUR BROTHER?
AS MANY TIMES AS I WANT! IT'S ALL TRUE!!
OW! OW!
DAHAHA HA!!
WHAM WHAM!!
THE TRUTH ABOUT THIS DRAGON STATUE IS...
...I BROKE IT FIRST!! BUT THEN HE SAID...
"THIS IS A WARNING TO KAIDO..."
"...UNTIL THE NEXT TIME I SHOW UP HERE"!!
MY FATHER WAS FURIOUS... BUT HE NEVER SAW ACE IN PERSON.

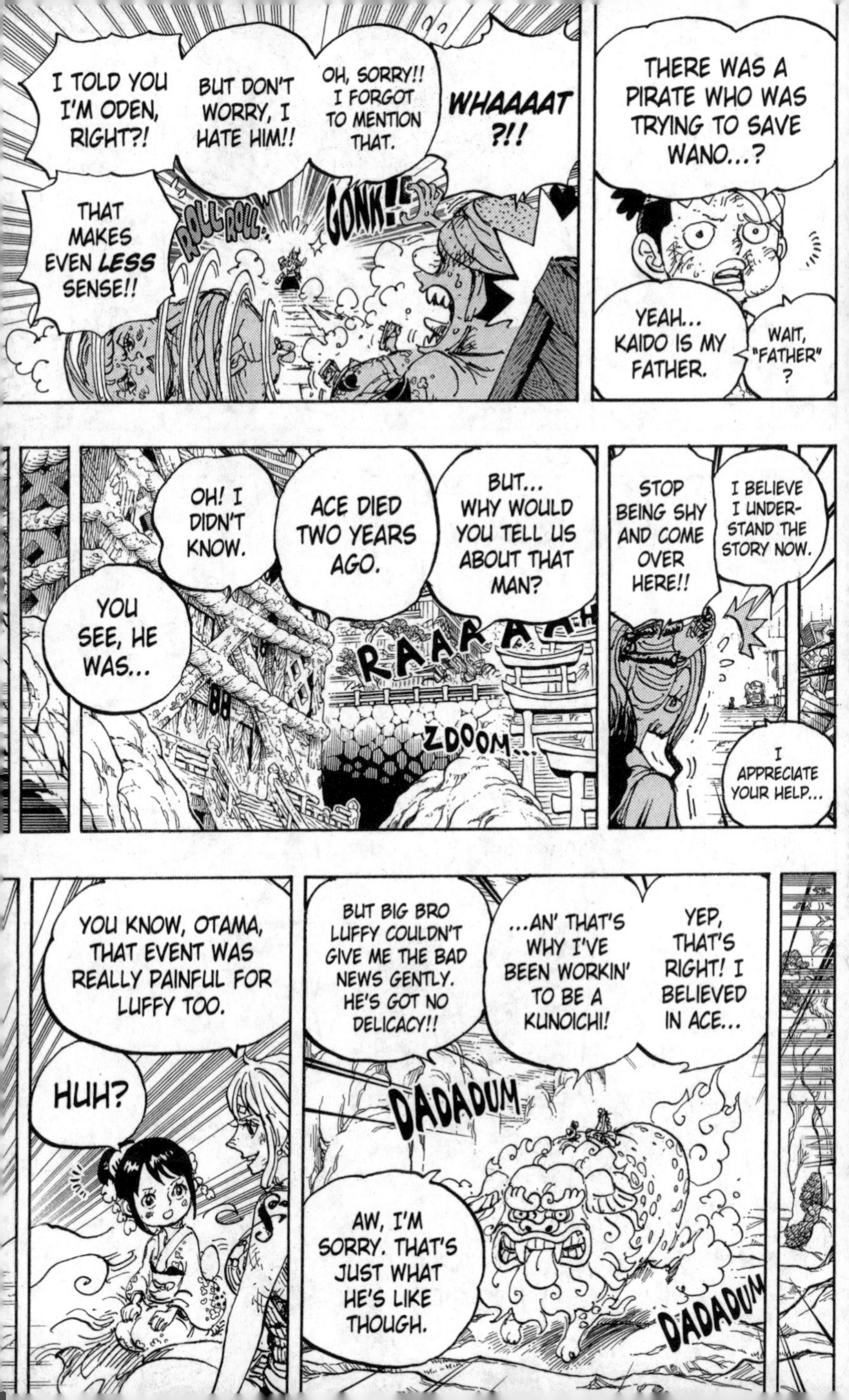
THERE WAS A PIRATE WHO WAS TRYING TO SAVE WANO...?
YEAH... KAIDO IS MY FATHER.
WAIT, "FATHER"?
WHAAAAT?!!
OH, SORRY!! I FORGOT TO MENTION THAT.
BUT DON'T WORRY, I HATE HIM!!
I TOLD YOU I'M ODEN, RIGHT?!
GONK!
ROLL ROLL
THAT MAKES EVEN LESS SENSE!!
I BELIEVE I UNDERSTAND THE STORY NOW.
STOP BEING SHY AND COME OVER HERE!!
I APPRECIATE YOUR HELP...
BUT... WHY WOULD YOU TELL US ABOUT THAT MAN?
ACE DIED TWO YEARS AGO.
OH! I DIDN'T KNOW.
YOU SEE, HE WAS...
RAAAAAH
ZDOOM...
YEP, THAT'S RIGHT! I BELIEVED IN ACE...
...AN' THAT'S WHY I'VE BEEN WORKIN' TO BE A KUNOICHI!
BUT BIG BRO LUFFY COULDN'T GIVE ME THE BAD NEWS GENTLY. HE'S GOT NO DELICACY!!
DADADUM
AW, I'M SORRY. THAT'S JUST WHAT HE'S LIKE THOUGH.
DADADUM
YOU KNOW, OTAMA, THAT EVENT WAS REALLY PAINFUL FOR LUFFY TOO.
HUH?

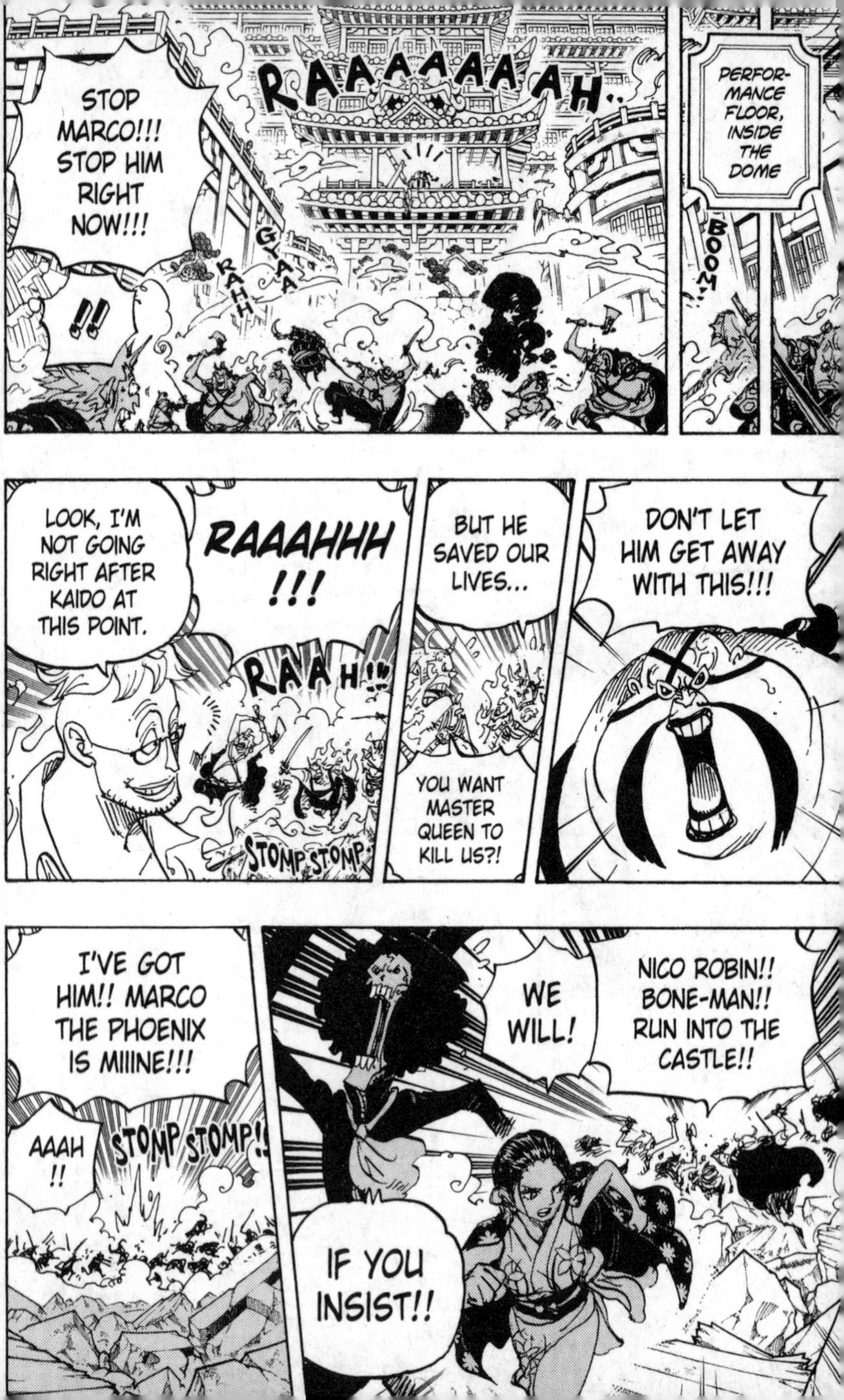
PERFORMANCE FLOOR, INSIDE THE DOME
BOOM
RAAAAAAAH..
STOP MARCO!!! STOP HIM RIGHT NOW!!!
GYAA
RAHH
!!
DON'T LET HIM GET AWAY WITH THIS!!!
BUT HE SAVED OUR LIVES...
YOU WANT MASTER QUEEN TO KILL US?!
RAAAHHH!!!
LOOK, I'M NOT GOING RIGHT AFTER KAIDO AT THIS POINT.
RAAH!!
STOMP STOMP
NICO ROBIN!! BONE-MAN!! RUN INTO THE CASTLE!!
WE WILL!
IF YOU INSIST!!
I'VE GOT HIM!! MARCO THE PHOENIX IS MIIINE!!!
AAAH!!
STOMP STOMP!!

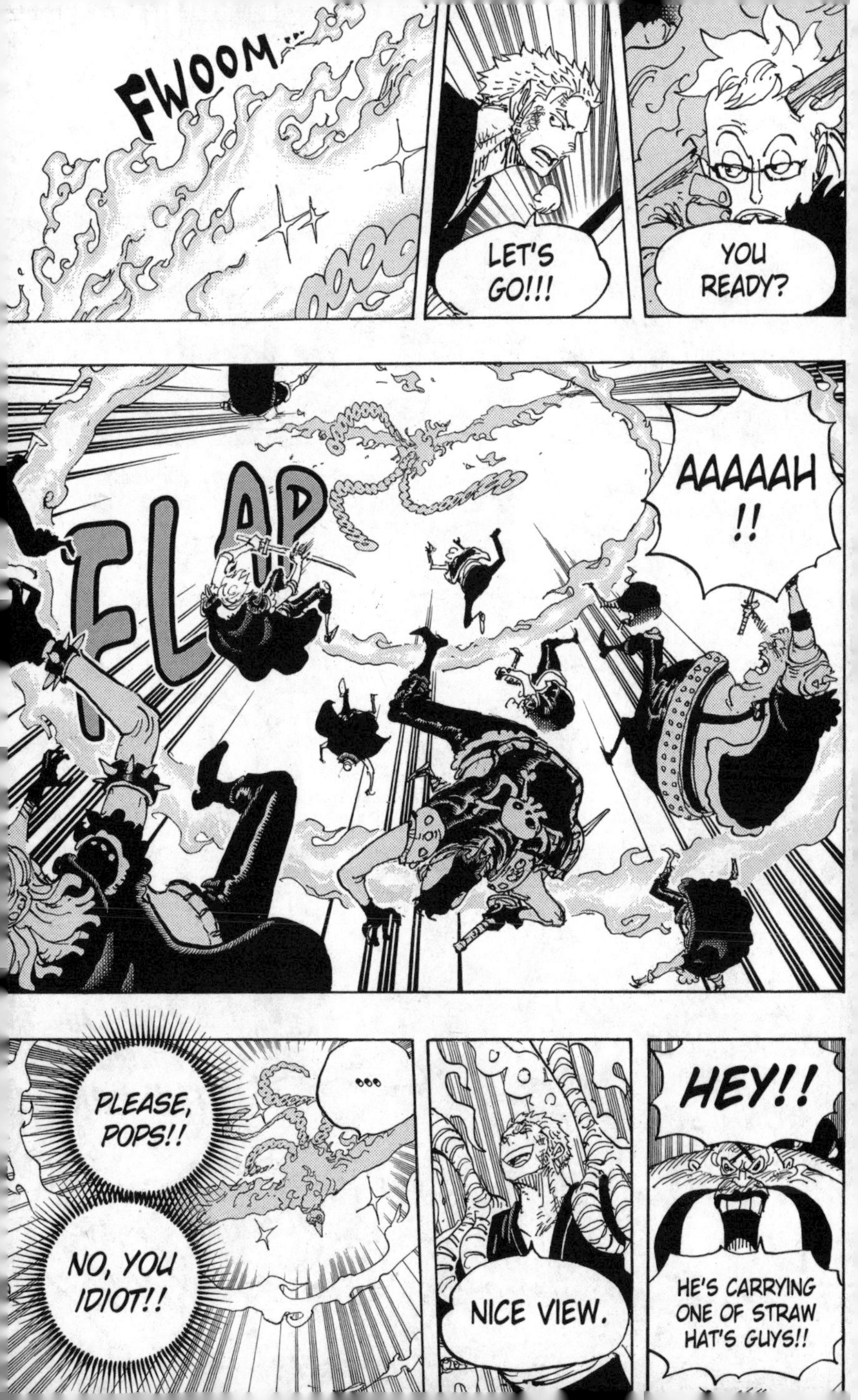
YOU READY?
LET'S GO!!!
FWOOM
AAAAAH!!
FLAP
HEY!!
HE'S CARRYING ONE OF STRAW HAT'S GUYS!!
NICE VIEW.
...
PLEASE, POPS!!
NO, YOU IDIOT!!

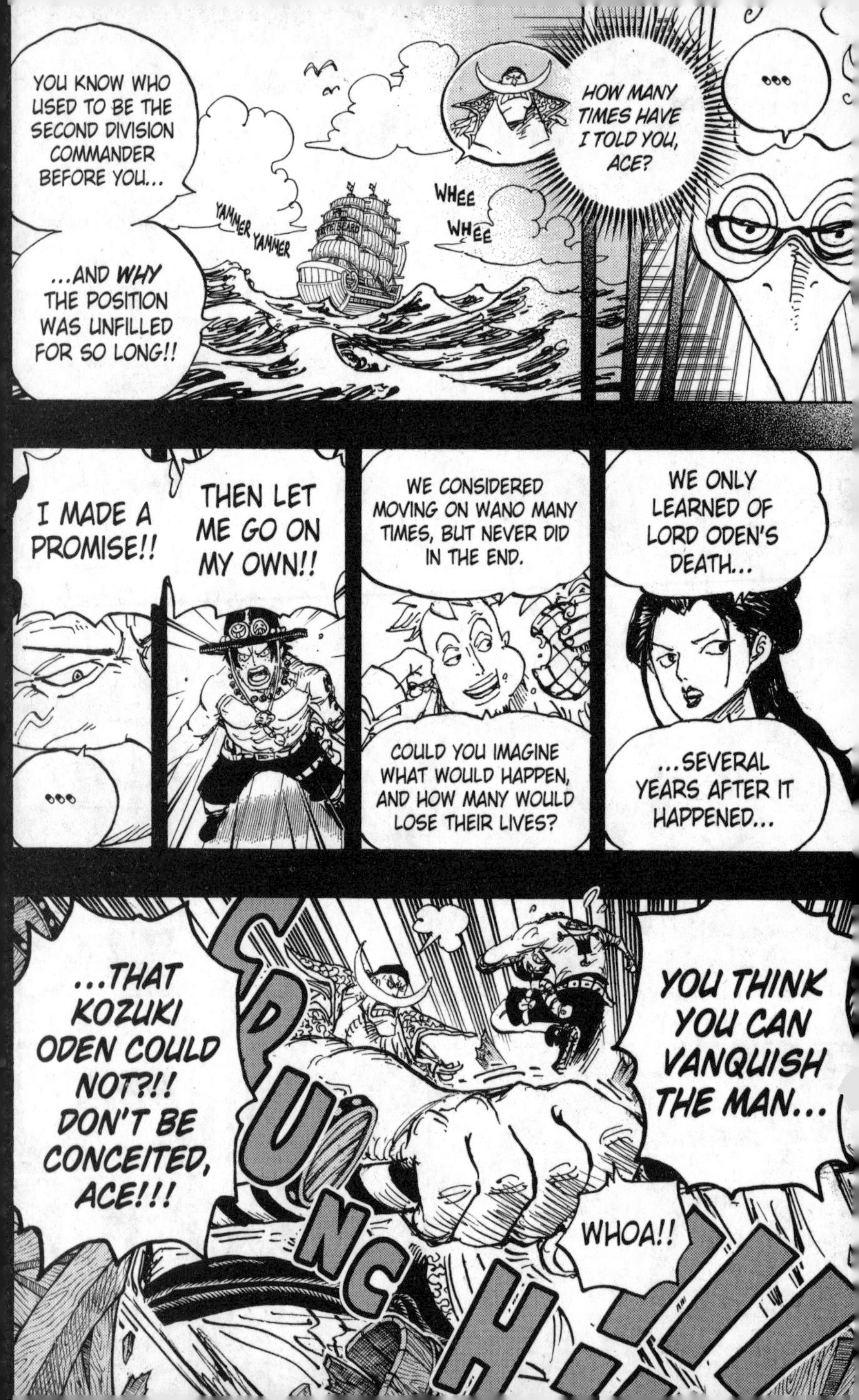
...
HOW MANY TIMES HAVE I TOLD YOU, ACE?
YOU KNOW WHO USED TO BE THE SECOND DIVISION COMMANDER BEFORE YOU...
WHEE WHEE
YAMMER YAMMER
...AND WHY THE POSITION WAS UNFILLED FOR SO LONG!!
WE ONLY LEARNED OF LORD ODEN'S DEATH...
...SEVERAL YEARS AFTER IT HAPPENED...
WE CONSIDERED MOVING ON WANO MANY TIMES, BUT NEVER DID IN THE END.
COULD YOU IMAGINE WHAT WOULD HAPPEN, AND HOW MANY WOULD LOSE THEIR LIVES?
THEN LET ME GO ON MY OWN!!
I MADE A PROMISE!!
...
YOU THINK YOU CAN VANQUISH THE MAN...
...THAT KOZUKI ODEN COULD NOT?!! DON'T BE CONCEITED, ACE!!!
WHOA!!
CRUNCH

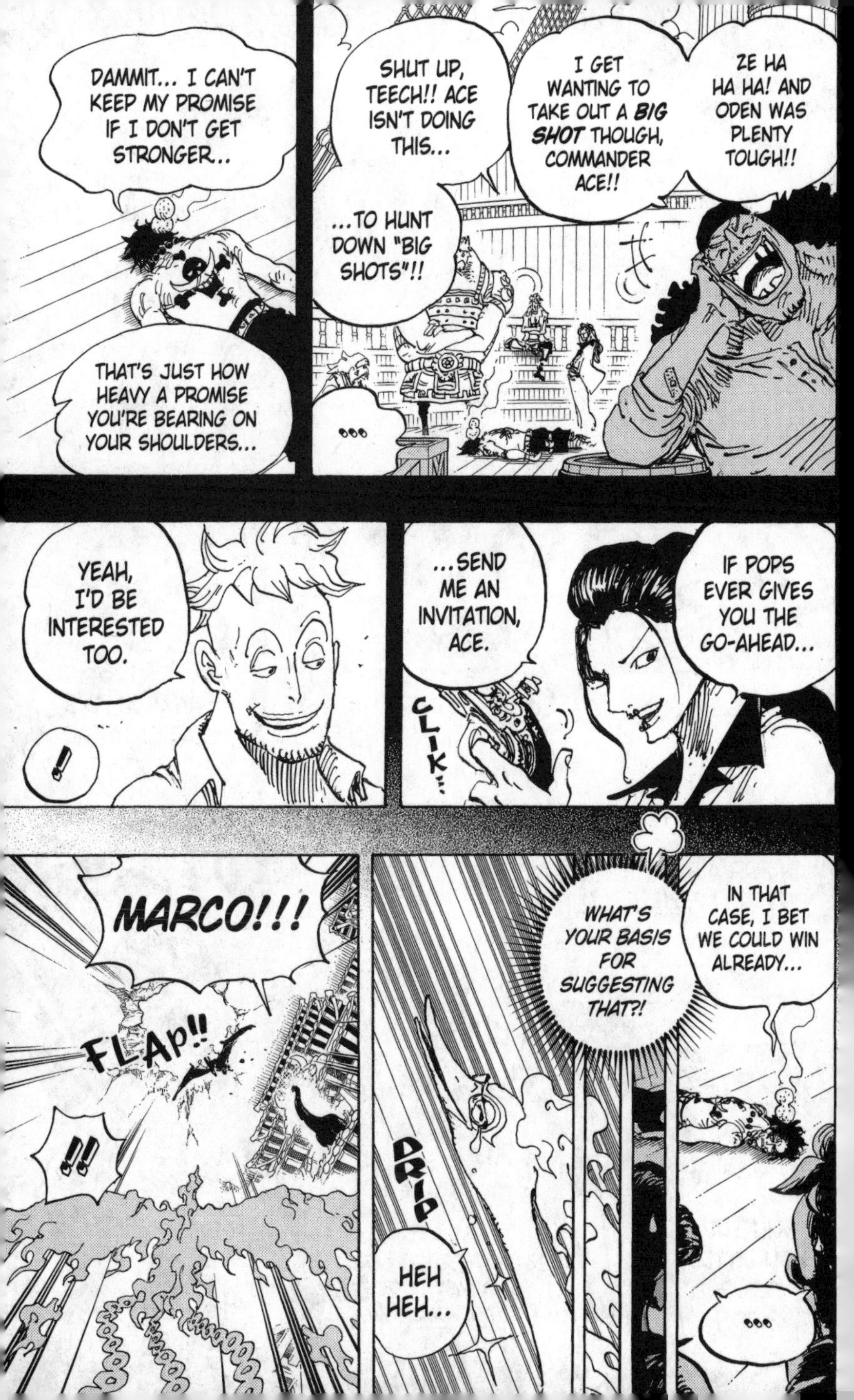
ZE HA HA HA! AND ODEN WAS PLENTY TOUGH!!
I GET WANTING TO TAKE OUT A BIG SHOT THOUGH, COMMANDER ACE!!
SHUT UP, TEECH!! ACE ISN'T DOING THIS...
...TO HUNT DOWN "BIG SHOTS"!!
...
DAMMIT... I CAN'T KEEP MY PROMISE IF I DON'T GET STRONGER...
THAT'S JUST HOW HEAVY A PROMISE YOU'RE BEARING ON YOUR SHOULDERS...
IF POPS EVER GIVES YOU THE GO-AHEAD...
...SEND ME AN INVITATION, ACE.
CLIK..
YEAH, I'D BE INTERESTED TOO.
!
IN THAT CASE, I BET WE COULD WIN ALREADY...
WHAT'S YOUR BASIS FOR SUGGESTING THAT?!
...
DRIP
HEH HEH...
MARCO!!!
FLAp!!
!!

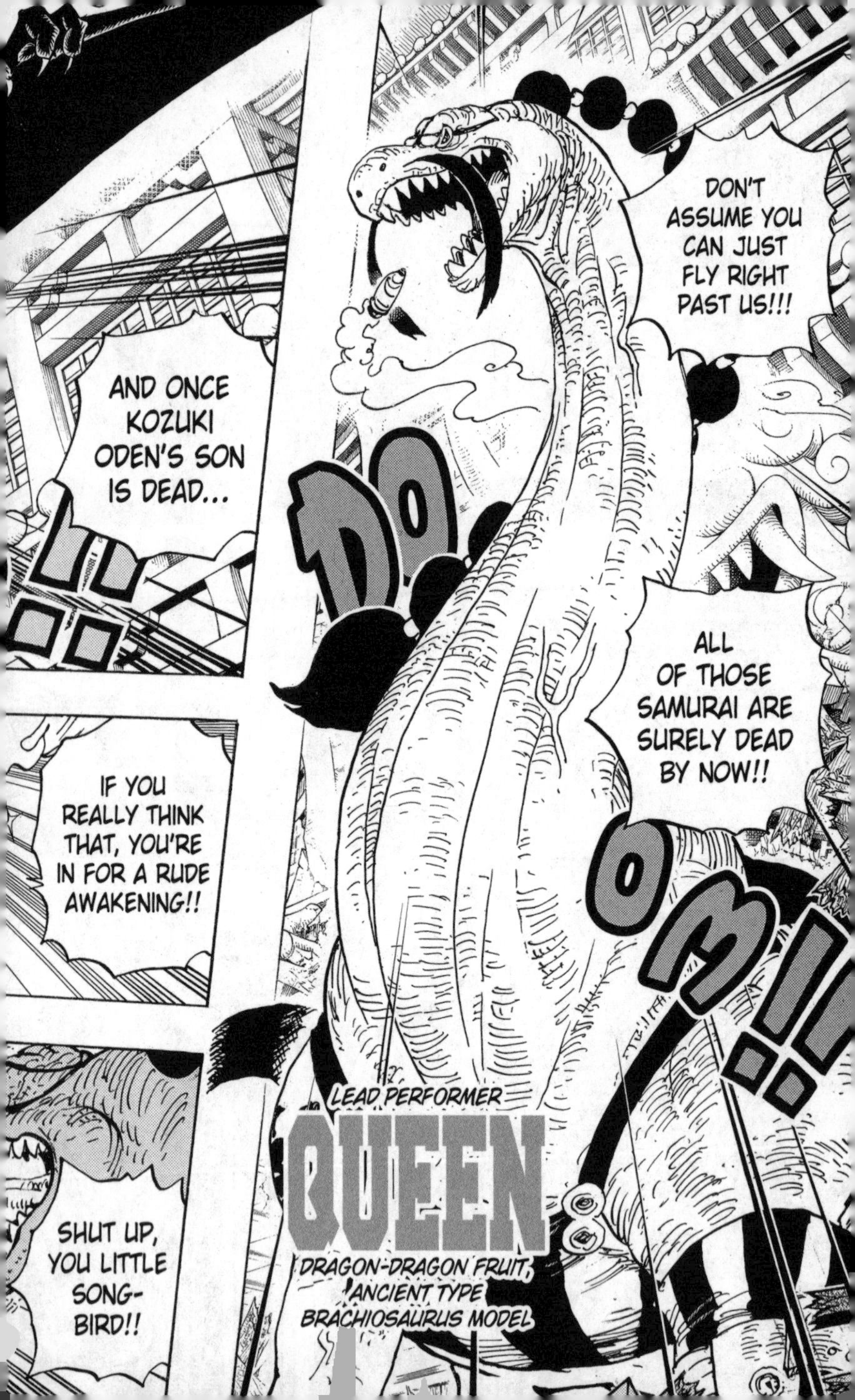
DON'T ASSUME YOU CAN JUST FLY RIGHT PAST US!!!
ALL OF THOSE SAMURAI ARE SURELY DEAD BY NOW!!
DOOM!!
LEAD PERFORMER
QUEEN
DRAGON-DRAGON FRUIT, ANCIENT TYPE BRACHIOSAURUS MODEL
AND ONCE KOZUKI ODEN'S SON IS DEAD...
IF YOU REALLY THINK THAT, YOU'RE IN FOR A RUDE AWAKENING!!
SHUT UP, YOU LITTLE SONG-BIRD!!

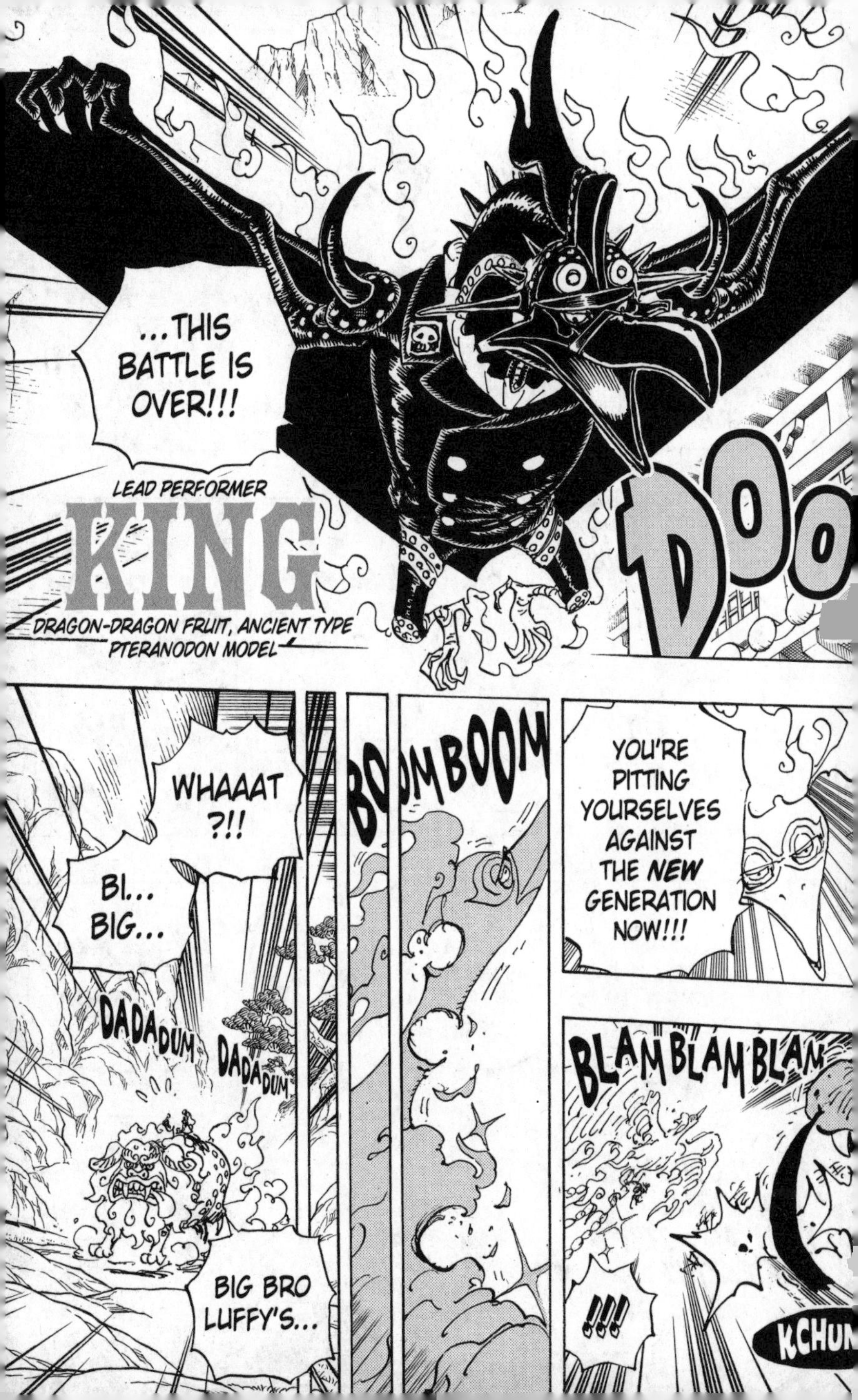
...THIS BATTLE IS OVER!!!
DOO
LEAD PERFORMER
KING
DRAGON-DRAGON FRUIT, ANCIENT TYPE PTERANODON MODEL
YOU'RE PITTING YOURSELVES AGAINST THE *NEW* GENERATION NOW!!!
BLAM BLAM BLAM
KCHUN
!!!
BOOM BOOM
WHAAAT ?!!
BI... BIG...
DADADUM DADADUM
BIG BRO LUFFY'S...

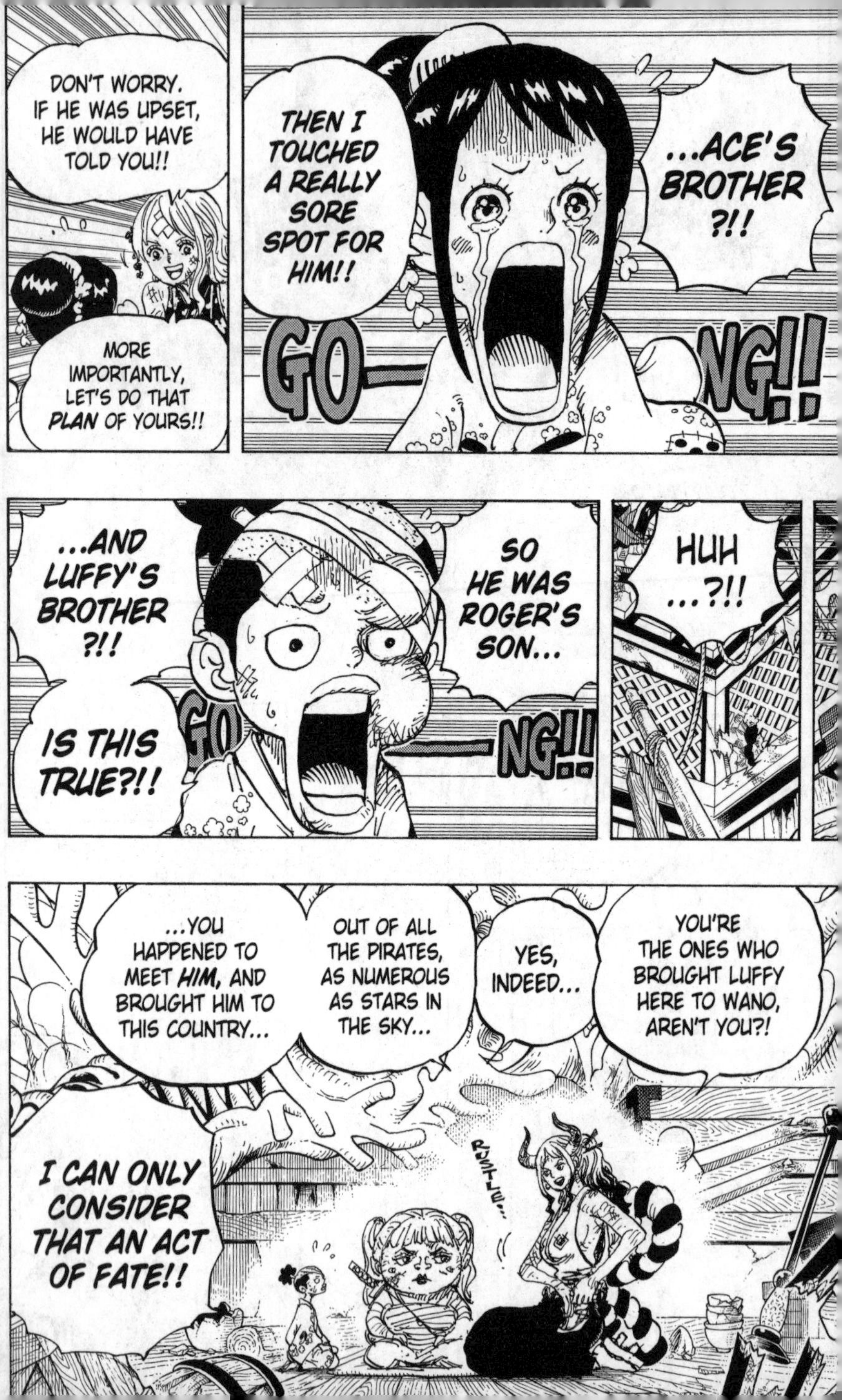
...ACE'S BROTHER ?!!
THEN I TOUCHED A REALLY SORE SPOT FOR HIM!!
GO—NG!!
DON'T WORRY. IF HE WAS UPSET, HE WOULD HAVE TOLD YOU!!
MORE IMPORTANTLY, LET'S DO THAT PLAN OF YOURS!!
HUH ...?!!
SO HE WAS ROGER'S SON...
...AND LUFFY'S BROTHER ?!!
GO—NG!!
IS THIS TRUE?!!
YOU'RE THE ONES WHO BROUGHT LUFFY HERE TO WANO, AREN'T YOU?!
YES, INDEED...
OUT OF ALL THE PIRATES, AS NUMEROUS AS STARS IN THE SKY...
...YOU HAPPENED TO MEET HIM, AND BROUGHT HIM TO THIS COUNTRY...
RUSTLE...
I CAN ONLY CONSIDER THAT AN ACT OF FATE!!

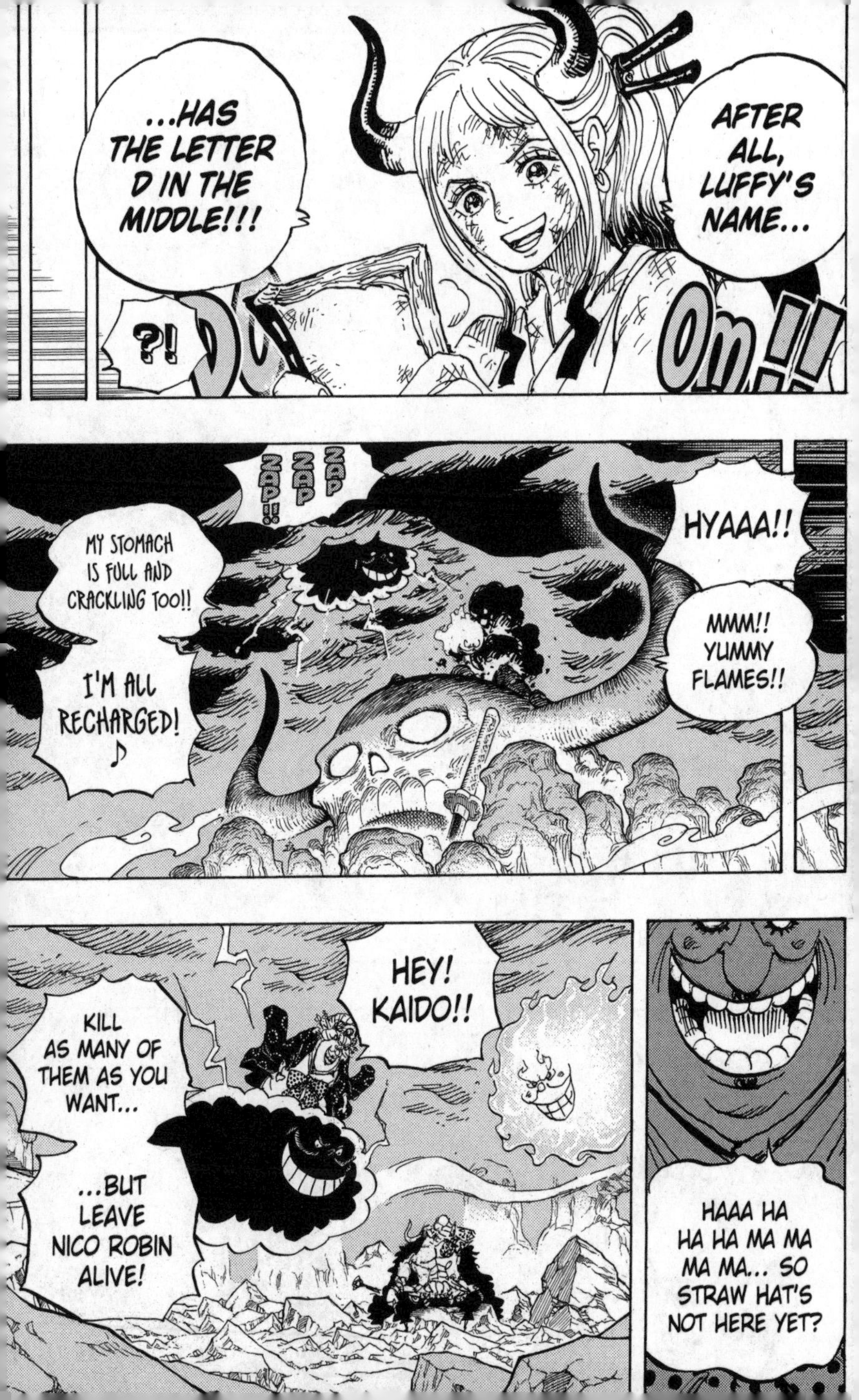
AFTER ALL, LUFFY'S NAME...
...HAS THE LETTER D IN THE MIDDLE!!!
DOOM!!
?!
HYAAA!!
MMM!! YUMMY FLAMES!!
ZAP ZAP ZAP!!
MY STOMACH IS FULL AND CRACKLING TOO!!
I'M ALL RECHARGED! ♪
HAAA HA HA HA MA MA MA MA... SO STRAW HAT'S NOT HERE YET?
HEY! KAIDO!!
KILL AS MANY OF THEM AS YOU WANT...
...BUT LEAVE NICO ROBIN ALIVE!

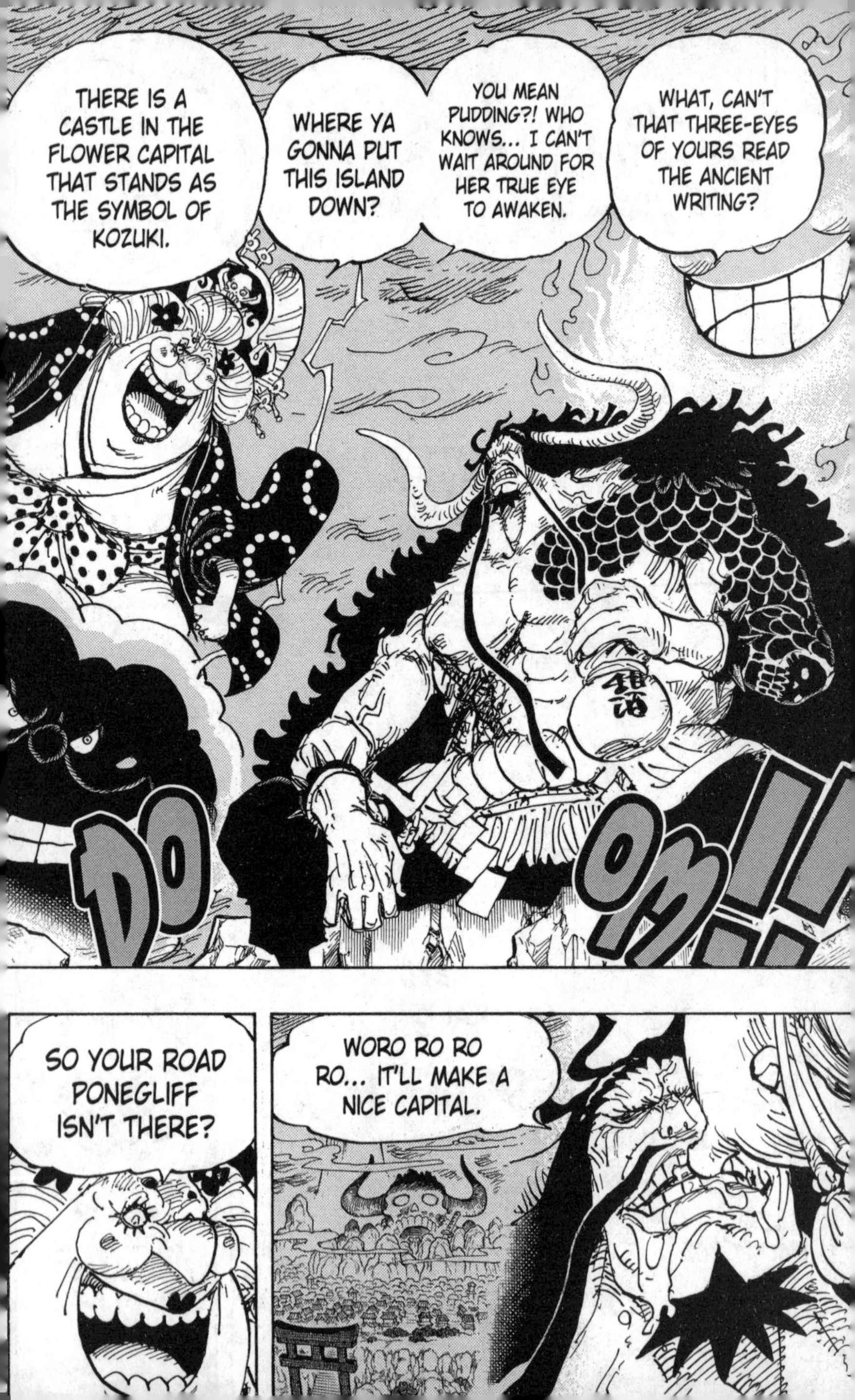
WHAT, CAN'T THAT THREE-EYES OF YOURS READ THE ANCIENT WRITING?
YOU MEAN PUDDING?! WHO KNOWS... I CAN'T WAIT AROUND FOR HER TRUE EYE TO AWAKEN.
WHERE YA GONNA PUT THIS ISLAND DOWN?
THERE IS A CASTLE IN THE FLOWER CAPITAL THAT STANDS AS THE SYMBOL OF KOZUKI.
DOOM!!
WORO RO RO RO... IT'LL MAKE A NICE CAPITAL.
SO YOUR ROAD PONEGLIFF ISN'T THERE?

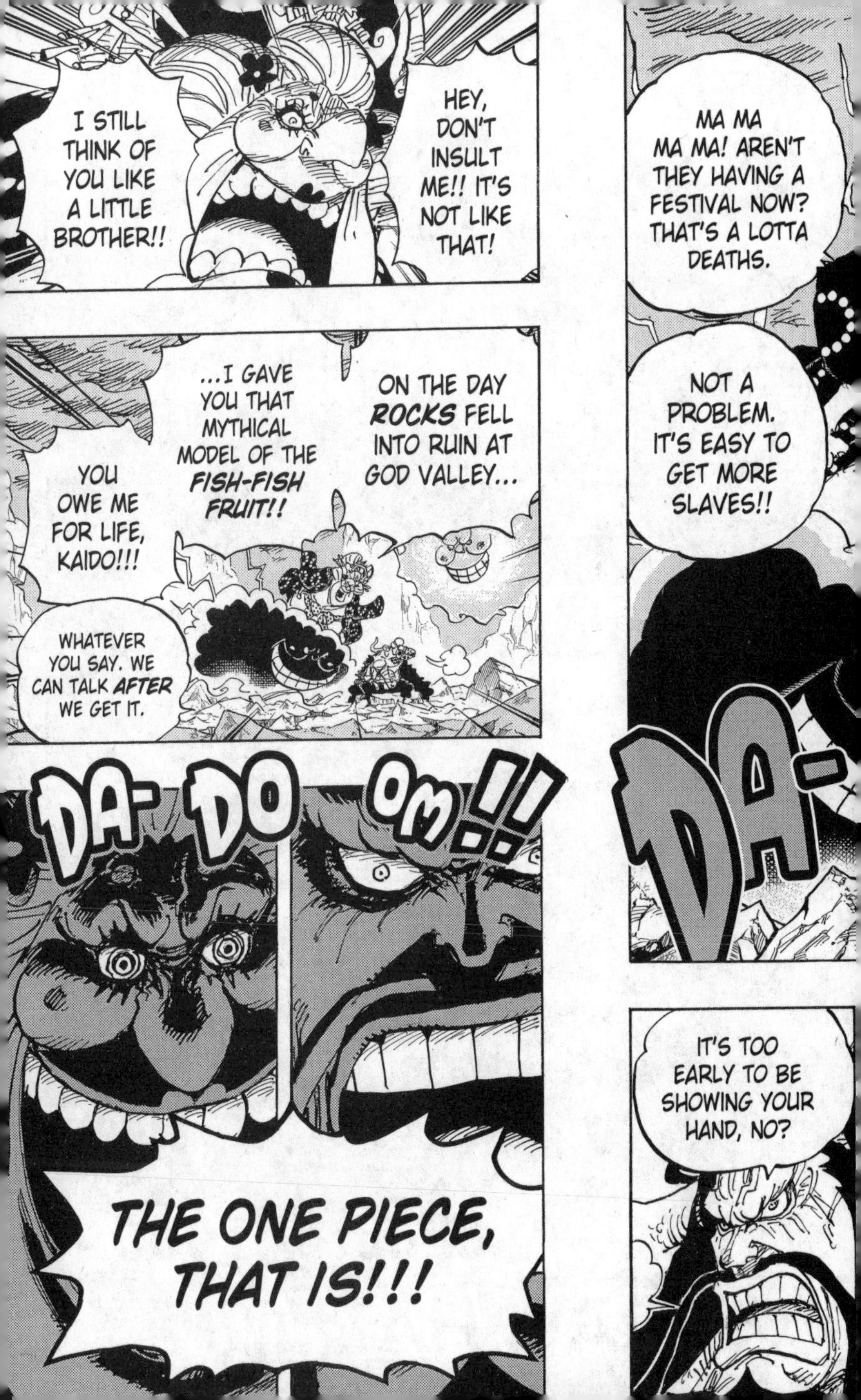
MA MA MA MA! AREN'T THEY HAVING A FESTIVAL NOW? THAT'S A LOTTA DEATHS.
NOT A PROBLEM. IT'S EASY TO GET MORE SLAVES!!
HEY, DON'T INSULT ME!! IT'S NOT LIKE THAT!
I STILL THINK OF YOU LIKE A LITTLE BROTHER!!
ON THE DAY ROCKS FELL INTO RUIN AT GOD VALLEY...
...I GAVE YOU THAT MYTHICAL MODEL OF THE FISH-FISH FRUIT!!
YOU OWE ME FOR LIFE, KAIDO!!!
WHATEVER YOU SAY. WE CAN TALK AFTER WE GET IT.
DA-
IT'S TOO EARLY TO BE SHOWING YOUR HAND, NO?
DA- DO OM!!
THE ONE PIECE, THAT IS!!!

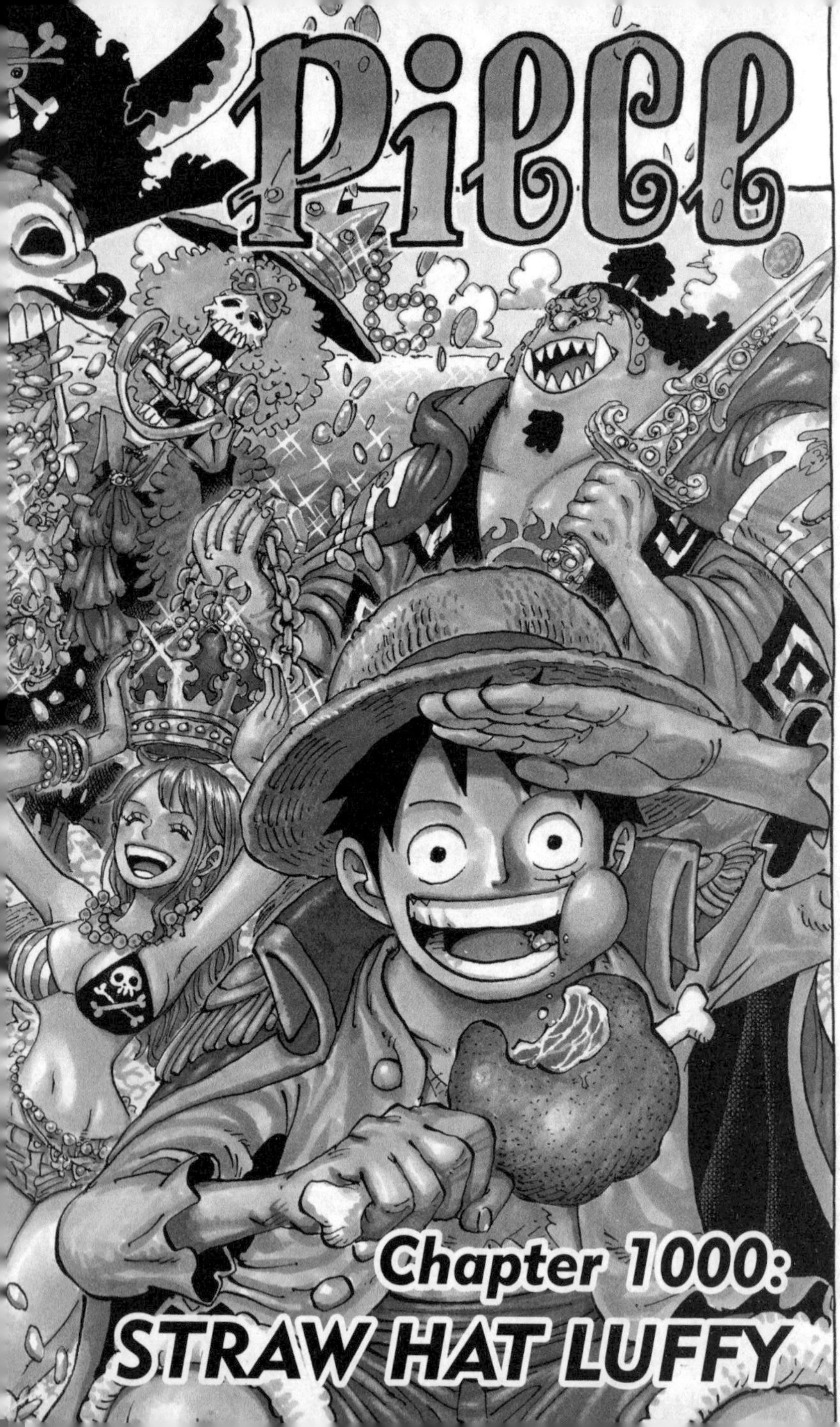
Piece
Chapter 1000:
STRAW HAT LUFFY

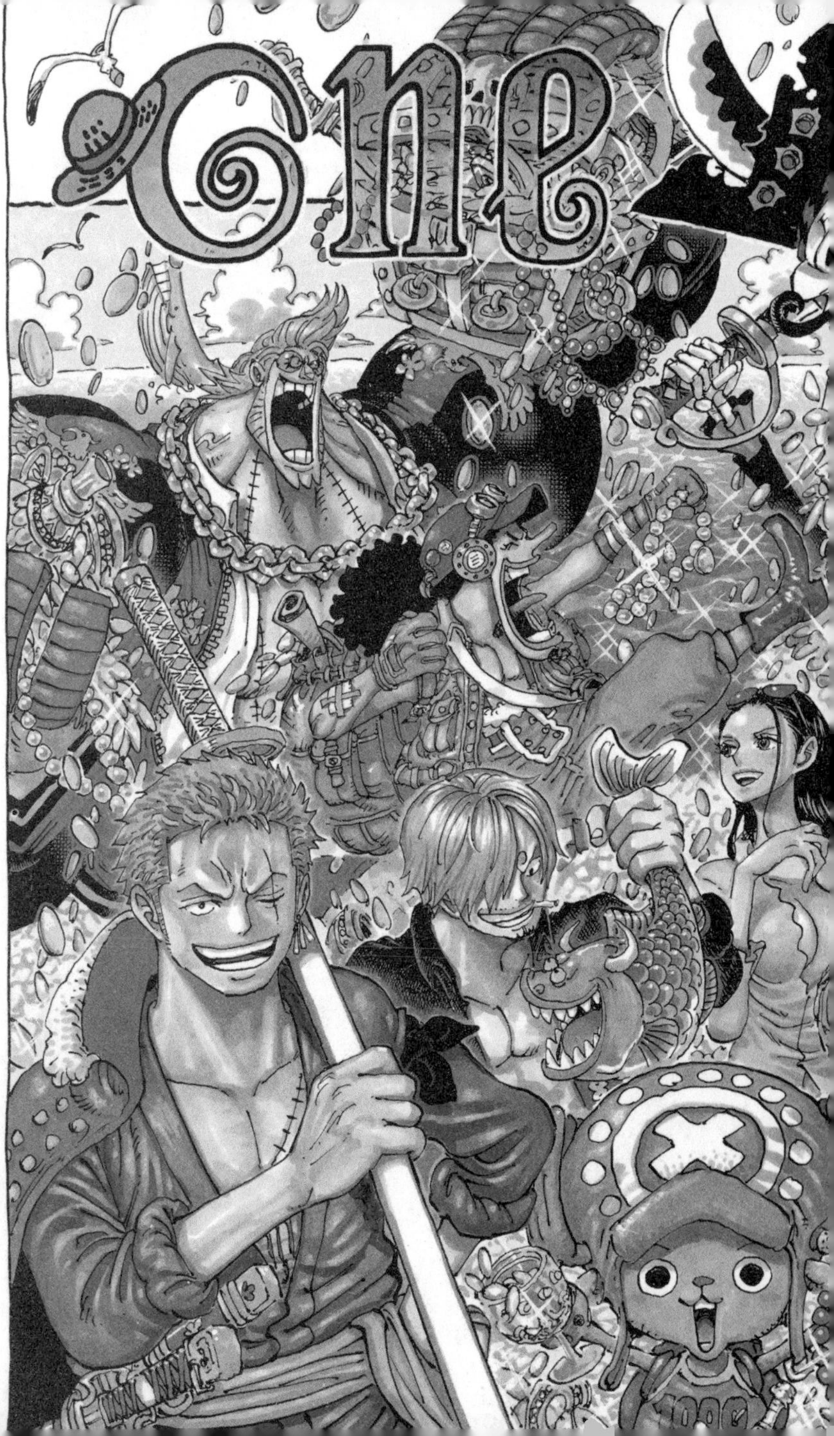
One

vol.99
ONE PIECE

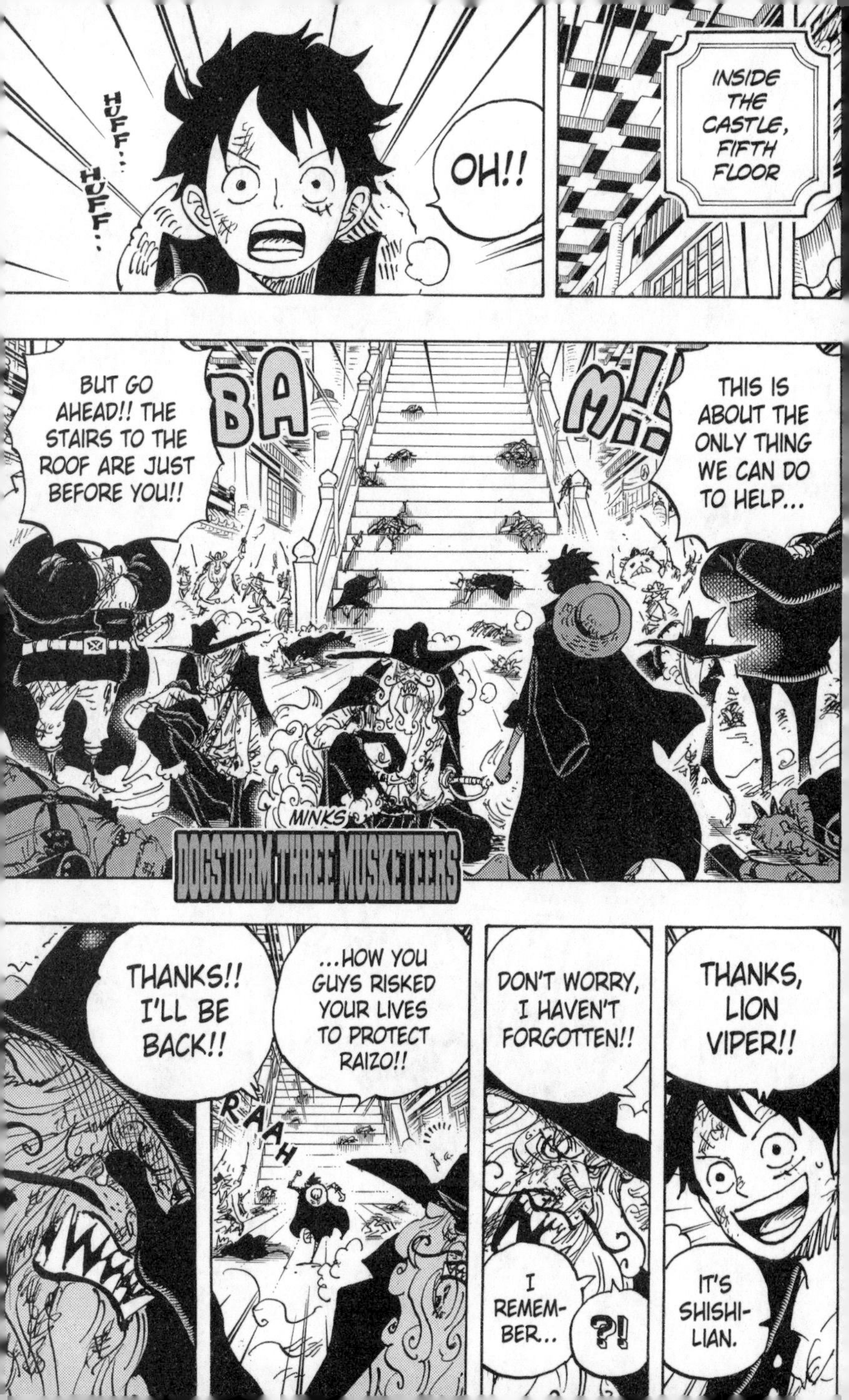
INSIDE THE CASTLE, FIFTH FLOOR
HUFF... HUFF...
OH!!
THIS IS ABOUT THE ONLY THING WE CAN DO TO HELP...
BAM!!
BUT GO AHEAD!! THE STAIRS TO THE ROOF ARE JUST BEFORE YOU!!
MINKS
DOGSTORM THREE MUSKETEERS
THANKS, LION VIPER!!
IT'S SHISHI-LIAN.
DON'T WORRY, I HAVEN'T FORGOTTEN!!
?!
I REMEMBER...
...HOW YOU GUYS RISKED YOUR LIVES TO PROTECT RAIZO!!
RAAAH
THANKS!! I'LL BE BACK!!

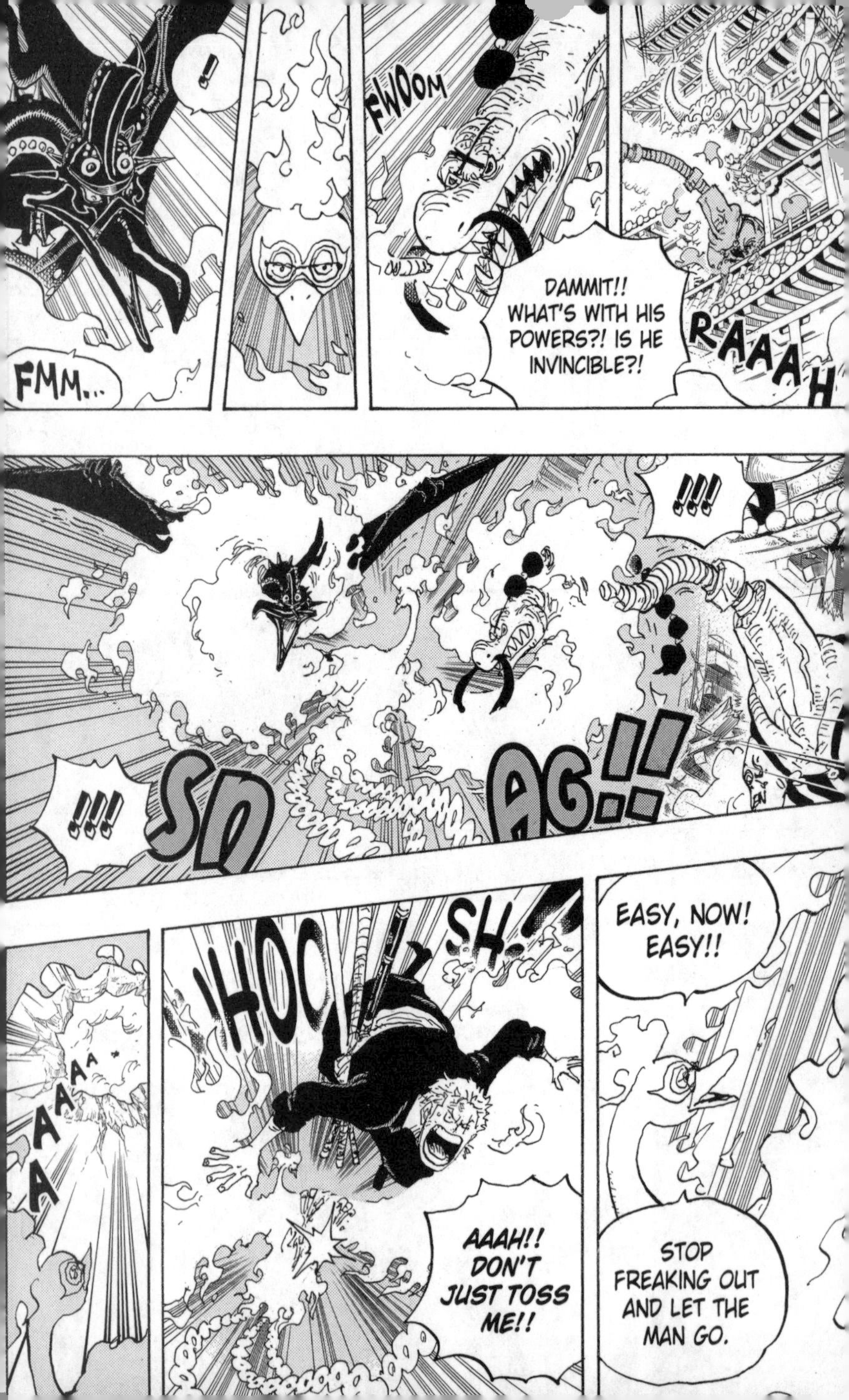
RAAAH
DAMMIT!! WHAT'S WITH HIS POWERS?! IS HE INVINCIBLE?!
FWOOM
!
FMM...
!!!
SNAG!!
!!!
EASY, NOW! EASY!!
STOP FREAKING OUT AND LET THE MAN GO.
WHOOSH!!
AAAH!! DON'T JUST TOSS ME!!
AAAAA

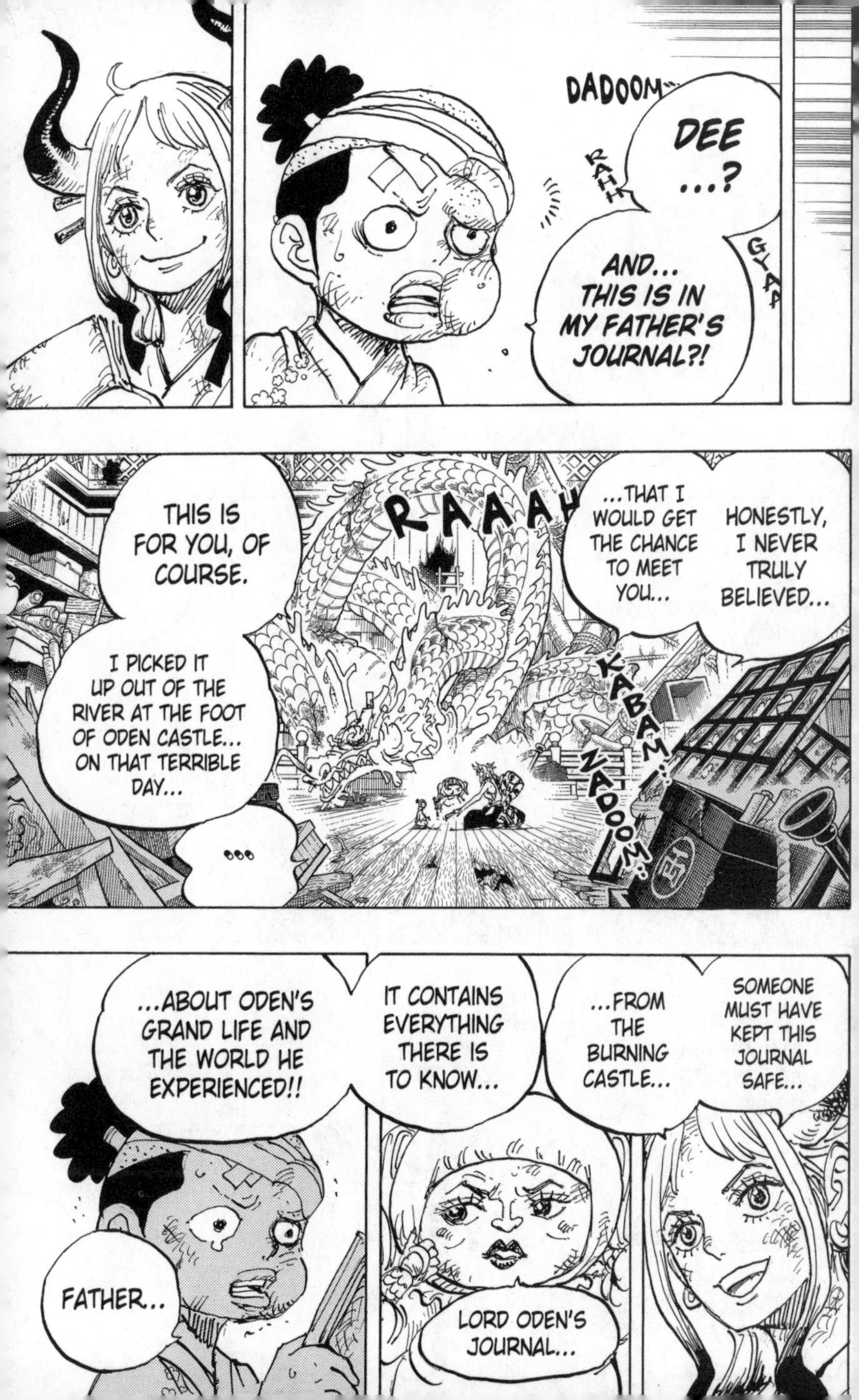
DADOOM
DEE ...?
RAHH
GYAA
AND... THIS IS IN MY FATHER'S JOURNAL?!
HONESTLY, I NEVER TRULY BELIEVED...
...THAT I WOULD GET THE CHANCE TO MEET YOU...
RAAAH
KABAM
ZADOOM
THIS IS FOR YOU, OF COURSE.
I PICKED IT UP OUT OF THE RIVER AT THE FOOT OF ODEN CASTLE... ON THAT TERRIBLE DAY...
...
SOMEONE MUST HAVE KEPT THIS JOURNAL SAFE...
...FROM THE BURNING CASTLE...
IT CONTAINS EVERYTHING THERE IS TO KNOW...
...ABOUT ODEN'S GRAND LIFE AND THE WORLD HE EXPERIENCED!!
LORD ODEN'S JOURNAL...
FATHER...

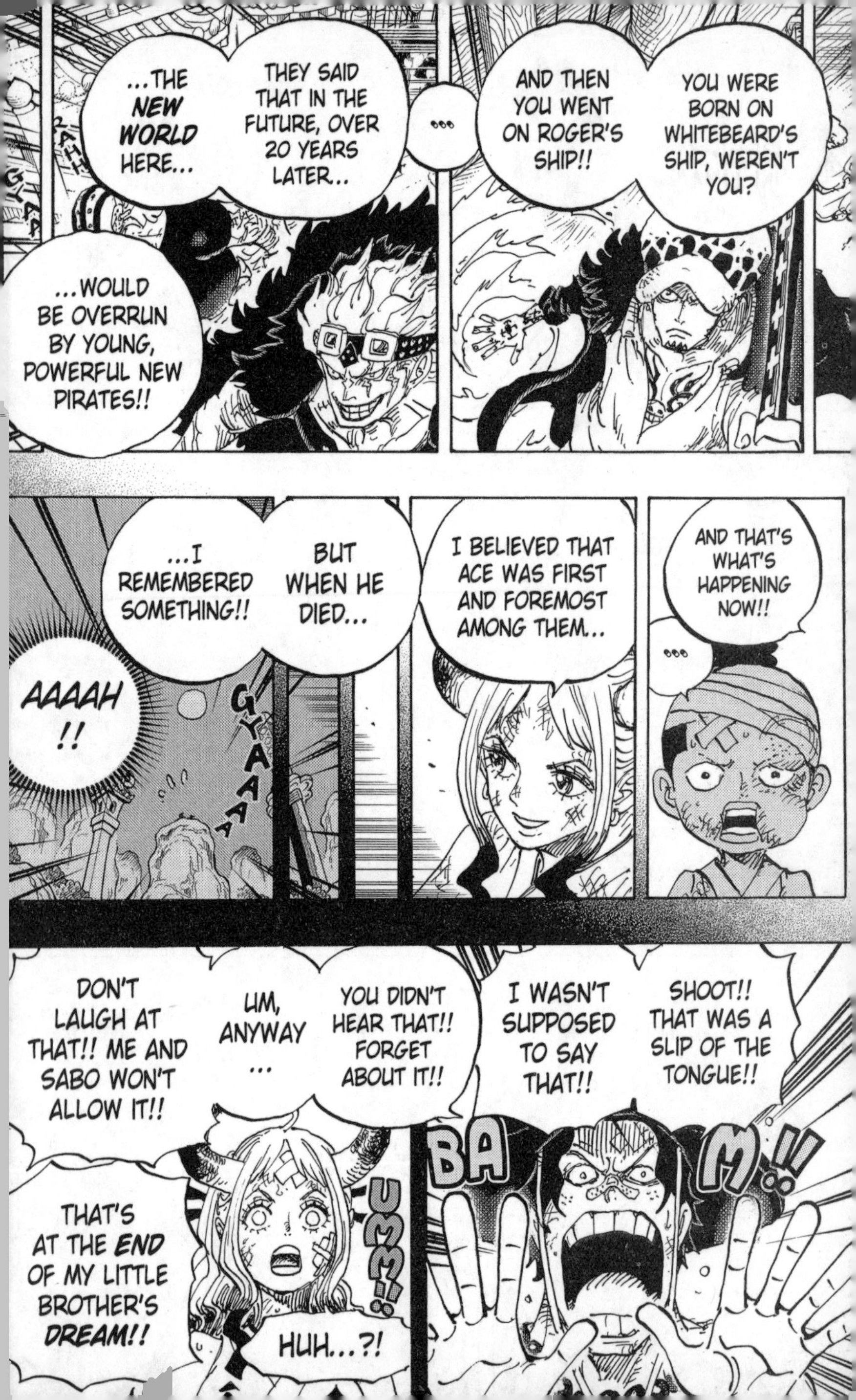
YOU WERE BORN ON WHITEBEARD'S SHIP, WEREN'T YOU?
AND THEN YOU WENT ON ROGER'S SHIP!!
...
THEY SAID THAT IN THE FUTURE, OVER 20 YEARS LATER...
...THE NEW WORLD HERE...
...WOULD BE OVERRUN BY YOUNG, POWERFUL NEW PIRATES!!
AND THAT'S WHAT'S HAPPENING NOW!!
...
I BELIEVED THAT ACE WAS FIRST AND FOREMOST AMONG THEM...
BUT WHEN HE DIED...
...I REMEMBERED SOMETHING!!
GYAAAA
AAAAH!!
SHOOT!! THAT WAS A SLIP OF THE TONGUE!!
I WASN'T SUPPOSED TO SAY THAT!!
BAM!!
YOU DIDN'T HEAR THAT!! FORGET ABOUT IT!!
UM, ANYWAY...
DON'T LAUGH AT THAT!! ME AND SABO WON'T ALLOW IT!!
UMM!!
THAT'S AT THE END OF MY LITTLE BROTHER'S DREAM!!
HUH...?!

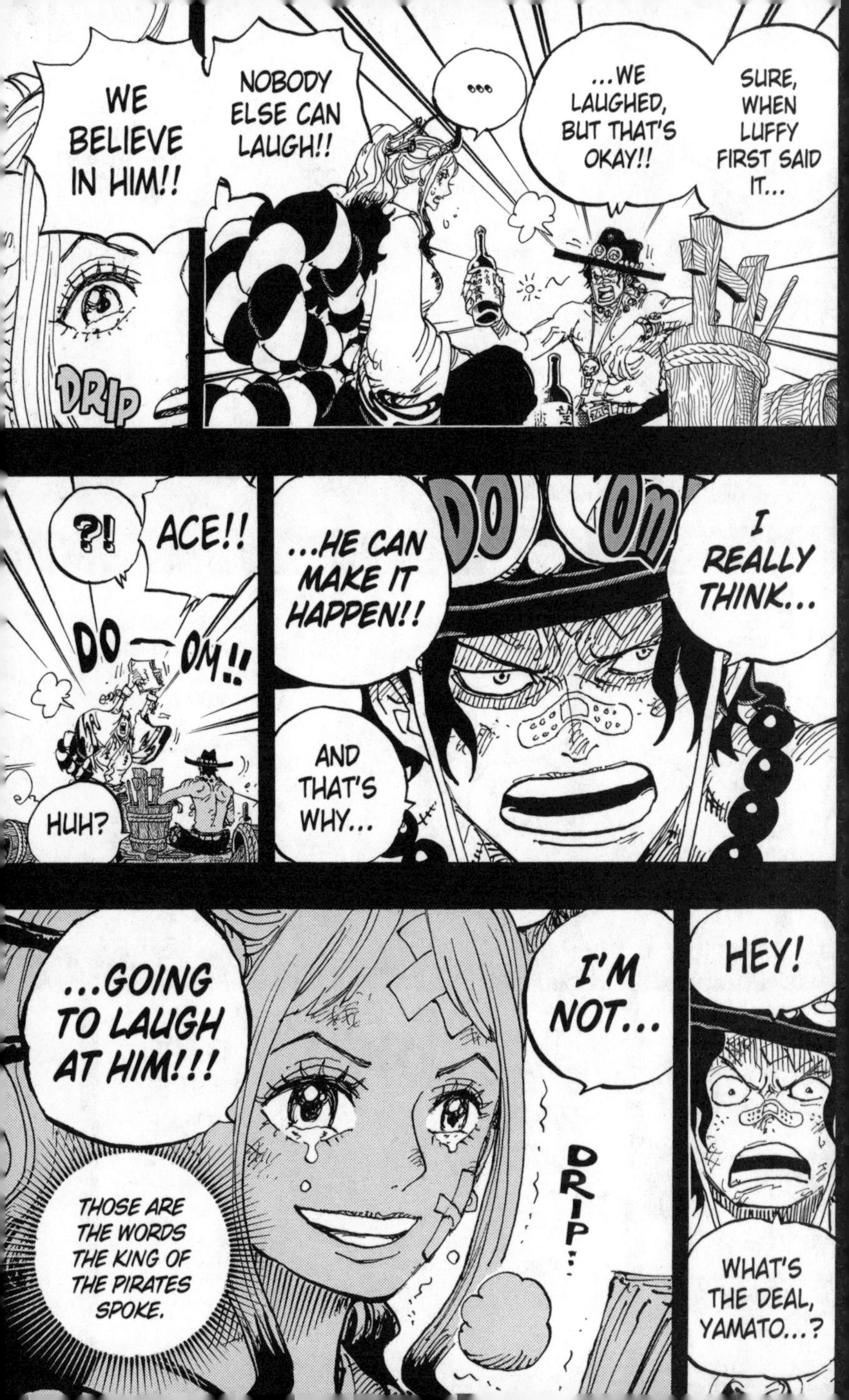
SURE, WHEN LUFFY FIRST SAID IT...
...WE LAUGHED, BUT THAT'S OKAY!!
...
NOBODY ELSE CAN LAUGH!!
WE BELIEVE IN HIM!!
DRIP
I REALLY THINK...
DO OM
...HE CAN MAKE IT HAPPEN!!
AND THAT'S WHY...
ACE!!
?!
DO—OM!!
HUH?
HEY!
WHAT'S THE DEAL, YAMATO...?
I'M NOT...
...GOING TO LAUGH AT HIM!!!
DRIP
THOSE ARE THE WORDS THE KING OF THE PIRATES SPOKE.

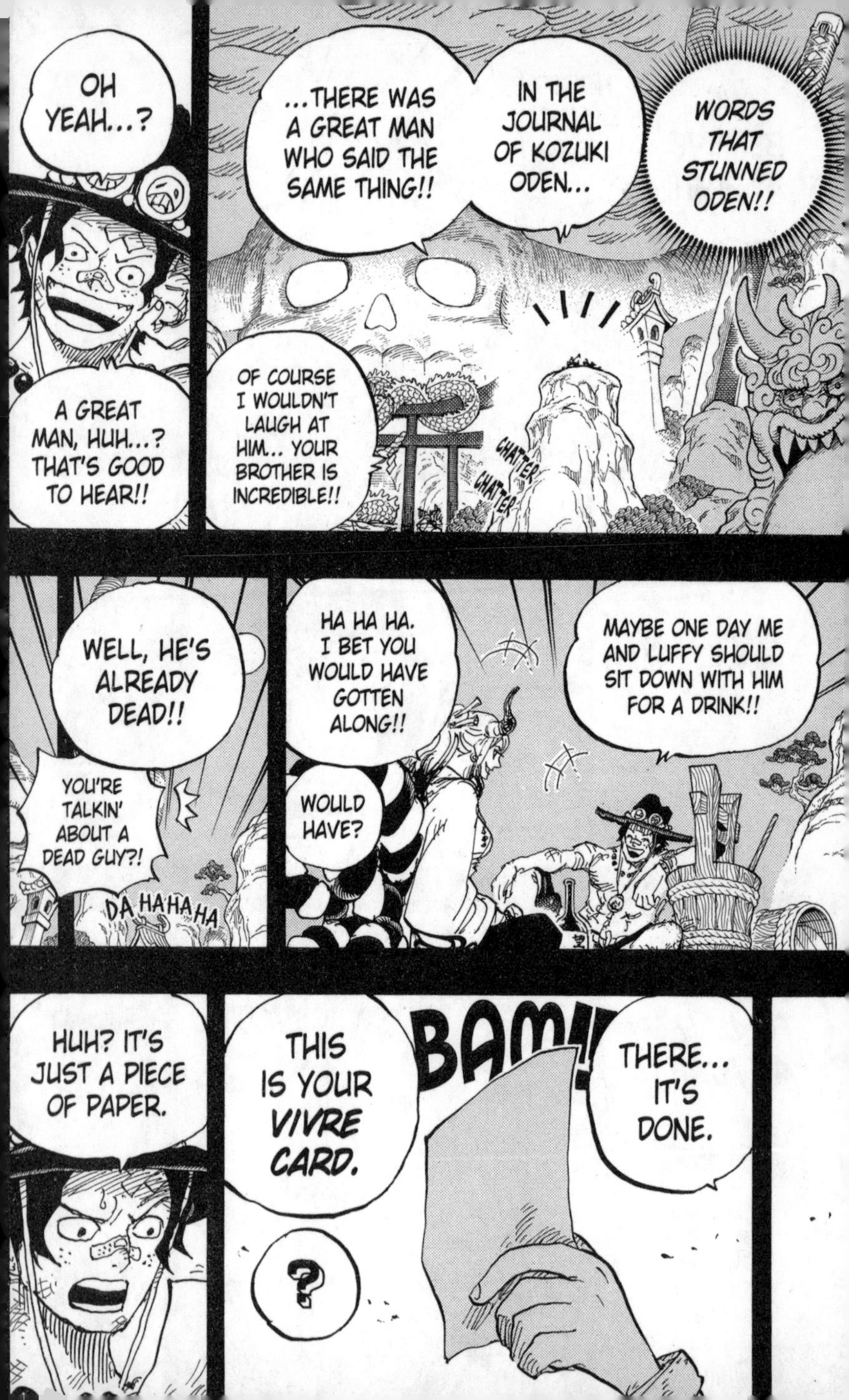
WORDS THAT STUNNED ODEN!!
IN THE JOURNAL OF KOZUKI ODEN...
...THERE WAS A GREAT MAN WHO SAID THE SAME THING!!
OF COURSE I WOULDN'T LAUGH AT HIM... YOUR BROTHER IS INCREDIBLE!!
CHATTER CHATTER
OH YEAH...?
A GREAT MAN, HUH...? THAT'S GOOD TO HEAR!!
MAYBE ONE DAY ME AND LUFFY SHOULD SIT DOWN WITH HIM FOR A DRINK!!
HA HA HA. I BET YOU WOULD HAVE GOTTEN ALONG!!
WOULD HAVE?
WELL, HE'S ALREADY DEAD!!
YOU'RE TALKIN' ABOUT A DEAD GUY?!
DA HA HA HA HA
THERE... IT'S DONE.
BAM!!
THIS IS YOUR VIVRE CARD.
?
HUH? IT'S JUST A PIECE OF PAPER.

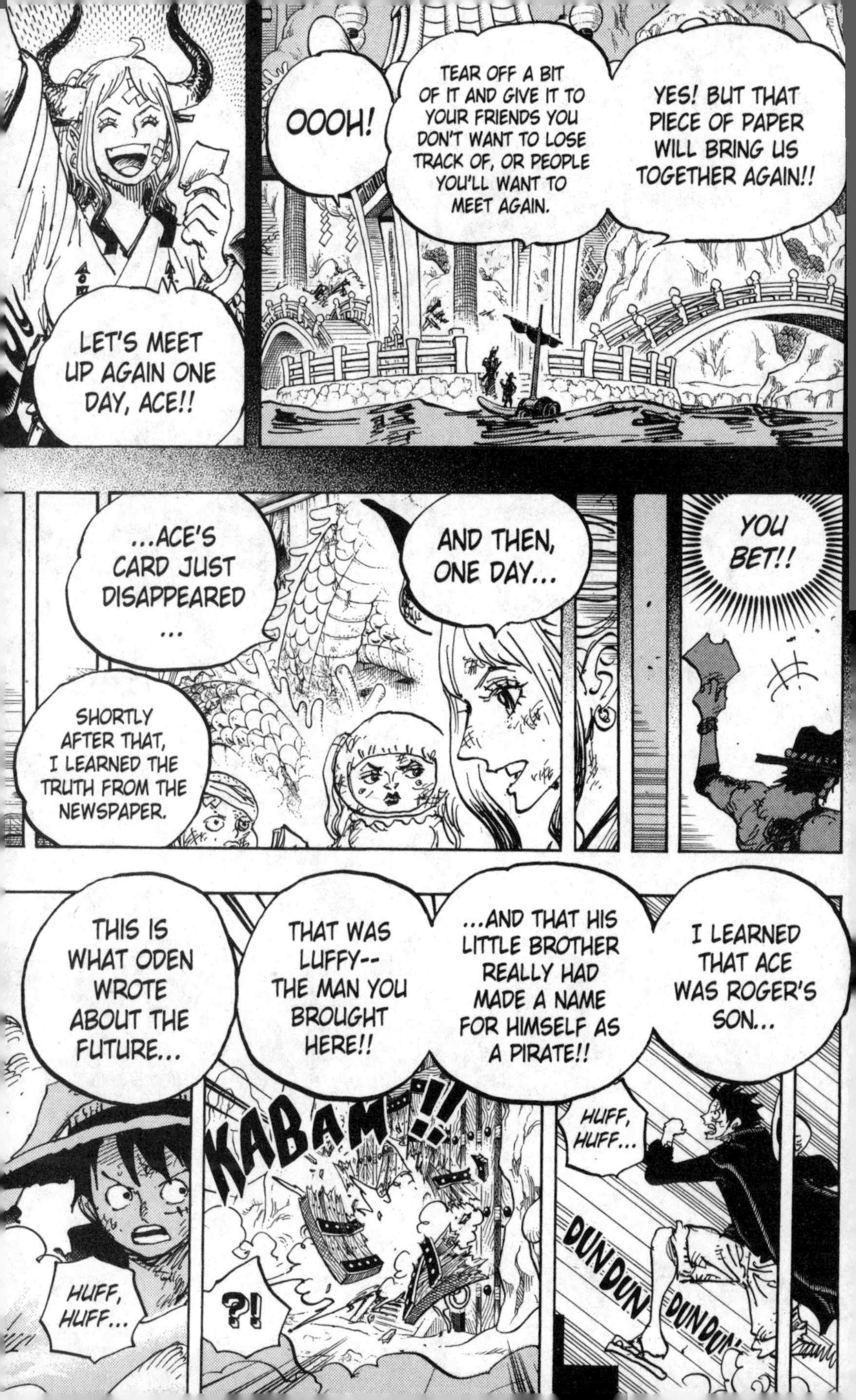
YES! BUT THAT PIECE OF PAPER WILL BRING US TOGETHER AGAIN!!
TEAR OFF A BIT OF IT AND GIVE IT TO YOUR FRIENDS YOU DON'T WANT TO LOSE TRACK OF, OR PEOPLE YOU'LL WANT TO MEET AGAIN.
OOOH!
LET'S MEET UP AGAIN ONE DAY, ACE!!
YOU BET!!
AND THEN, ONE DAY...
...ACE'S CARD JUST DISAPPEARED ...
SHORTLY AFTER THAT, I LEARNED THE TRUTH FROM THE NEWSPAPER.
I LEARNED THAT ACE WAS ROGER'S SON...
...AND THAT HIS LITTLE BROTHER REALLY HAD MADE A NAME FOR HIMSELF AS A PIRATE!!
THAT WAS LUFFY-- THE MAN YOU BROUGHT HERE!!
THIS IS WHAT ODEN WROTE ABOUT THE FUTURE...
HUFF, HUFF...
DUN DUN
DUN DUN
KABAM!!
?!
HUFF, HUFF...

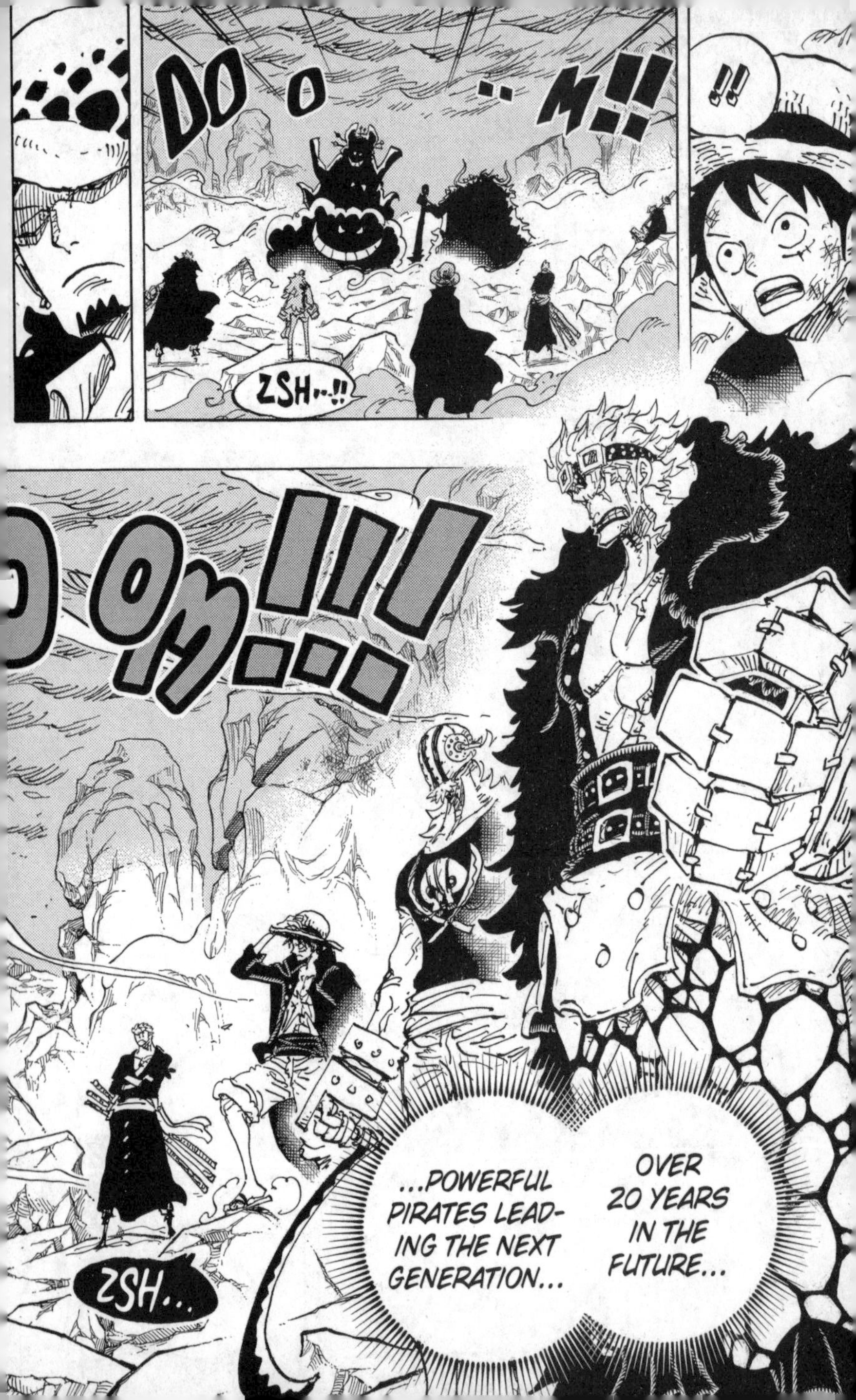
!!
DO O ..M!!
ZSH--!!
OVER 20 YEARS IN THE FUTURE...
...POWERFUL PIRATES LEAD-ING THE NEXT GENERATION...
DOOM...!!!
ZSH...

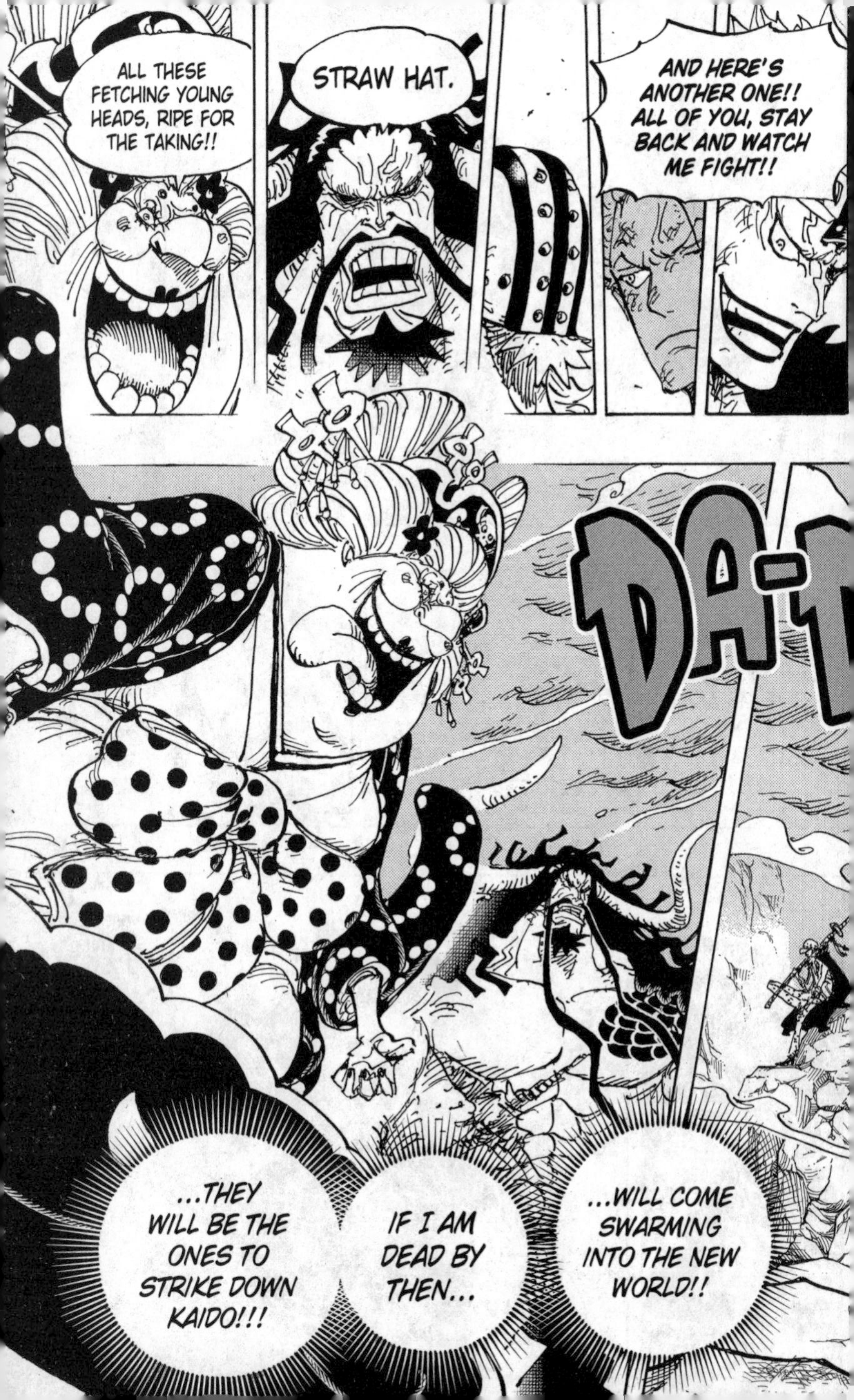
AND HERE'S ANOTHER ONE!! ALL OF YOU, STAY BACK AND WATCH ME FIGHT!!
STRAW HAT.
ALL THESE FETCHING YOUNG HEADS, RIPE FOR THE TAKING!!
DA-
...WILL COME SWARMING INTO THE NEW WORLD!!
IF I AM DEAD BY THEN...
...THEY WILL BE THE ONES TO STRIKE DOWN KAIDO!!!

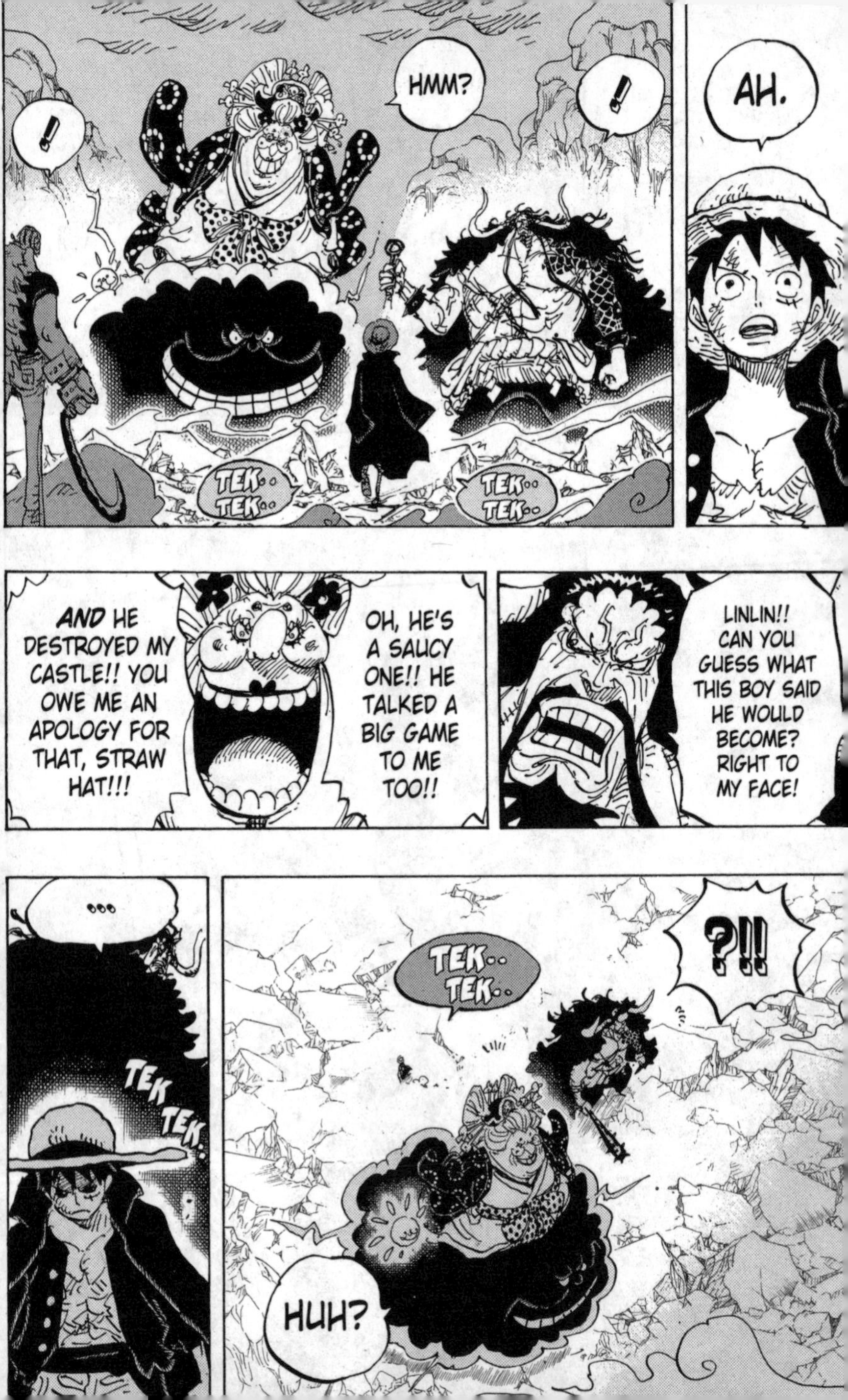
AH.
!
HMM?
!
TEK.. TEK..
TEK.. TEK..
LINLIN!! CAN YOU GUESS WHAT THIS BOY SAID HE WOULD BECOME? RIGHT TO MY FACE!
OH, HE'S A SAUCY ONE!! HE TALKED A BIG GAME TO ME TOO!!
AND HE DESTROYED MY CASTLE!! YOU OWE ME AN APOLOGY FOR THAT, STRAW HAT!!!
?!!
TEK.. TEK..
HUH?
...
TEK TEK

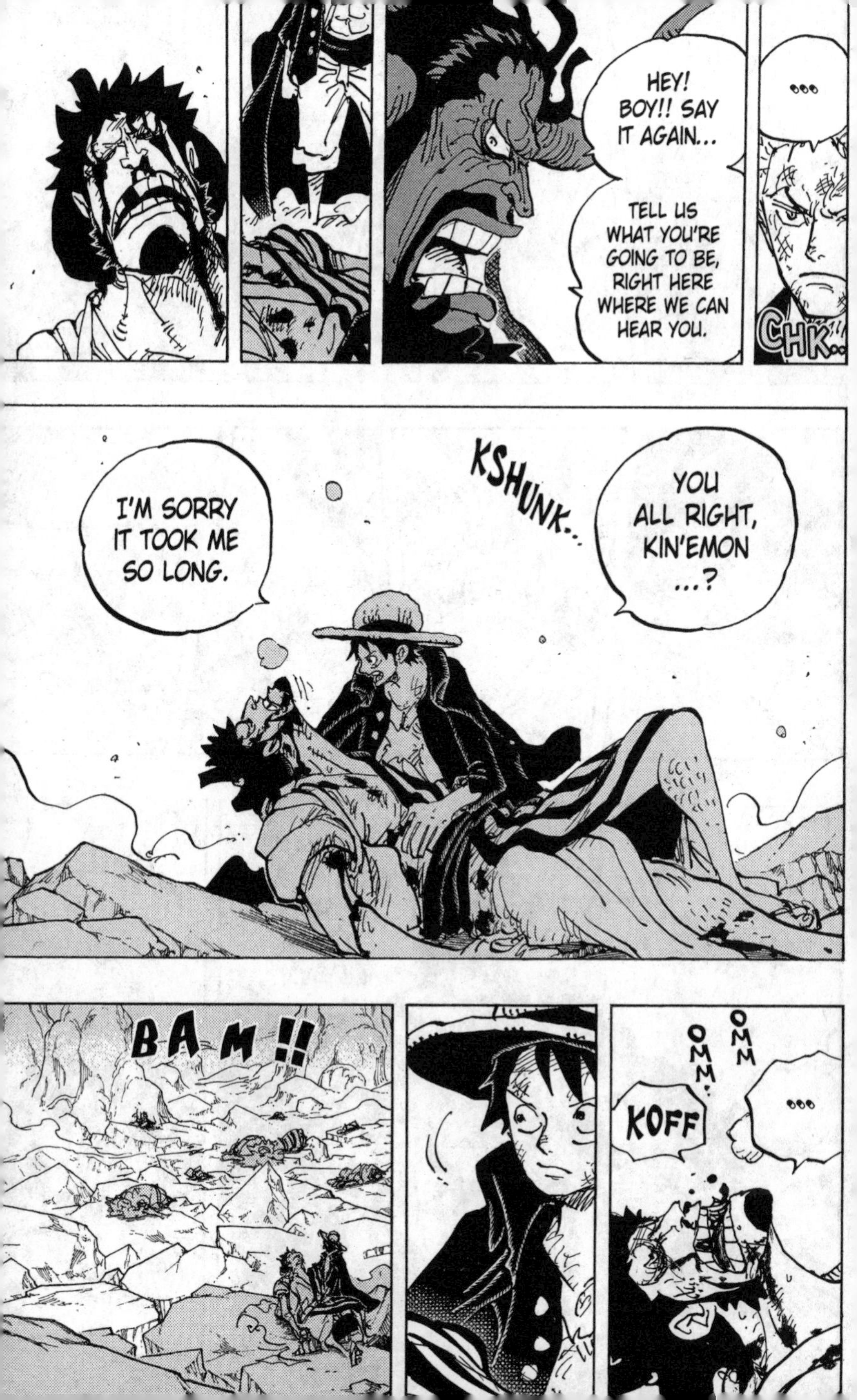
...
CHK...
HEY! BOY!! SAY IT AGAIN...
TELL US WHAT YOU'RE GOING TO BE, RIGHT HERE WHERE WE CAN HEAR YOU.
YOU ALL RIGHT, KIN'EMON ...?
KSHUNK...
I'M SORRY IT TOOK ME SO LONG.
...
OMM
OMM.
KOFF
BAM!!

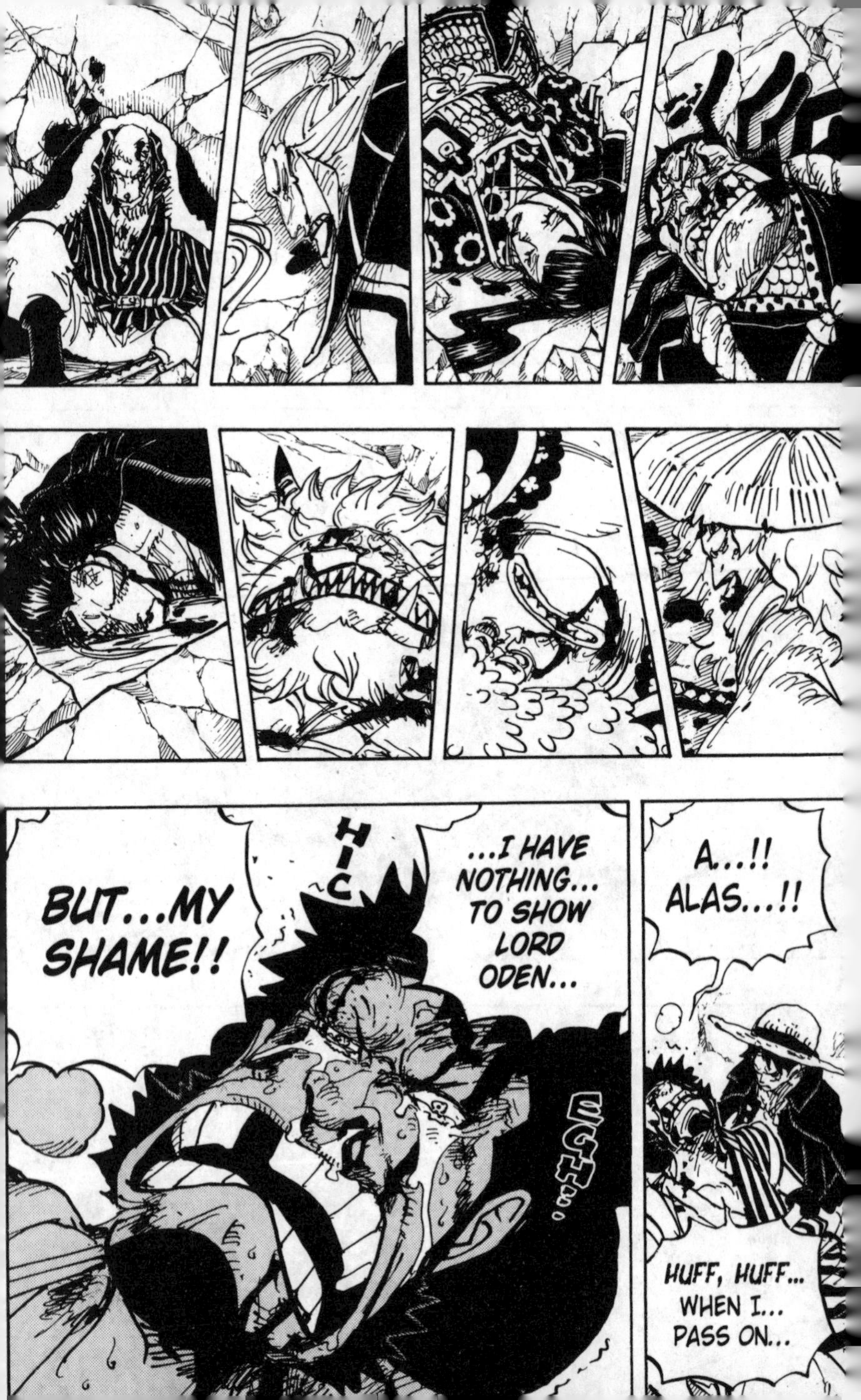
A...!! ALAS...!!
HUFF, HUFF... WHEN I... PASS ON...
...I HAVE NOTHING... TO SHOW LORD ODEN...
HIC
BUT...MY SHAME!!
EGGH...

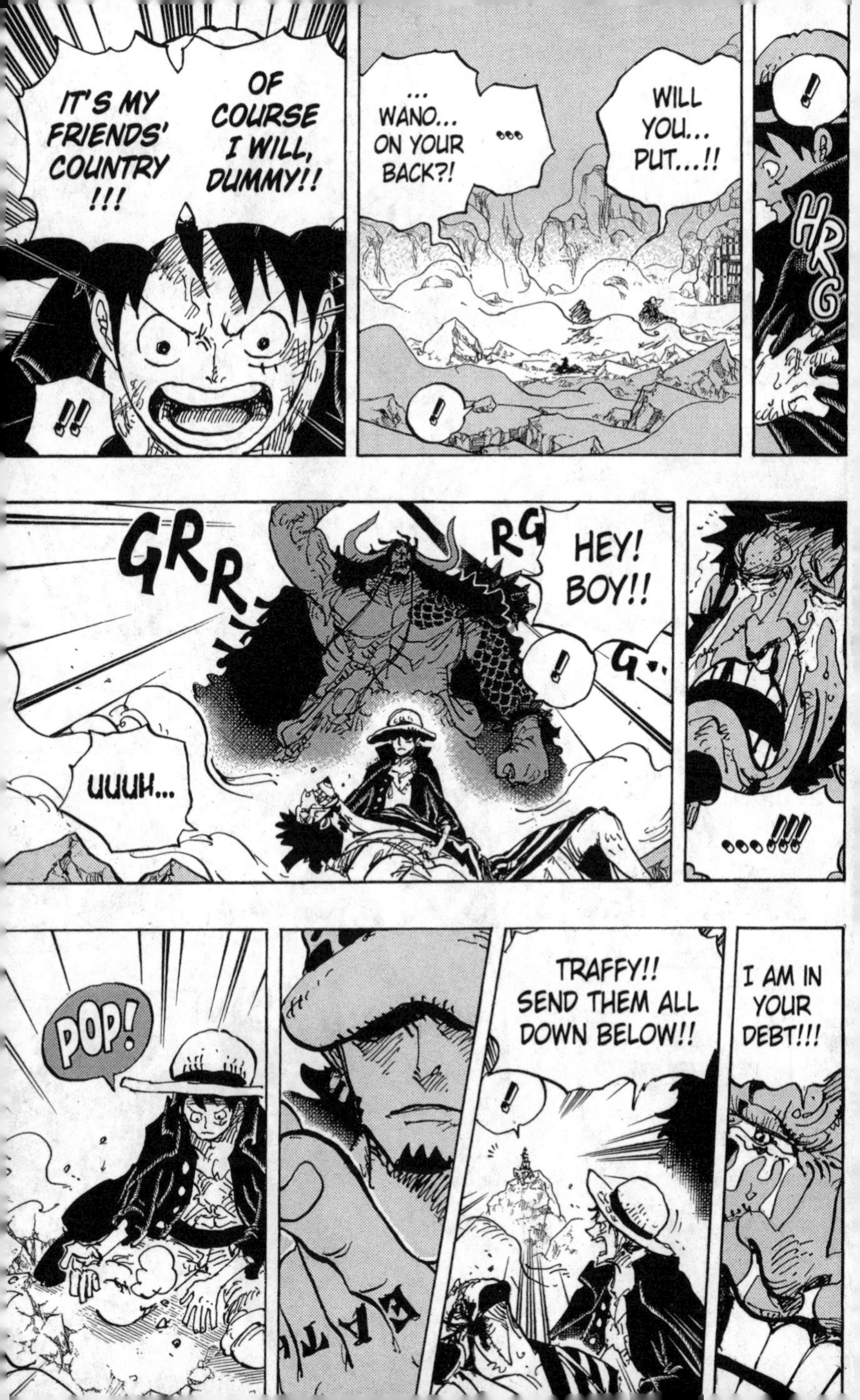
!
HRG
WILL YOU... PUT...!!
...
... WANO... ON YOUR BACK?!
!
OF COURSE I WILL, DUMMY!!
IT'S MY FRIENDS' COUNTRY !!!
!!
...!!!
HEY! BOY!!
RG
G..
!
GRR
UUUH...
I AM IN YOUR DEBT!!!
TRAFFY!! SEND THEM ALL DOWN BELOW!!
!
POP!

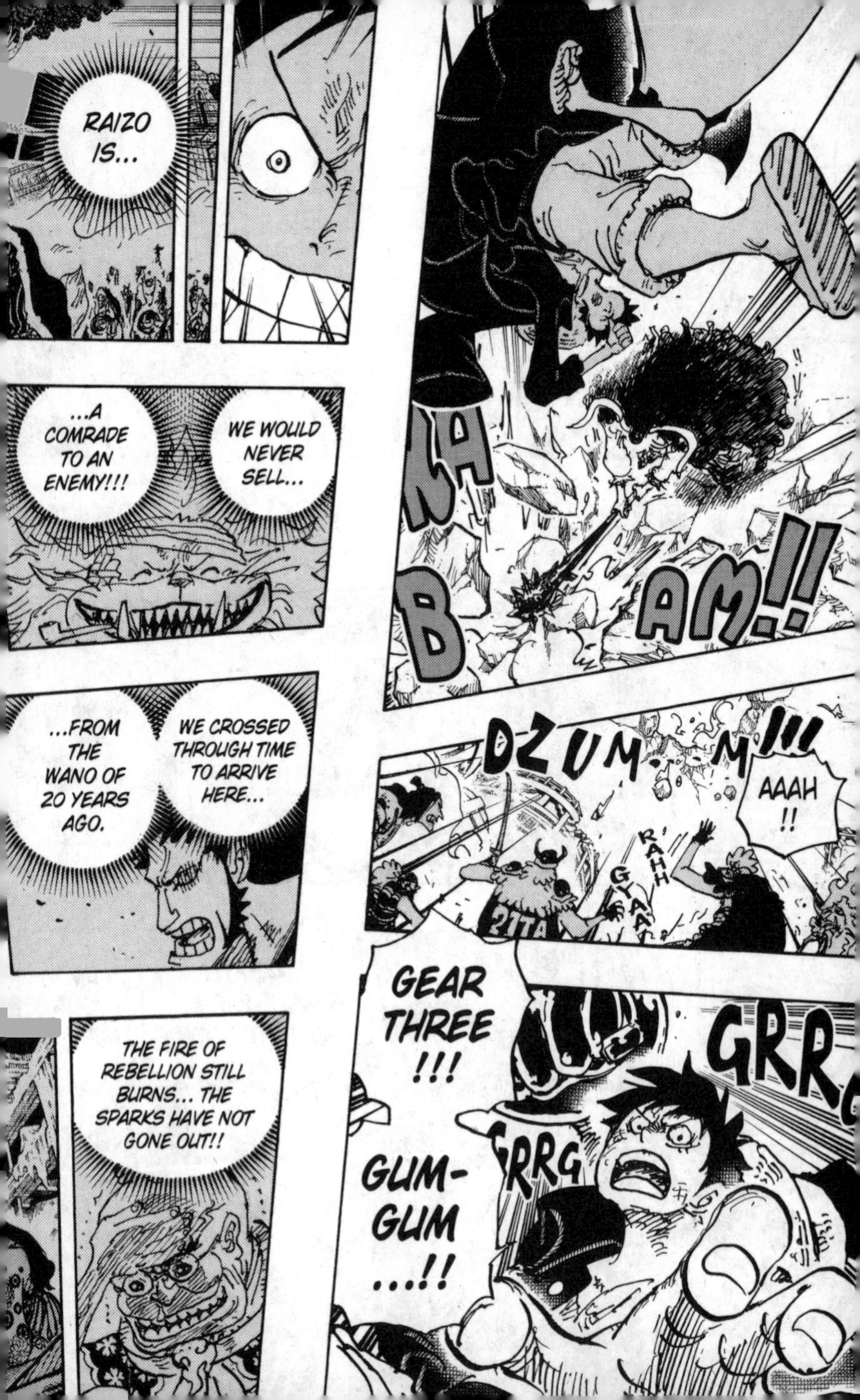

BAM!!
DZUMM!!!
AAAH!!
RAHH
GYAA
GEAR THREE!!!
GRRG
GRRG
GUM-GUM...!!
RAIZO IS...
WE WOULD NEVER SELL...
...A COMRADE TO AN ENEMY!!!
WE CROSSED THROUGH TIME TO ARRIVE HERE...
...FROM THE WANO OF 20 YEARS AGO.
THE FIRE OF REBELLION STILL BURNS... THE SPARKS HAVE NOT GONE OUT!!

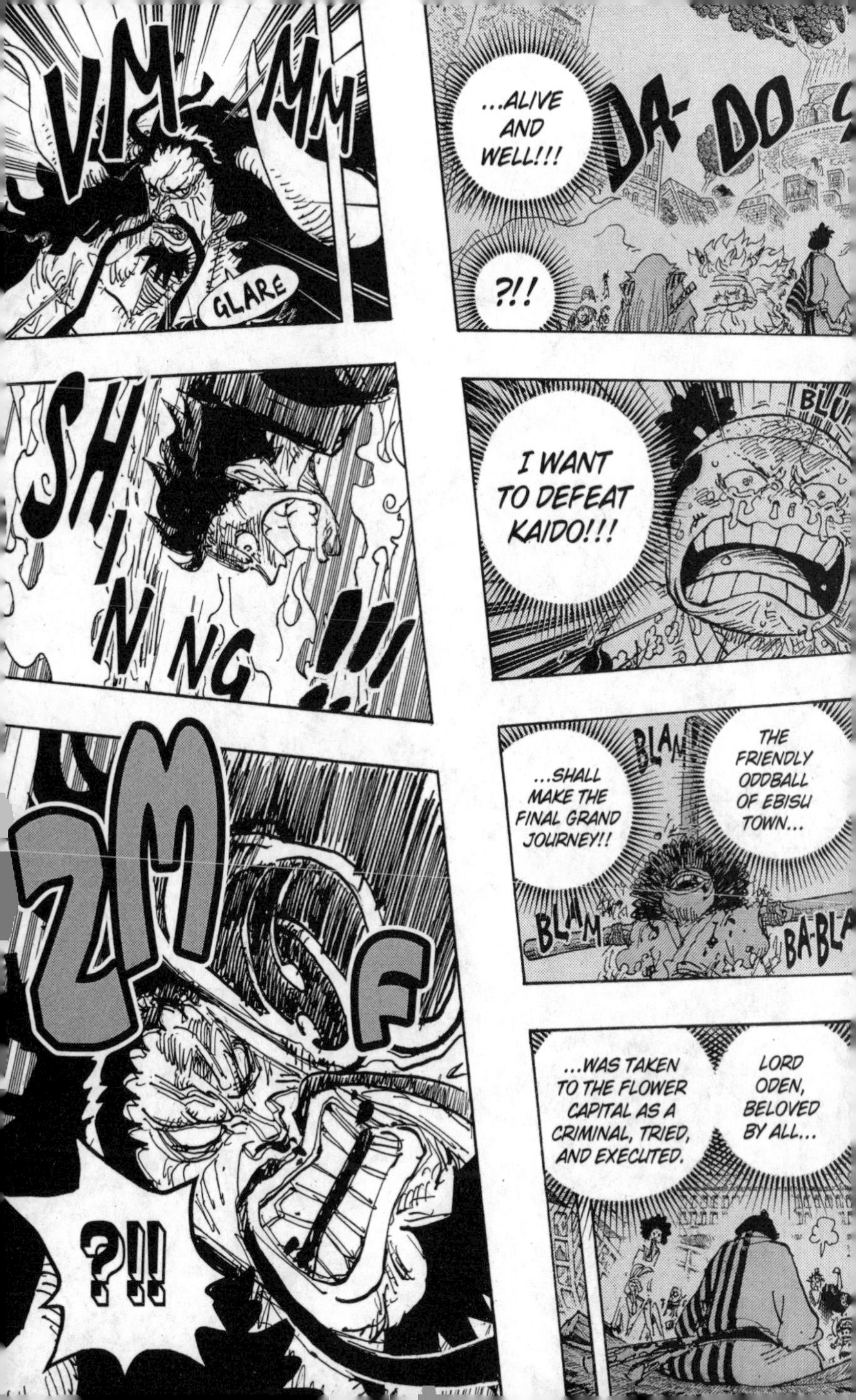

DA-DO
...ALIVE AND WELL!!!
?!!
BLU
I WANT TO DEFEAT KAIDO!!!
THE FRIENDLY ODDBALL OF EBISU TOWN...
BLAM
...SHALL MAKE THE FINAL GRAND JOURNEY!!
BA-BLA
BLAM
LORD ODEN, BELOVED BY ALL...
...WAS TAKEN TO THE FLOWER CAPITAL AS A CRIMINAL, TRIED, AND EXECUTED.
VM-MM
GLARE
SHINNNG!!!
ZM
SF
?!!

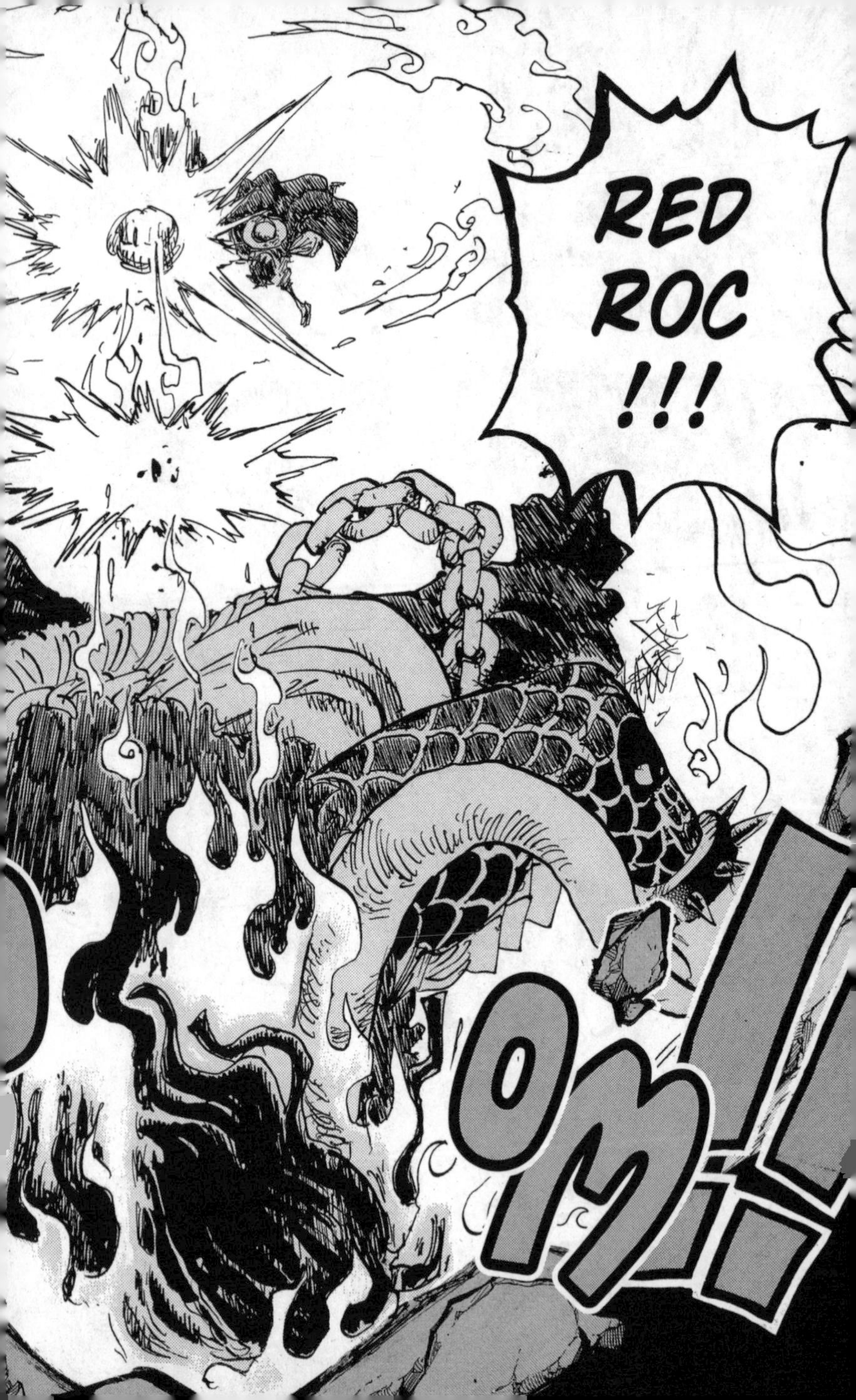
RED ROC !!!

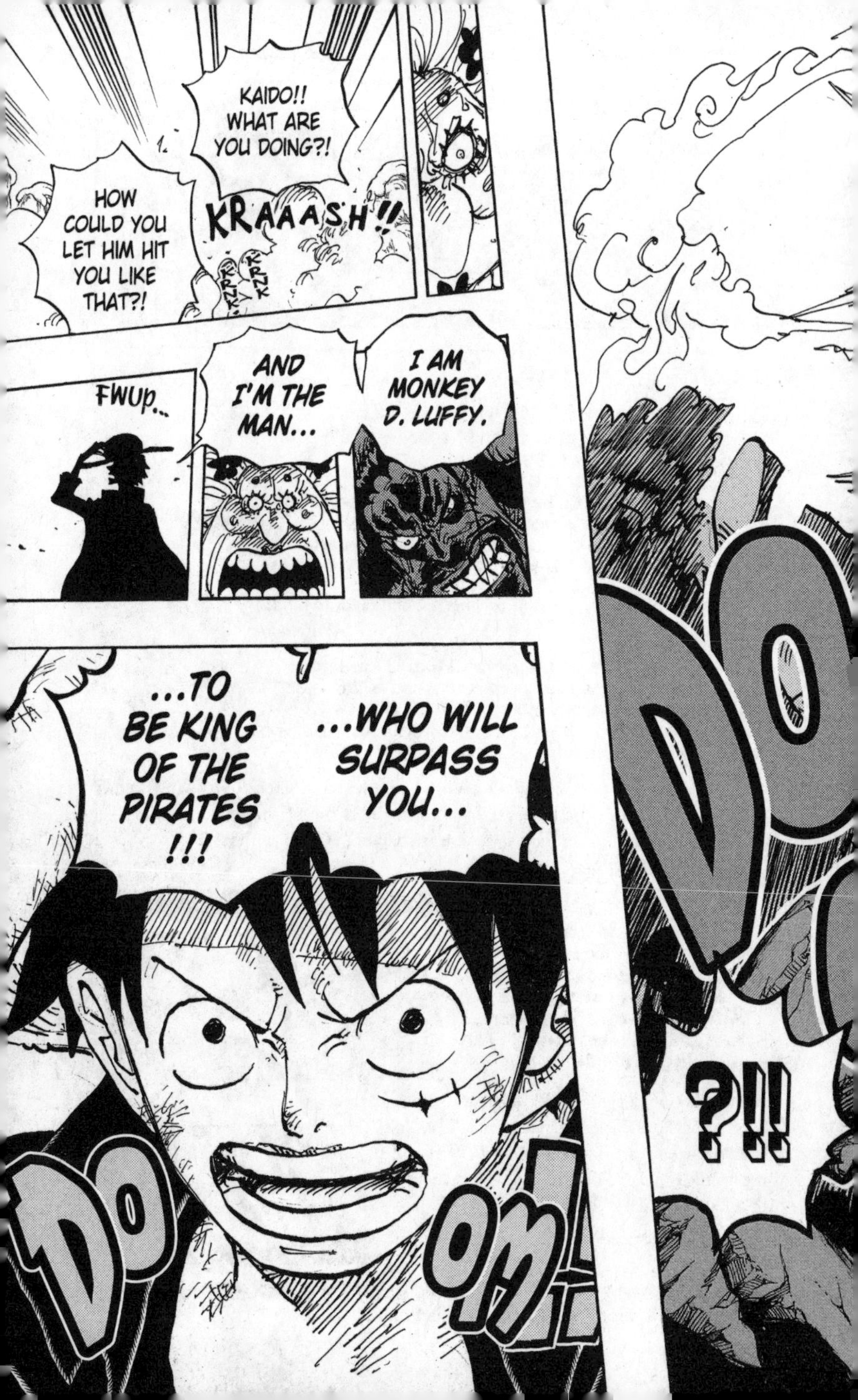
DO
?!!
KAIDO!! WHAT ARE YOU DOING?!
KRAAASH!!
HOW COULD YOU LET HIM HIT YOU LIKE THAT?!
KRNK KRNK
I AM MONKEY D. LUFFY.
AND I'M THE MAN...
FWUp...
...WHO WILL SURPASS YOU...
...TO BE KING OF THE PIRATES!!!
DOOM!

SBS Question Corner

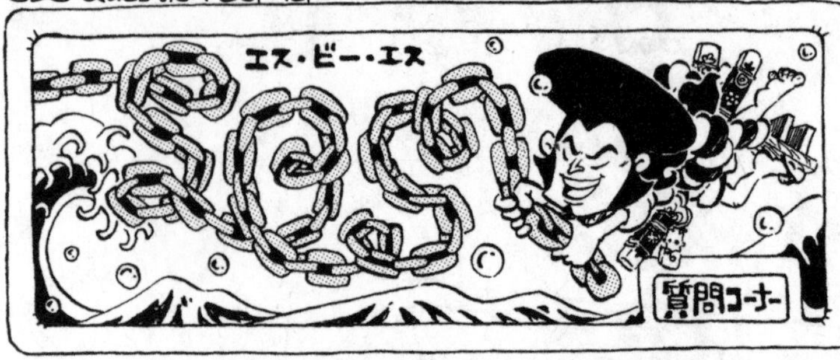
エス・ビー・エス
質問コーナー

(I ♡ OP, Ishikawa)

Q: Please draw a personification of everyone's favorite, Yamato's side-boob!! --Yashirai

A: Okay, I'm good at this... Hey, I can't do that!! What is the personification of a side-boob?! (Well, I tried anyway.) Honestly, the number of postcards and letters I got about side-boob this, side-boob that! Next volume is volume 100, you guys! I'm not taking any of your dirty questions and prompts! We're going fully wholesome next time!!

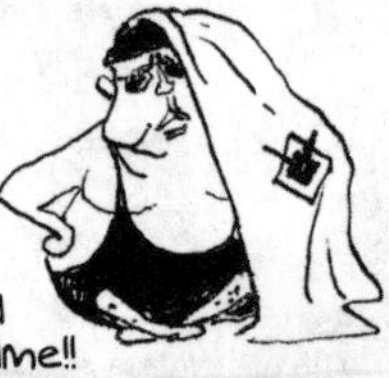

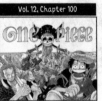

Q: Odacchi! Please tell us Yamato's age, height, and favorite food!

--Pumpkin

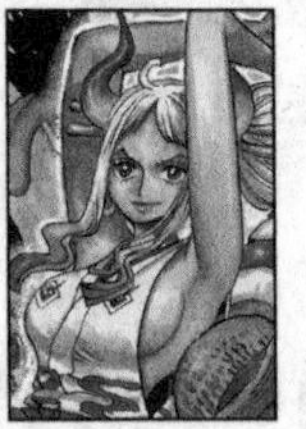

A: Now this is a proper question. I would love to answer questions like these. Yamato is 28 (born same year as Momonosuke), 9'8" tall (that's 2 Luffys) and loves to eat oden, of course. And also salmon (raw, whole).

Q: Hello, Oda Sensei. Congratulations on reaching the milestone of chapter 1,000!! I was wondering, did you make the layout of the chapter 1,000 cover illustration the same as chapter 100's on purpose?! I got goosebumps when I noticed that!!

--Kinosan

Chapter 1000

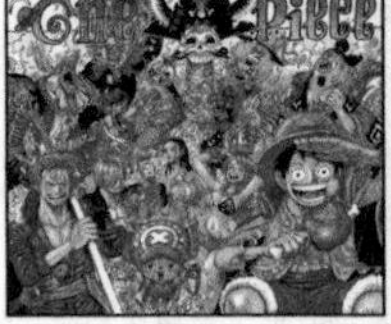
One Piece

Vol. 12, Chapter 100

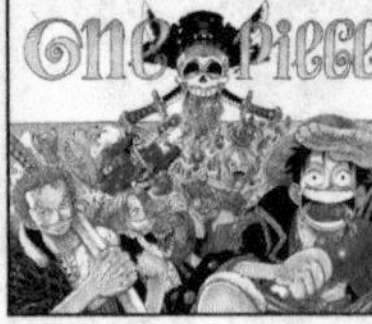
One Piece

A: That's right! Longtime readers might have noticed that, but people who are newer to the series probably haven't seen that one before. They were both such big milestones, I felt inspired to go back to it!

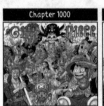

Q: In chapter 966, Roger and Rayleigh are holding Momonosuke and Hiyori and saying, "I haven't spent time with a baby in ages" and "Reminds me of the old days." Whose baby were they holding in the past?! I didn't see many women on Roger's ship…

--Count Deeno

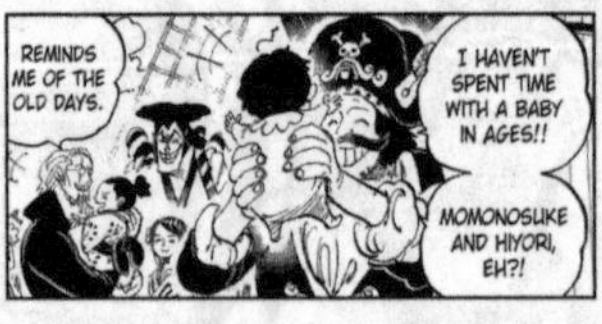
I HAVEN'T SPENT TIME WITH A BABY IN AGES!!
REMINDS ME OF THE OLD DAYS.
MOMONOSUKE AND HIYORI, EH?!

A: Huh? They said that? Weird... Uh...ignore that!! Please don't think about it! Fwee fwee fwoo♪ (whistling)

Chapter 1001:
BATTLE OF MONSTERS ON ONIGASHIMA

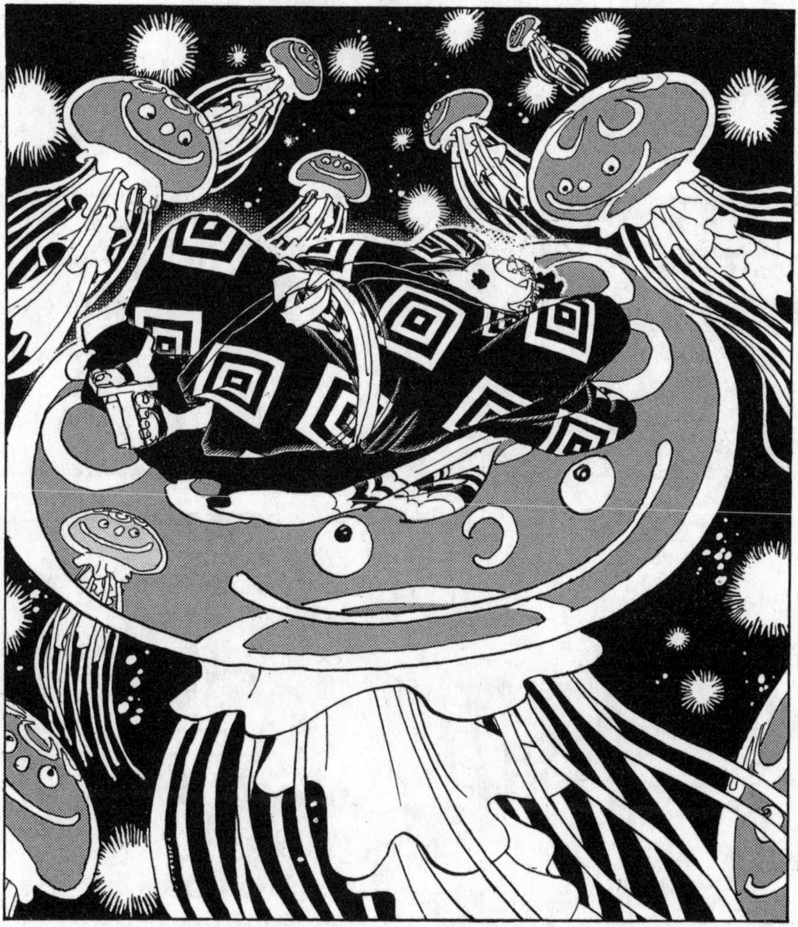

READER REQUEST: "JIMBEI RESTING LUXURIOUSLY ON A JELLYFISH BED" BY P.N. TOSHIKIYA

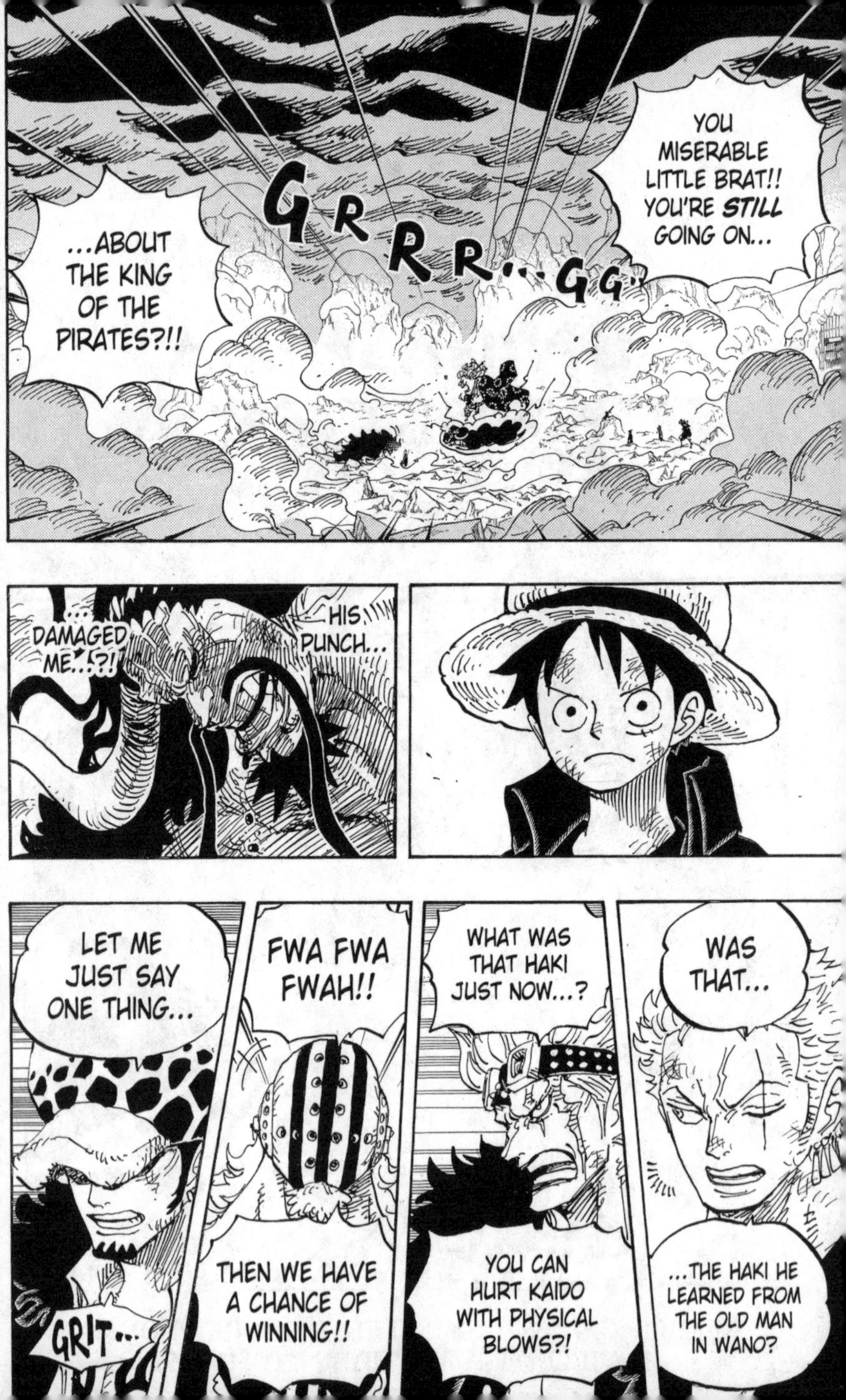
YOU MISERABLE LITTLE BRAT!! YOU'RE STILL GOING ON...
GRRRR...GG
...ABOUT THE KING OF THE PIRATES?!!
HIS PUNCH...
...DAMAGED ME...?!
WAS THAT...
...THE HAKI HE LEARNED FROM THE OLD MAN IN WANO?
WHAT WAS THAT HAKI JUST NOW...?
YOU CAN HURT KAIDO WITH PHYSICAL BLOWS?!
FWA FWA FWAH!!
THEN WE HAVE A CHANCE OF WINNING!!
LET ME JUST SAY ONE THING...
GRIT...

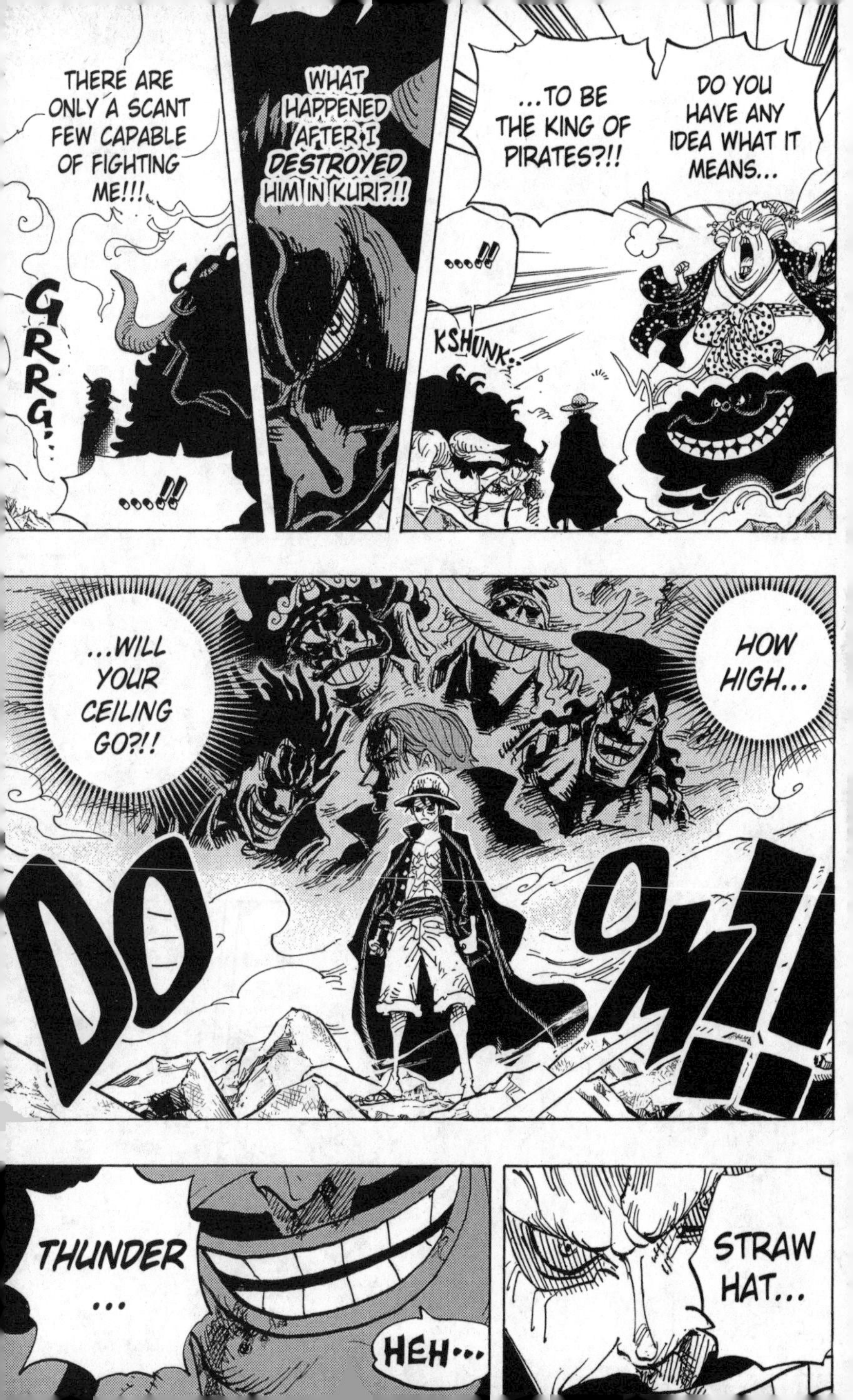
DO YOU HAVE ANY IDEA WHAT IT MEANS...
...TO BE THE KING OF PIRATES?!!
...!!
KSHUNK..
WHAT HAPPENED AFTER I DESTROYED HIM IN KURI?!!
THERE ARE ONLY A SCANT FEW CAPABLE OF FIGHTING ME!!!
GRRG...
...!!
HOW HIGH...
...WILL YOUR CEILING GO?!!
DOOM!!
STRAW HAT...
THUNDER ...
HEH...

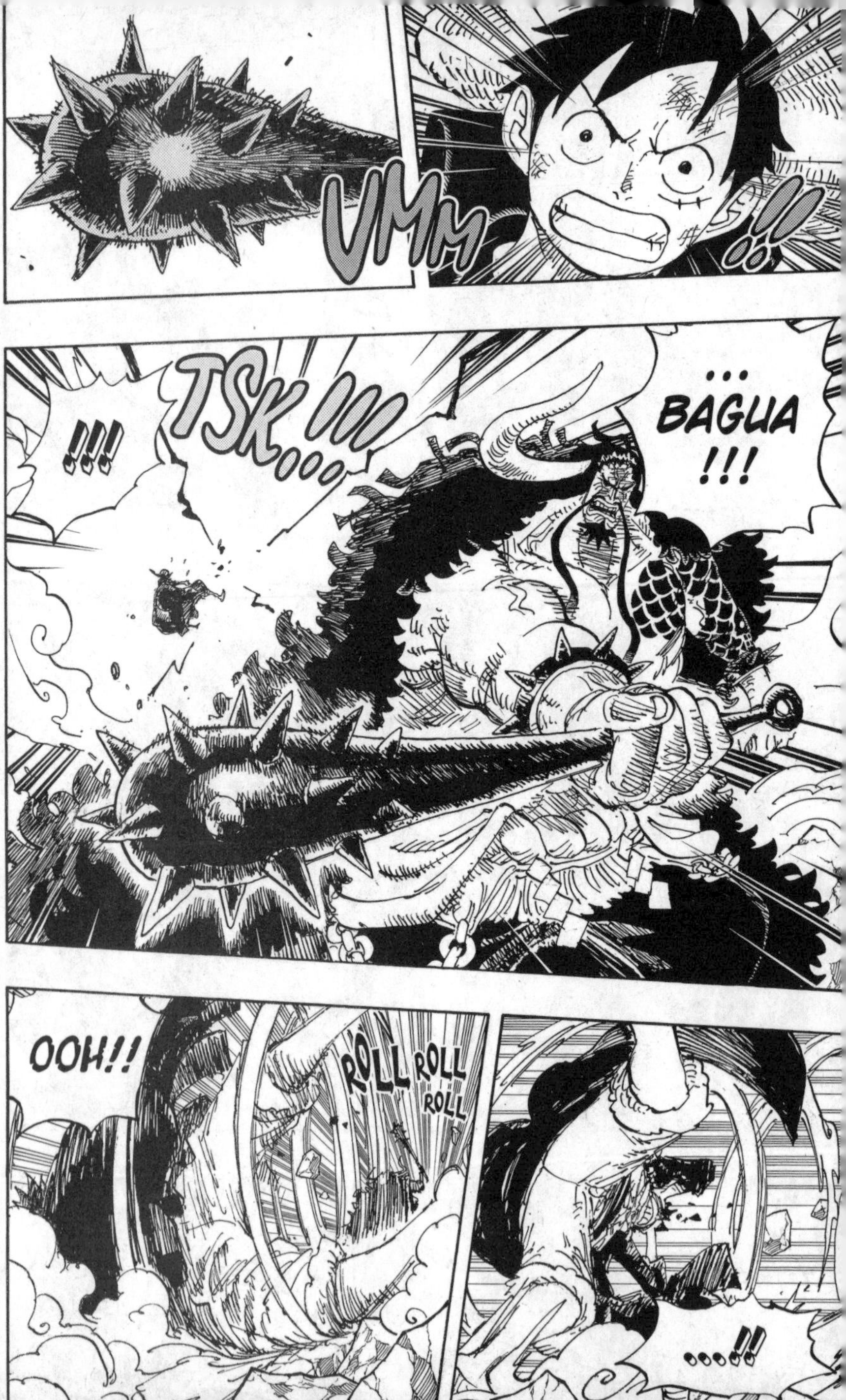
!!
VMM
... BAGUA !!!
TSK...!!!
!!!
....!!
ROLL ROLL ROLL
OOH!!

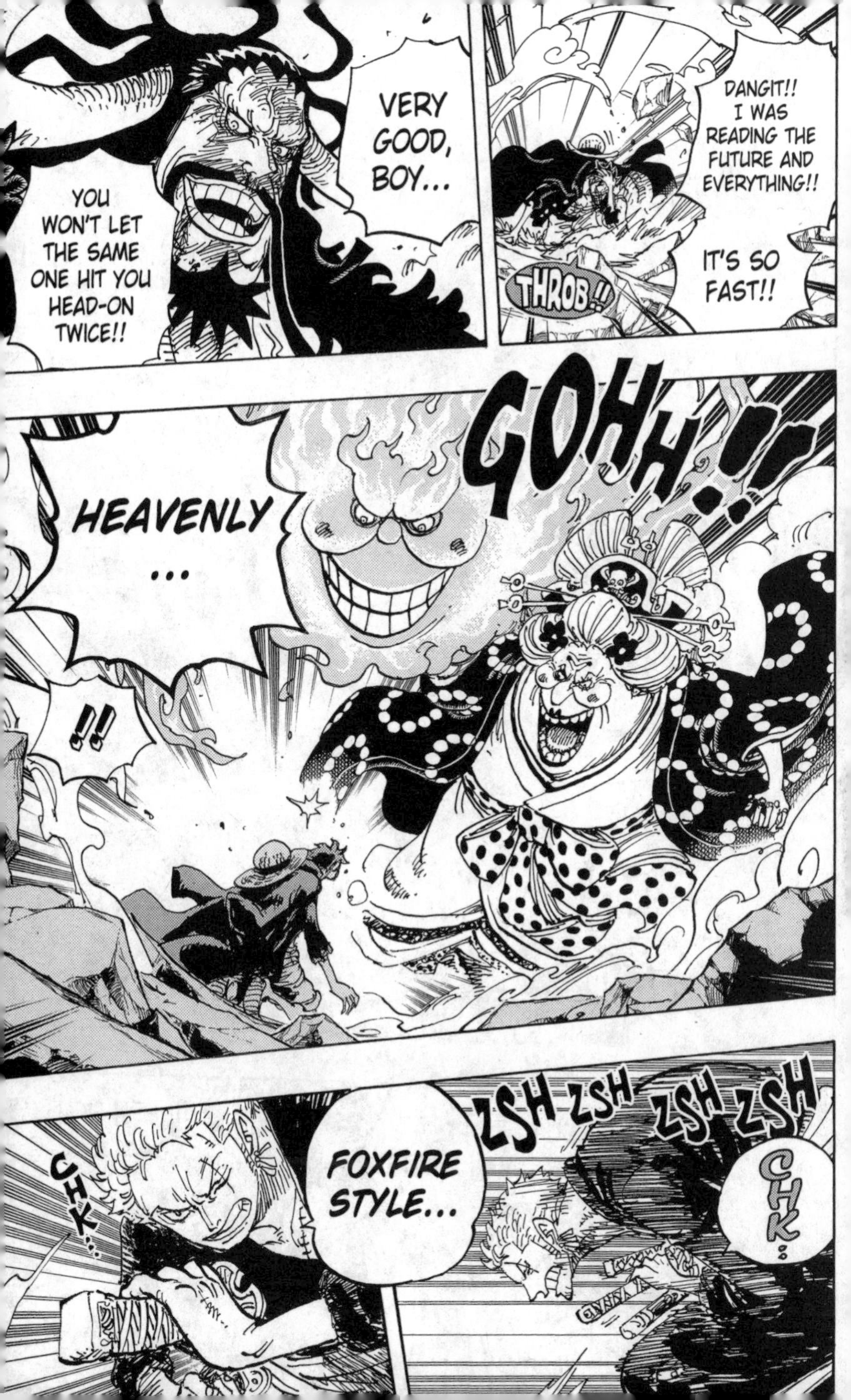
DANGIT!! I WAS READING THE FUTURE AND EVERYTHING!!
IT'S SO FAST!!
THROB!!
VERY GOOD, BOY...
YOU WON'T LET THE SAME ONE HIT YOU HEAD-ON TWICE!!
GOHH!!
HEAVENLY ...
!!
ZSH ZSH ZSH ZSH
CHK..
FOXFIRE STYLE...
CHK...

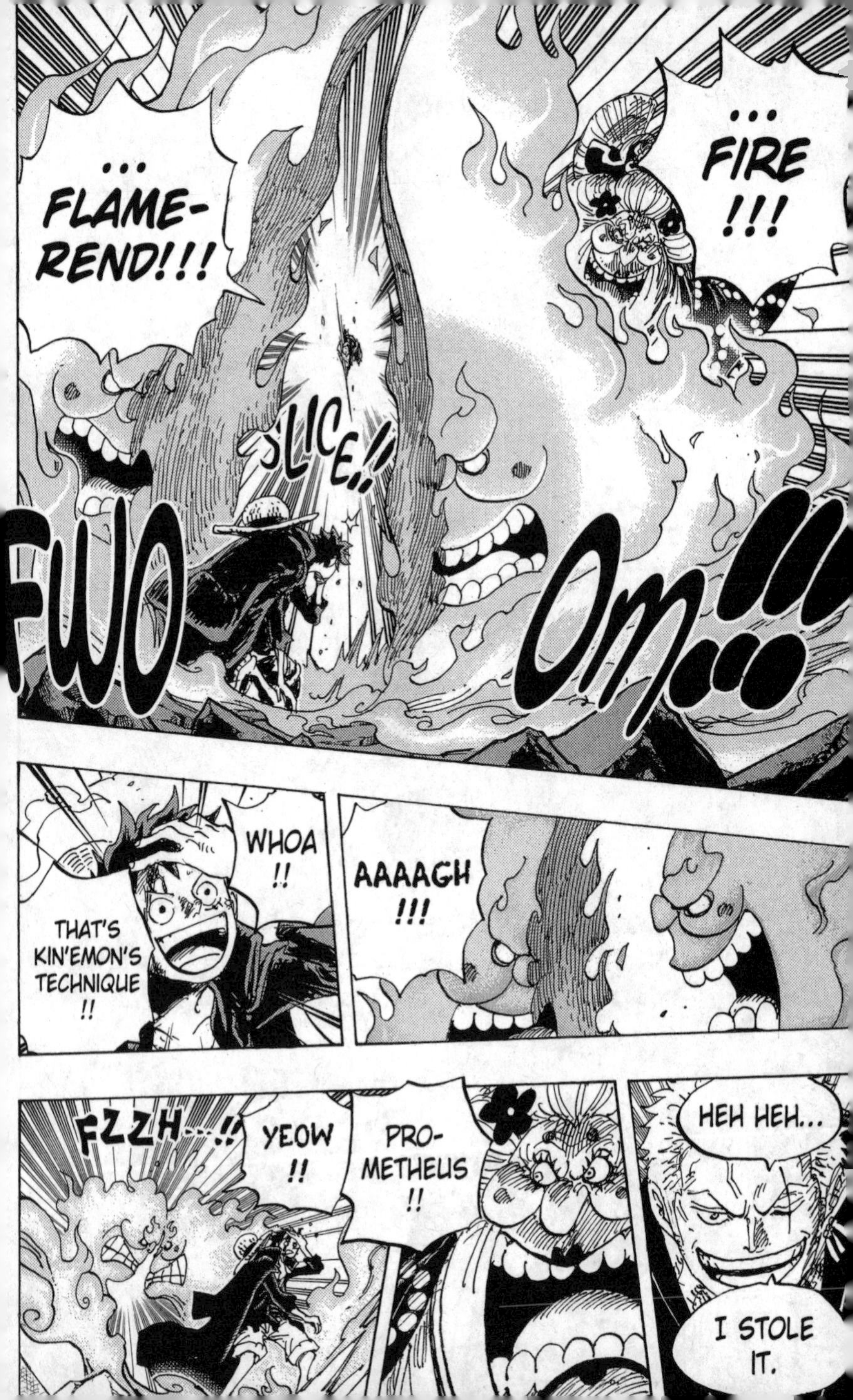

... FIRE !!!
... FLAME-REND!!!
SLICE!!
FUOOM...!!!
AAAAGH !!!
WHOA !!
THAT'S KIN'EMON'S TECHNIQUE !!
HEH HEH...
I STOLE IT.
PRO-METHEUS !!
YEOW !!
FZZH...!!

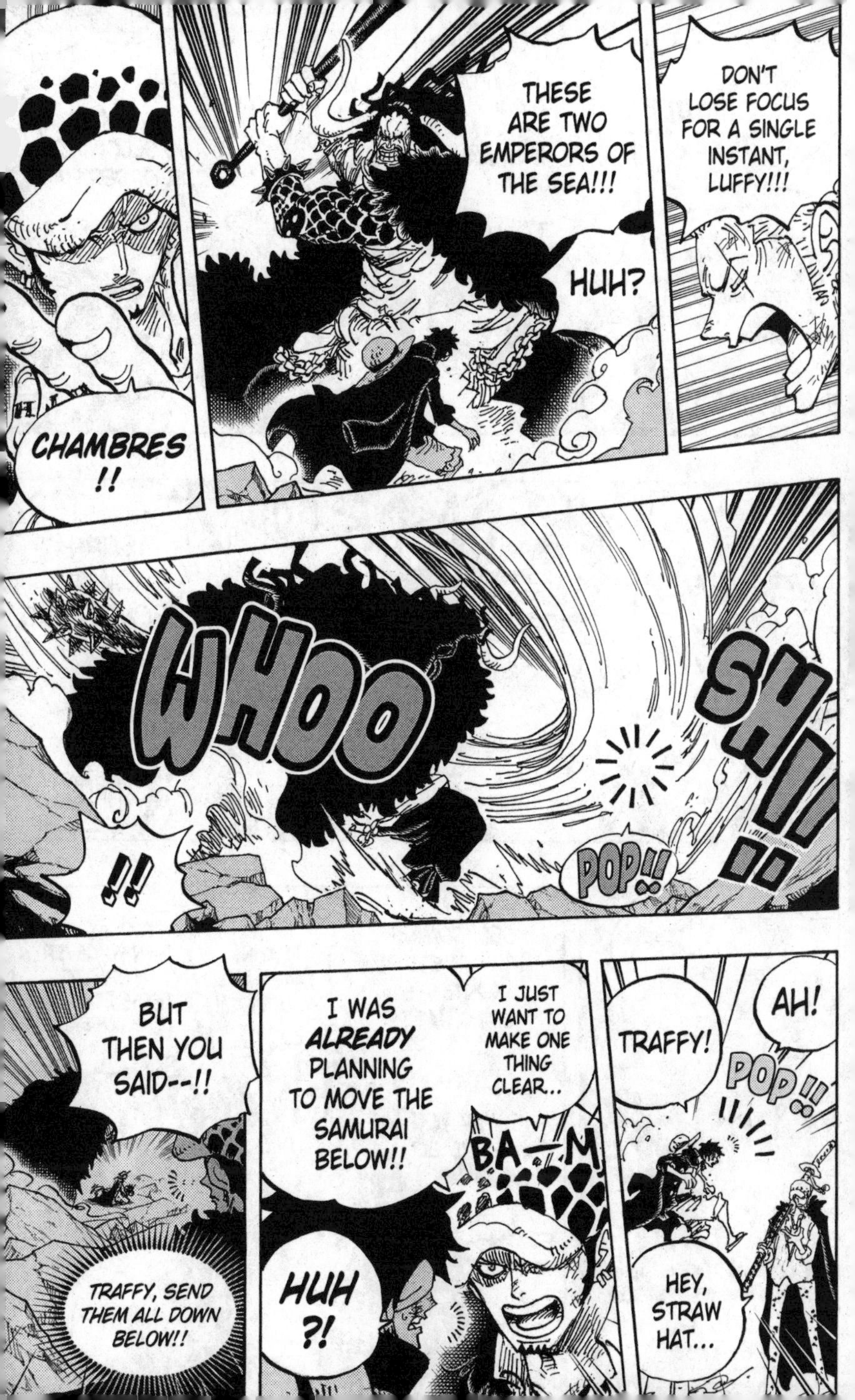
DON'T LOSE FOCUS FOR A SINGLE INSTANT, LUFFY!!!
THESE ARE TWO EMPERORS OF THE SEA!!!
HUH?
CHAMBRES !!
WHOOSH!!
POP!!
!!
AH!
TRAFFY!
POP!!
HEY, STRAW HAT...
I JUST WANT TO MAKE ONE THING CLEAR...
BA—M
I WAS *ALREADY* PLANNING TO MOVE THE SAMURAI BELOW!!
HUH ?!
BUT THEN YOU SAID--!!
TRAFFY, SEND THEM ALL DOWN BELOW!!

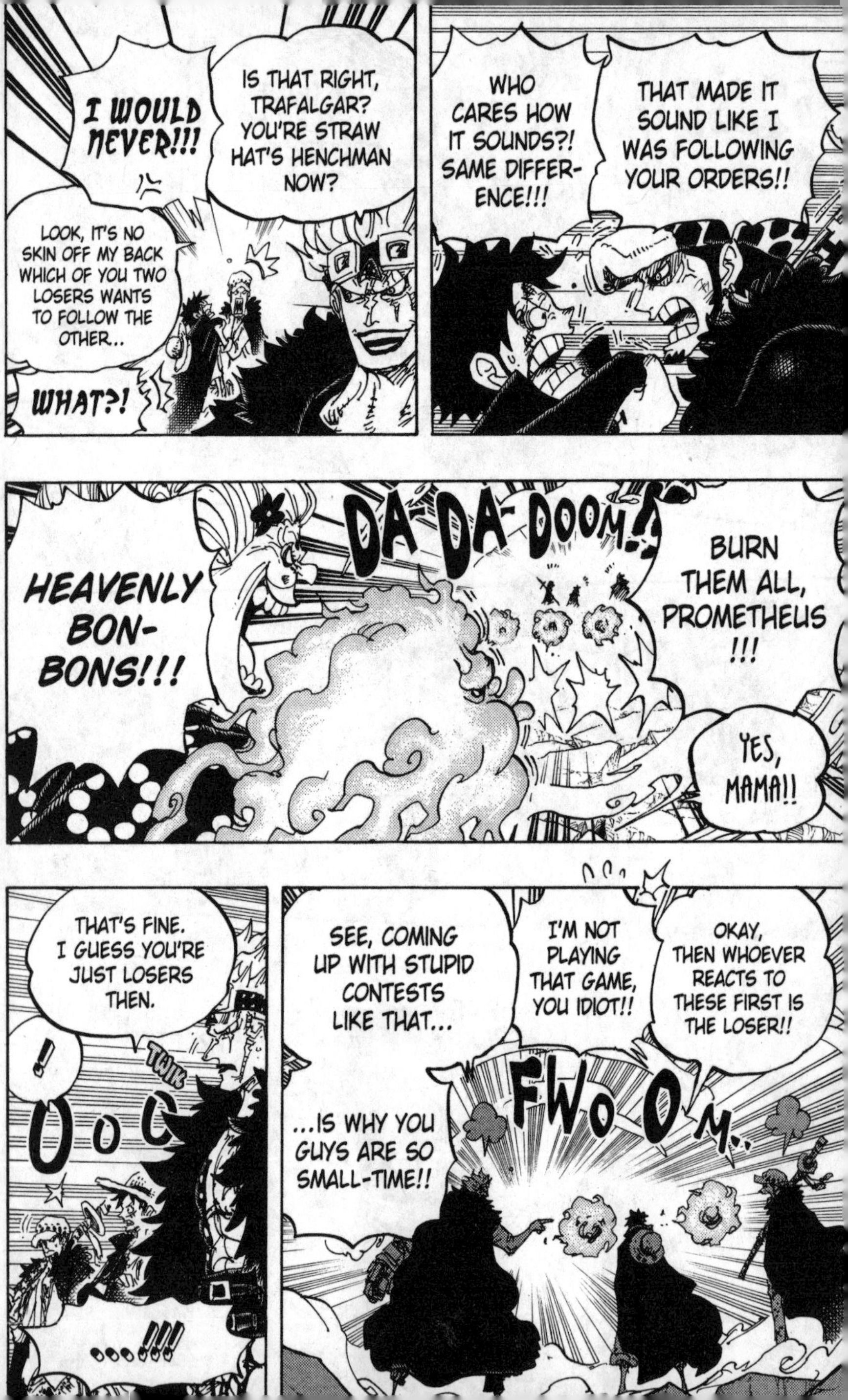
THAT MADE IT SOUND LIKE I WAS FOLLOWING YOUR ORDERS!!
WHO CARES HOW IT SOUNDS?! SAME DIFFER-ENCE!!!
IS THAT RIGHT, TRAFALGAR? YOU'RE STRAW HAT'S HENCHMAN NOW?
I WOULD NEVER!!!
LOOK, IT'S NO SKIN OFF MY BACK WHICH OF YOU TWO LOSERS WANTS TO FOLLOW THE OTHER...
WHAT?!
BURN THEM ALL, PROMETHEUS!!!
DA-DA-DOOM
HEAVENLY BON-BONS!!!
YES, MAMA!!
OKAY, THEN WHOEVER REACTS TO THESE FIRST IS THE LOSER!!
I'M NOT PLAYING THAT GAME, YOU IDIOT!!
SEE, COMING UP WITH STUPID CONTESTS LIKE THAT...
FWOOM
...IS WHY YOU GUYS ARE SO SMALL-TIME!!
THAT'S FINE. I GUESS YOU'RE JUST LOSERS THEN.
TWIK
!
...!!!

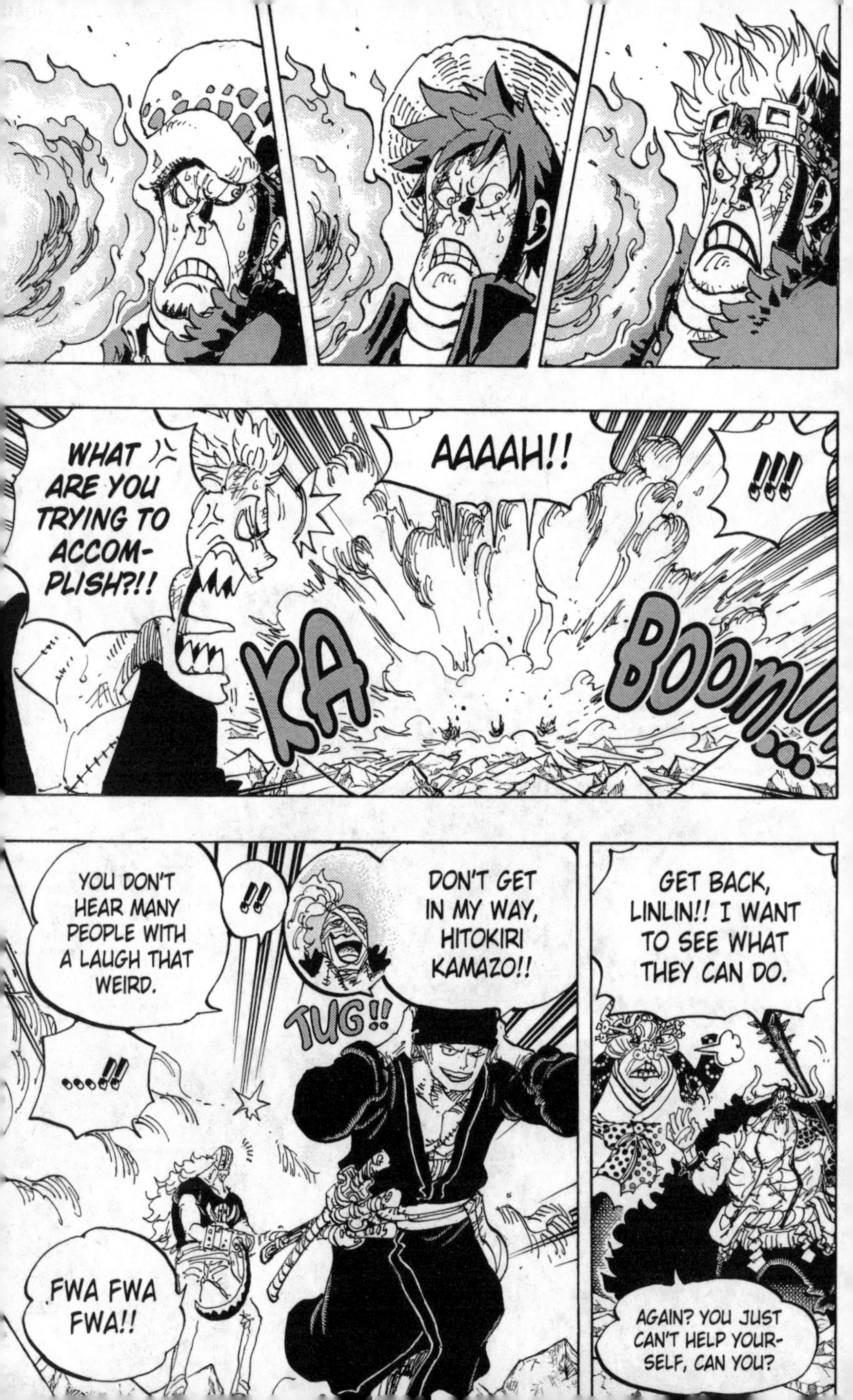
!!!
AAAAH!!
WHAT ARE YOU TRYING TO ACCOMPLISH?!!
KA BOOM...
GET BACK, LINLIN!! I WANT TO SEE WHAT THEY CAN DO.
AGAIN? YOU JUST CAN'T HELP YOURSELF, CAN YOU?
DON'T GET IN MY WAY, HITOKIRI KAMAZO!!
!!
YOU DON'T HEAR MANY PEOPLE WITH A LAUGH THAT WEIRD.
TUG!!
....!!
FWA FWA FWA!!

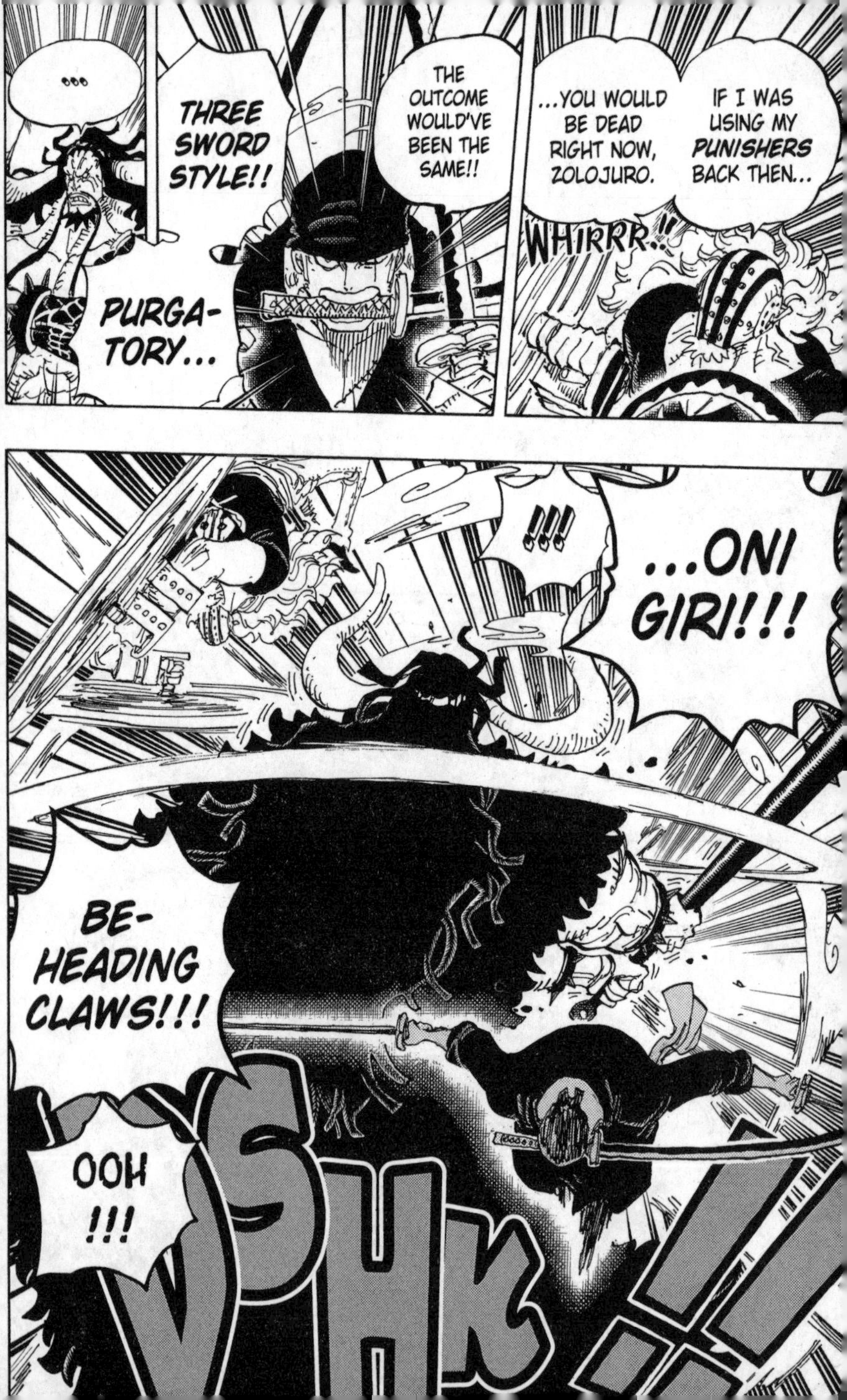
IF I WAS USING MY PUNISHERS BACK THEN...
...YOU WOULD BE DEAD RIGHT NOW, ZOLOJURO.
WHIRRR..!!
THE OUTCOME WOULD'VE BEEN THE SAME!!
THREE SWORD STYLE!!
PURGA-TORY...
...
!!!
...ONI GIRI!!!
BE-HEADING CLAWS!!!
OOH !!!
VSHK!!

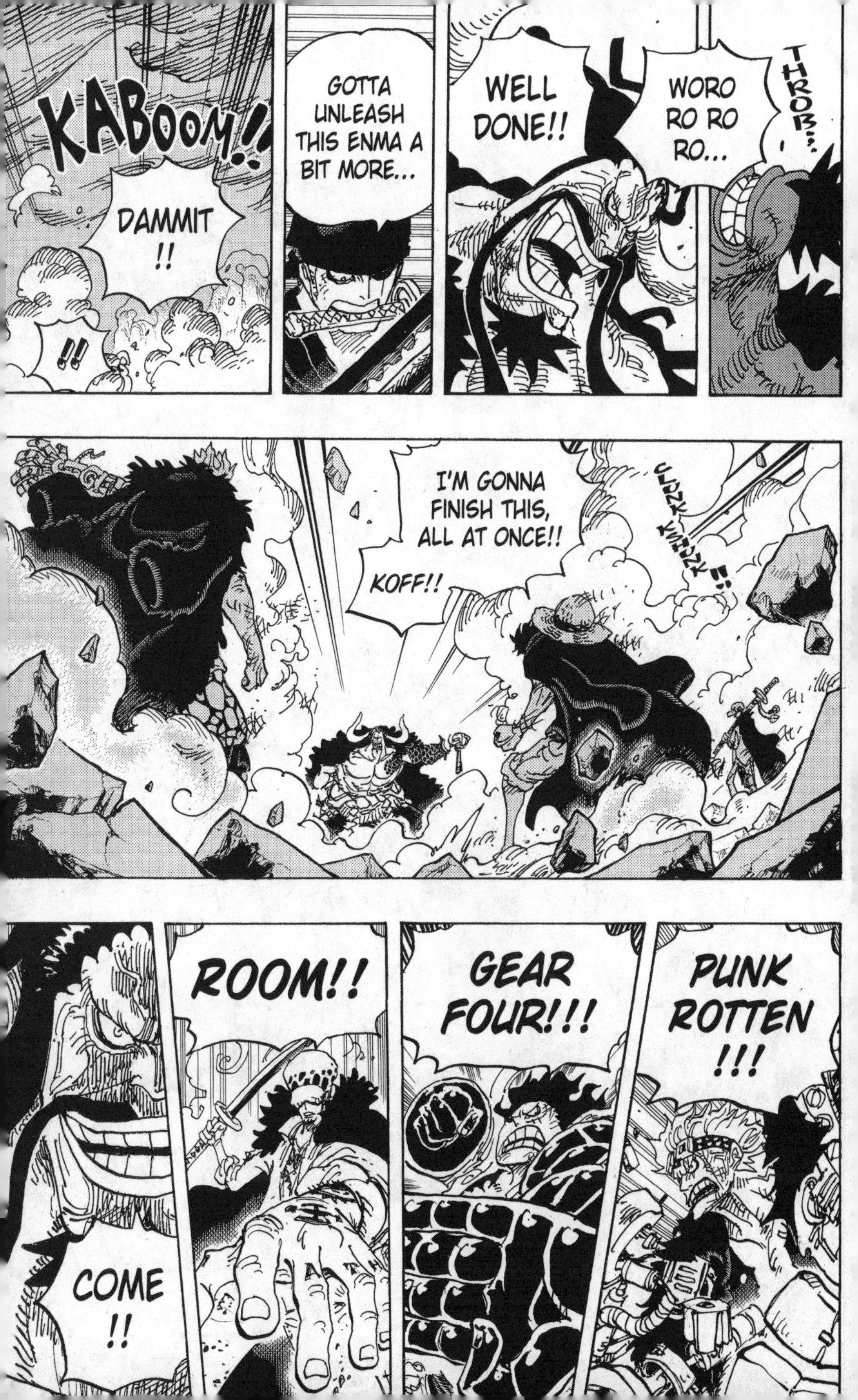
THROB!!
WORO RO RO RO...
WELL DONE!!
GOTTA UNLEASH THIS ENMA A BIT MORE...
KABOOM!!
DAMMIT!!
!!
CLUNK KLINK!!
I'M GONNA FINISH THIS, ALL AT ONCE!!
KOFF!!
PUNK ROTTEN!!!
GEAR FOUR!!!
ROOM!!
COME!!

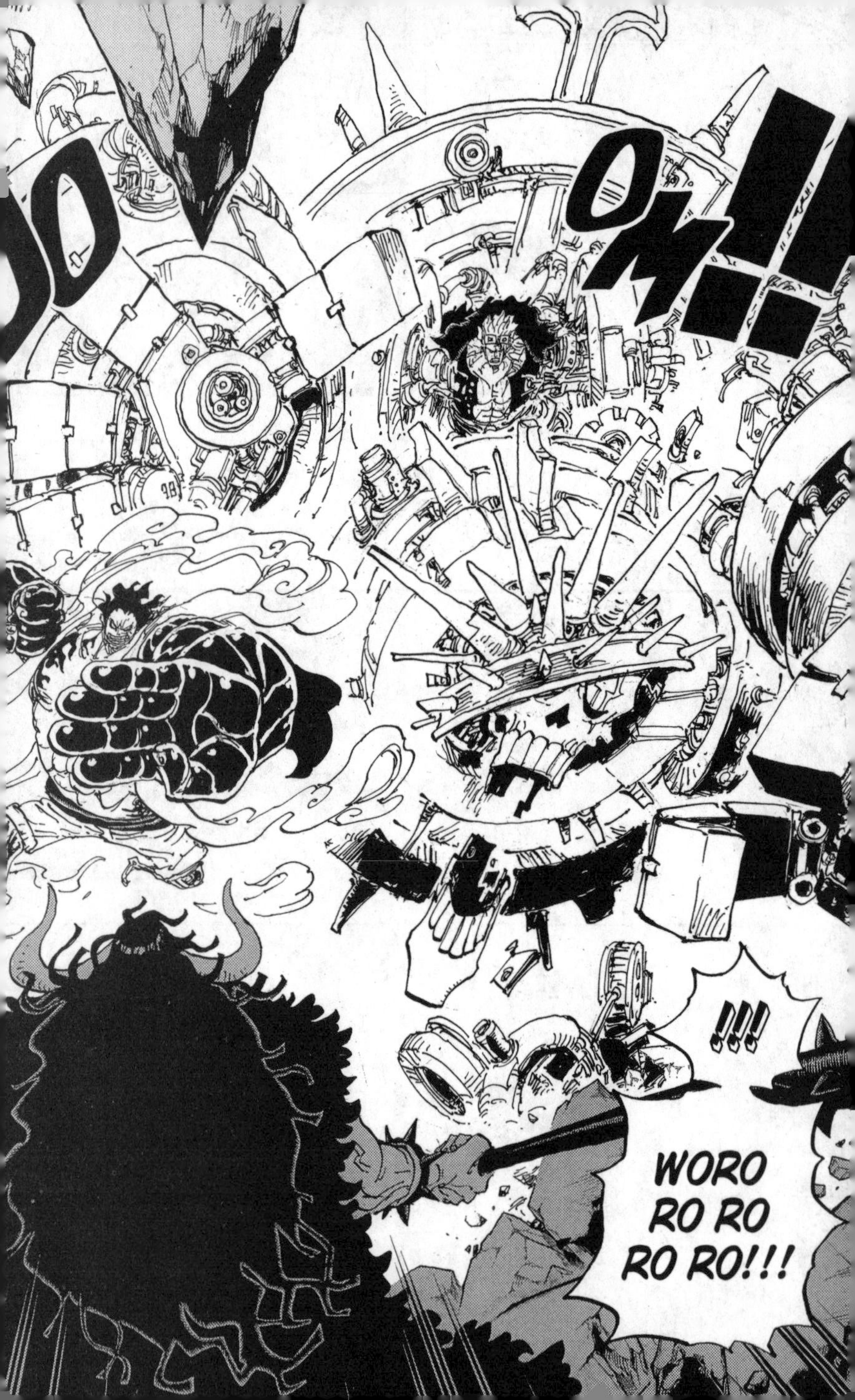
DOON!!
!!!
WORO RO RO RO RO!!!

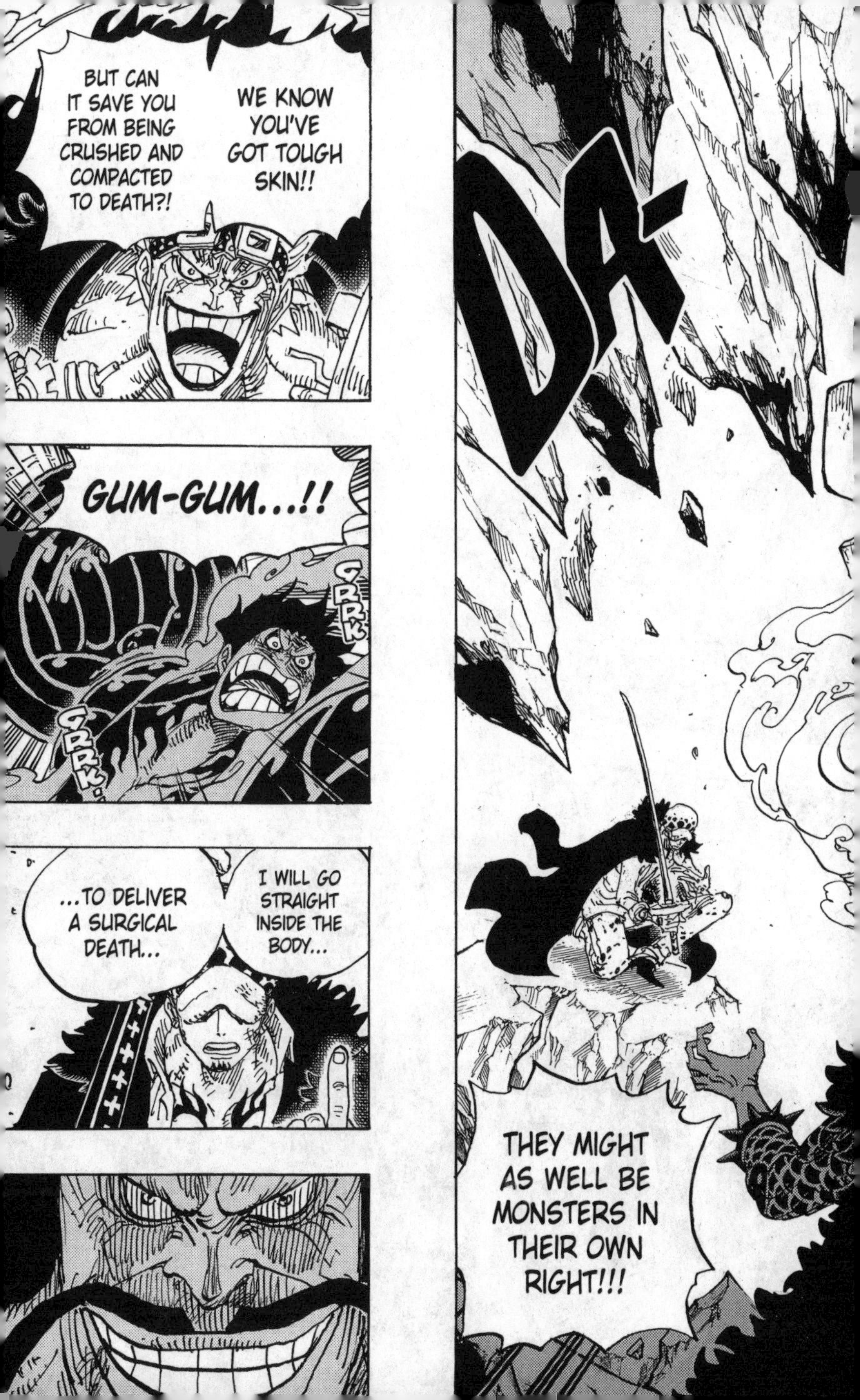
DA-
THEY MIGHT AS WELL BE MONSTERS IN THEIR OWN RIGHT!!!
WE KNOW YOU'VE GOT TOUGH SKIN!!
BUT CAN IT SAVE YOU FROM BEING CRUSHED AND COMPACTED TO DEATH?!
GUM-GUM...!!
GRRK
GRRK
I WILL GO STRAIGHT INSIDE THE BODY...
...TO DELIVER A SURGICAL DEATH...

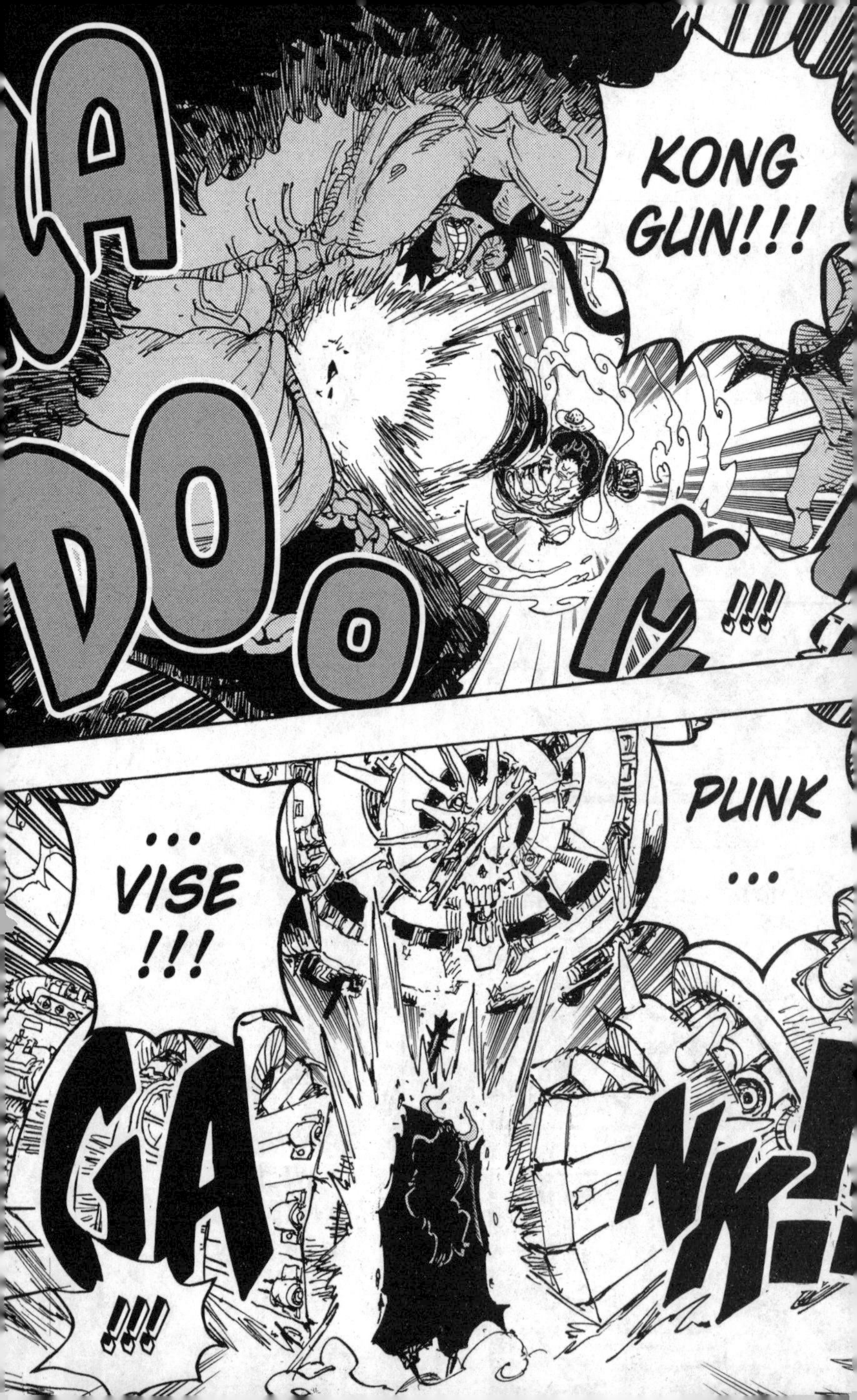
KONG GUN!!!
PUNK ...
... VISE !!!

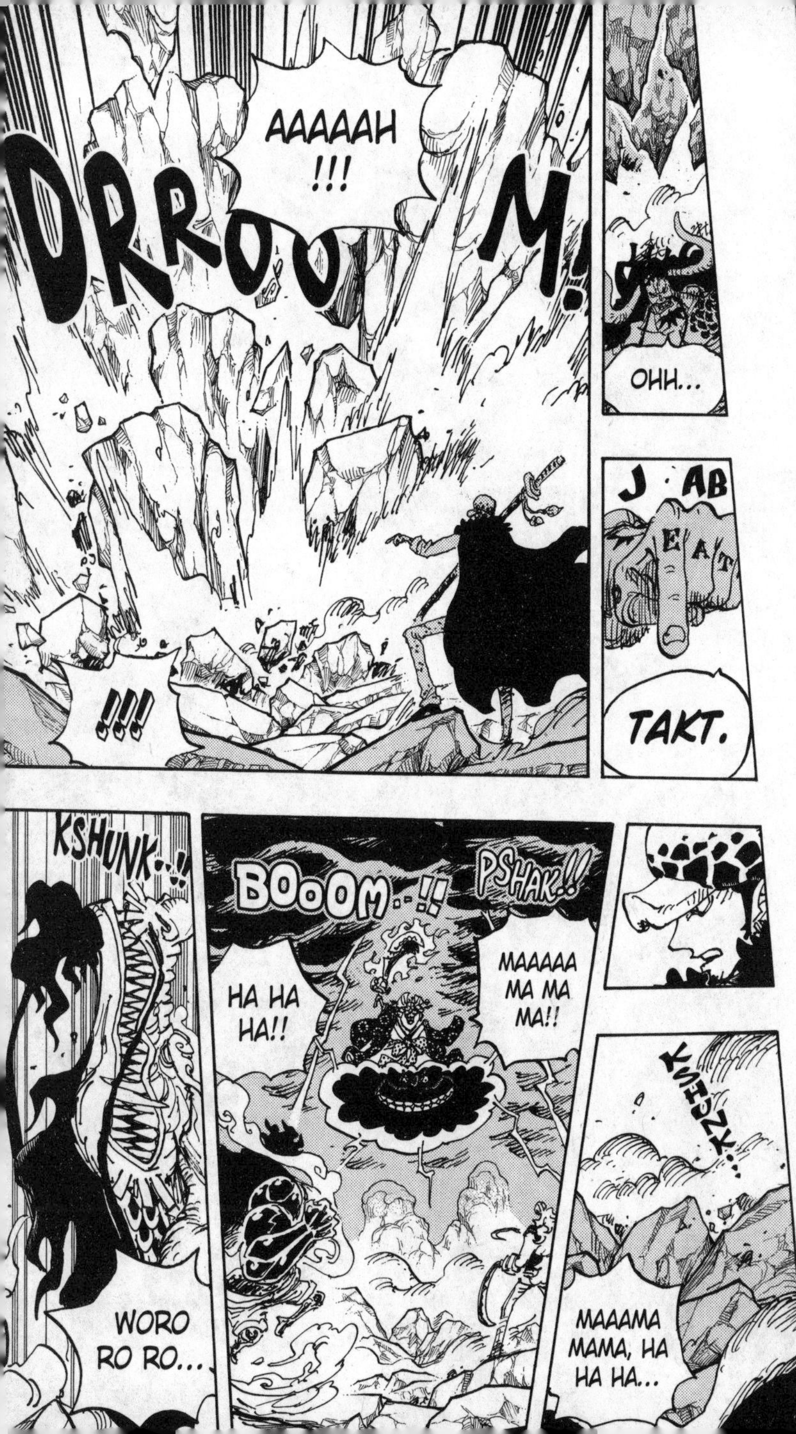
OHH...
J AB
E A T
TAKT.
AAAAAH !!!
DRROOOM!
!!!
KSHUNK...
MAAAMA MAMA, HA HA HA...
PSHAK!!
MAAAAA MA MA MA!!
BOOOM..!!
HA HA HA!!
KSHUNK..!!
WORO RO RO...

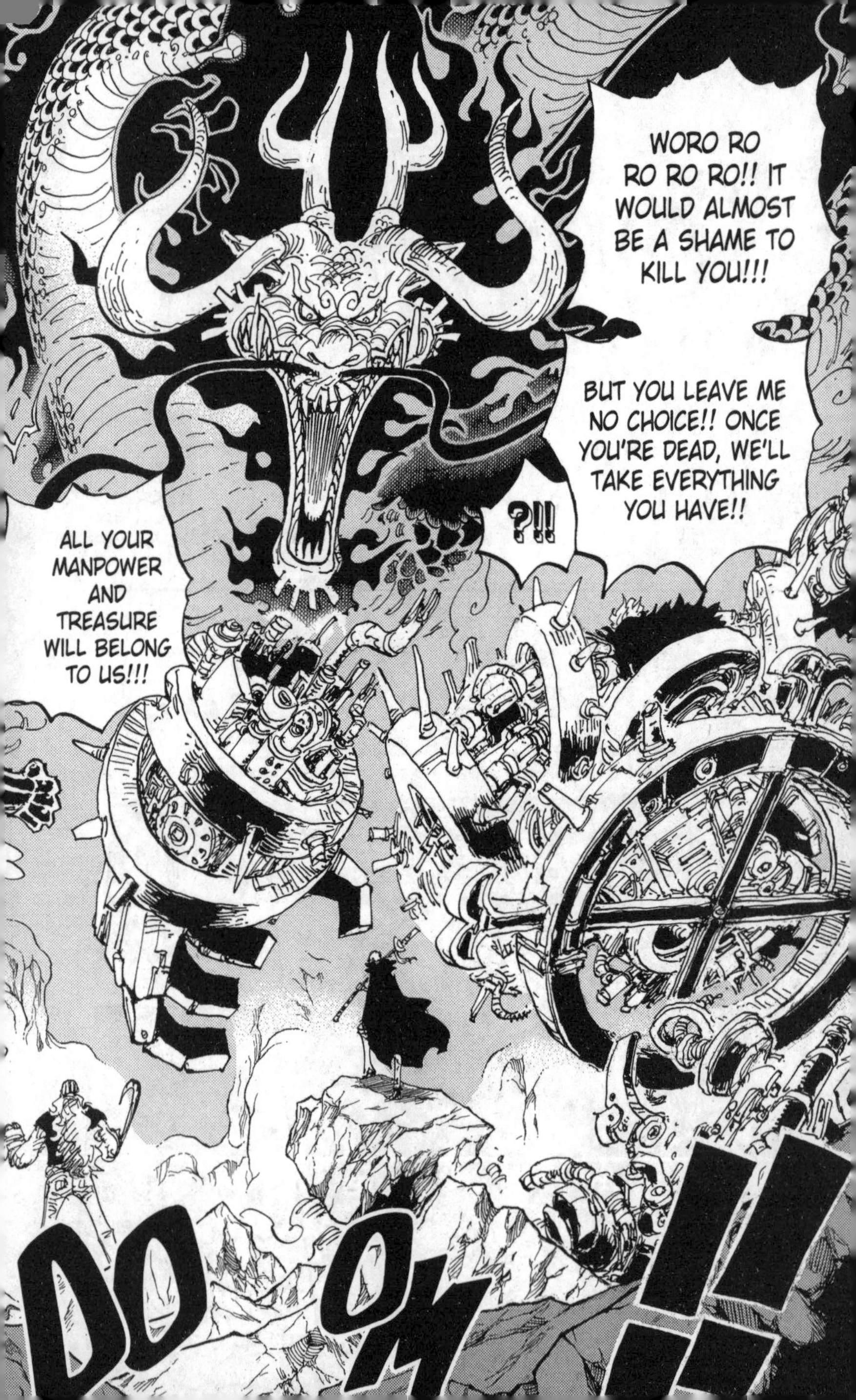
WORO RO RO RO RO!! IT WOULD ALMOST BE A SHAME TO KILL YOU!!!
BUT YOU LEAVE ME NO CHOICE!! ONCE YOU'RE DEAD, WE'LL TAKE EVERYTHING YOU HAVE!!
?!!
ALL YOUR MANPOWER AND TREASURE WILL BELONG TO US!!!
DOOM!!

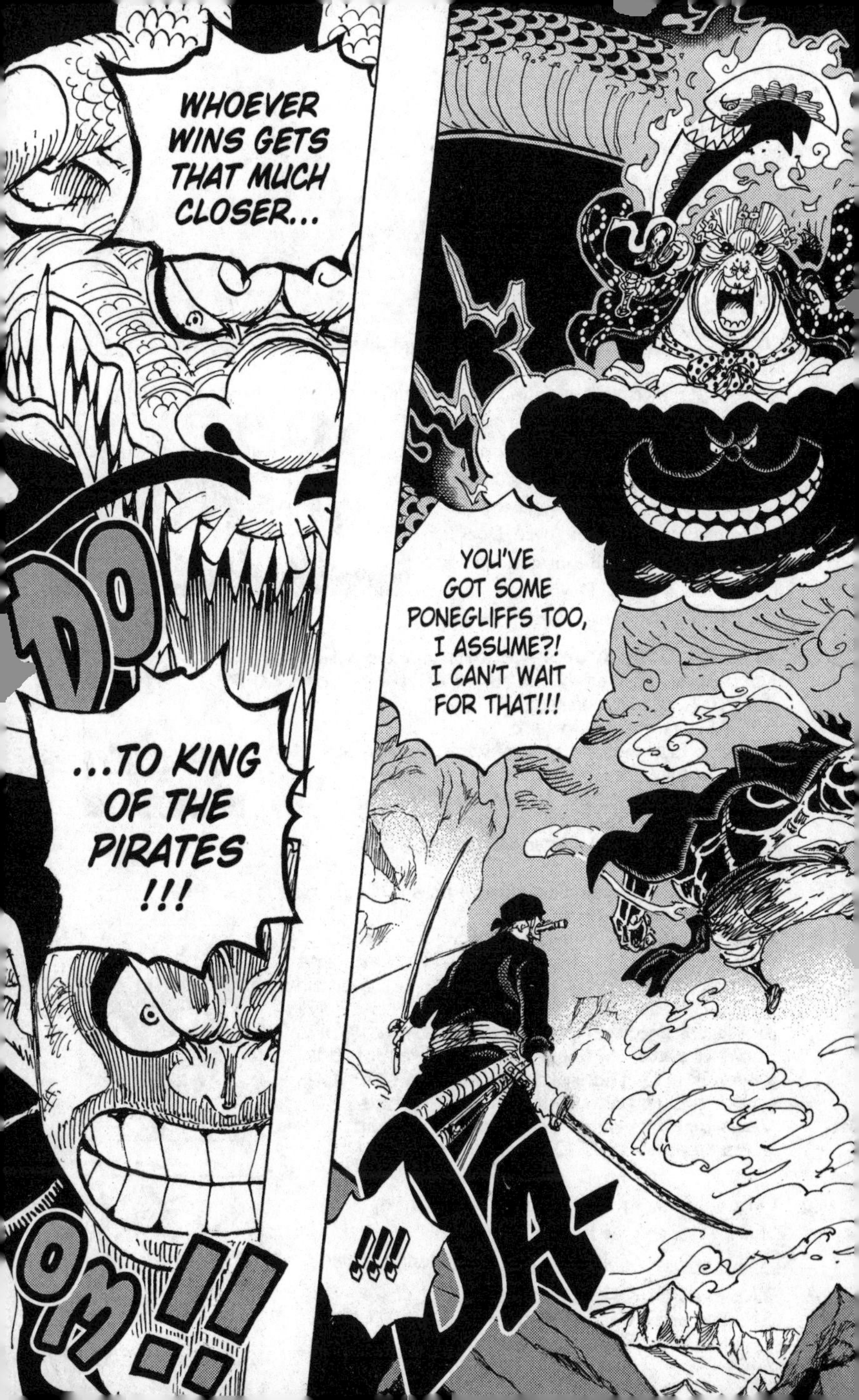
YOU'VE GOT SOME PONEGLIFFS TOO, I ASSUME?! I CAN'T WAIT FOR THAT!!!
!!!
WHOEVER WINS GETS THAT MUCH CLOSER...
...TO KING OF THE PIRATES!!!
DOOM!!

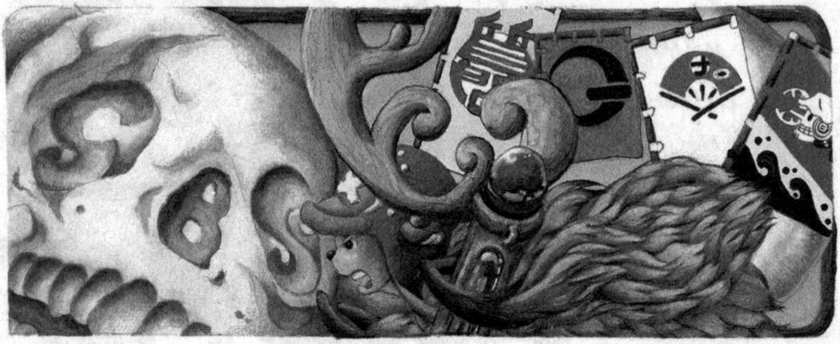

(Takahisa Fujiwara, Nara)

Q: Odacchi, I noticed that when everyone's getting funky on the performance floor in chapter 978, there's a giraffe-based Gifter who's different from Kaku or the Headliner named Hamlet. Does that mean Smile fruits are able to create many of the same powers over and over? Does it not matter if there's already a user of that power from a natural Devil Fruit?

--Taro in the Dark

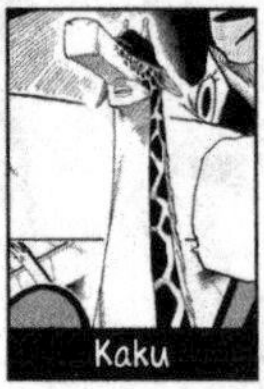

Kaku

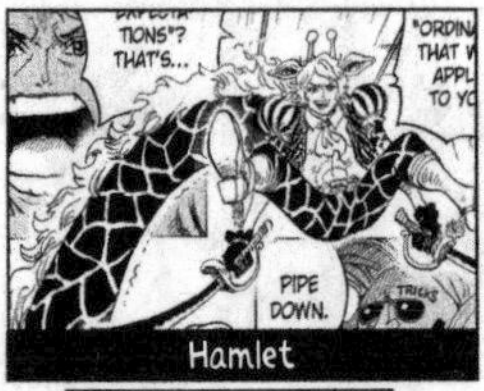
THAT'S...
PIPE DOWN.

Hamlet

A: All right. Smile fruits are artificial Devil Fruits, so they're not at all like the real thing. Let's go through the process.

★ SAD on Punk Hazard
Liquid containing various animal bloodline elements.

★ Smile Factory on Dressrosa
Feeding SAD to plants causes them to grow strange fruit.

★ On Wano
The imported fruit has a 10% chance of giving animal powers.

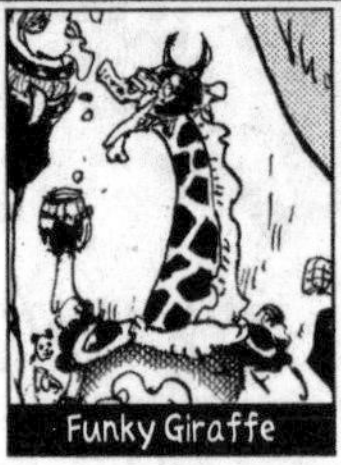

Funky Giraffe

In other words, they have nothing to do with real Devil Fruits. That's why there are multiple Gifters of the same animal. Bloodline Elements can only be extracted from a living biological specimen, which is why Smile fruits don't create Mythical, Logia, or Paramythia types. That's the limit of Caesar's scientific powers. But perhaps the super-genius Vegapunk has been conducting research that goes beyond this... Or perhaps not...

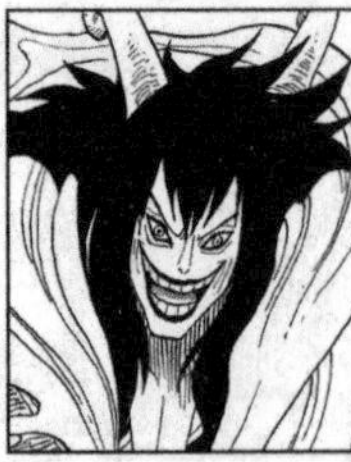

Q: Odacchi! What's the difference between the Spider-Spider Fruit and the Bug-Bug Fruit?

--Shun Ootsuki

A: The Bug-Bug Fruit gives insect powers. Spiders are arachnids, not insects. That's why it's the Spider-Spider Fruit.

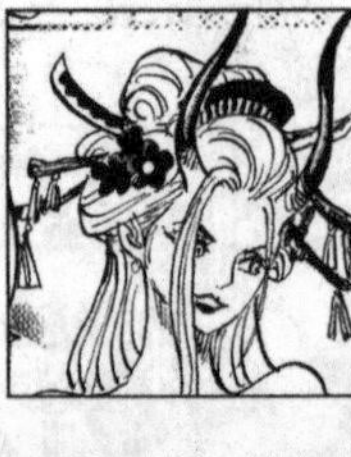

Chapter 1002:
FOUR EMPERORS VS. NEW GENERATION

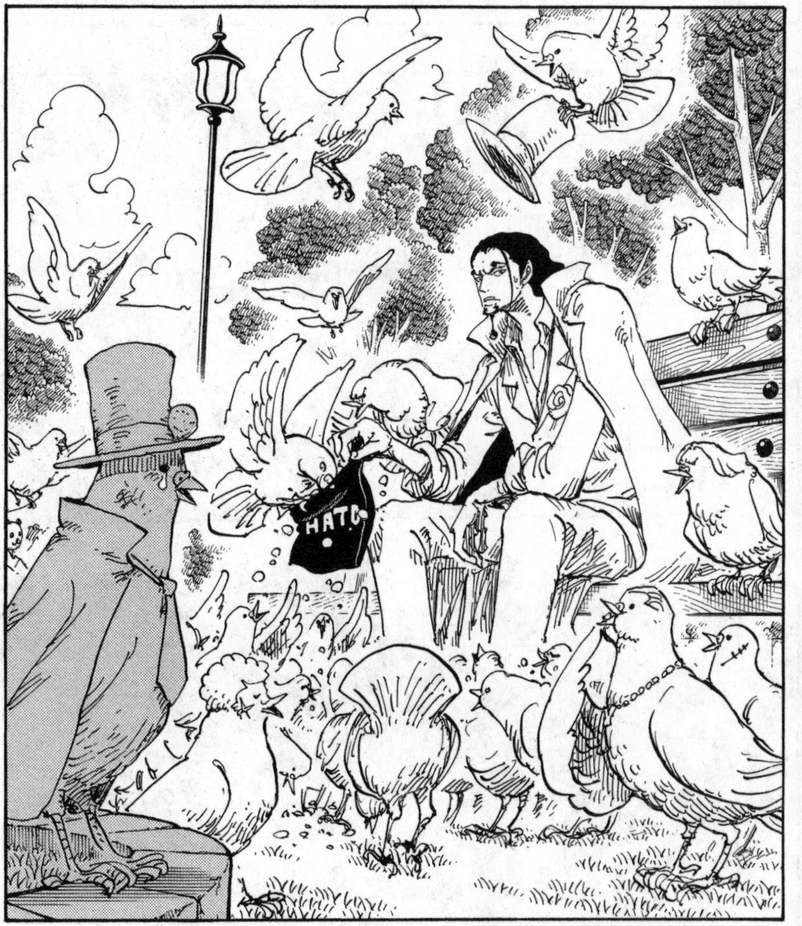

READER REQUEST: "LUCCI FEEDING PIGEONS IN THE PARK" BY P.N. X-5GO

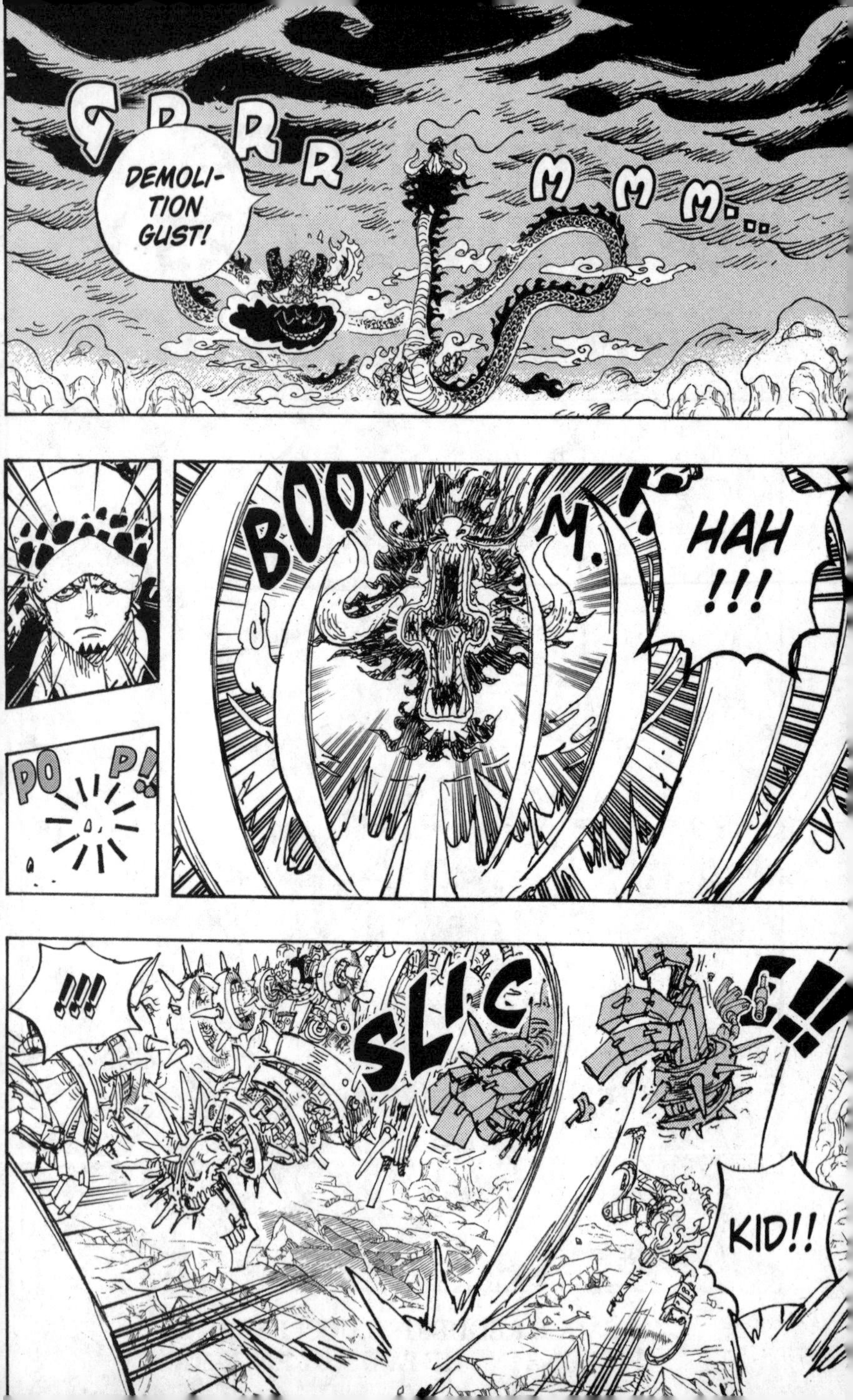
GRRRMMM...
DEMOLITION GUST!
BOOM.
HAH!!!
POP!!
SLICE!!
KID!!
!!!

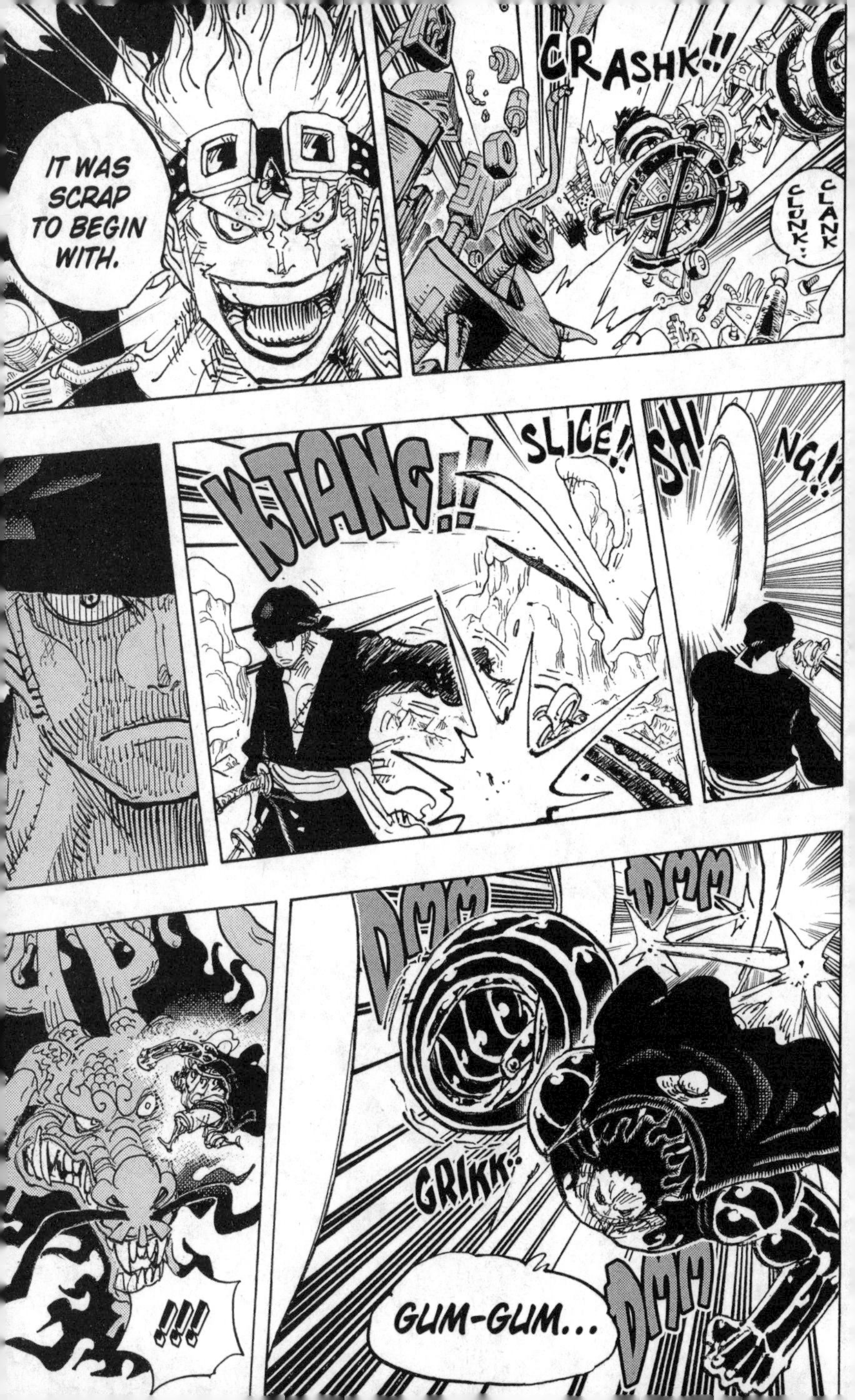
CRASHK!!
CLANK
CLUNK...
IT WAS SCRAP TO BEGIN WITH.
SHING!!
SLICE!!
KTANG!!
DMM
DMM
GRIKK..
DMM
GUM-GUM...
!!!

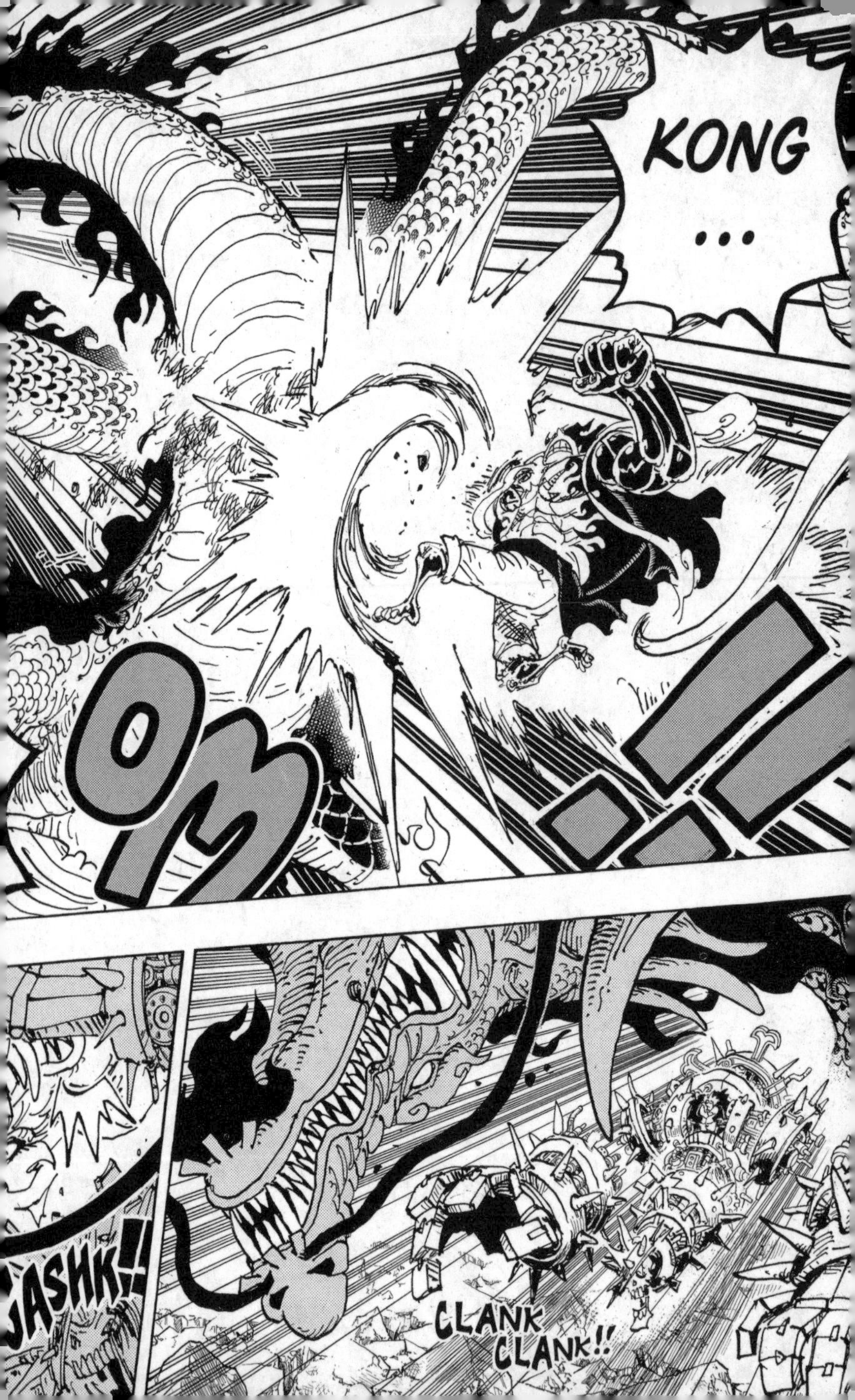
KONG
...
CLANK
CLANK!!
GASHK!!

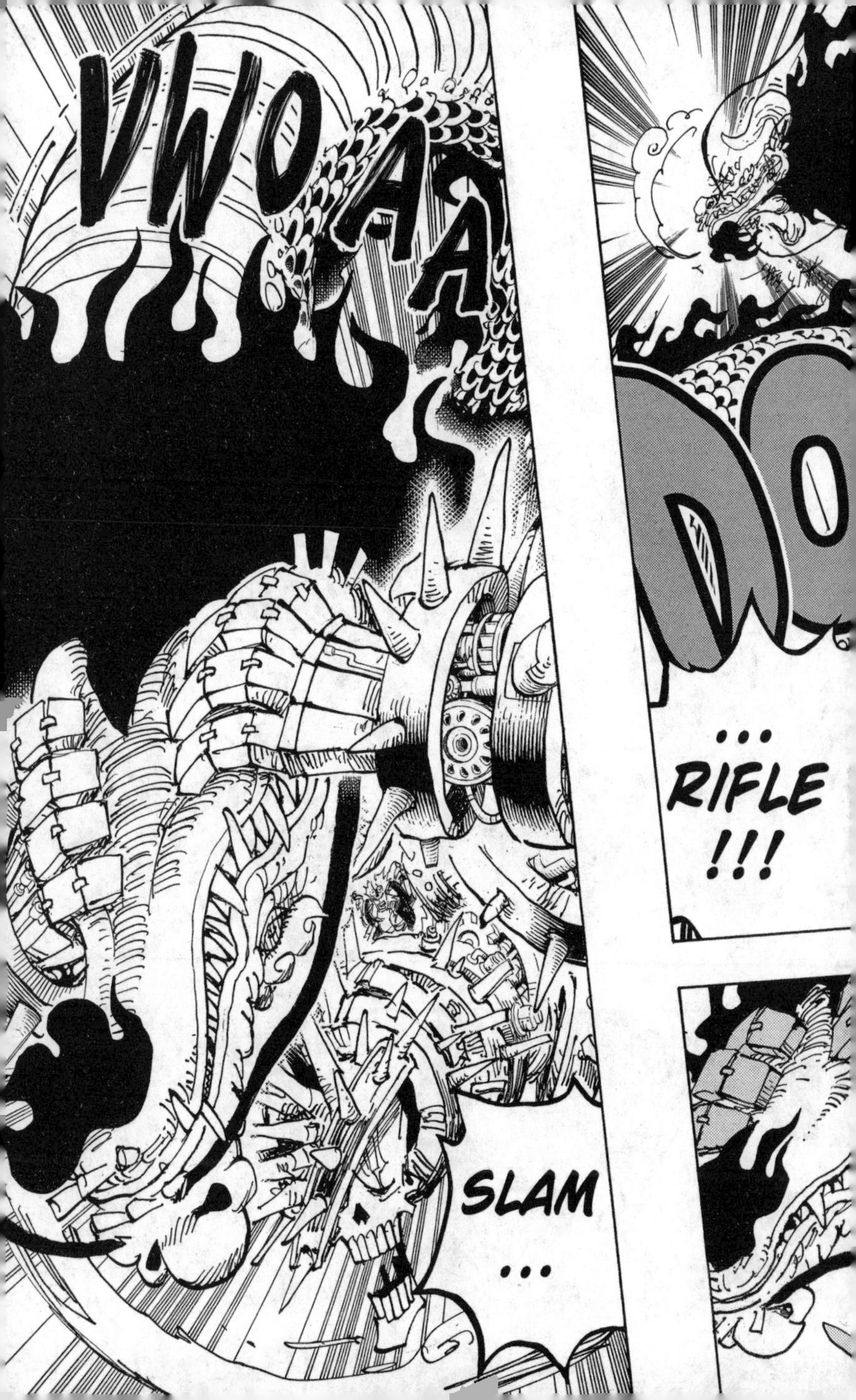
DO
... RIFLE !!!
VWOAA
SLAM ...

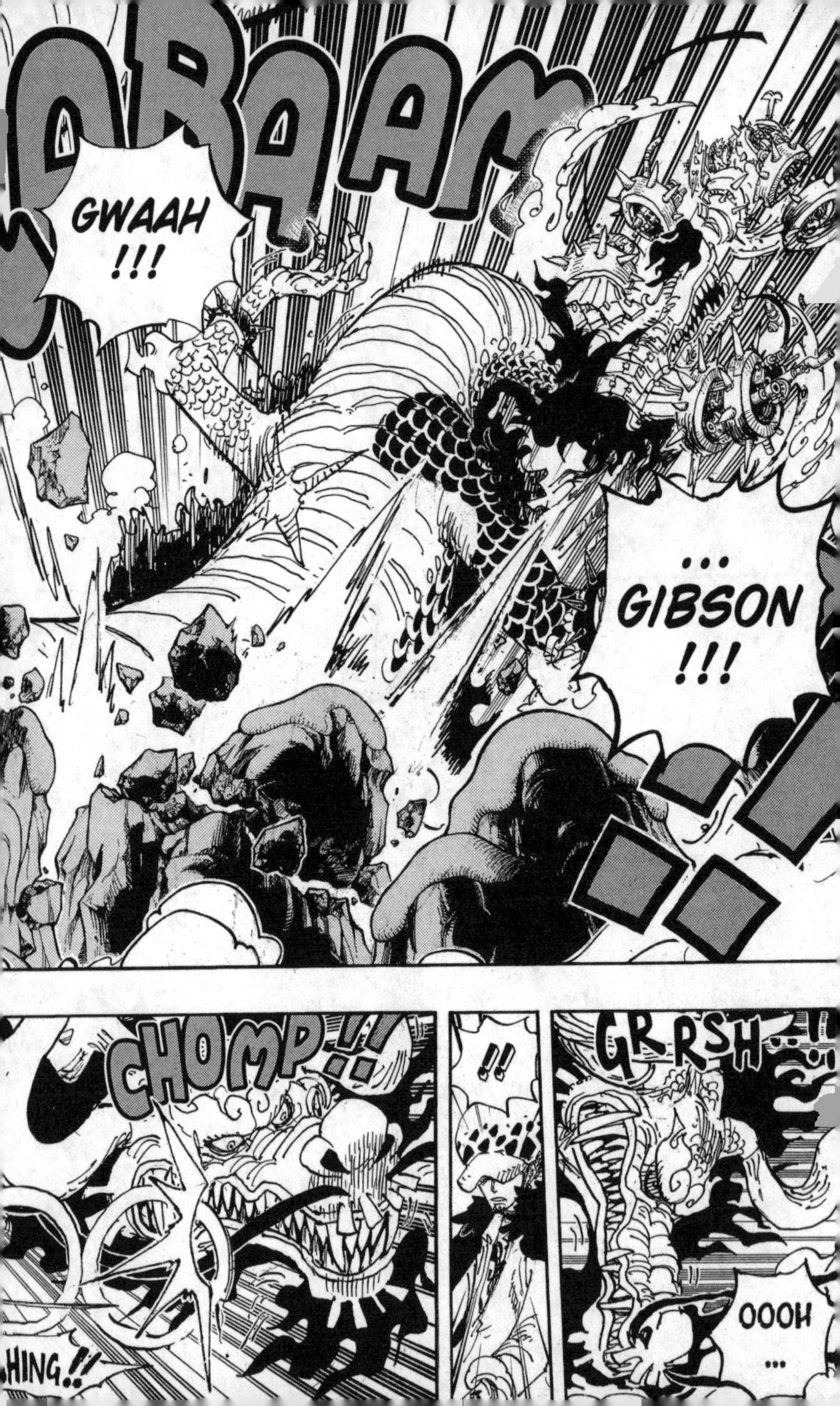
DRAAM
GWAAH!!!
...GIBSON!!!
GRRSH...!!
OOOH...
!!
CHOMP!!
HING!!

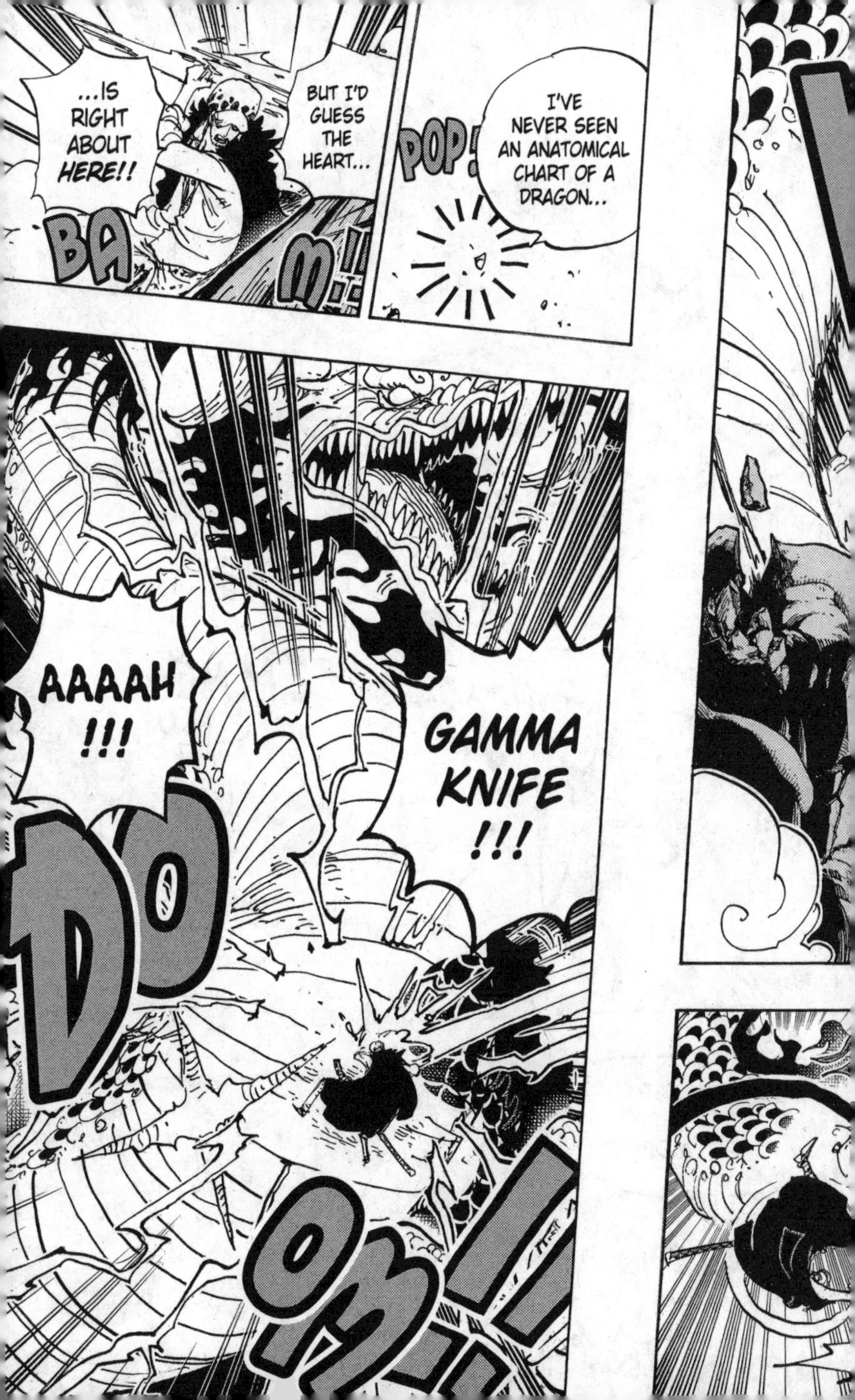

I'VE NEVER SEEN AN ANATOMICAL CHART OF A DRAGON...
POP!
BUT I'D GUESS THE HEART...
...IS RIGHT ABOUT HERE!!
BAM!!
GAMMA KNIFE!!!
AAAAH!!!
DOOM!!

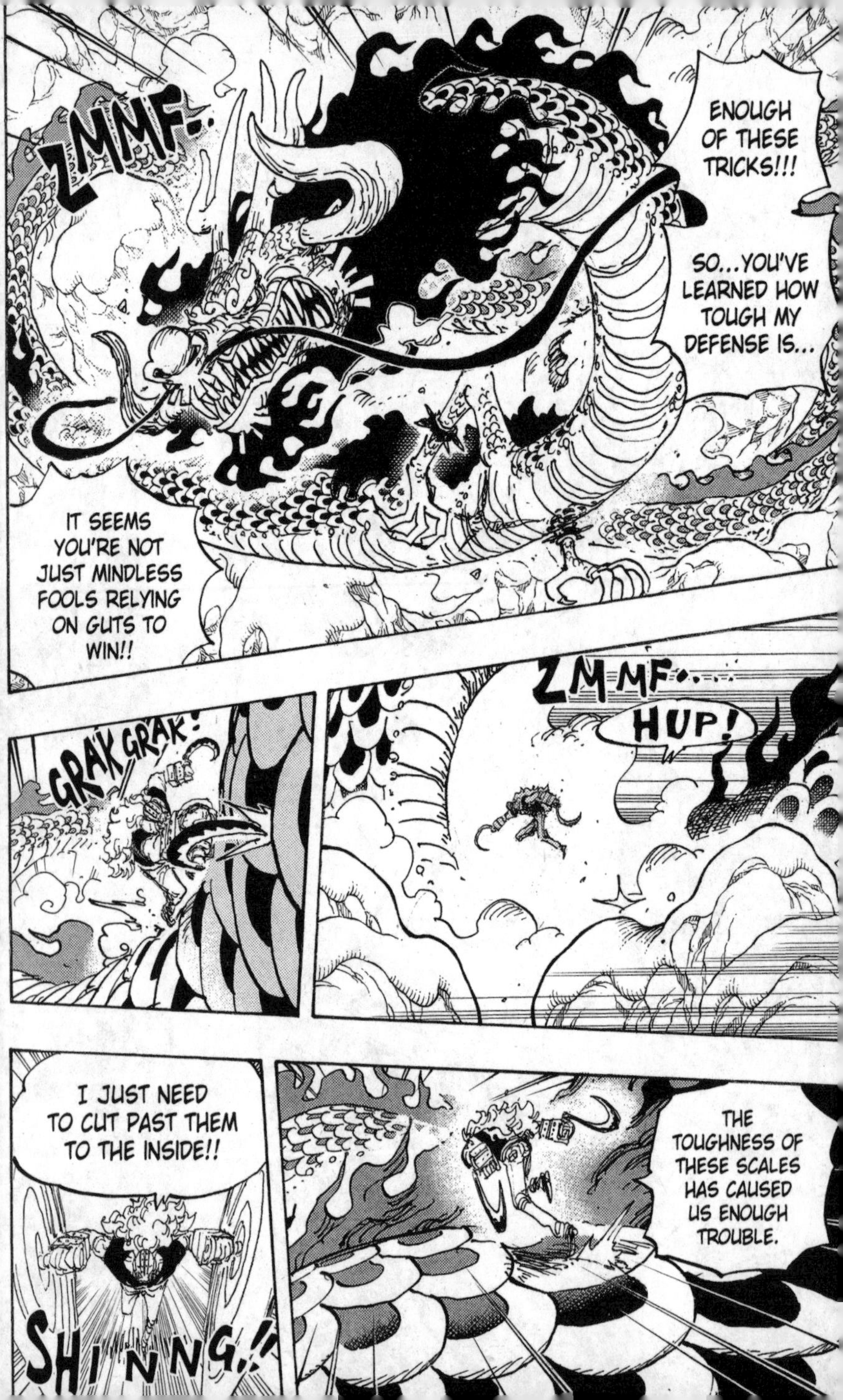
ENOUGH OF THESE TRICKS!!!
ZMMF...
SO...YOU'VE LEARNED HOW TOUGH MY DEFENSE IS...
IT SEEMS YOU'RE NOT JUST MINDLESS FOOLS RELYING ON GUTS TO WIN!!
ZMMF......
HUP!
GRAK GRAK!
THE TOUGHNESS OF THESE SCALES HAS CAUSED US ENOUGH TROUBLE.
I JUST NEED TO CUT PAST THEM TO THE INSIDE!!
SHINNG!!

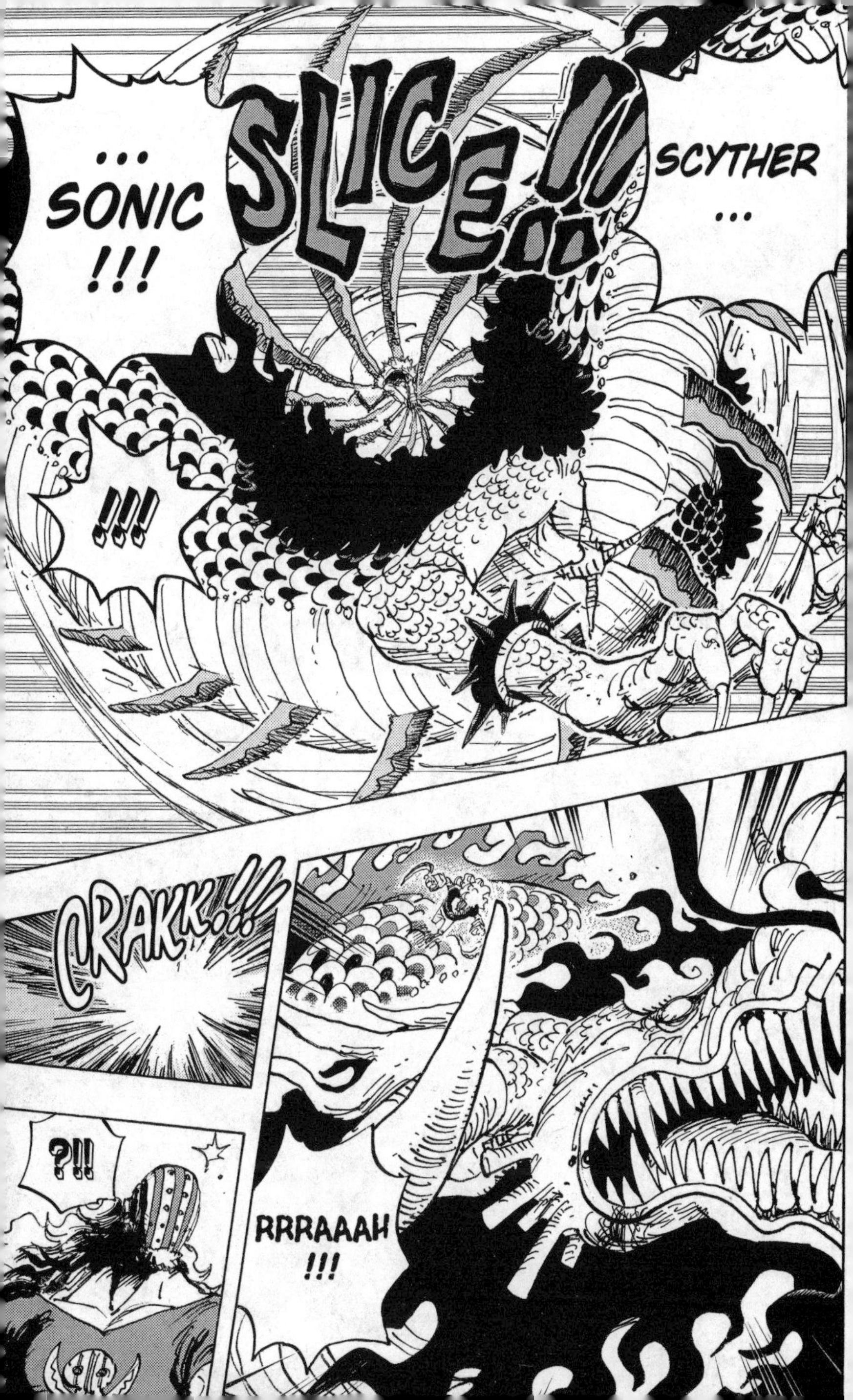
SCYTHER ...
SLICE!!
... SONIC !!!
!!!
RRRAAAH !!!
CRAKK!!
?!!

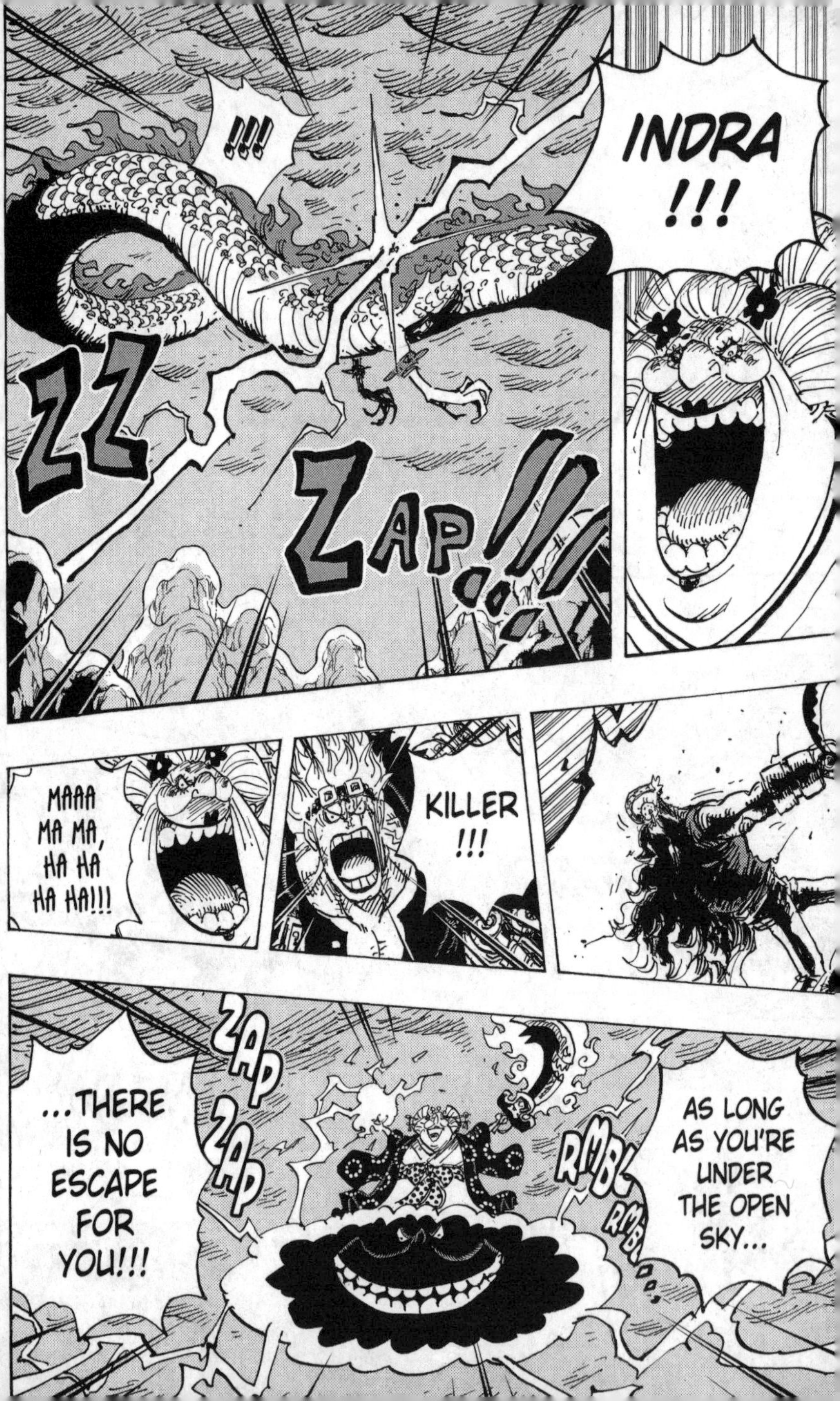
INDRA !!!
!!!
ZZ
ZAP!!
KILLER !!!
MAAA MA MA, HA HA HA HA!!!
AS LONG AS YOU'RE UNDER THE OPEN SKY...
RMBL
RMBL
ZAP
ZAP
...THERE IS NO ESCAPE FOR YOU!!!

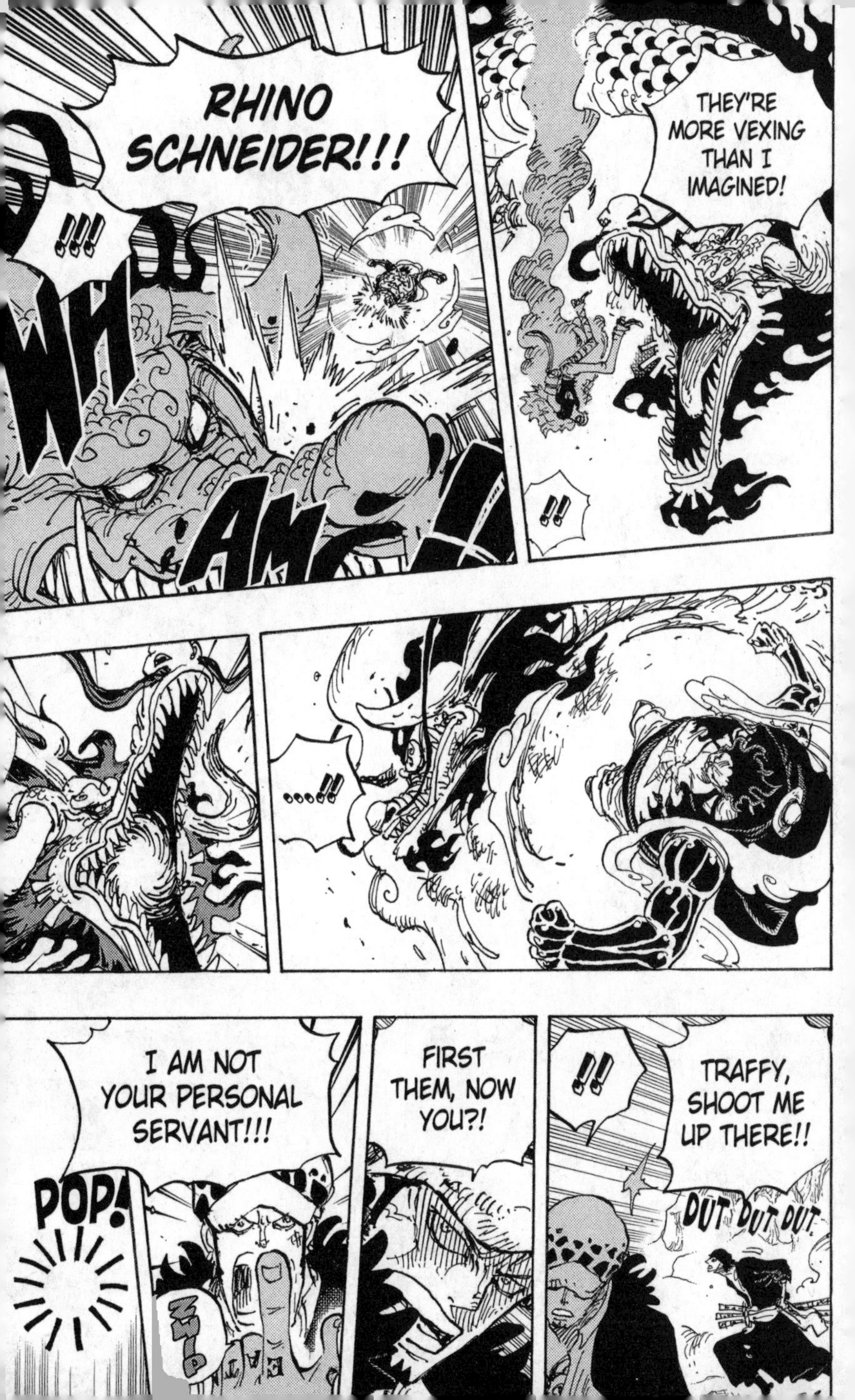
THEY'RE MORE VEXING THAN I IMAGINED!
!!
RHINO SCHNEIDER!!!
!!!
....!!
!!
TRAFFY, SHOOT ME UP THERE!!
DUT DUT DUT
FIRST THEM, NOW YOU?!
I AM NOT YOUR PERSONAL SERVANT!!!
POP!

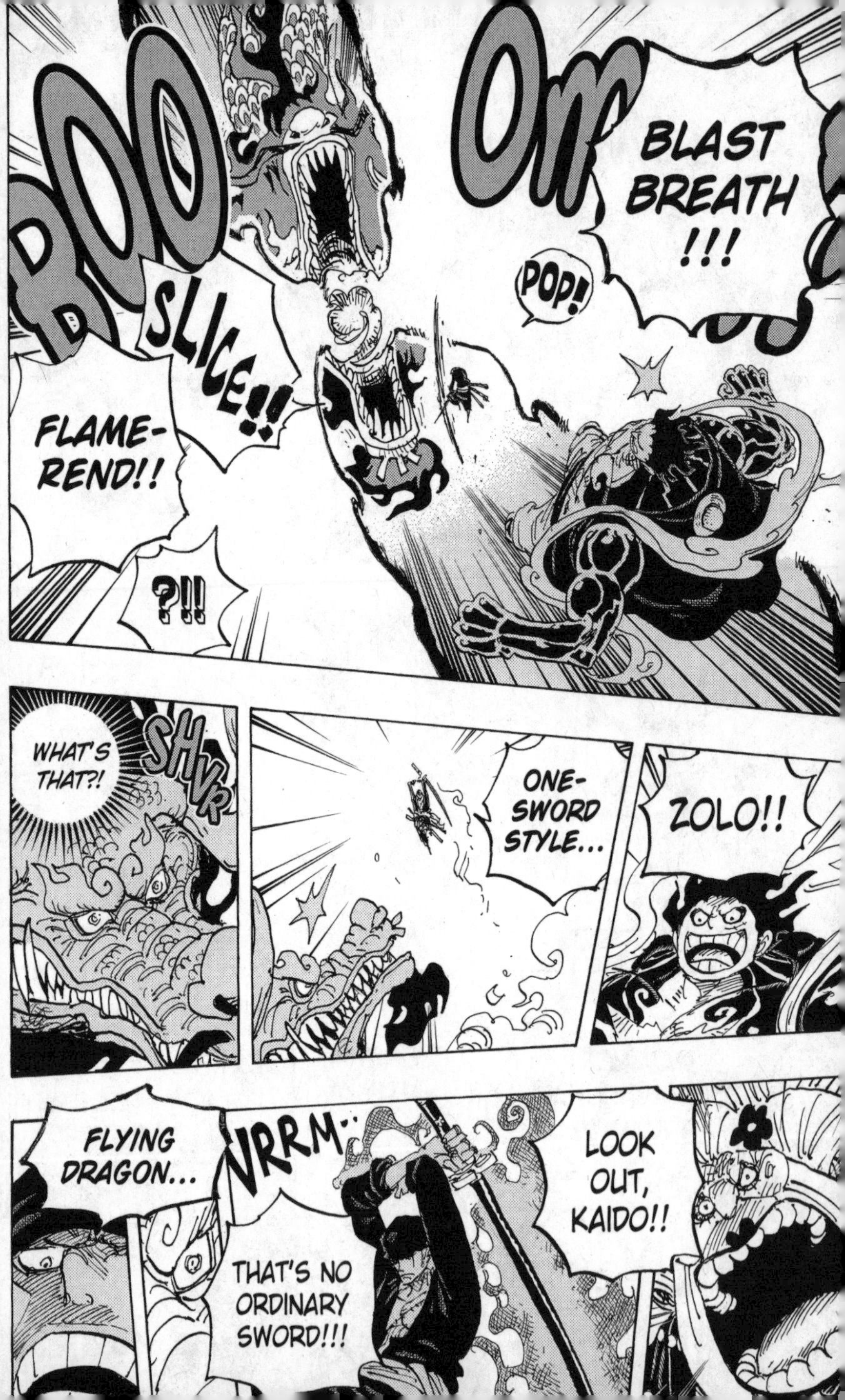
BLAST BREATH!!!
BOOOM
POP!
SLICE!!
FLAME-REND!!
?!!
ZOLO!!
ONE-SWORD STYLE...
WHAT'S THAT?!
SHVR
LOOK OUT, KAIDO!!
THAT'S NO ORDINARY SWORD!!!
VRRM
FLYING DRAGON...

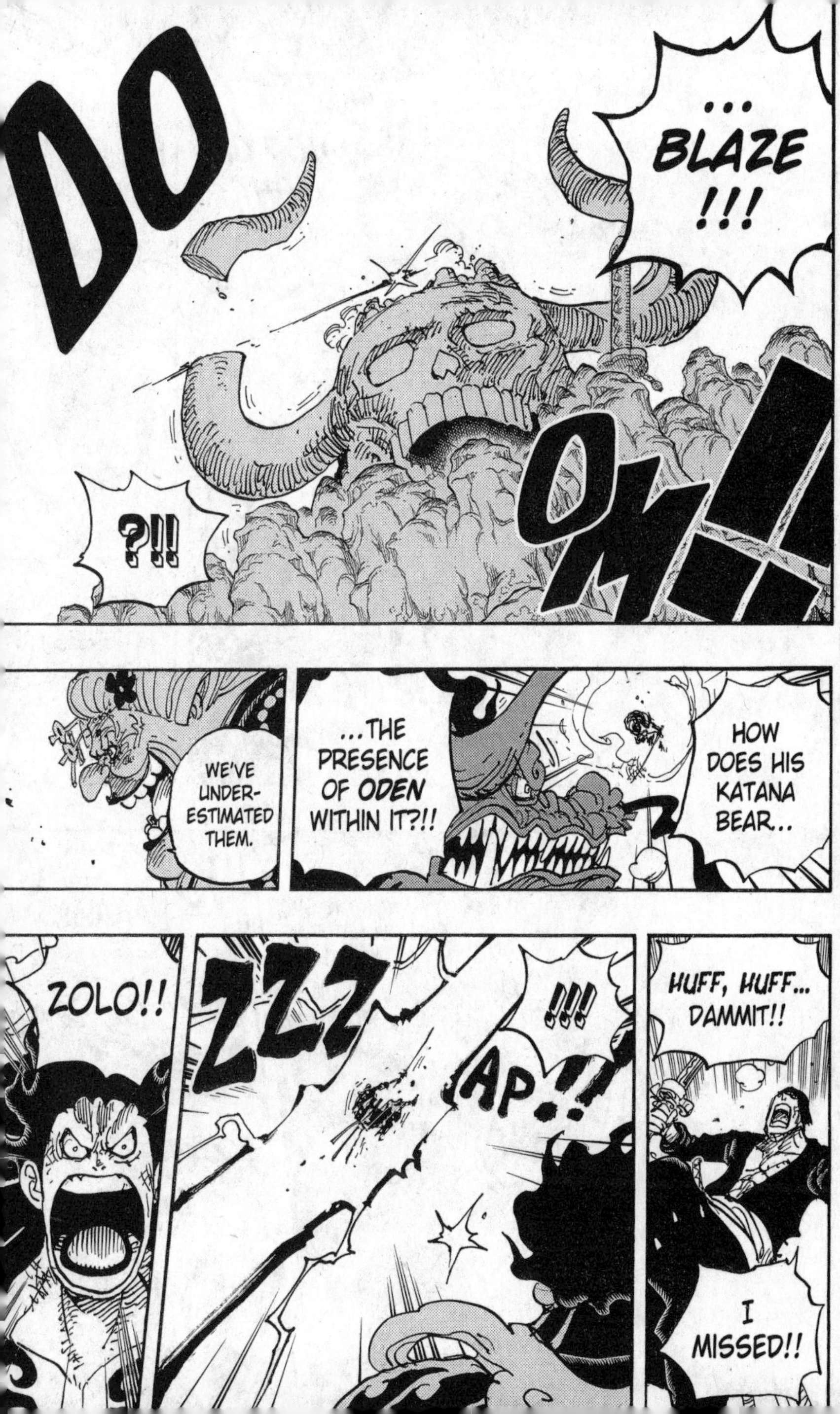

...BLAZE !!!
DO
OM!!
?!!
HOW DOES HIS KATANA BEAR...
...THE PRESENCE OF ODEN WITHIN IT?!!
WE'VE UNDER-ESTIMATED THEM.
HUFF, HUFF... DAMMIT!!
I MISSED!!
!!!
ZZZ
AP!!
ZOLO!!

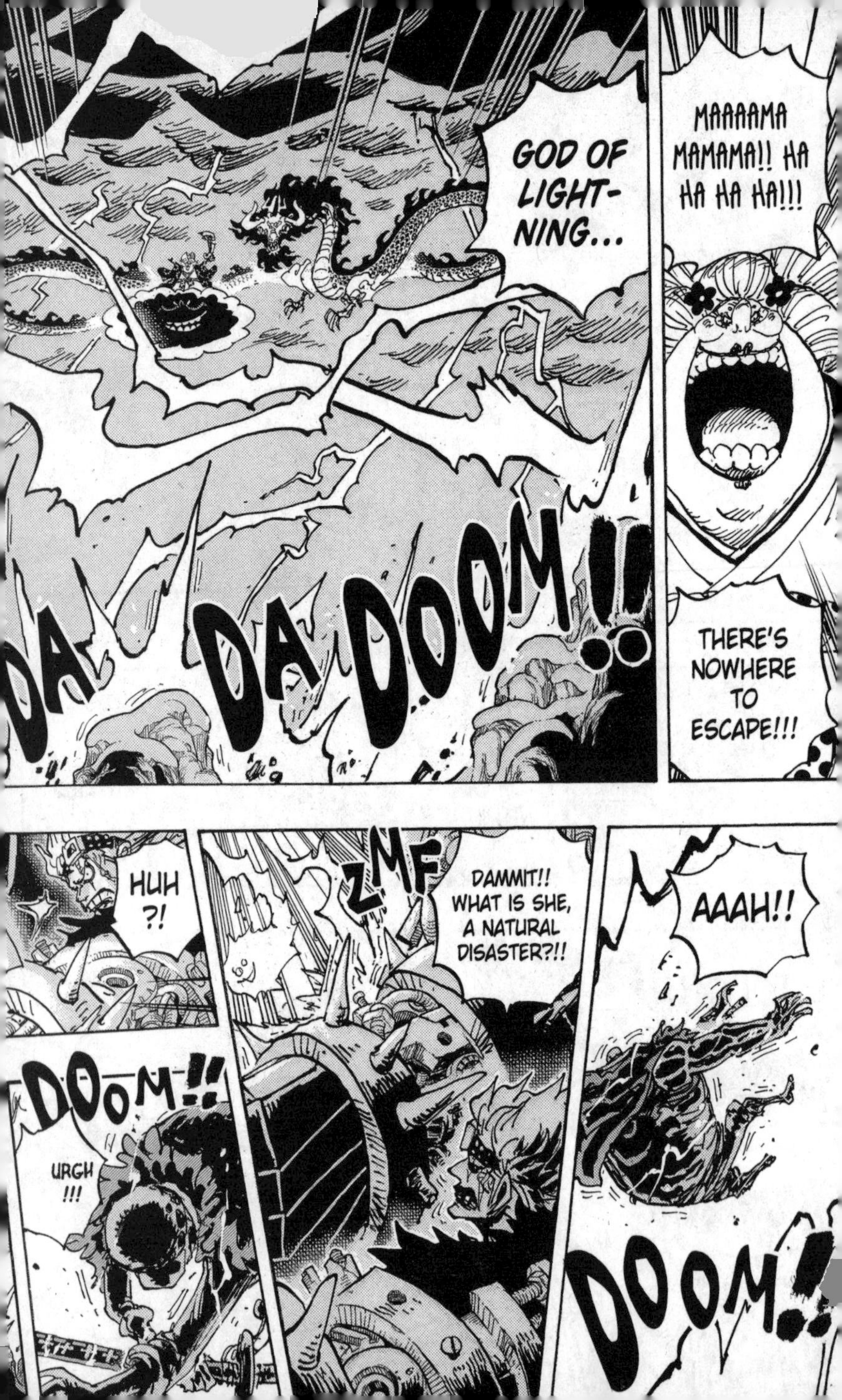

MAAAAMA MAMAMA!! HA HA HA HA!!!
THERE'S NOWHERE TO ESCAPE!!!
GOD OF LIGHTNING...
DA DA DOOM!!
AAAH!!
DOOM!!
ZMF
DAMMIT!! WHAT IS SHE, A NATURAL DISASTER?!!
HUH ?!
DOOM!!
URGH !!!

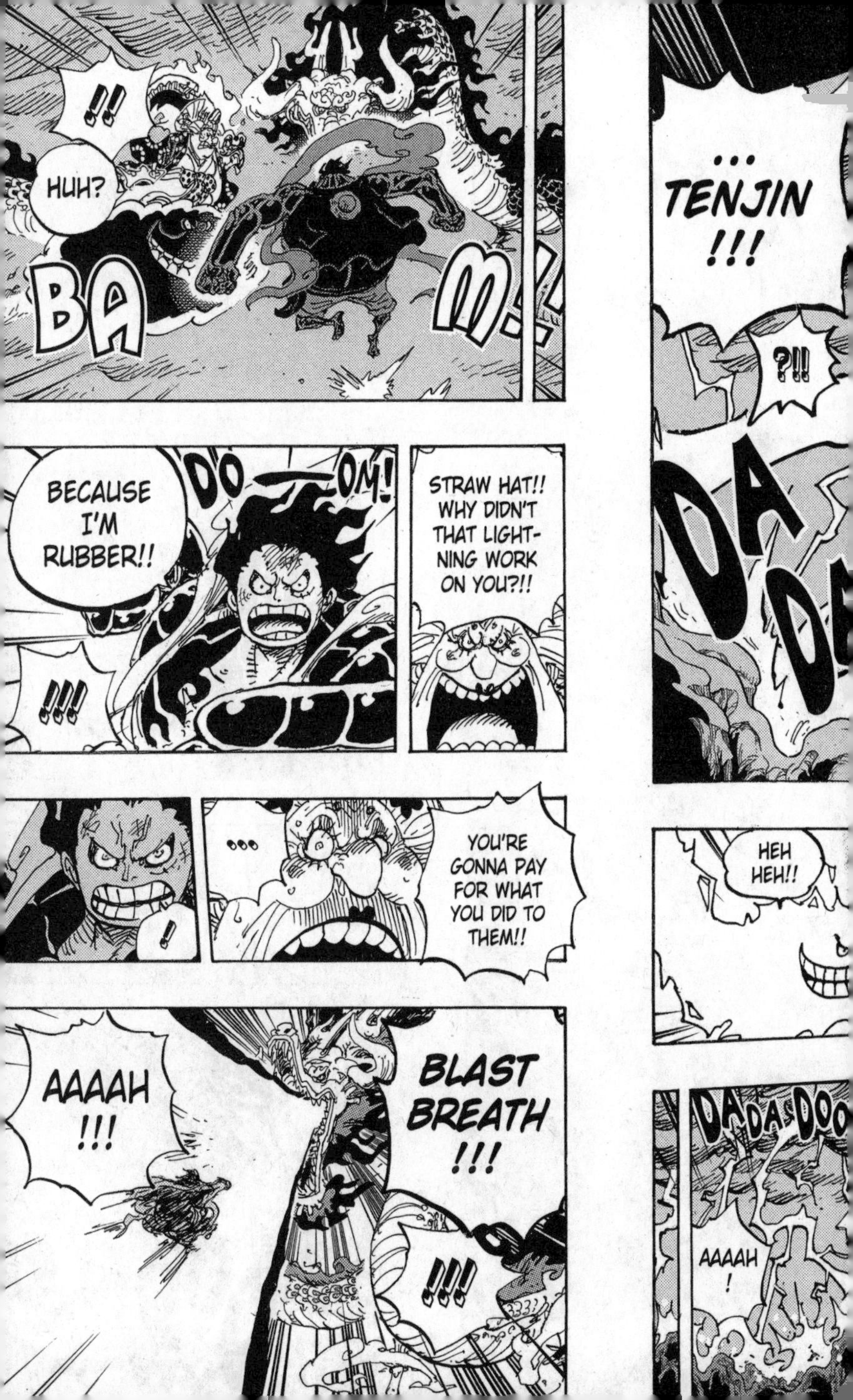
...TENJIN !!!
?!!
DADO
HEH HEH!!
DADASDOO
AAAAH !
!!
HUH?
BAM!!
STRAW HAT!! WHY DIDN'T THAT LIGHT-NING WORK ON YOU?!!
DO—OM!
BECAUSE I'M RUBBER!!
!!!
YOU'RE GONNA PAY FOR WHAT YOU DID TO THEM!!
...
!
BLAST BREATH !!!
AAAAH !!!
!!!

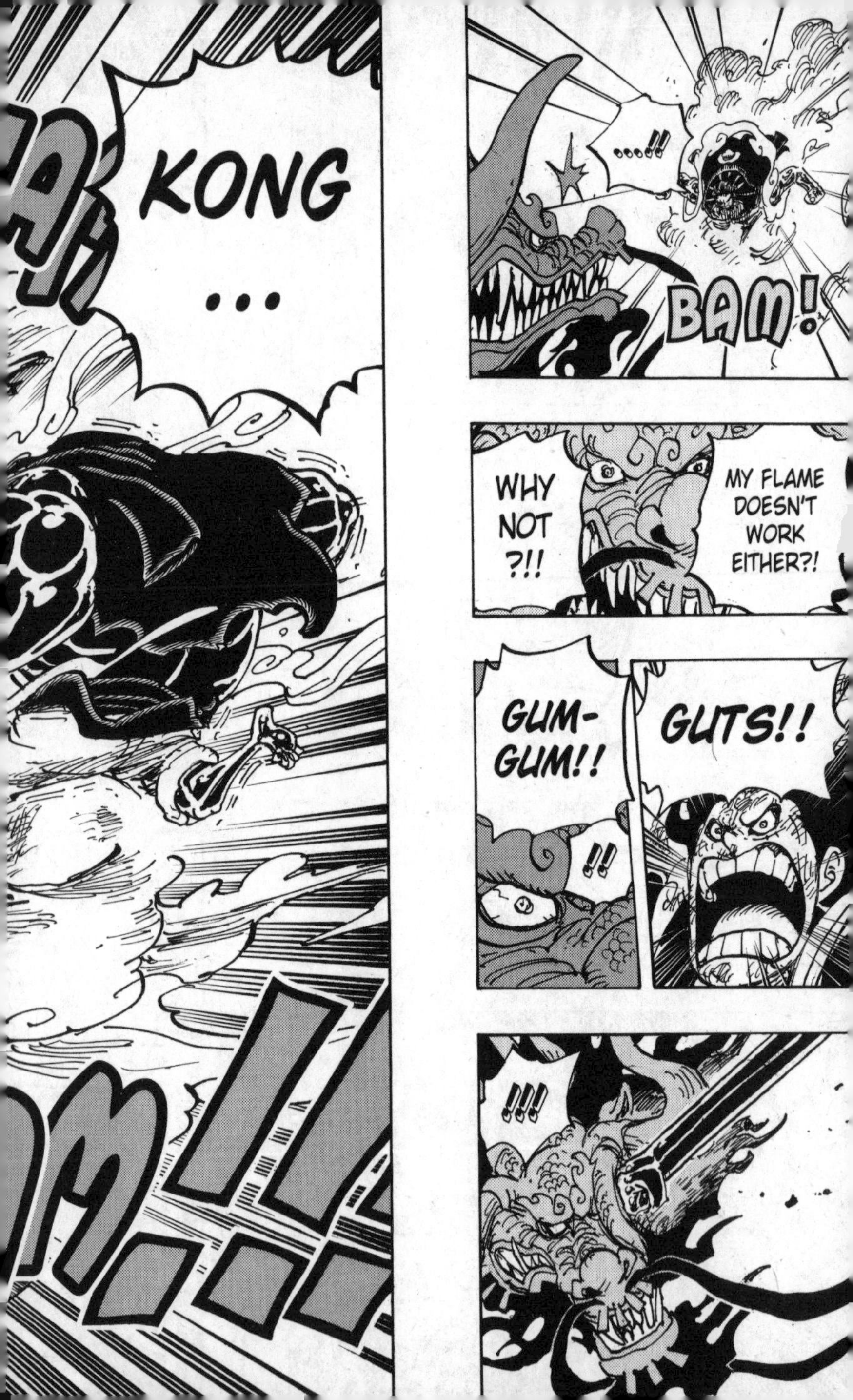
....!!
BAM!
MY FLAME DOESN'T WORK EITHER?!
WHY NOT ?!!
GUTS!!
GUM-GUM!!
!!
!!!
KONG
...

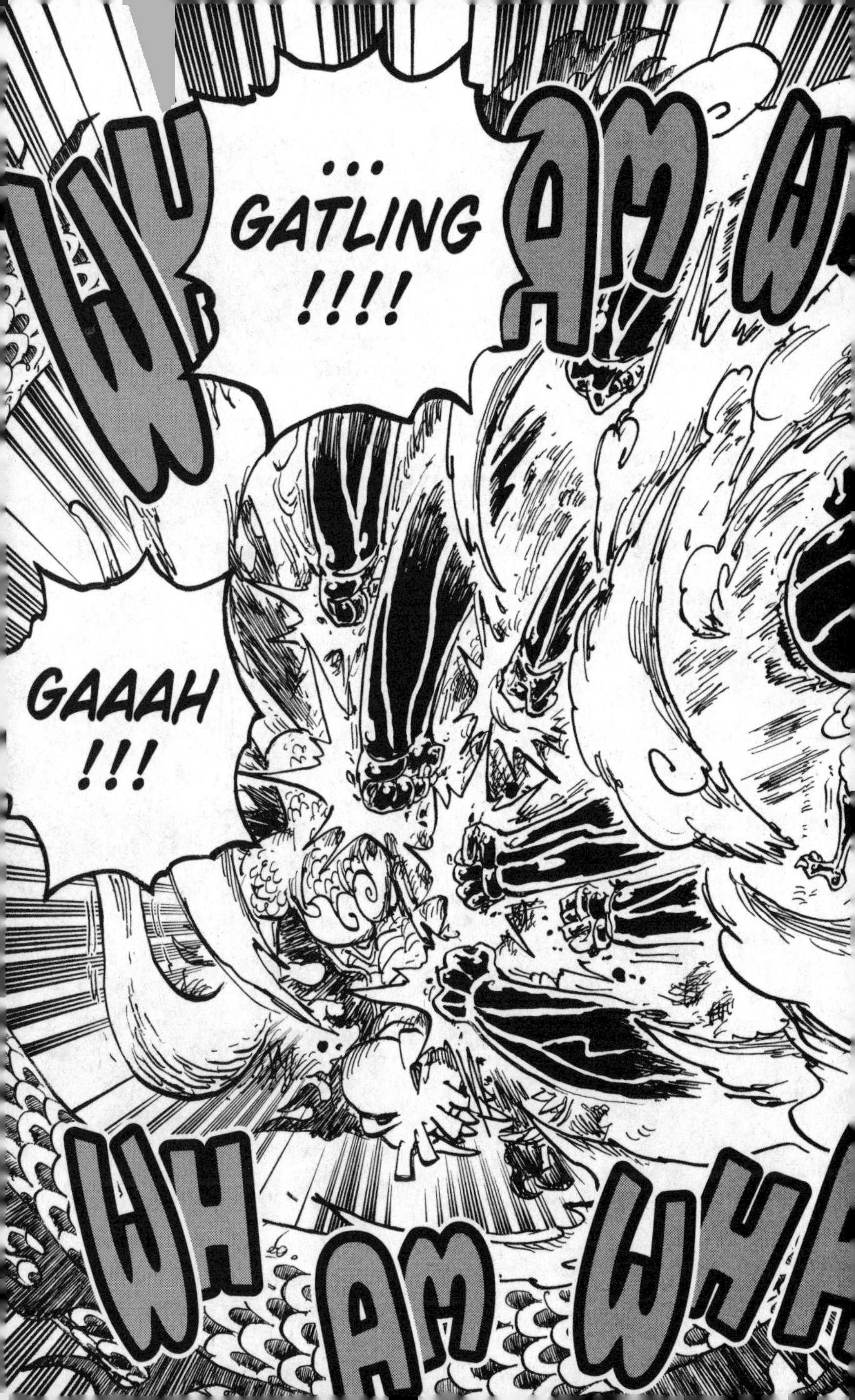
... GATLING !!!!
GAAAH !!!

SBS Question Corner

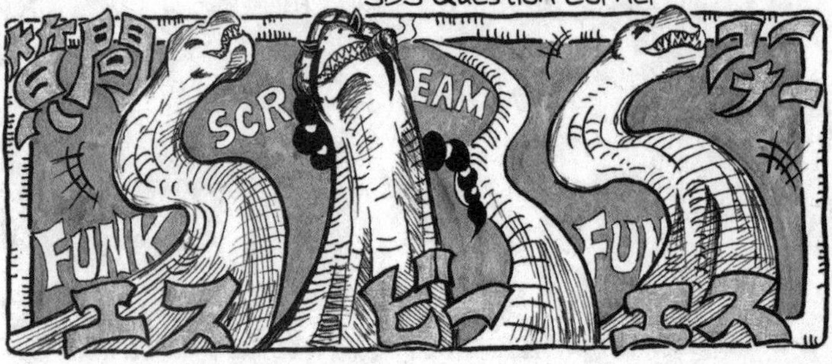
SCR
EAM
FUNK
FUN

(Mr. Anonymous, Tokyo)

Q: Question for Oda Sensei! What are your three favorite Smile user designs?

--Taro

A: Ah, I see. Man, those Smile Fruit users are funny, huh? Are they bozos or what?! Wow, this is a hard question to answer! Well, I'll start with #3 and that's **Speed**, a.k.a. **Horselina**! When you hear the word "centaur," you think of a big burly horse man, but I wanted to make her a sexy lady. Since simple horse legs wouldn't really fit the bill, I tried to emphasize her thighs to look more human, and yet she has that wacky horse face when she smiles. It's the unexpected difference between the two sides that makes her lovable.

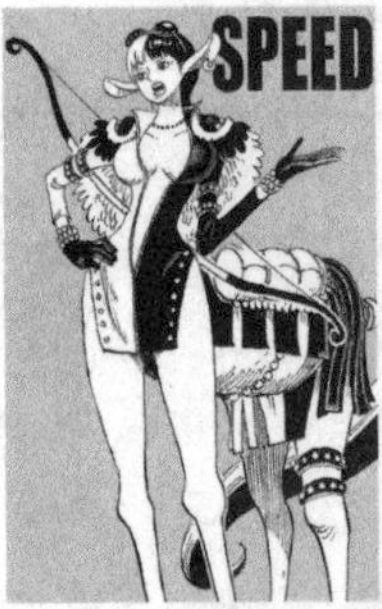
SPEED

Next up, #2! The signature member of the "Why are you growing that way?" series, **Hamlet**!! The poor giraffe neck is trembling from supporting his weight. It's an absolute failure of biology, and yet his speech is very positive and princely. You gotta love this guy.

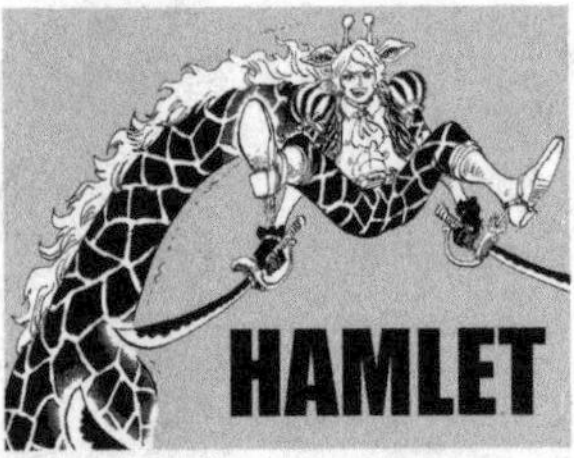
HAMLET

Lastly, #1!! The man with the lion on his tummy, **Holdem**! You might say that the entire reason I invented the Smile Fruits was to draw this man. A long time ago, there was a robot anime called *Future Robot Daltanious*. It had a lion robot and a human robot that fused together into a bigger robot with the lion's face on its chest!! When I was a kid, it was the coolest thing. I wanted the Chogokin figure so bad! And that desire led me to create this character here in my own story!! LOL. Oh, that reminds me that I also loved a centaur robot toy called Daibajin. Maybe that's why I like Horselina so much? Basically, all Smile users are combining robots!! They're awesome!!

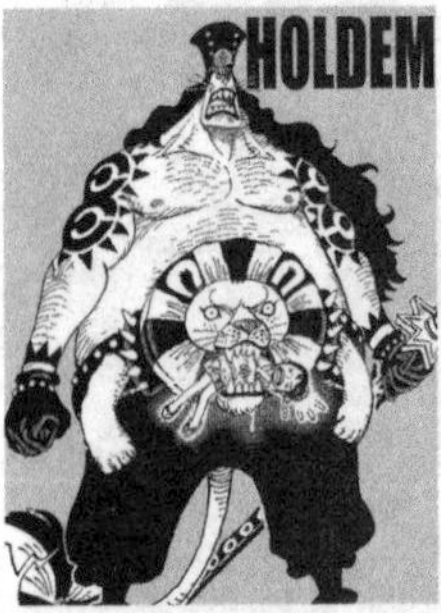
HOLDEM

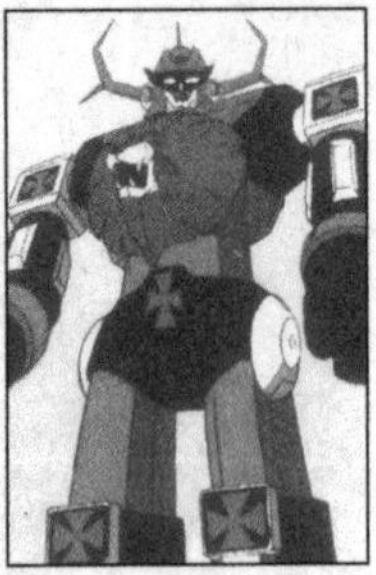

© Toei

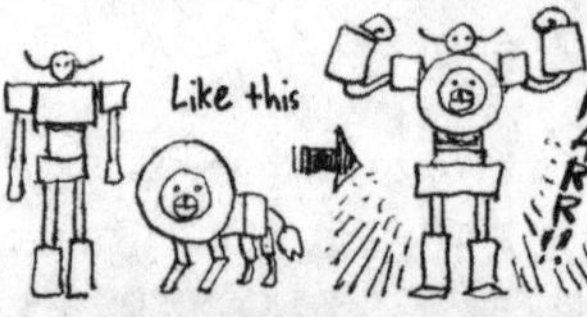
Like this
RARR!!

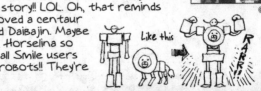

Chapter 1003:
NIGHT ON THE BOARD

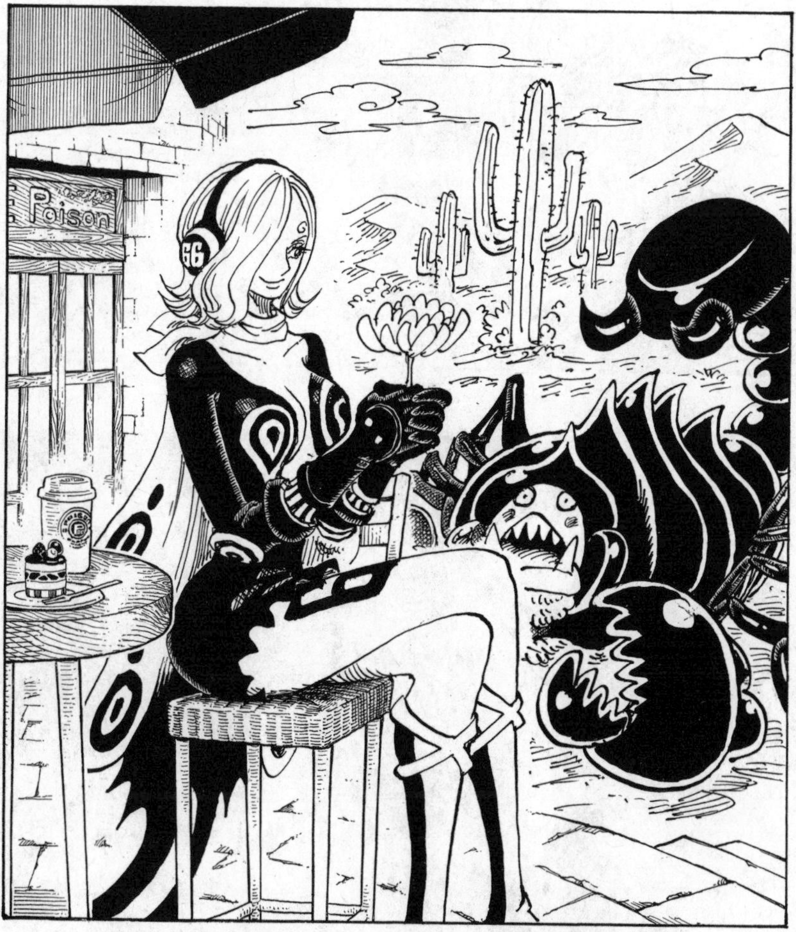
Poison

READER REQUEST: "REIJU RECEIVING THE AFFECTIONS OF A SCORPION WITH A CACTUS FLOWER" BY NODA SKYWALKER

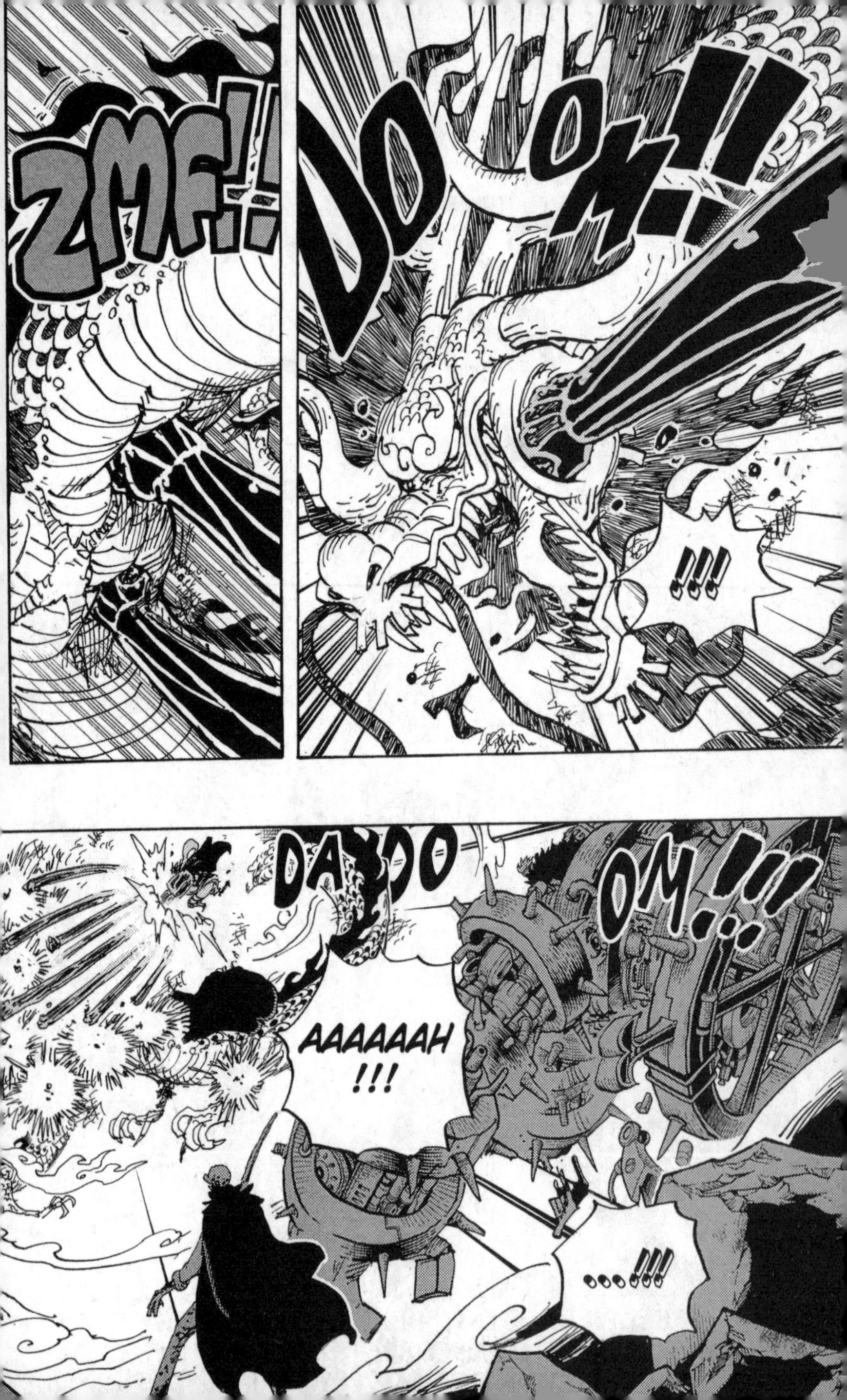
DOON!!
!!!
ZMF!!
DADOOM!!!
AAAAAH!!!
...!!!

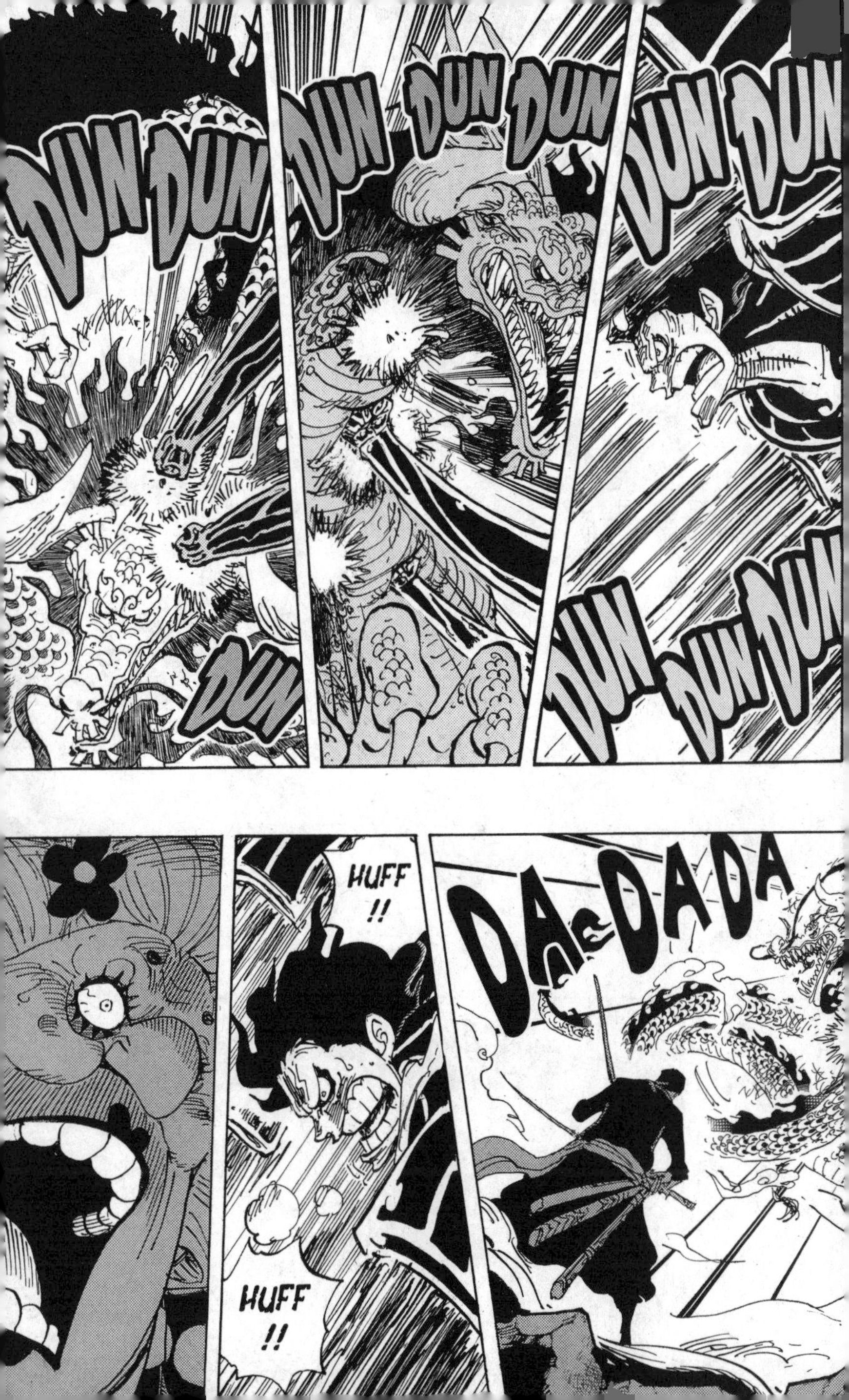
DUN DUN
DUN DUN DUN
DUN DUN DUN
DUN DUN
DUN
DADADA
HUFF !!
HUFF !!

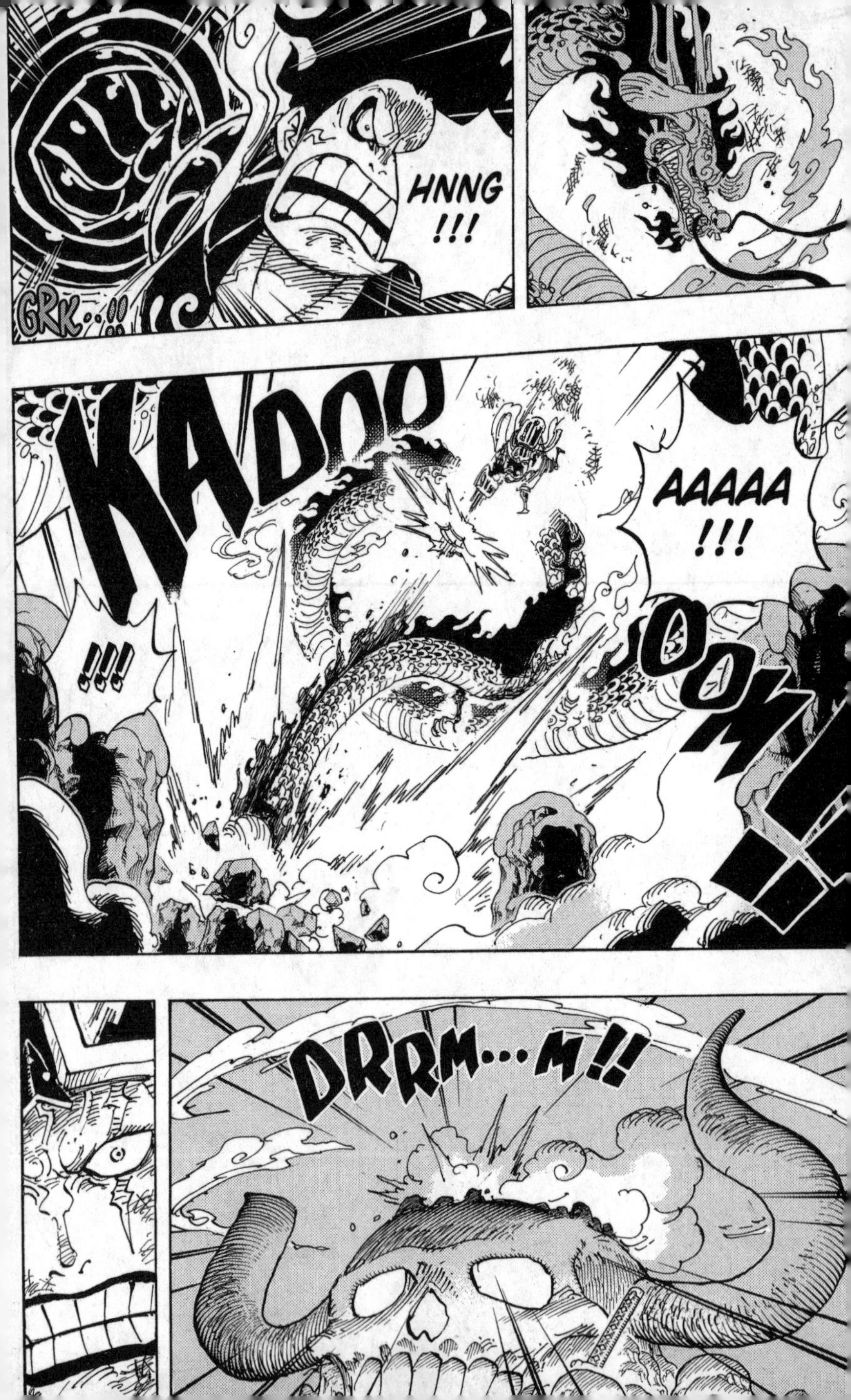
HNNG !!!
GRK..!!
AAAAA !!!
KADOO
OOOM!!
!!!
DRRM...M!!

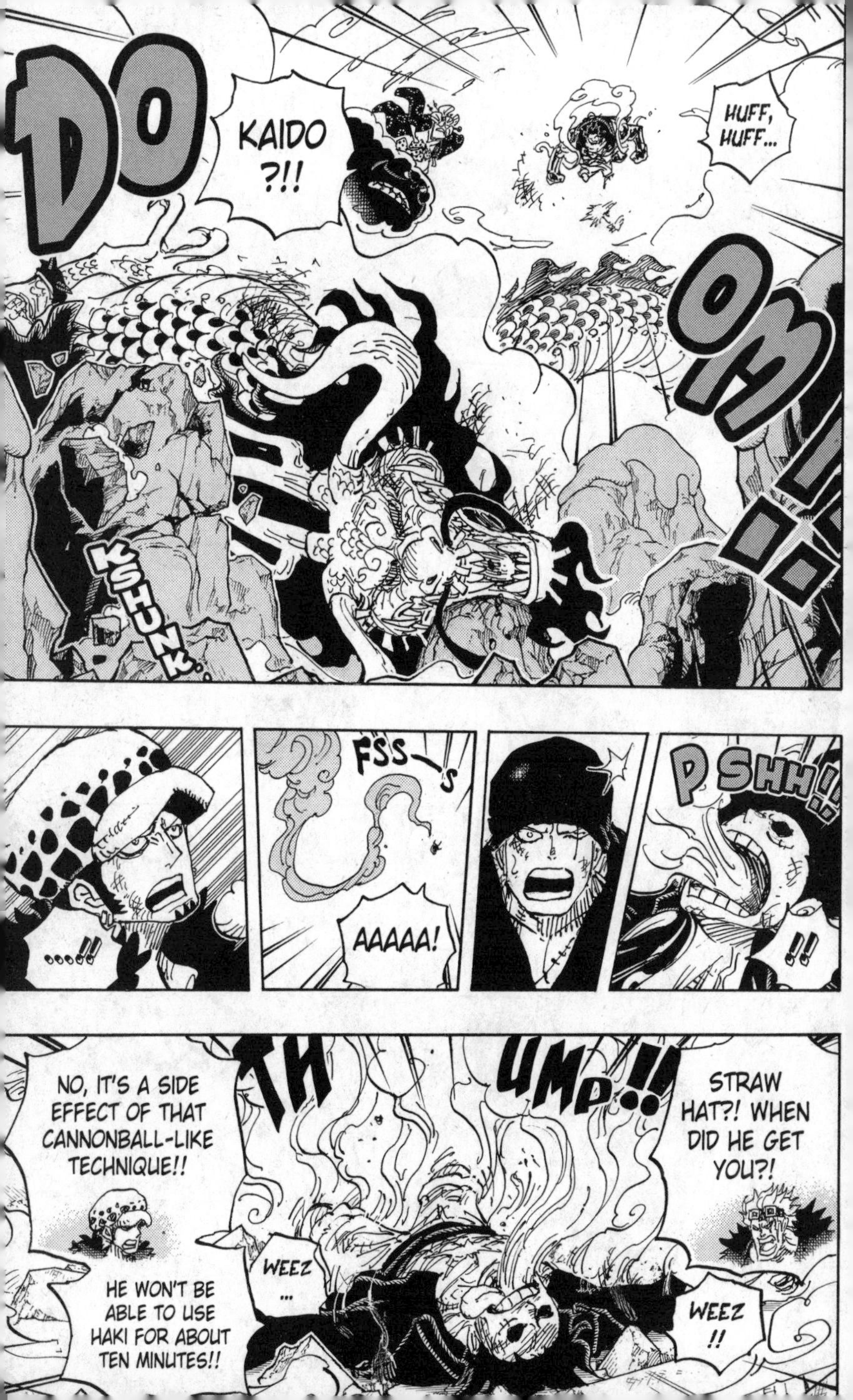
DOOM!!
HUFF, HUFF...
KAIDO ?!!
KSHUNK
PSHH!!
!!
FSS—S
AAAAA!
....!!
STRAW HAT?! WHEN DID HE GET YOU?!
WEEZ !!
THUMP!!
WEEZ ...
NO, IT'S A SIDE EFFECT OF THAT CANNONBALL-LIKE TECHNIQUE!!
HE WON'T BE ABLE TO USE HAKI FOR ABOUT TEN MINUTES!!

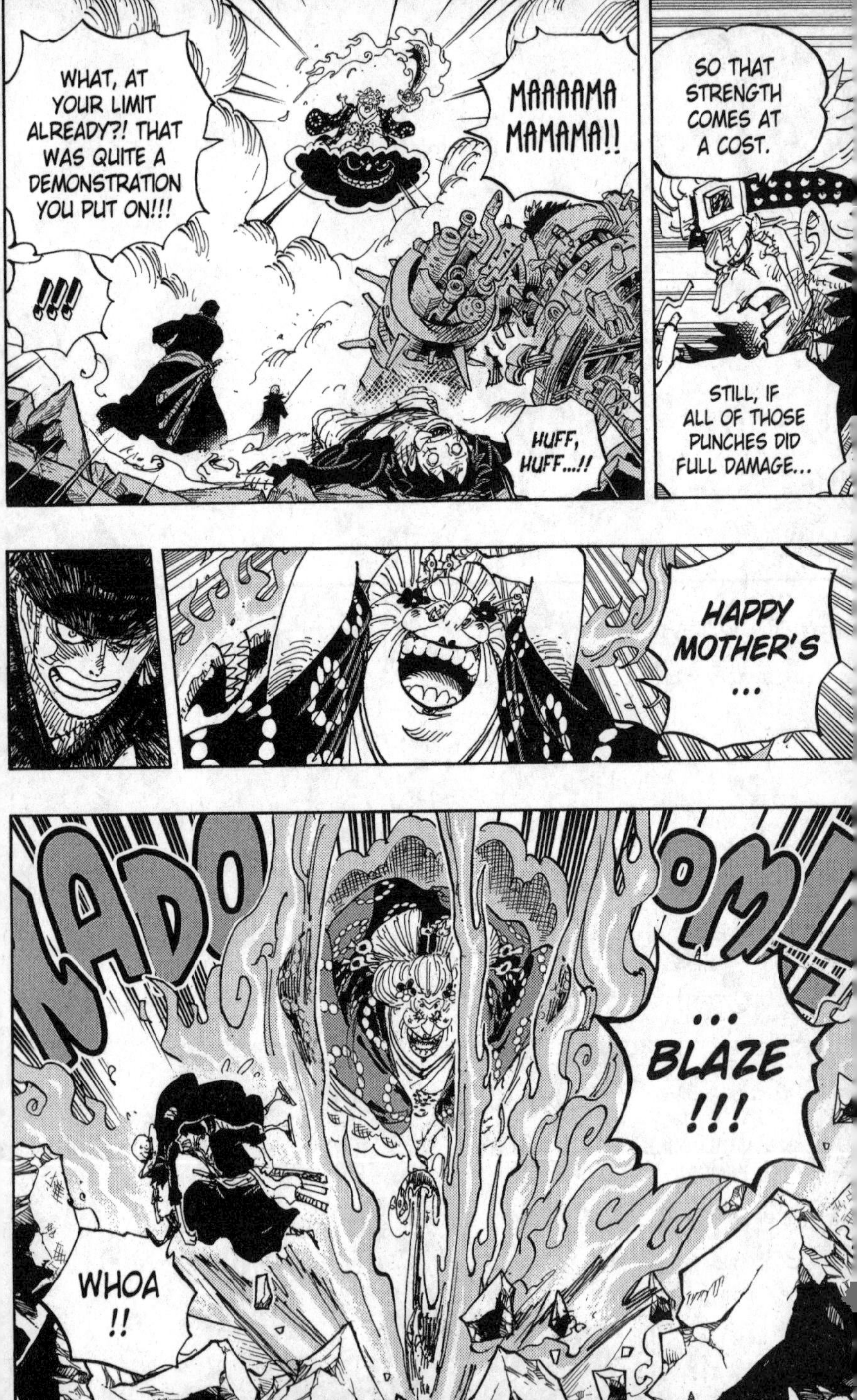
SO THAT STRENGTH COMES AT A COST.
STILL, IF ALL OF THOSE PUNCHES DID FULL DAMAGE...
MAAAAMA MAMAMA!!
WHAT, AT YOUR LIMIT ALREADY?! THAT WAS QUITE A DEMONSTRATION YOU PUT ON!!!
!!!
HUFF, HUFF...!!
HAPPY MOTHER'S ...
... BLAZE !!!
WHOA !!

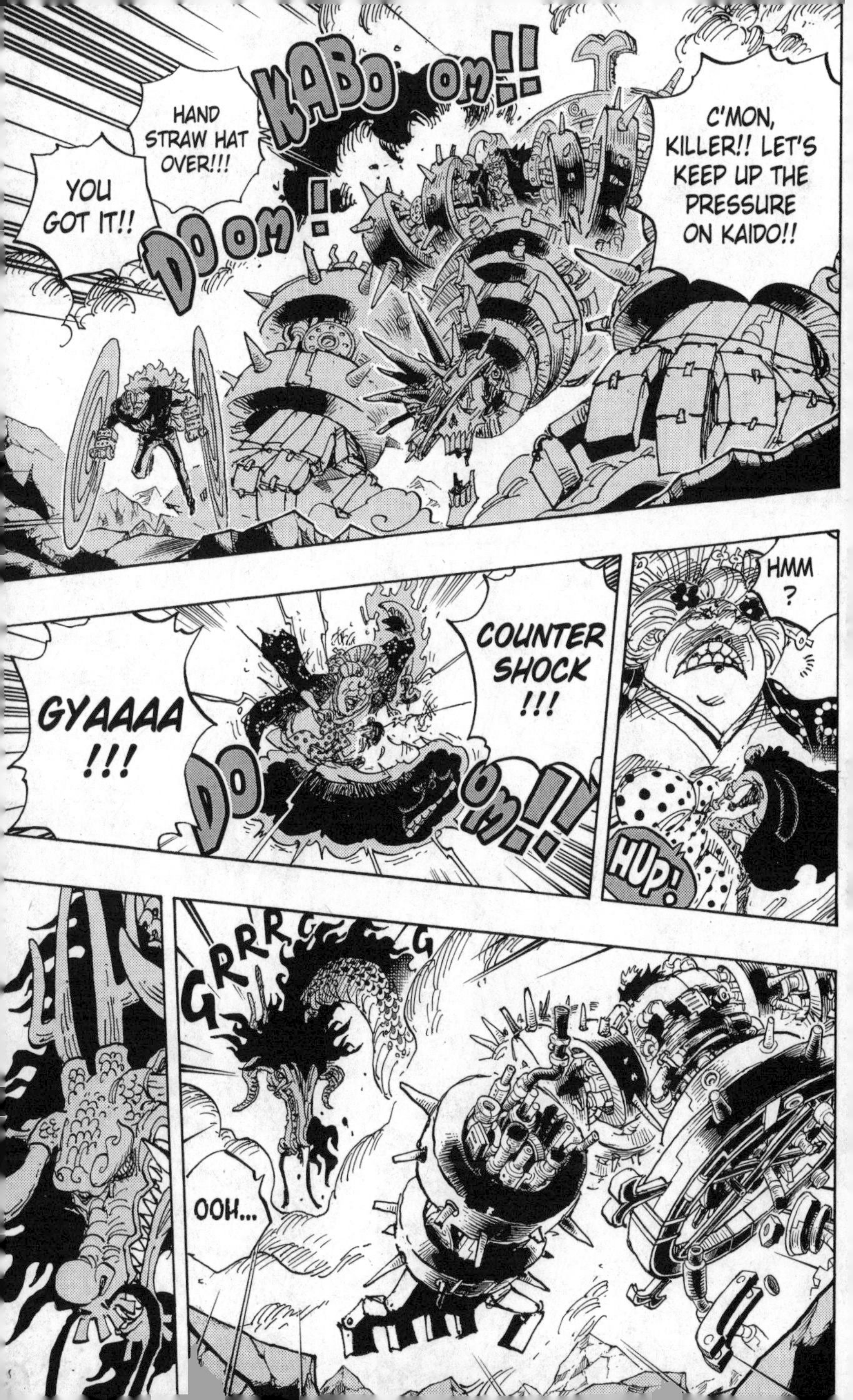
C'MON, KILLER!! LET'S KEEP UP THE PRESSURE ON KAIDO!!
KABOOM!!
DOOM!!
HAND STRAW HAT OVER!!!
YOU GOT IT!!
HMM?
HUP!
COUNTER SHOCK!!!
DOOM!!
GYAAAA!!!
GRRRG G
OOH...

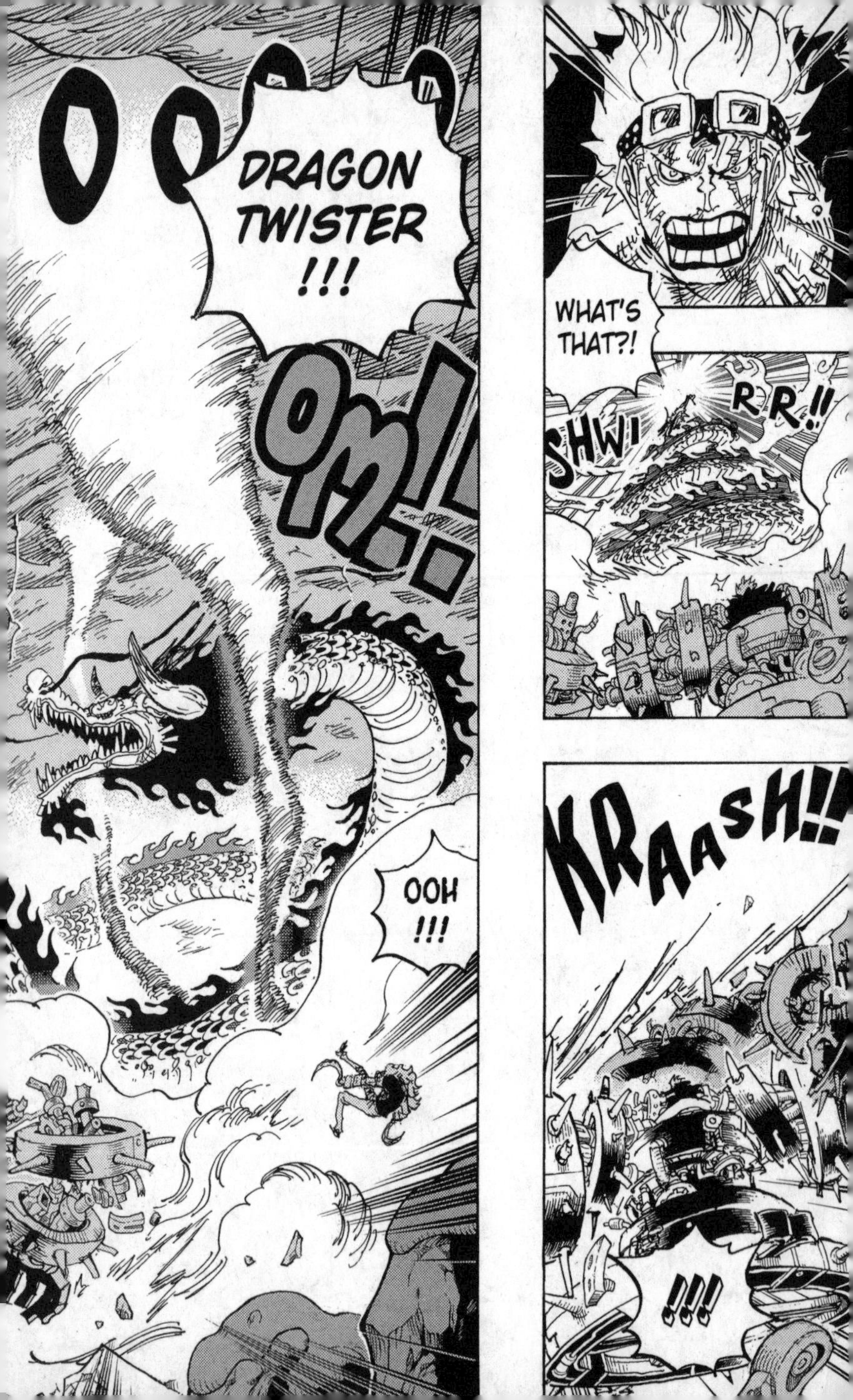
WHAT'S THAT?!
SHWI RR!!
KRAASH!!
!!!
DRAGON TWISTER !!!
OOH !!!

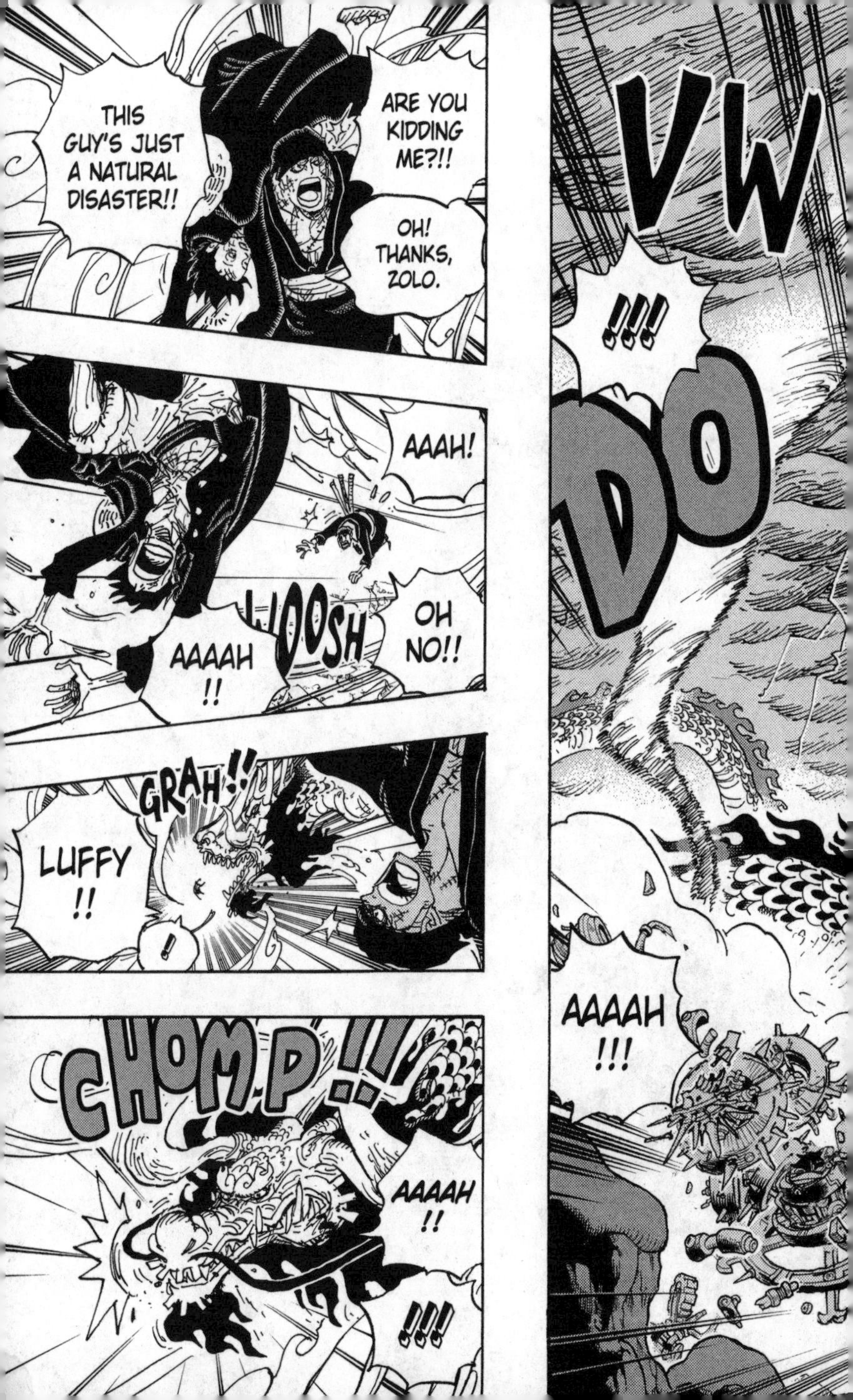
VW
!!!
DO
AAAAH
!!!
ARE YOU KIDDING ME?!!
THIS GUY'S JUST A NATURAL DISASTER!!
OH! THANKS, ZOLO.
AAAH!
OH NO!!
WOOSH
AAAAH
!!
GRAH!!
LUFFY
!!
!
CHOMP!!!
AAAAH
!!
!!!

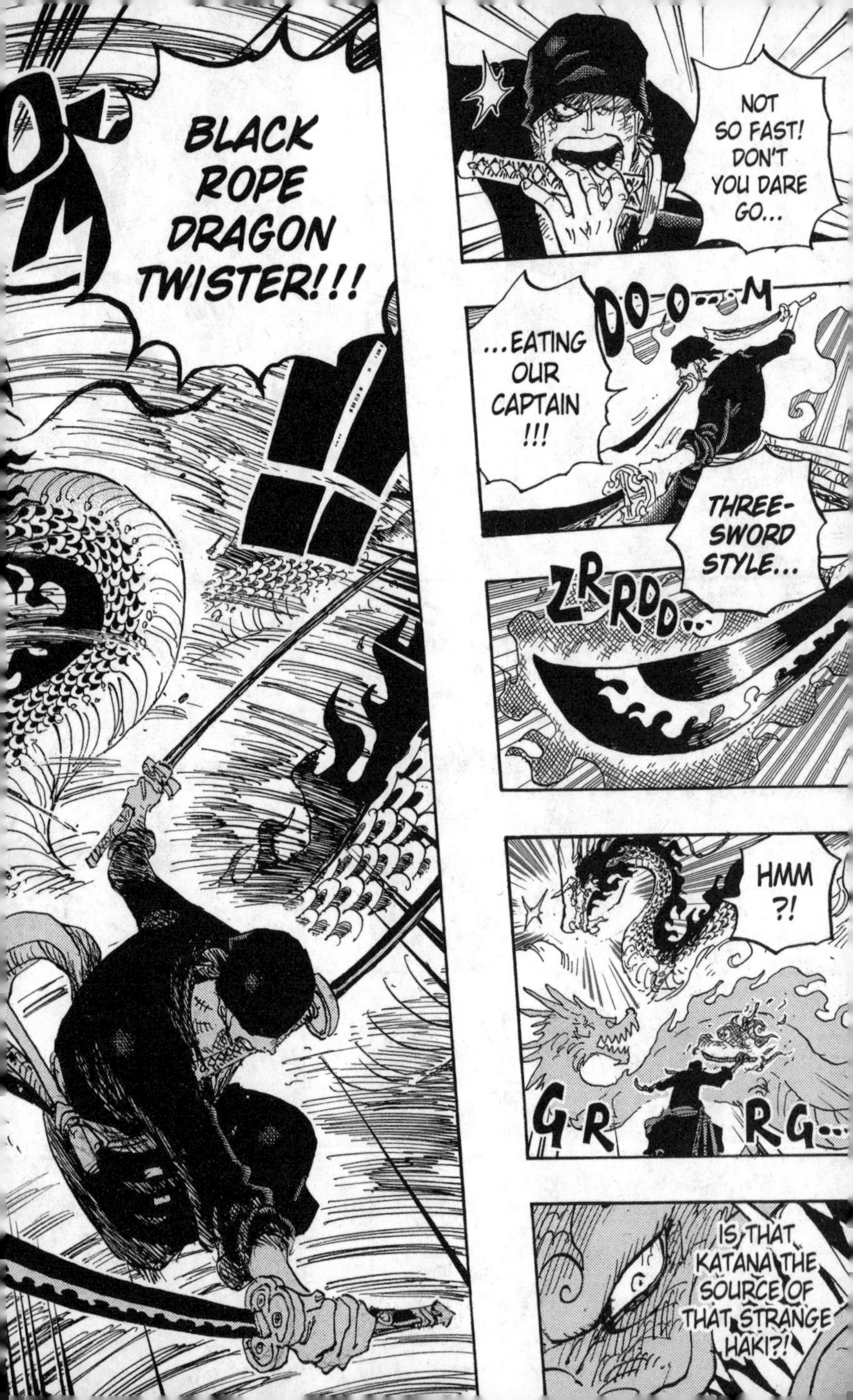
NOT SO FAST! DON'T YOU DARE GO...
DOO-O-...M
...EATING OUR CAPTAIN !!!
THREE-SWORD STYLE...
ZRRDD...
HMM ?!
GR RG...
IS THAT KATANA THE SOURCE OF THAT STRANGE HAKI?!
BLACK ROPE DRAGON TWISTER!!!

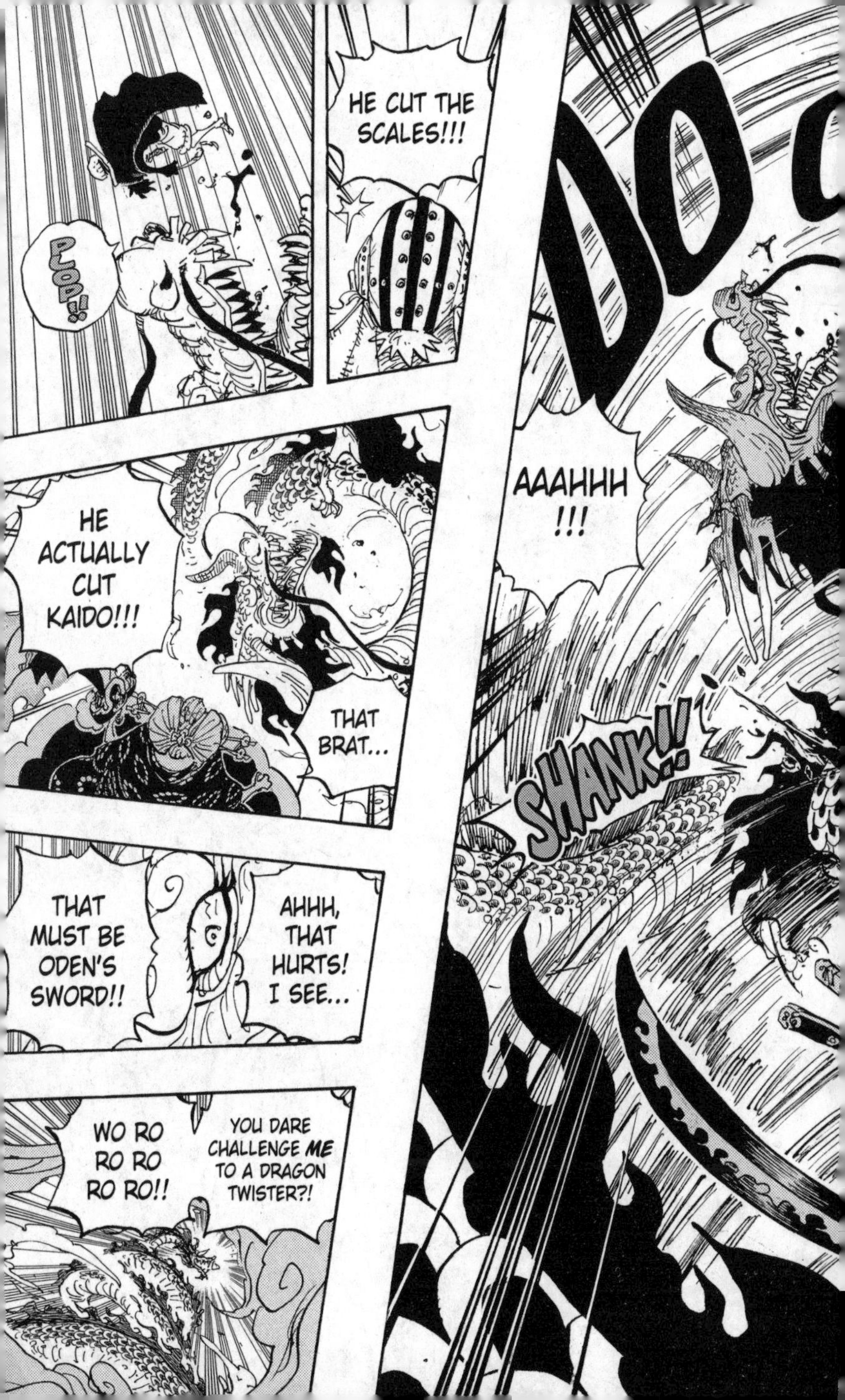
AAAHHH !!!
SHANK!!
HE CUT THE SCALES!!!
PLOP!!
HE ACTUALLY CUT KAIDO!!!
THAT BRAT...
AHHH, THAT HURTS! I SEE...
THAT MUST BE ODEN'S SWORD!!
YOU DARE CHALLENGE *ME* TO A DRAGON TWISTER?!
WO RO RO RO RO RO!!

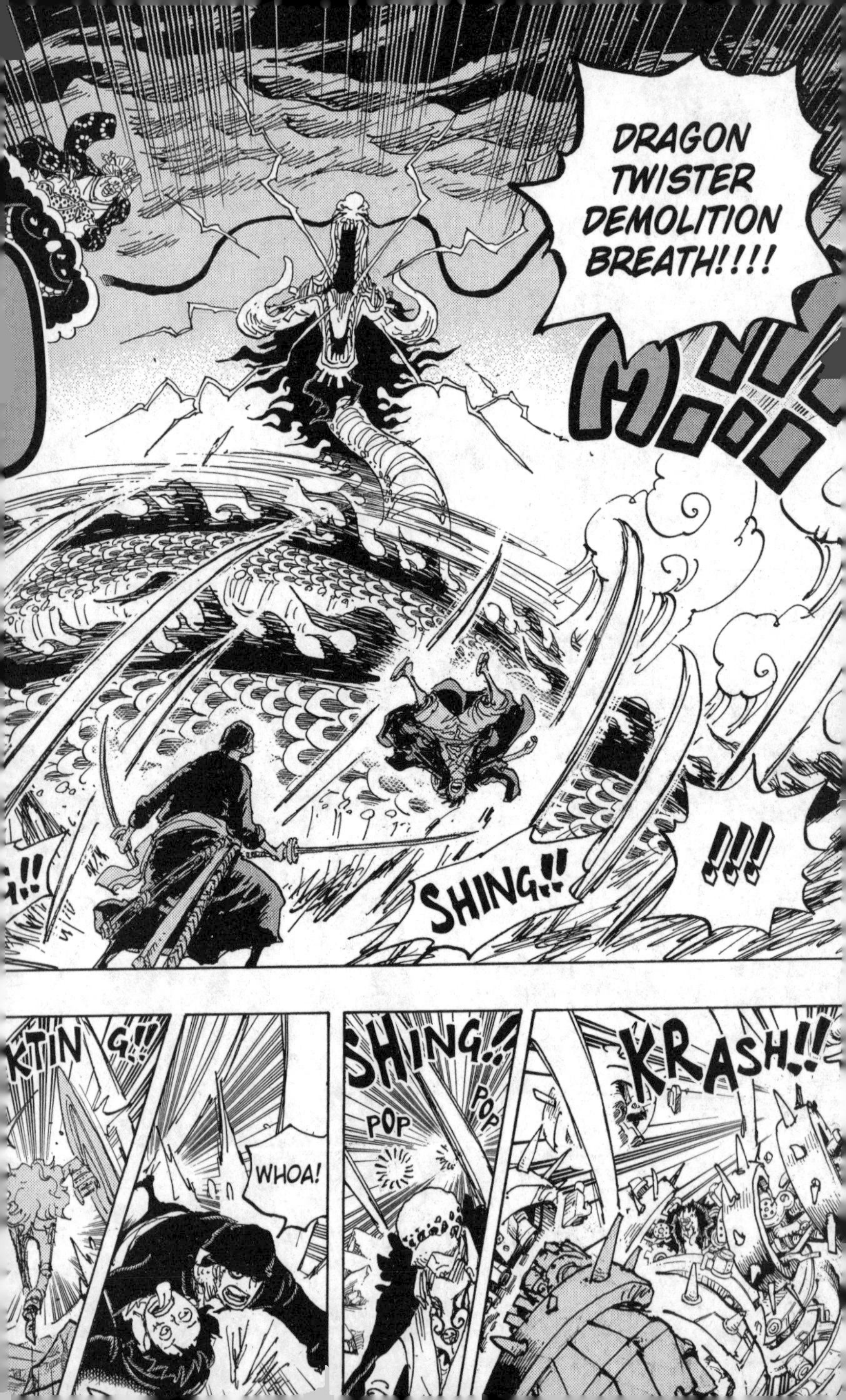
DRAGON TWISTER DEMOLITION BREATH!!!!
!!!
SHING!!
KRASH!!
SHING!!
POP
POP
WHOA!
KTING!!

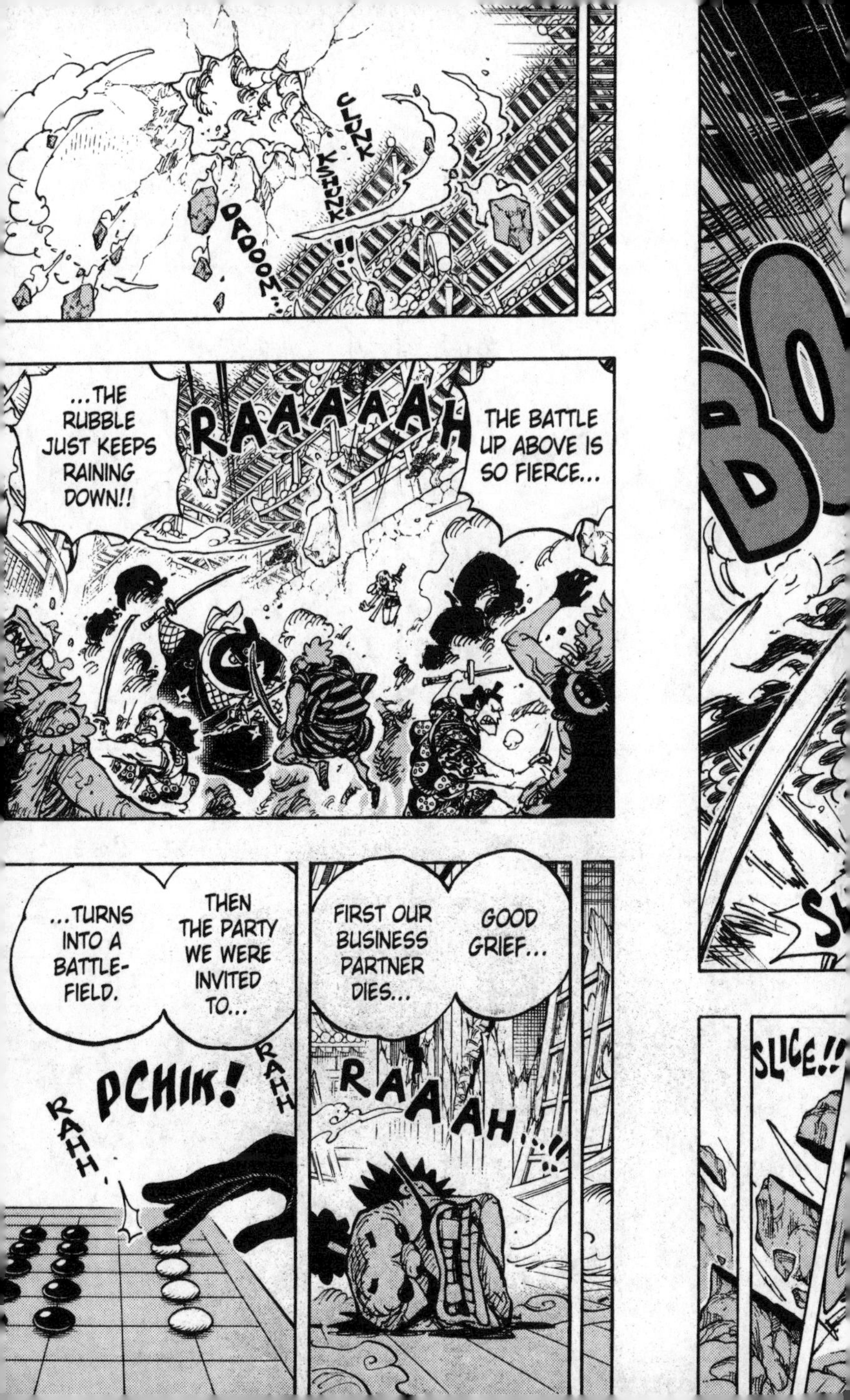
BO
SH
SLICE!!
CLUNK
KSHUNK!!
DADOOM...
THE BATTLE UP ABOVE IS SO FIERCE...
RAAAAAH
...THE RUBBLE JUST KEEPS RAINING DOWN!!
GOOD GRIEF...
FIRST OUR BUSINESS PARTNER DIES...
RAAAH...!!
THEN THE PARTY WE WERE INVITED TO...
...TURNS INTO A BATTLE-FIELD.
RAHH
PCHIK!
RAHH

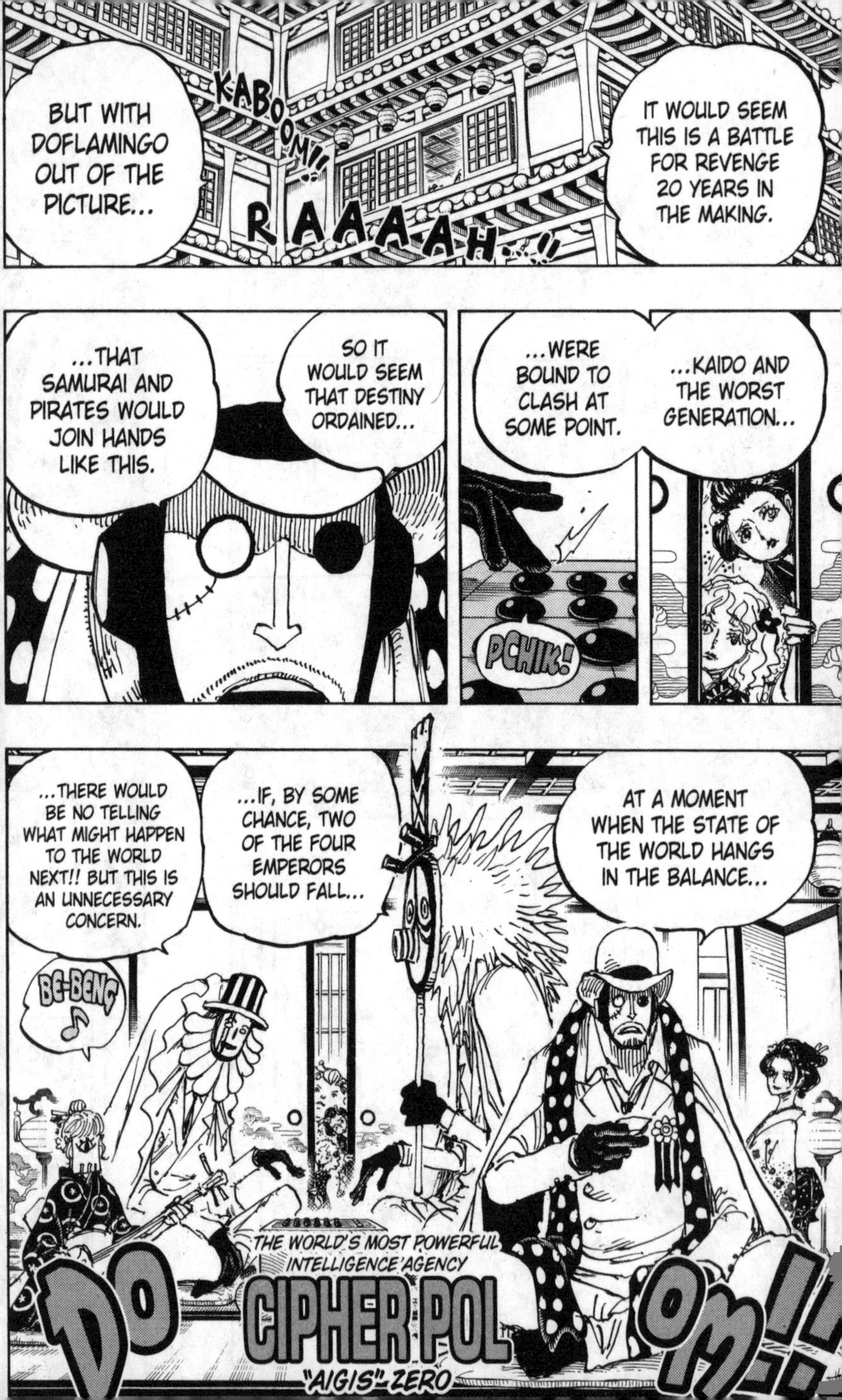
IT WOULD SEEM THIS IS A BATTLE FOR REVENGE 20 YEARS IN THE MAKING.
KABOOM!!
RAAAAH!!
BUT WITH DOFLAMINGO OUT OF THE PICTURE...
...KAIDO AND THE WORST GENERATION...
...WERE BOUND TO CLASH AT SOME POINT.
PCHIK!
SO IT WOULD SEEM THAT DESTINY ORDAINED...
...THAT SAMURAI AND PIRATES WOULD JOIN HANDS LIKE THIS.
AT A MOMENT WHEN THE STATE OF THE WORLD HANGS IN THE BALANCE...
...IF, BY SOME CHANCE, TWO OF THE FOUR EMPERORS SHOULD FALL...
...THERE WOULD BE NO TELLING WHAT MIGHT HAPPEN TO THE WORLD NEXT!! BUT THIS IS AN UNNECESSARY CONCERN.
BE-BENG ♪
THE WORLD'S MOST POWERFUL INTELLIGENCE AGENCY
CIPHER POL
"AIGIS" ZERO
DOOM!!

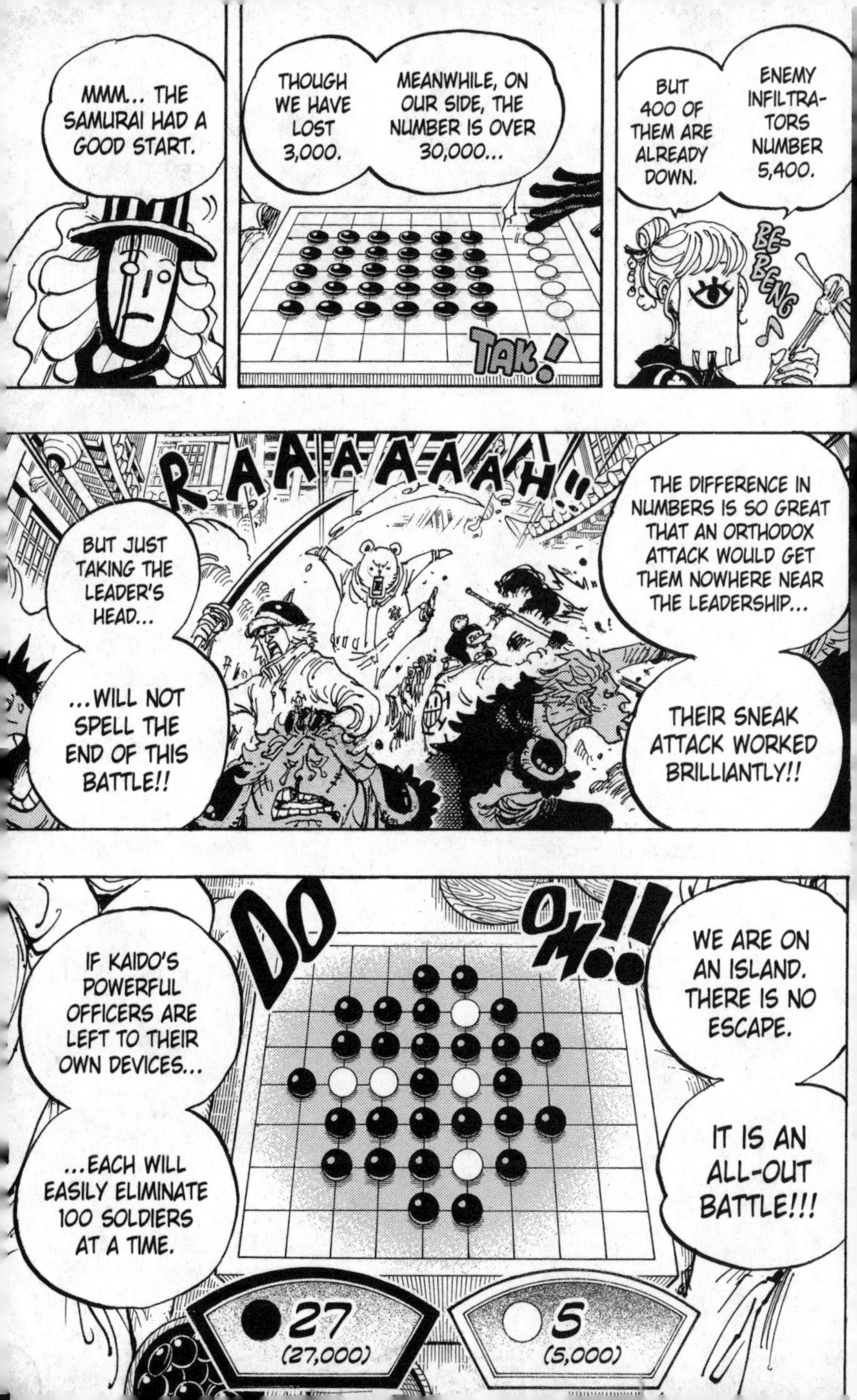
ENEMY INFILTRATORS NUMBER 5,400.
BUT 400 OF THEM ARE ALREADY DOWN.
BE-BENG
MEANWHILE, ON OUR SIDE, THE NUMBER IS OVER 30,000...
THOUGH WE HAVE LOST 3,000.
TAK!
MMM... THE SAMURAI HAD A GOOD START.
RAAAAAAAH!!
THE DIFFERENCE IN NUMBERS IS SO GREAT THAT AN ORTHODOX ATTACK WOULD GET THEM NOWHERE NEAR THE LEADERSHIP...
THEIR SNEAK ATTACK WORKED BRILLIANTLY!!
BUT JUST TAKING THE LEADER'S HEAD...
...WILL NOT SPELL THE END OF THIS BATTLE!!
DOOM!!
WE ARE ON AN ISLAND. THERE IS NO ESCAPE.
IT IS AN ALL-OUT BATTLE!!!
IF KAIDO'S POWERFUL OFFICERS ARE LEFT TO THEIR OWN DEVICES...
...EACH WILL EASILY ELIMINATE 100 SOLDIERS AT A TIME.
27 (27,000)
5 (5,000)

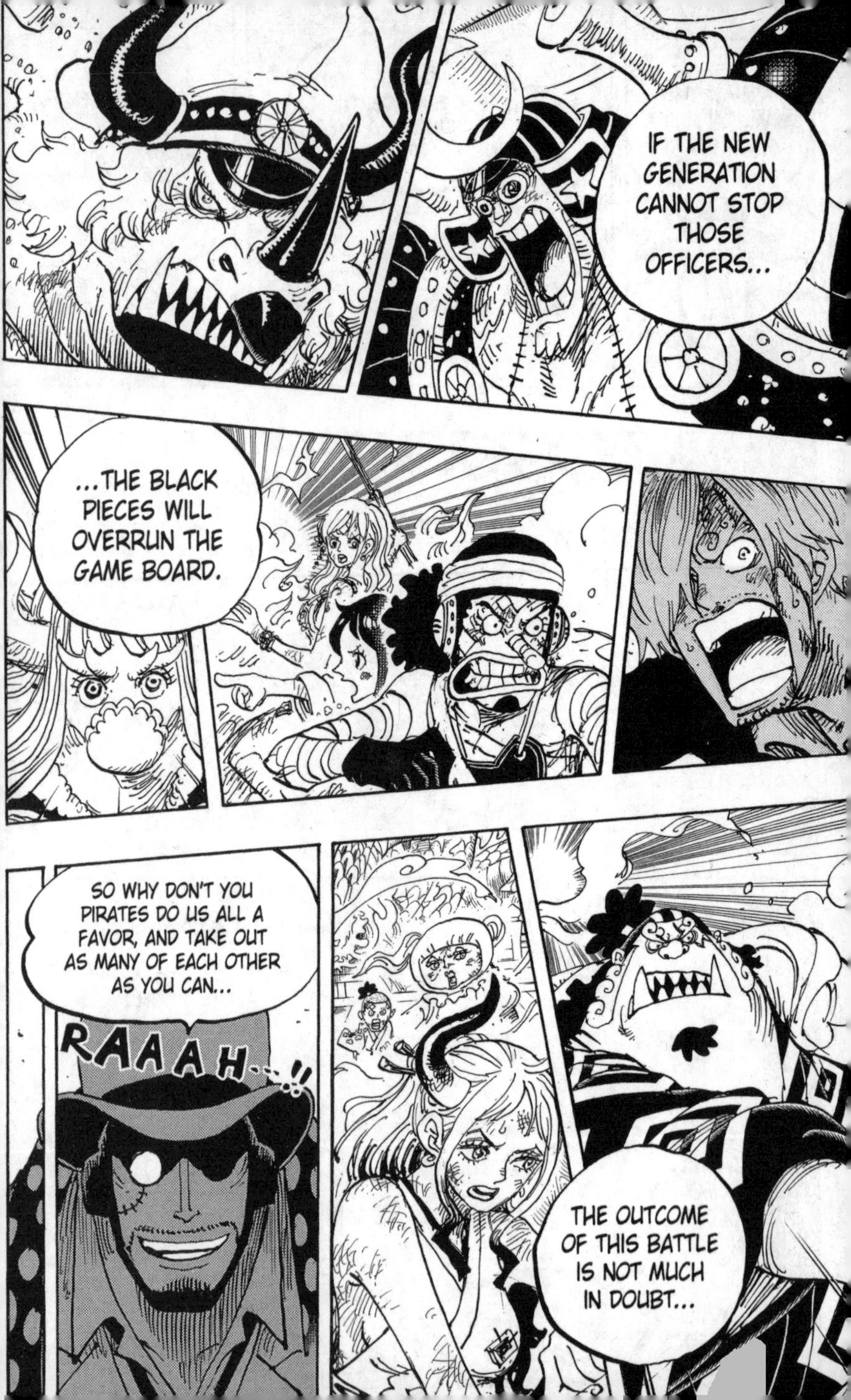

IF THE NEW GENERATION CANNOT STOP THOSE OFFICERS...
...THE BLACK PIECES WILL OVERRUN THE GAME BOARD.
THE OUTCOME OF THIS BATTLE IS NOT MUCH IN DOUBT...
SO WHY DON'T YOU PIRATES DO US ALL A FAVOR, AND TAKE OUT AS MANY OF EACH OTHER AS YOU CAN...
RAAAH...!!

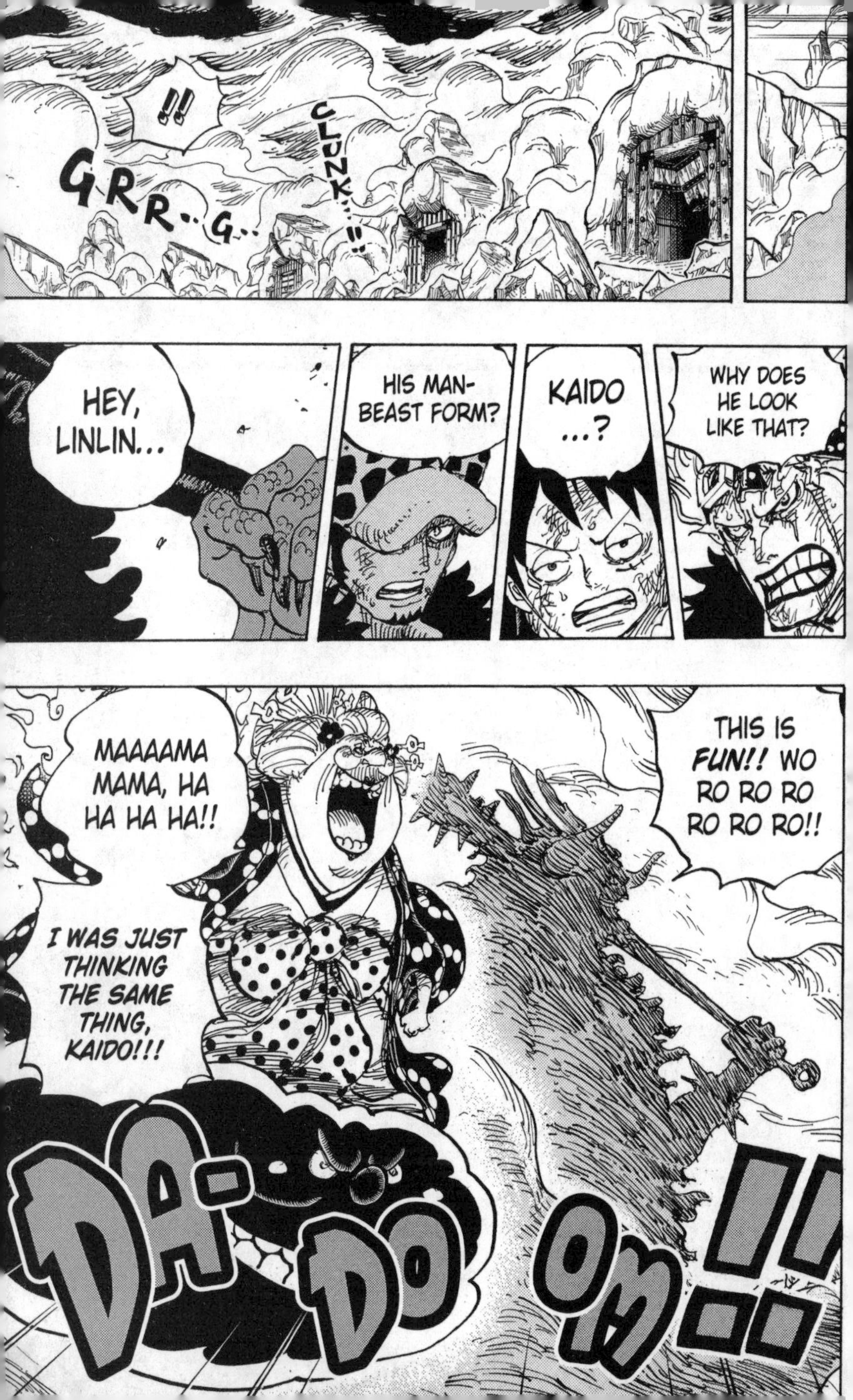

CLUNK...!!
!!
GRRR..G..
WHY DOES HE LOOK LIKE THAT?
KAIDO ...?
HIS MAN-BEAST FORM?
HEY, LINLIN...
THIS IS *FUN!!* WO RO RO RO RO RO RO!!
MAAAAMA MAMA, HA HA HA HA!!
I WAS JUST THINKING THE SAME THING, KAIDO!!!
DA-DO OM..!!

質問コーナー♪
エスビーエス

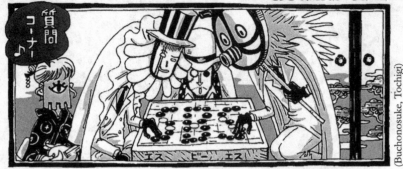

(Buchonosuke, Tochigi)

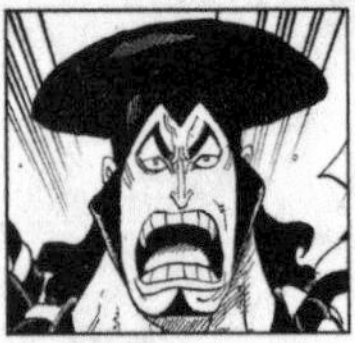

Q: What style of topknot is Kozuki Oden sporting? What's the name of it? Is it the "Perfect Fit for Wano Pillows" knot?

--Taro in the Dark

A: Perfect fit for Wano pillows? It's the other way around! Japanese culture can be such a funny thing. Do you know what pillows were like back in the days when people tied up their hair like that? Since the hair was tied on top, the pillows looked like this. In fact, I remember my grandma using one of them.

Like this
zzz..
Perfect fit!!

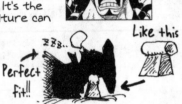

← Now, Oden originally looked like this in my planning sketches. The parts from top to bottom are a chewy konnyaku cake, hard-boiled egg, and ganmodoki tofu fritter, all ingredients in an oden hot-pot. Only the ganmodoki survived! In other words, this would be a "tremendously tasteful tofu topknot."

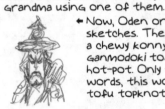

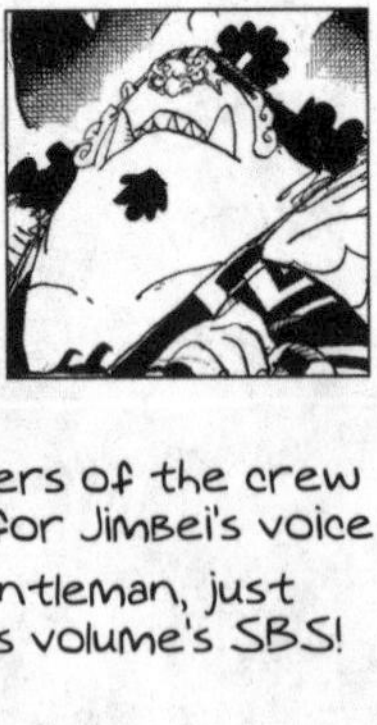

Q: A question for Odacchi… Or more accurately, a suggestion!! A while ago, you did an "SBS with the Voice Actors" series, where you took questions for the voice actors of the Straw Hats! Well, how about we bring that back for the newest member of the crew, Jimbei's actor Katsuhisa Hoki?

--Pitera

A: Ooh, that's good. That was a long time ago, LOL. It started with Luffy's Mayumi Tanaka in volume 52, and ended in volume 64, with the nine members of the crew at the time. So we're going to take questions for Jimbei's voice actor, **Katsuhisa Hoki!!** He's a classy, dandy gentleman, just like Jimbei! Ask him anything! And that's it for this volume's SBS! Next up, volume 100!!

Chapter 1004:

MILLET DUMPLINGS

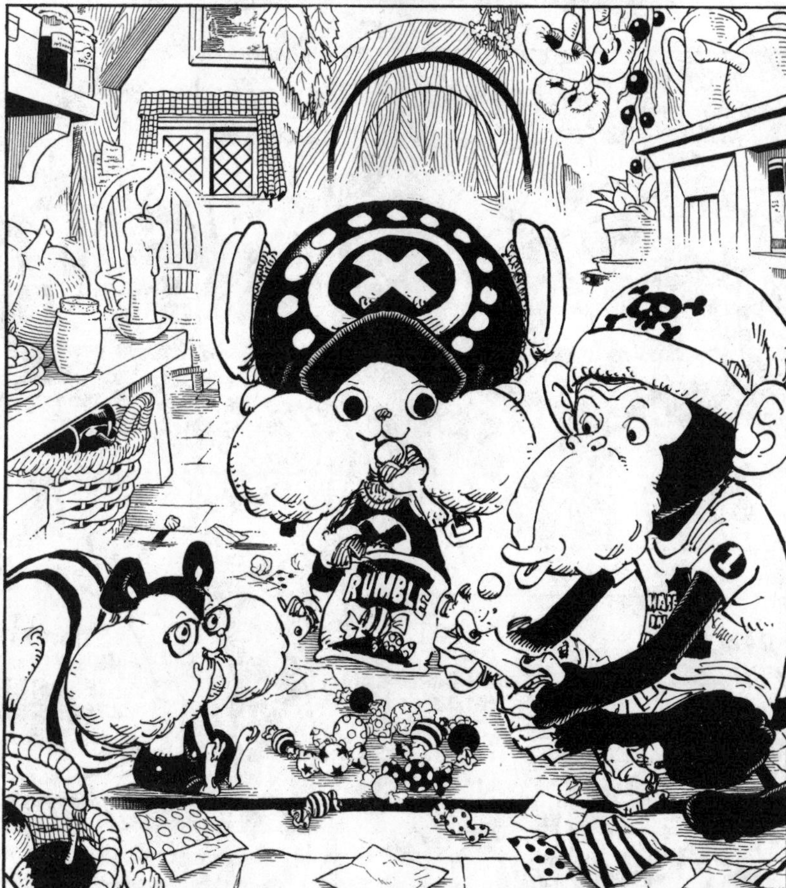

RUMBLE

READER REQUEST: "CHOPPER HANDING OUT RUMBLE BALL CANDIES TO A SQUIRREL AND MONKEY PACKING THEIR CHEEKS" BY HIYU MORI

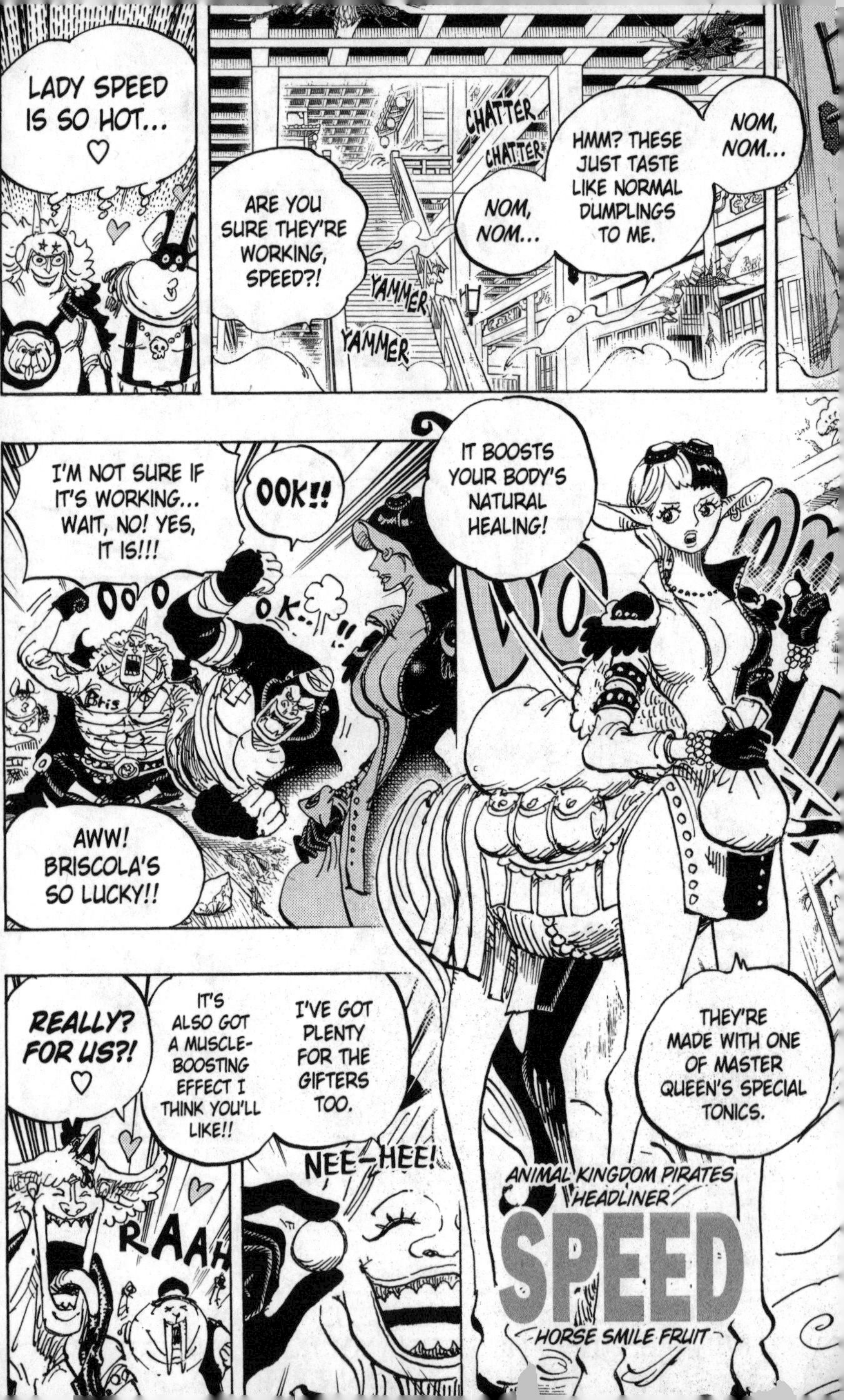
NOM, NOM...
HMM? THESE JUST TASTE LIKE NORMAL DUMPLINGS TO ME.
NOM, NOM...
CHATTER
CHATTER
ARE YOU SURE THEY'RE WORKING, SPEED?!
YAMMER
YAMMER
LADY SPEED IS SO HOT... ♡
IT BOOSTS YOUR BODY'S NATURAL HEALING!
THEY'RE MADE WITH ONE OF MASTER QUEEN'S SPECIAL TONICS.
ANIMAL KINGDOM PIRATES HEADLINER
SPEED
HORSE SMILE FRUIT
OOK!!
I'M NOT SURE IF IT'S WORKING... WAIT, NO! YES, IT IS!!!
OOOOK!!
AWW! BRISCOLA'S SO LUCKY!!
I'VE GOT PLENTY FOR THE GIFTERS TOO.
IT'S ALSO GOT A MUSCLE-BOOSTING EFFECT I THINK YOU'LL LIKE!!
NEE-HEE!
REALLY? FOR US?! ♡
RAAAH

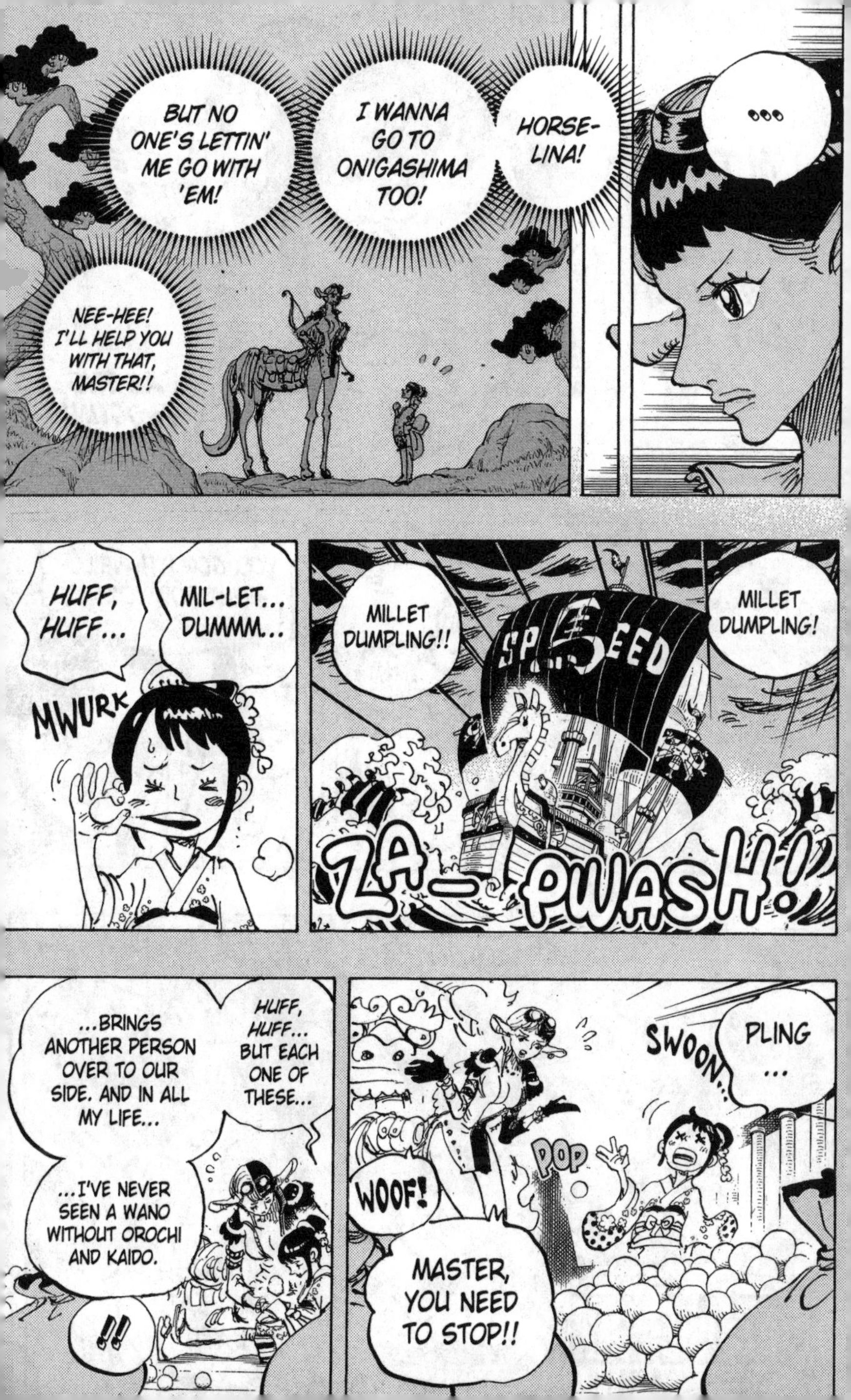
...
HORSE-LINA!
I WANNA GO TO ONIGASHIMA TOO!
BUT NO ONE'S LETTIN' ME GO WITH 'EM!
NEE-HEE! I'LL HELP YOU WITH THAT, MASTER!!
MILLET DUMPLING!
MILLET DUMPLING!!
SP...EED
ZA-PWASH!
MIL-LET... DUMMM...
HUFF, HUFF...
MWURK
PLING ...
SWOON...
POP
WOOF!
MASTER, YOU NEED TO STOP!!
HUFF, HUFF... BUT EACH ONE OF THESE...
...BRINGS ANOTHER PERSON OVER TO OUR SIDE. AND IN ALL MY LIFE...
...I'VE NEVER SEEN A WANO WITHOUT OROCHI AND KAIDO.
!!

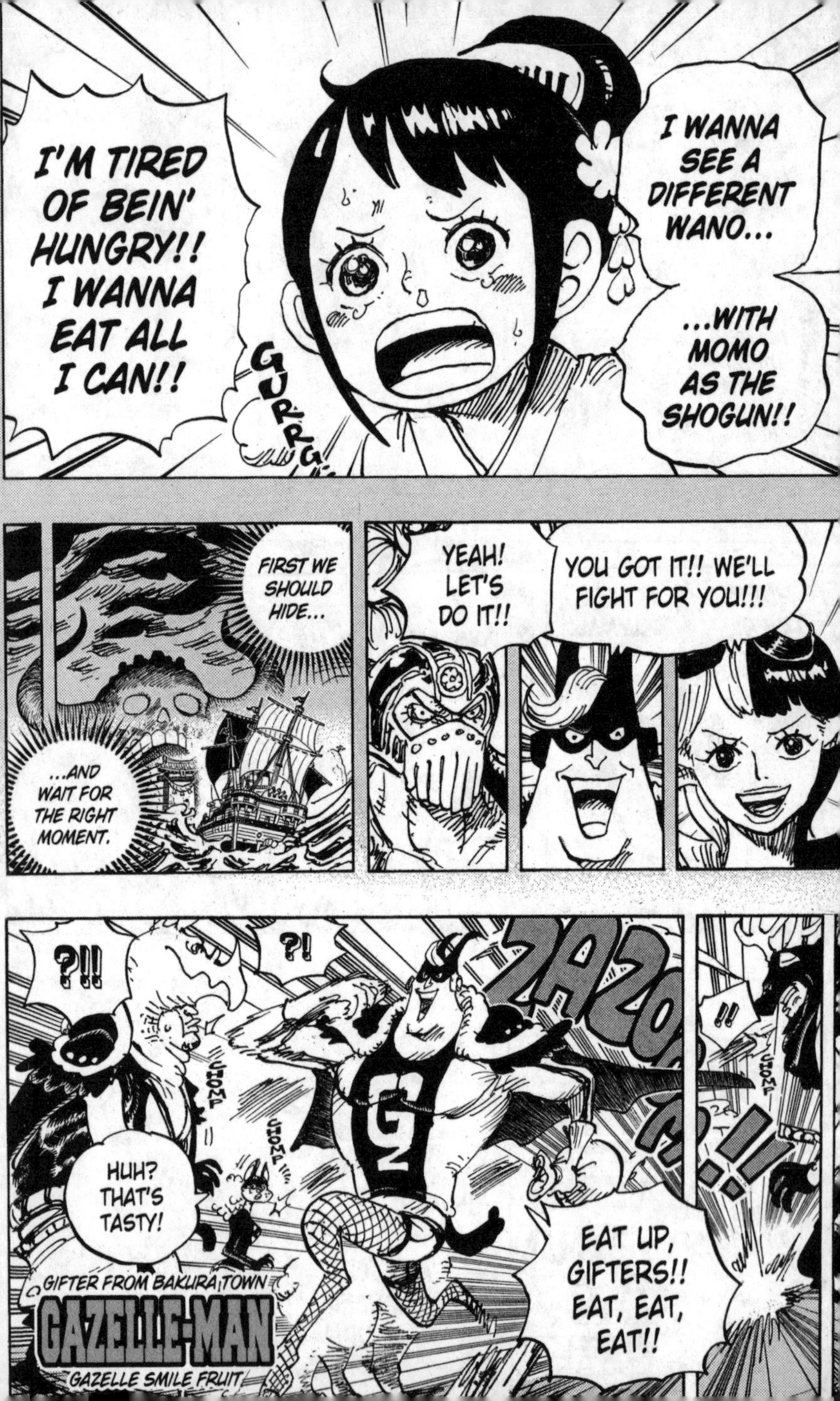
I WANNA SEE A DIFFERENT WANO...
...WITH MOMO AS THE SHOGUN!!
I'M TIRED OF BEIN' HUNGRY!! I WANNA EAT ALL I CAN!!
GURRRG...
YOU GOT IT!! WE'LL FIGHT FOR YOU!!!
YEAH! LET'S DO IT!!
FIRST WE SHOULD HIDE...
...AND WAIT FOR THE RIGHT MOMENT.
!!
CHOMP
?!
?!!
CHOMP
CHOMP
HUH? THAT'S TASTY!
EAT UP, GIFTERS!! EAT, EAT, EAT!!
GIFTER FROM BAKURA TOWN
GAZELLE-MAN
GAZELLE SMILE FRUIT

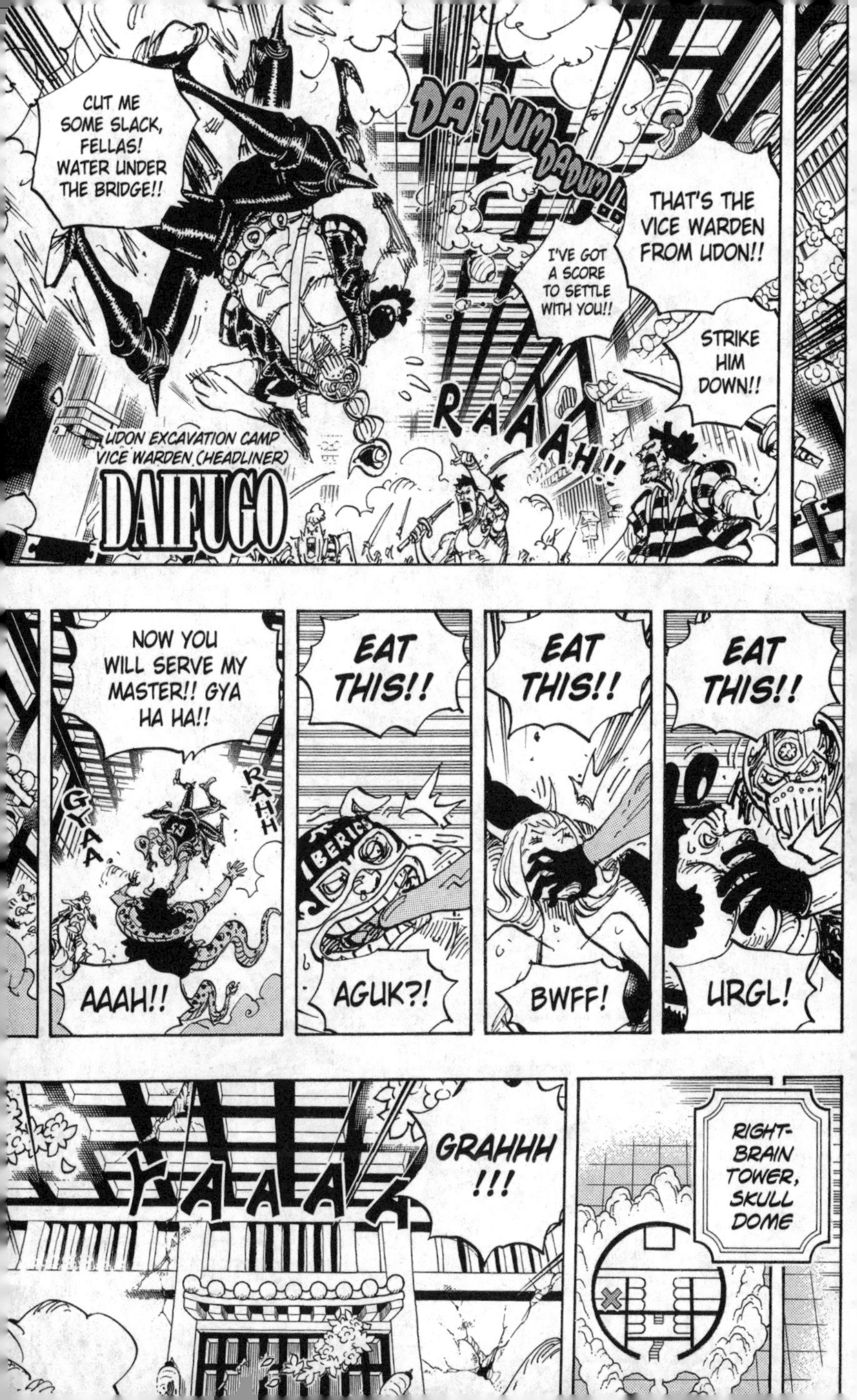
THAT'S THE VICE WARDEN FROM UDON!!
STRIKE HIM DOWN!!
DA DUM DADUM!!
I'VE GOT A SCORE TO SETTLE WITH YOU!!
CUT ME SOME SLACK, FELLAS! WATER UNDER THE BRIDGE!!
RAAAAH!!
UDON EXCAVATION CAMP VICE WARDEN (HEADLINER)
DAIFUGO
EAT THIS!!
URGL!
EAT THIS!!
BWFF!
EAT THIS!!
AGUK?!
NOW YOU WILL SERVE MY MASTER!! GYA HA HA!!
RAHH
GYAA
AAAH!!
RIGHT-BRAIN TOWER, SKULL DOME
GRAHHH!!!
YAAAA

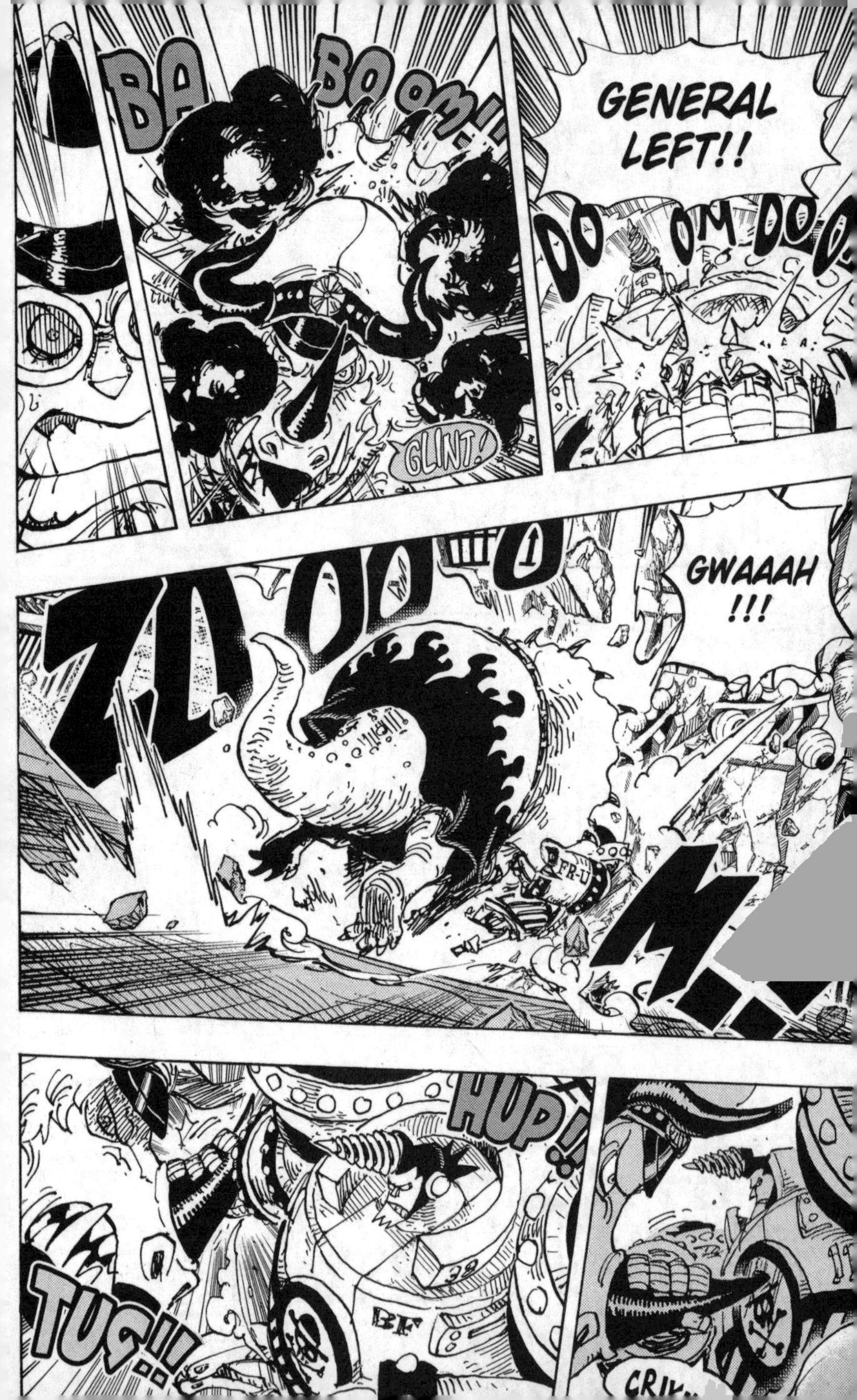
GENERAL LEFT!!
DOOM DOO
BABOOM!!
GLINT!
GWAAAH!!!
ZDOOOM...
CRIK...
HUP!!
TUG!!

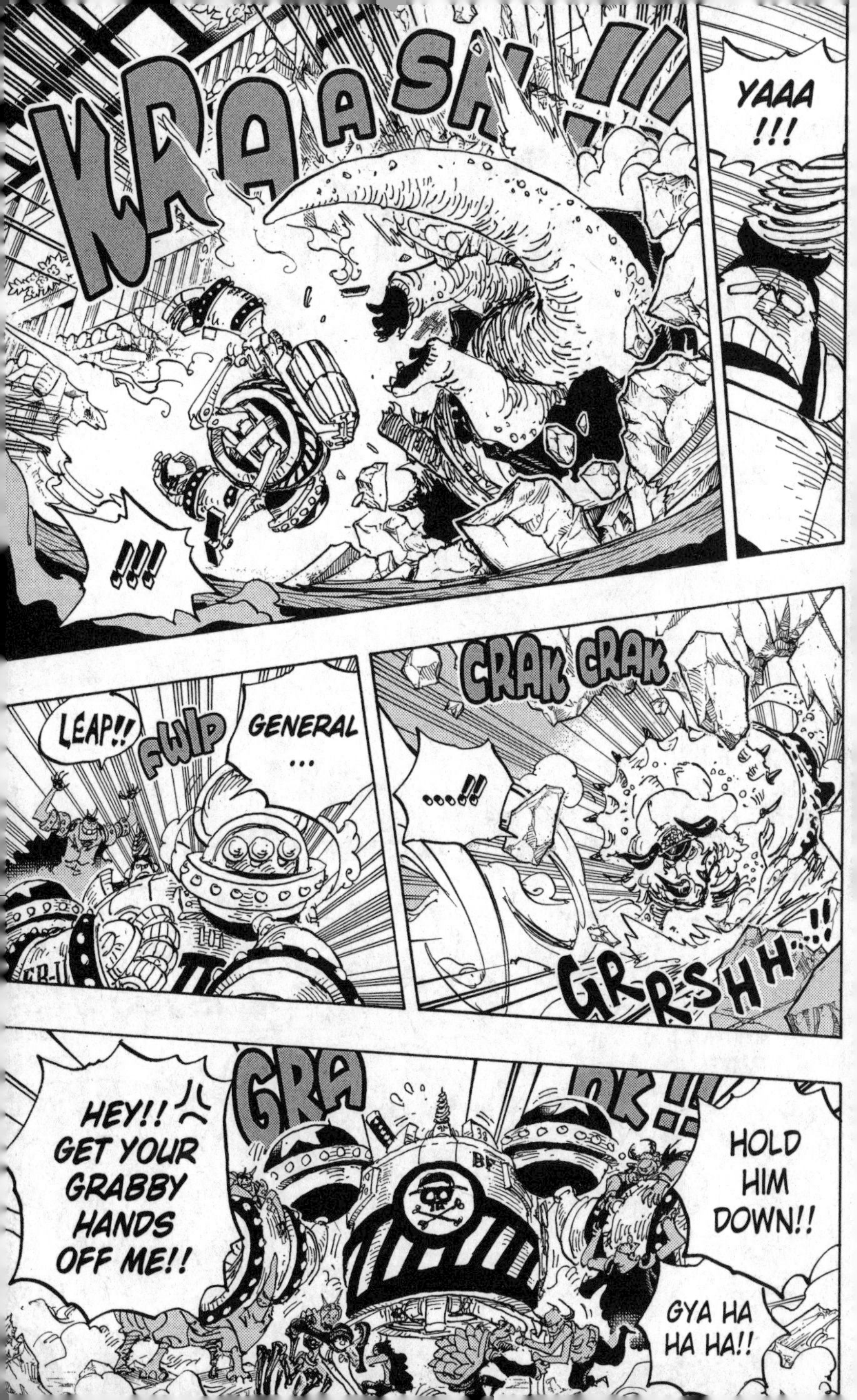
YAAA !!!
KRAASH!!!
!!!
CRAK CRAK
....!!
GRRSHH..!!
GENERAL ...
FWIP
LEAP!!
GRA
OK!!
HOLD HIM DOWN!!
GYA HA HA HA!!
HEY!! GET YOUR GRABBY HANDS OFF ME!!

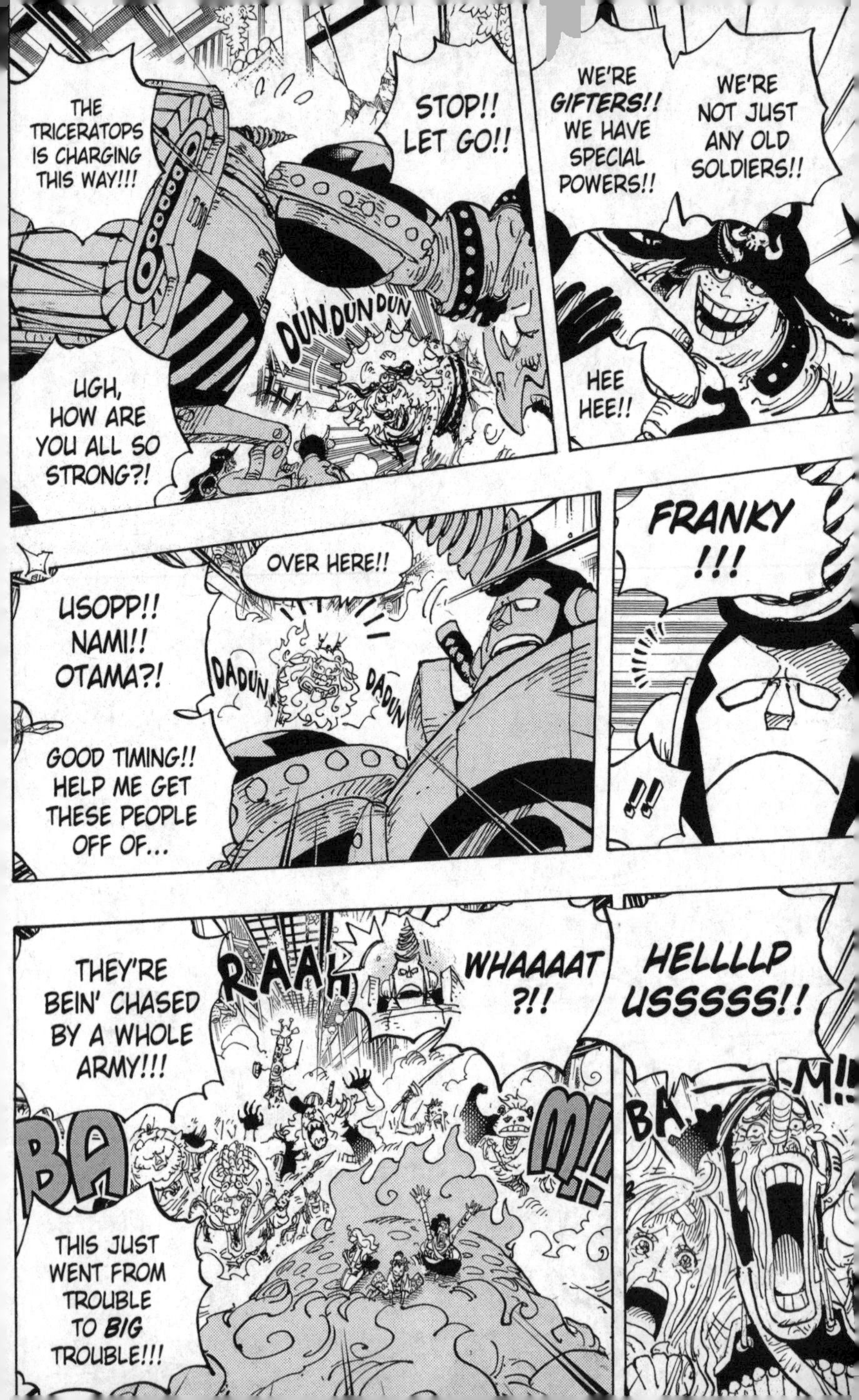

WE'RE NOT JUST ANY OLD SOLDIERS!!
WE'RE GIFTERS!! WE HAVE SPECIAL POWERS!!
HEE HEE!!
STOP!! LET GO!!
THE TRICERATOPS IS CHARGING THIS WAY!!!
DUN DUN DUN
UGH, HOW ARE YOU ALL SO STRONG?!
FRANKY!!!
!!
OVER HERE!!
USOPP!! NAMI!! OTAMA?!
DADUN DADUN
GOOD TIMING!! HELP ME GET THESE PEOPLE OFF OF...
HELLLLP USSSSS!!
BA—M!!
WHAAAAT?!!
RAAH
THEY'RE BEIN' CHASED BY A WHOLE ARMY!!!
BA M!!
THIS JUST WENT FROM TROUBLE TO *BIG* TROUBLE!!!

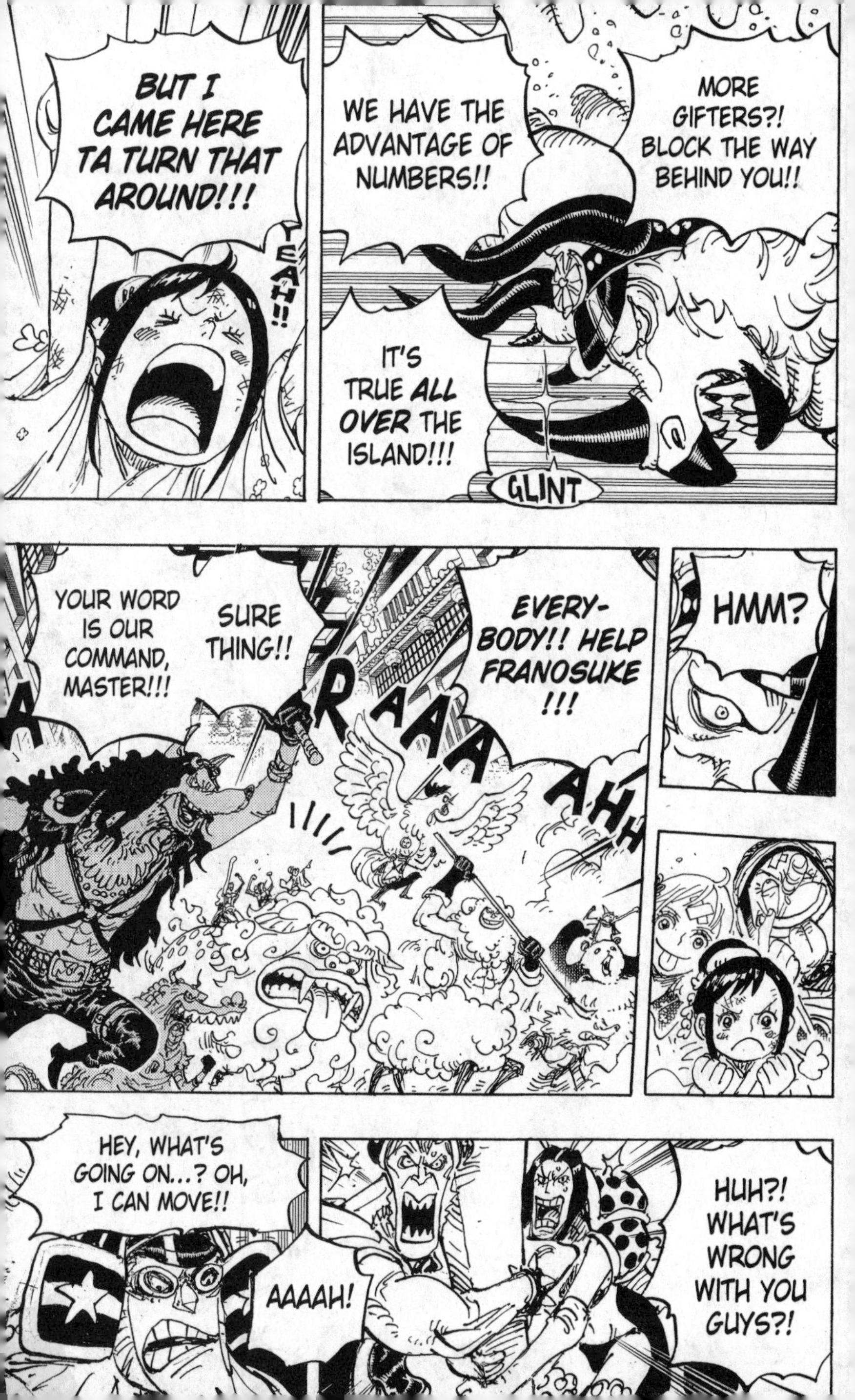
MORE GIFTERS?! BLOCK THE WAY BEHIND YOU!!
WE HAVE THE ADVANTAGE OF NUMBERS!!
IT'S TRUE ALL OVER THE ISLAND!!!
GLINT
BUT I CAME HERE TA TURN THAT AROUND!!!
YEAH!!
HMM?
EVERY-BODY!! HELP FRANOSUKE!!!
SURE THING!!
YOUR WORD IS OUR COMMAND, MASTER!!!
RAAAAHH
HUH?! WHAT'S WRONG WITH YOU GUYS?!
AAAAH!
HEY, WHAT'S GOING ON...? OH, I CAN MOVE!!

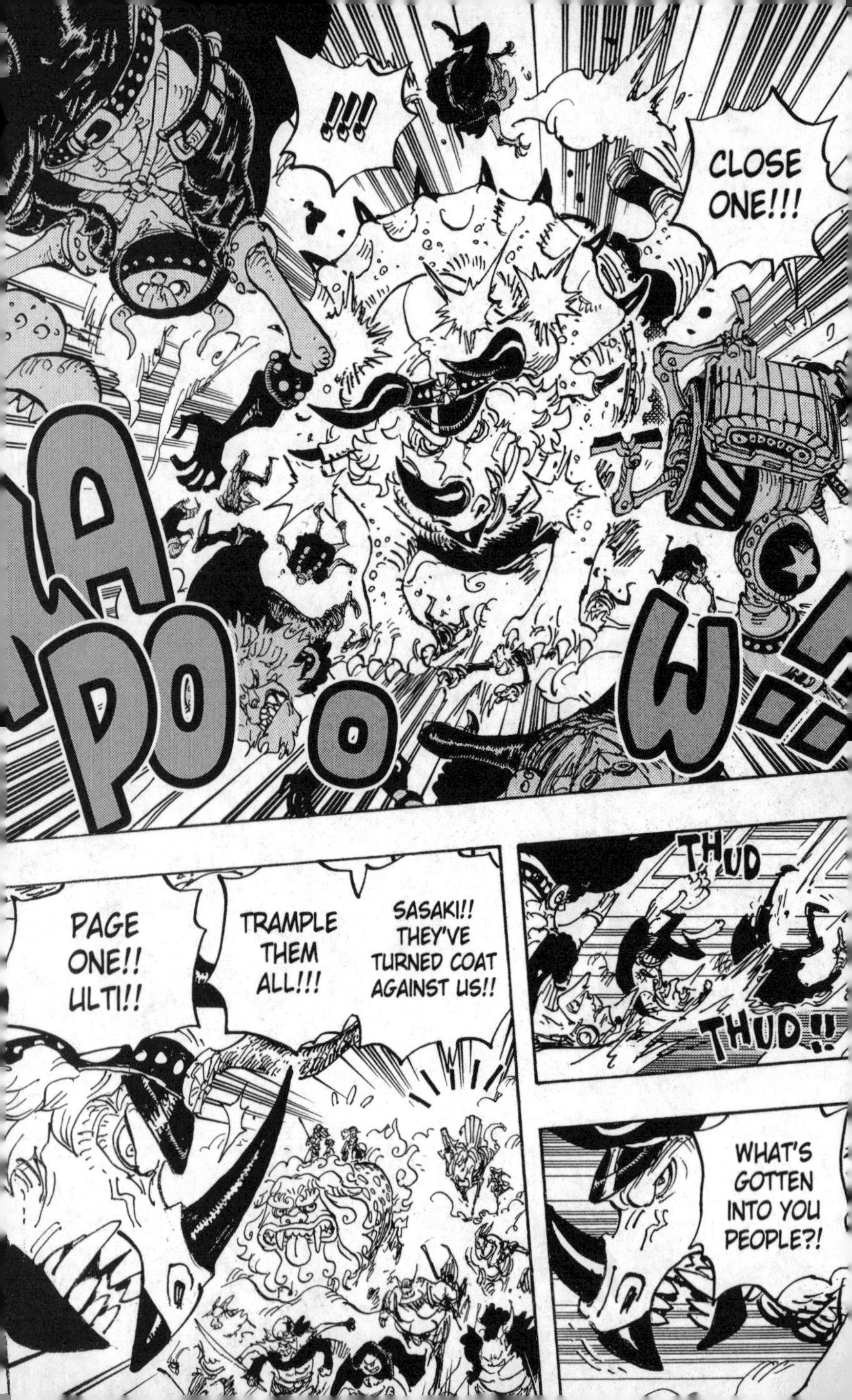
!!!
CLOSE ONE!!!
APOOW!!
THUD
THUD!!
WHAT'S GOTTEN INTO YOU PEOPLE?!
SASAKI!! THEY'VE TURNED COAT AGAINST US!!
TRAMPLE THEM ALL!!!
PAGE ONE!! ULTI!!

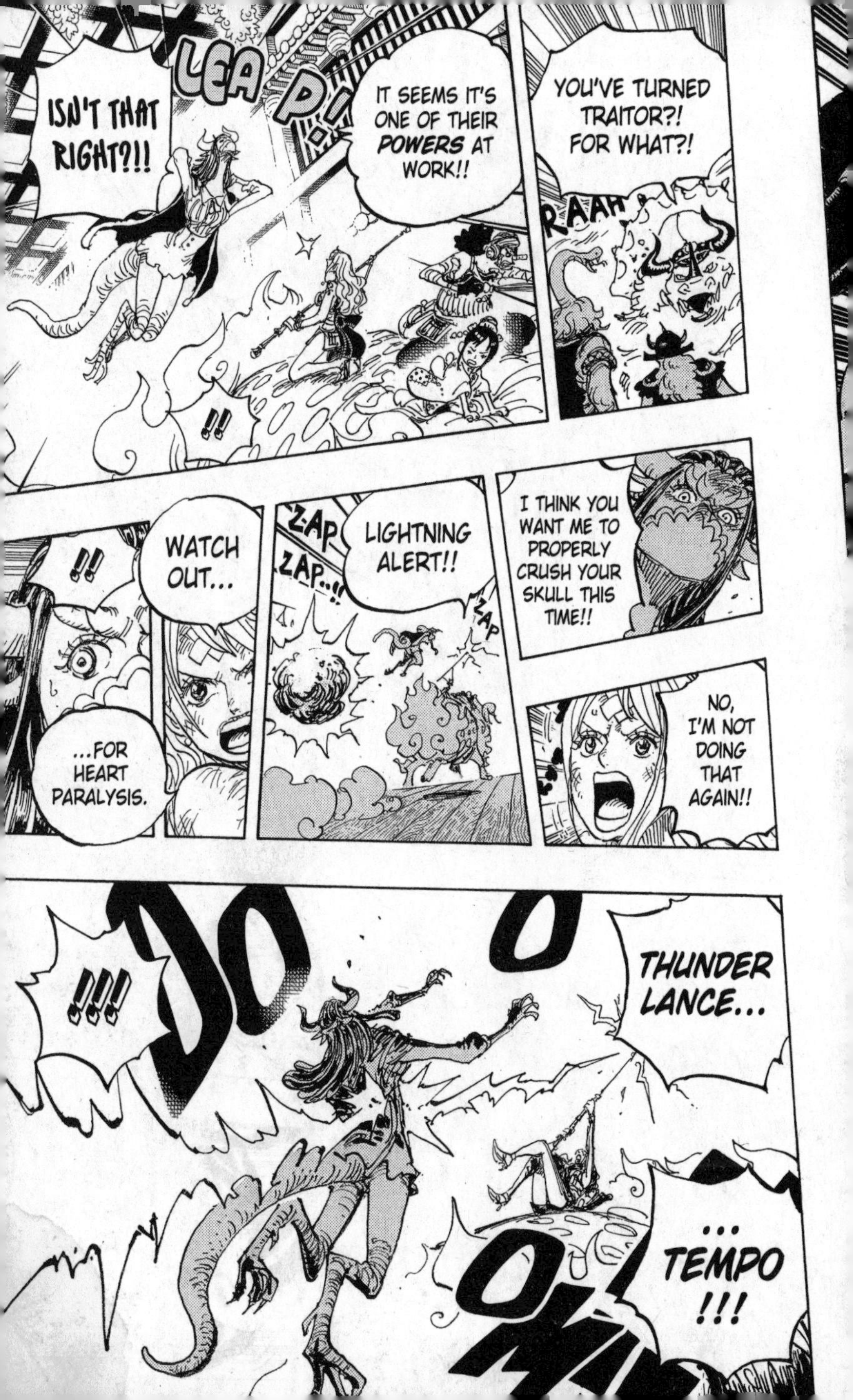
YOU'VE TURNED TRAITOR?! FOR WHAT?!
RAAH
IT SEEMS IT'S ONE OF THEIR POWERS AT WORK!!
LEA P!
ISN'T THAT RIGHT?!!
!!
I THINK YOU WANT ME TO PROPERLY CRUSH YOUR SKULL THIS TIME!!
NO, I'M NOT DOING THAT AGAIN!!
ZAP
LIGHTNING ALERT!!
ZAP
ZAP..!!
WATCH OUT...
!!
...FOR HEART PARALYSIS.
THUNDER LANCE...
O
DO
!!!
...TEMPO !!!
OM

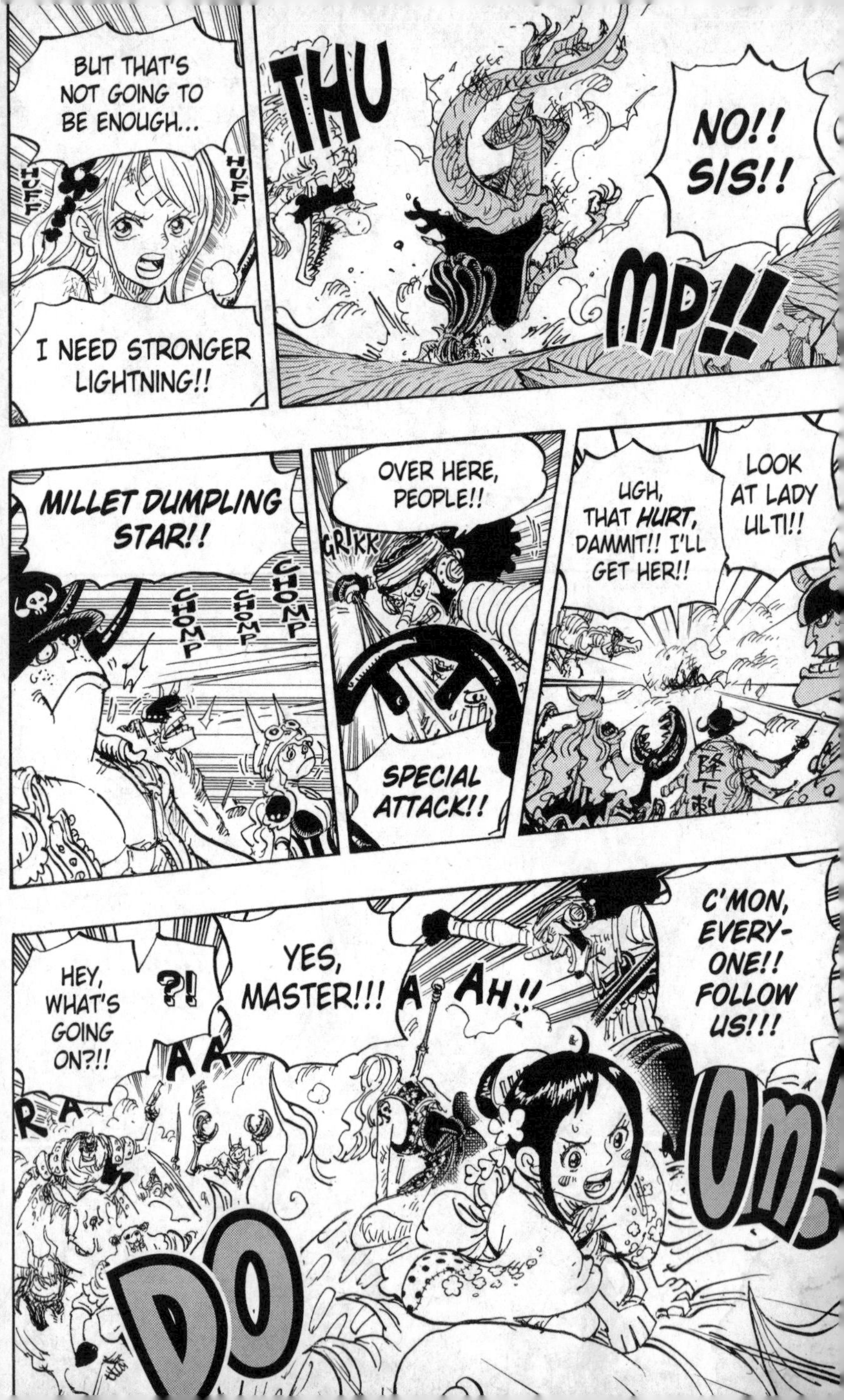
NO!! SIS!!
THU
MP!!
BUT THAT'S NOT GOING TO BE ENOUGH...
HUFF
HUFF
I NEED STRONGER LIGHTNING!!
LOOK AT LADY ULTI!!
UGH, THAT HURT, DAMMIT!! I'LL GET HER!!
OVER HERE, PEOPLE!!
GRIKK
SPECIAL ATTACK!!
MILLET DUMPLING STAR!!
CHOMP
CHOMP
CHOMP
C'MON, EVERY-ONE!! FOLLOW US!!!
A AH!!
YES, MASTER!!!
?!
HEY, WHAT'S GOING ON?!!
R A AA
DO
OM

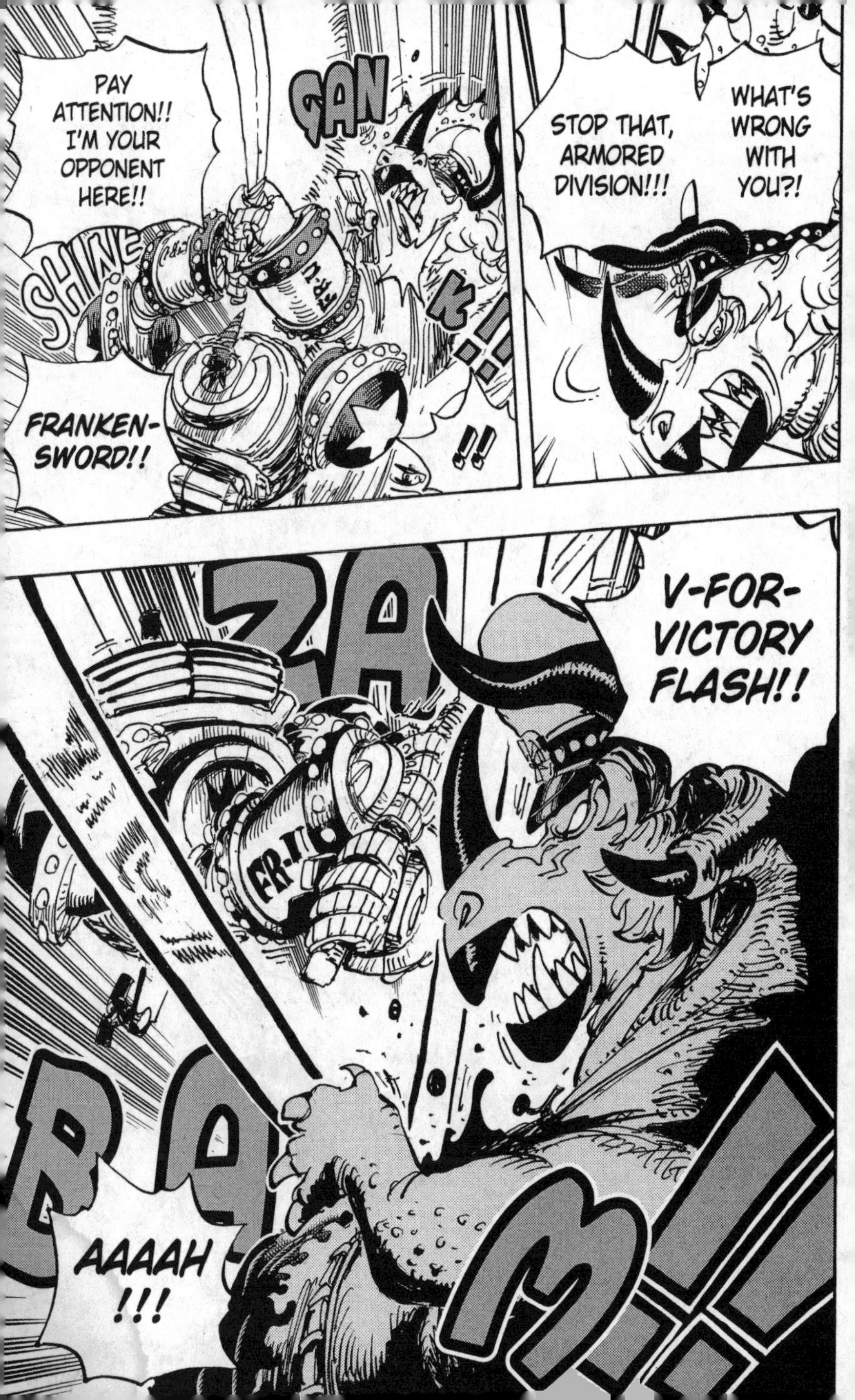
WHAT'S WRONG WITH YOU?!
STOP THAT, ARMORED DIVISION!!!
PAY ATTENTION!! I'M YOUR OPPONENT HERE!!
GAN
K!!
SHINE
FRANKEN-SWORD!!
!!
V-FOR-VICTORY FLASH!!
ZA
BA
AAAAH!!!

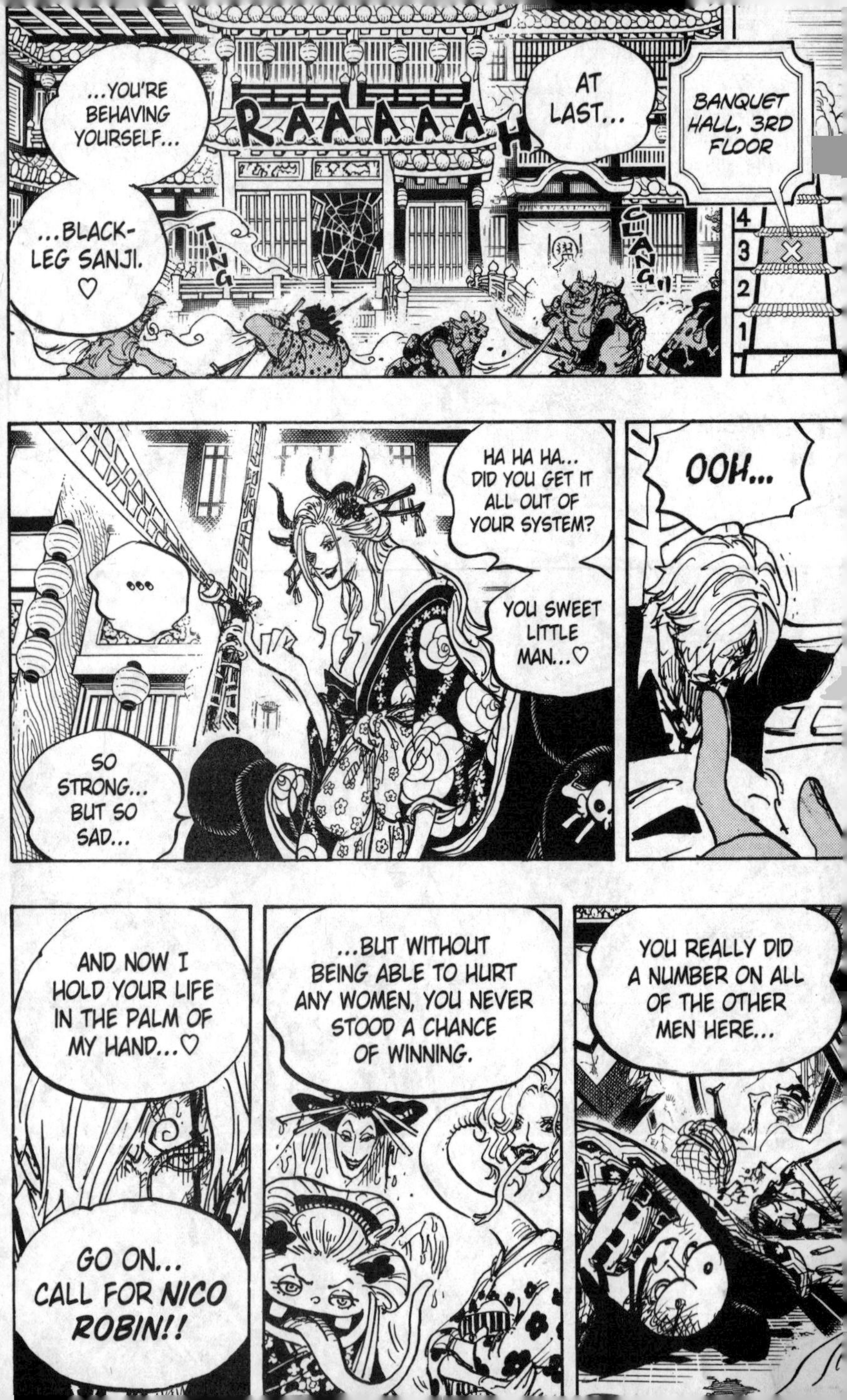
BANQUET HALL, 3RD FLOOR
AT LAST...
RAAAAAAH
CLANG
...YOU'RE BEHAVING YOURSELF...
TING
...BLACK-LEG SANJI. ♡
OOH...
HA HA HA... DID YOU GET IT ALL OUT OF YOUR SYSTEM?
YOU SWEET LITTLE MAN...♡
...
SO STRONG... BUT SO SAD...
YOU REALLY DID A NUMBER ON ALL OF THE OTHER MEN HERE...
...BUT WITHOUT BEING ABLE TO HURT ANY WOMEN, YOU NEVER STOOD A CHANCE OF WINNING.
AND NOW I HOLD YOUR LIFE IN THE PALM OF MY HAND...♡
GO ON... CALL FOR NICO ROBIN!!

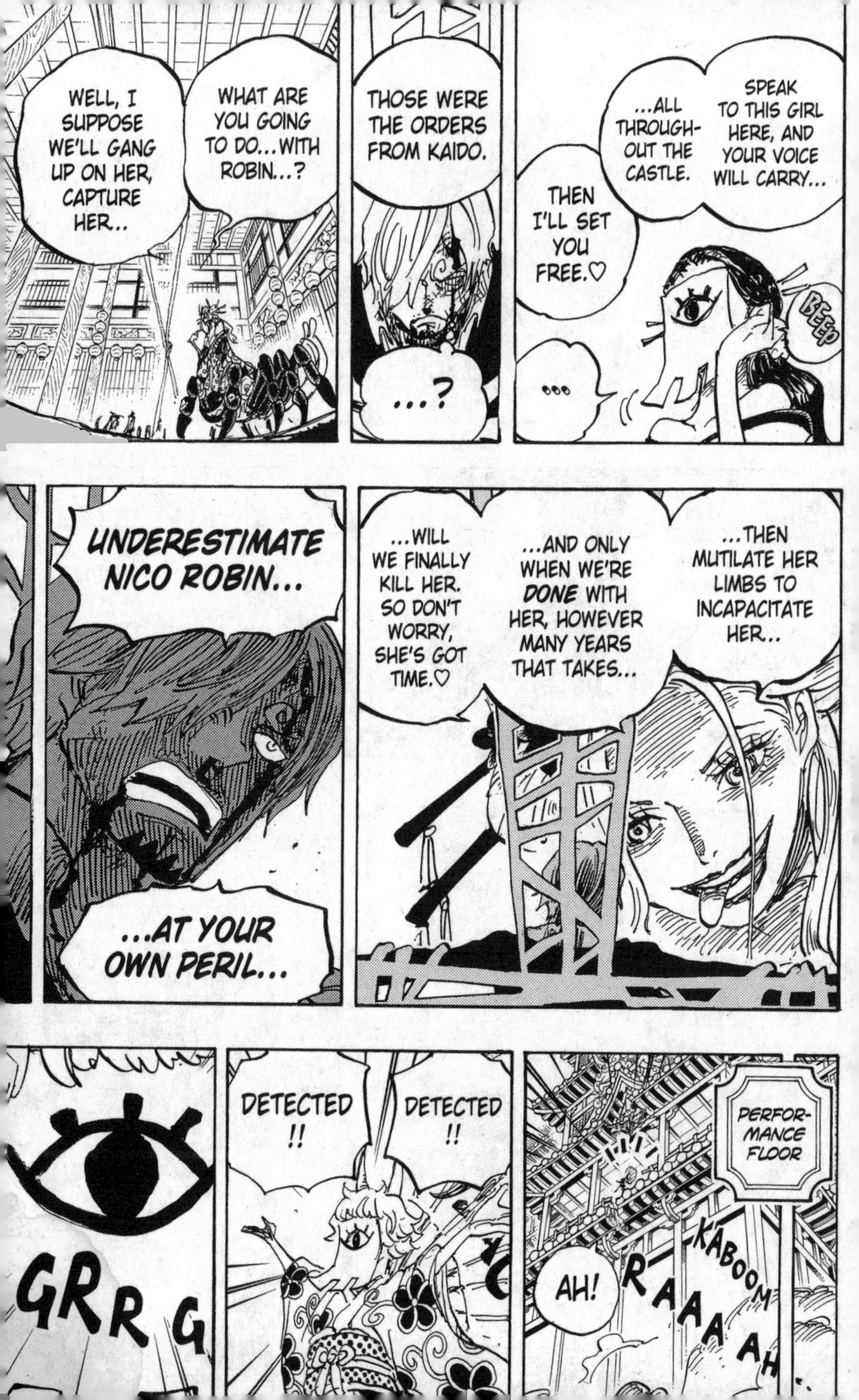
SPEAK TO THIS GIRL HERE, AND YOUR VOICE WILL CARRY...
...ALL THROUGHOUT THE CASTLE.
THEN I'LL SET YOU FREE.♡
BEEP
...
THOSE WERE THE ORDERS FROM KAIDO.
...?
WHAT ARE YOU GOING TO DO...WITH ROBIN...?
WELL, I SUPPOSE WE'LL GANG UP ON HER, CAPTURE HER...
...THEN MUTILATE HER LIMBS TO INCAPACITATE HER...
...AND ONLY WHEN WE'RE *DONE* WITH HER, HOWEVER MANY YEARS THAT TAKES...
...WILL WE FINALLY KILL HER. SO DON'T WORRY, SHE'S GOT TIME.♡
UNDERESTIMATE NICO ROBIN...
...AT YOUR OWN PERIL...
PERFORMANCE FLOOR
KABOOM
RAAAAAH
AH!
DETECTED !!
DETECTED !!
GRRG

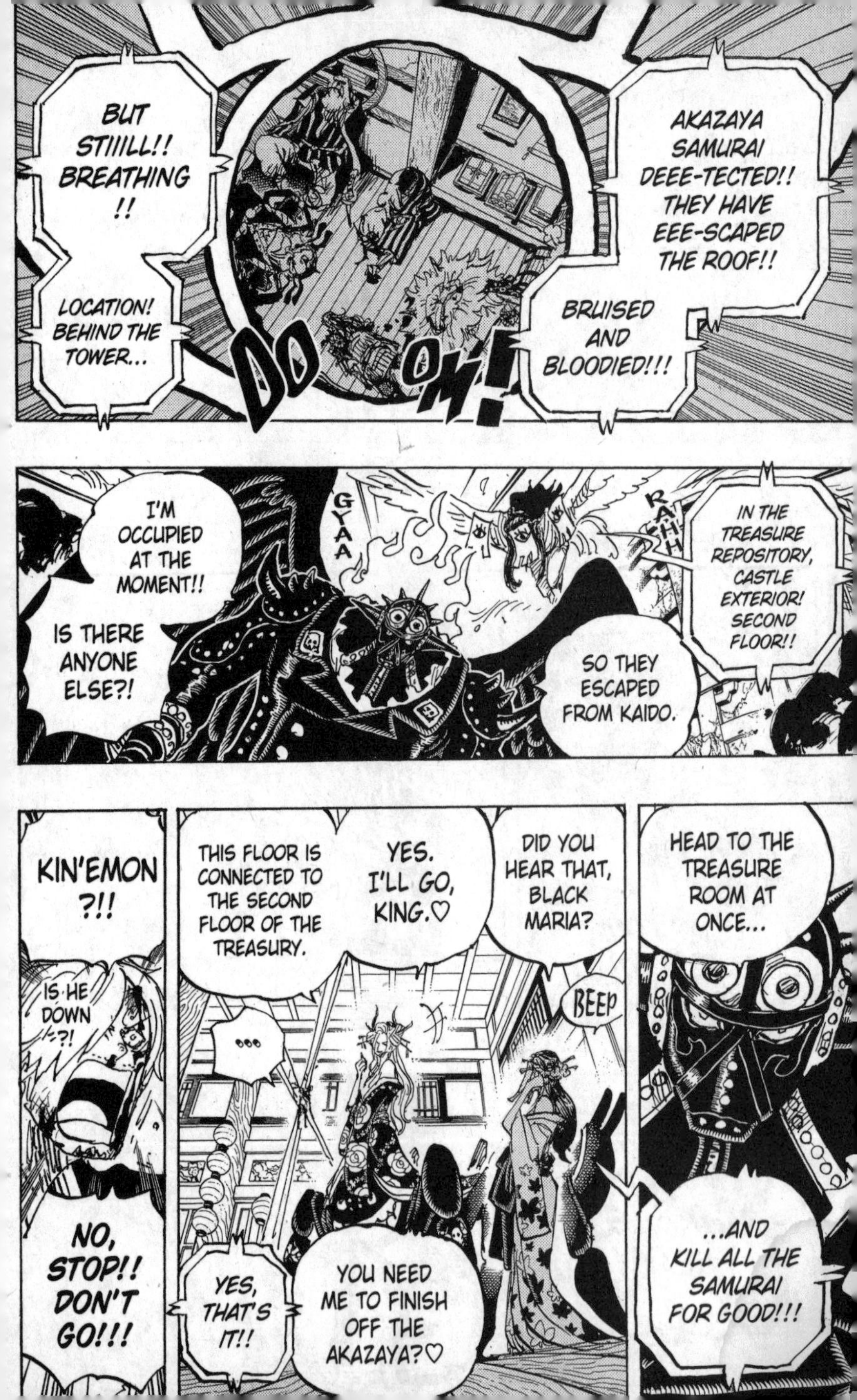
AKAZAYA SAMURAI DEEE-TECTED!! THEY HAVE EEE-SCAPED THE ROOF!!
BRUISED AND BLOODIED!!!
BUT STIIIILL!! BREATHING !!
LOCATION! BEHIND THE TOWER...
DOOM!
IN THE TREASURE REPOSITORY, CASTLE EXTERIOR! SECOND FLOOR!!
RAHH
GYAA
SO THEY ESCAPED FROM KAIDO.
I'M OCCUPIED AT THE MOMENT!!
IS THERE ANYONE ELSE?!
HEAD TO THE TREASURE ROOM AT ONCE...
...AND KILL ALL THE SAMURAI FOR GOOD!!!
DID YOU HEAR THAT, BLACK MARIA?
BEEP
YES. I'LL GO, KING.♡
THIS FLOOR IS CONNECTED TO THE SECOND FLOOR OF THE TREASURY.
...
YOU NEED ME TO FINISH OFF THE AKAZAYA?♡
YES, THAT'S IT!!
KIN'EMON ?!!
IS HE DOWN ?!
NO, STOP!! DON'T GO!!!

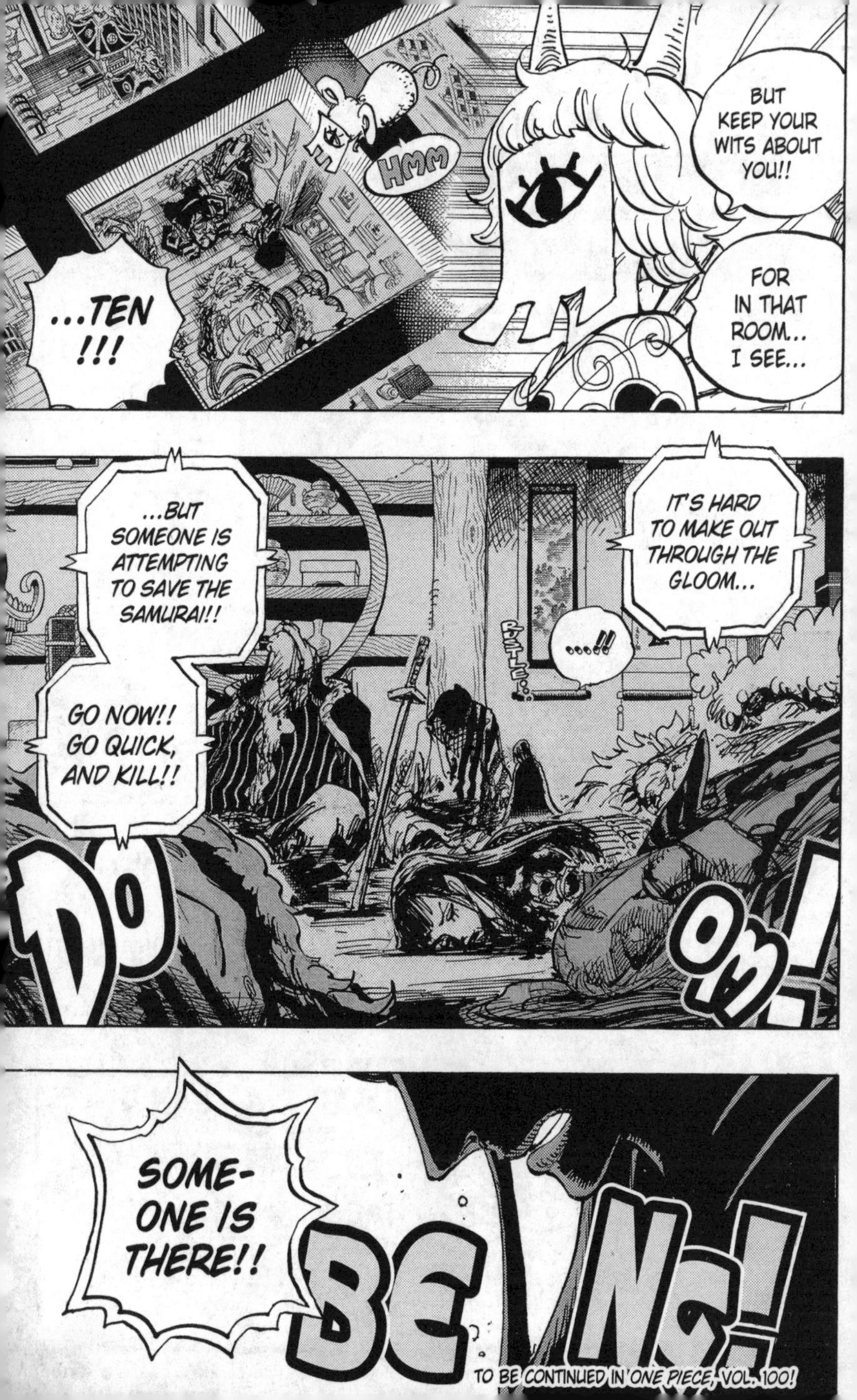
BUT KEEP YOUR WITS ABOUT YOU!!
FOR IN THAT ROOM... I SEE...
HMM
...TEN !!!
IT'S HARD TO MAKE OUT THROUGH THE GLOOM...
....!!
RUSTLE
...BUT SOMEONE IS ATTEMPTING TO SAVE THE SAMURAI!!
GO NOW!! GO QUICK, AND KILL!!
DO OM!
BE NG!
SOME-ONE IS THERE!!
TO BE CONTINUED IN ONE PIECE, VOL. 100!

WT100 (World Top 100) Final Results!!

Over 12 million votes cast worldwide!!

The seventh character popularity poll is the first worldwide poll! Who's tops around the globe?!

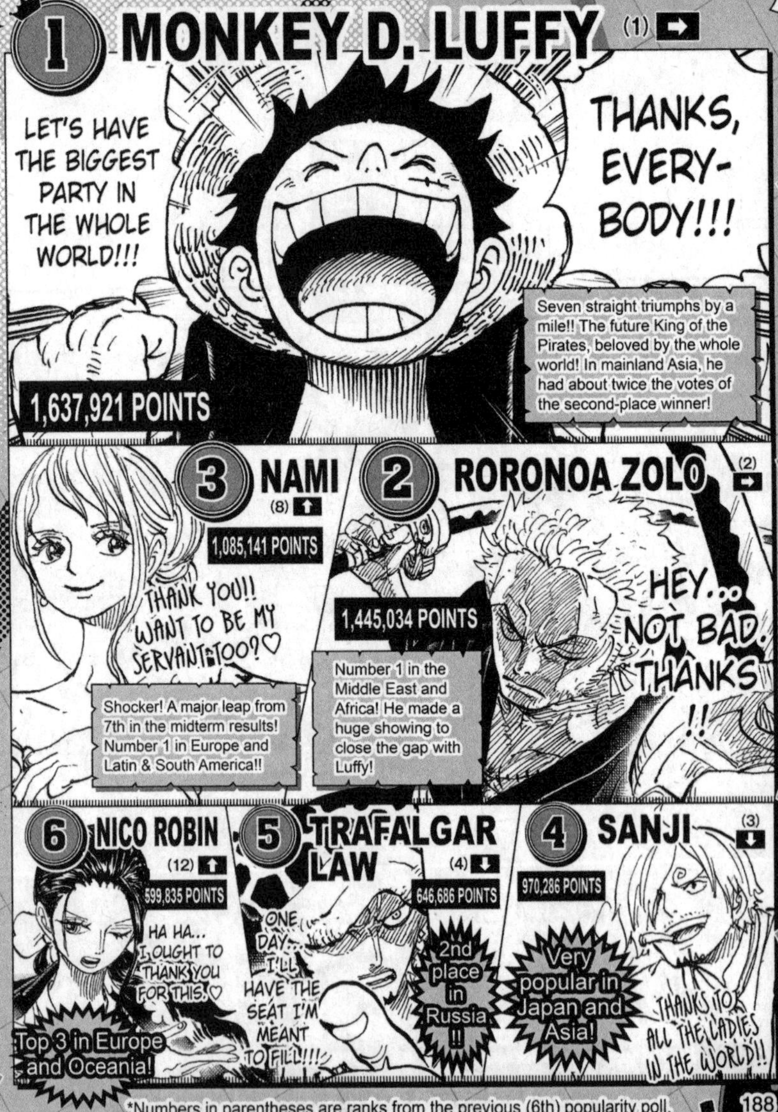
1 MONKEY D. LUFFY (1)
THANKS, EVERY-BODY!!!
LET'S HAVE THE BIGGEST PARTY IN THE WHOLE WORLD!!!
Seven straight triumphs by a mile!! The future King of the Pirates, beloved by the whole world! In mainland Asia, he had about twice the votes of the second-place winner!
1,637,921 POINTS
2 RORONOA ZOLO (2)
HEY... NOT BAD. THANKS!!
1,445,034 POINTS
Number 1 in the Middle East and Africa! He made a huge showing to close the gap with Luffy!
3 NAMI (8)
1,085,141 POINTS
THANK YOU!! WANT TO BE MY SERVANT TOO?♡
Shocker! A major leap from 7th in the midterm results! Number 1 in Europe and Latin & South America!!
4 SANJI (3)
970,286 POINTS
THANKS FOR ALL THE LADIES IN THE WORLD!!
Very popular in Japan and Asia!
5 TRAFALGAR LAW (4)
646,686 POINTS
ONE DAY... I'LL HAVE THE SEAT I'M MEANT TO FILL!!!
2nd place in Russia!!
6 NICO ROBIN (12)
599,835 POINTS
HA HA... I OUGHT TO THANK YOU FOR THIS.♡
Top 3 in Europe and Oceania!

*Numbers in parentheses are ranks from the previous (6th) popularity poll.

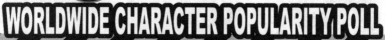

THE 1ST ONE PIECE WORLDWIDE CHARACTER POPULARITY POLL

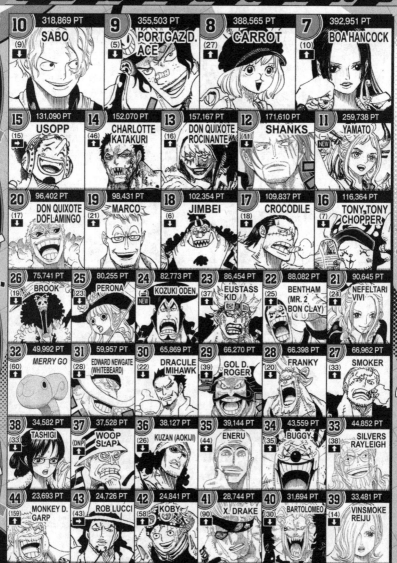

Rank	Points	Character	Previous rank	Change
7	392,951 PT	BOA HANCOCK	(10)	↑
8	388,565 PT	CARROT	(27)	↑
9	355,503 PT	PORTGAZ D. ACE	(5)	↓
10	318,869 PT	SABO	(9)	↓
11	259,738 PT	YAMATO	(—)	NEW
12	171,610 PT	SHANKS	(11)	↓
13	157,167 PT	DON QUIXOTE ROCINANTE	(16)	↑
14	152,070 PT	CHARLOTTE KATAKURI	(46)	↑
15	131,090 PT	USOPP	(15)	→
16	116,364 PT	TONY TONY CHOPPER	(7)	↓
17	109,837 PT	CROCODILE	(18)	↑
18	102,354 PT	JIMBEI	(6)	↓
19	98,431 PT	MARCO	(21)	↑
20	96,402 PT	DON QUIXOTE DOFLAMINGO	(17)	↓
21	90,645 PT	NEFELTARI VIVI	(24)	↑
22	88,082 PT	BENTHAM (MR. 2 BON CLAY)	(25)	↑
23	86,454 PT	EUSTASS KID	(37)	↑
24	82,773 PT	KOZUKI ODEN	(—)	NEW
25	80,255 PT	PERONA	(23)	↓
26	75,741 PT	BROOK	(19)	↓
27	66,962 PT	SMOKER	(33)	↑
28	66,398 PT	FRANKY	(20)	↓
29	66,270 PT	GOL D. ROGER	(39)	↑
30	65,869 PT	DRACULE MIHAWK	(22)	↓
31	59,957 PT	EDWARD NEWGATE (WHITEBEARD)	(28)	↓
32	49,992 PT	MERRY GO	(60)	↑
33	44,852 PT	SILVERS RAYLEIGH	(38)	↑
34	43,559 PT	BUGGY	(35)	↑
35	39,144 PT	ENERU	(44)	↑
36	38,127 PT	KUZAN (AOKIJI)	(26)	↓
37	37,528 PT	WOOP SLAP	(DNP)	↑
38	34,582 PT	TASHIGI	(33)	↓
39	33,481 PT	VINSMOKE REIJU	(14)	↓
40	31,694 PT	BARTOLOMEO	(30)	↓
41	28,744 PT	X. DRAKE	(90)	↑
42	24,841 PT	KOBY	(58)	↑
43	24,726 PT	ROB LUCCI	(43)	→
44	23,693 PT	MONKEY D. GARP	(159)	↑

Next up, results for #45-100!

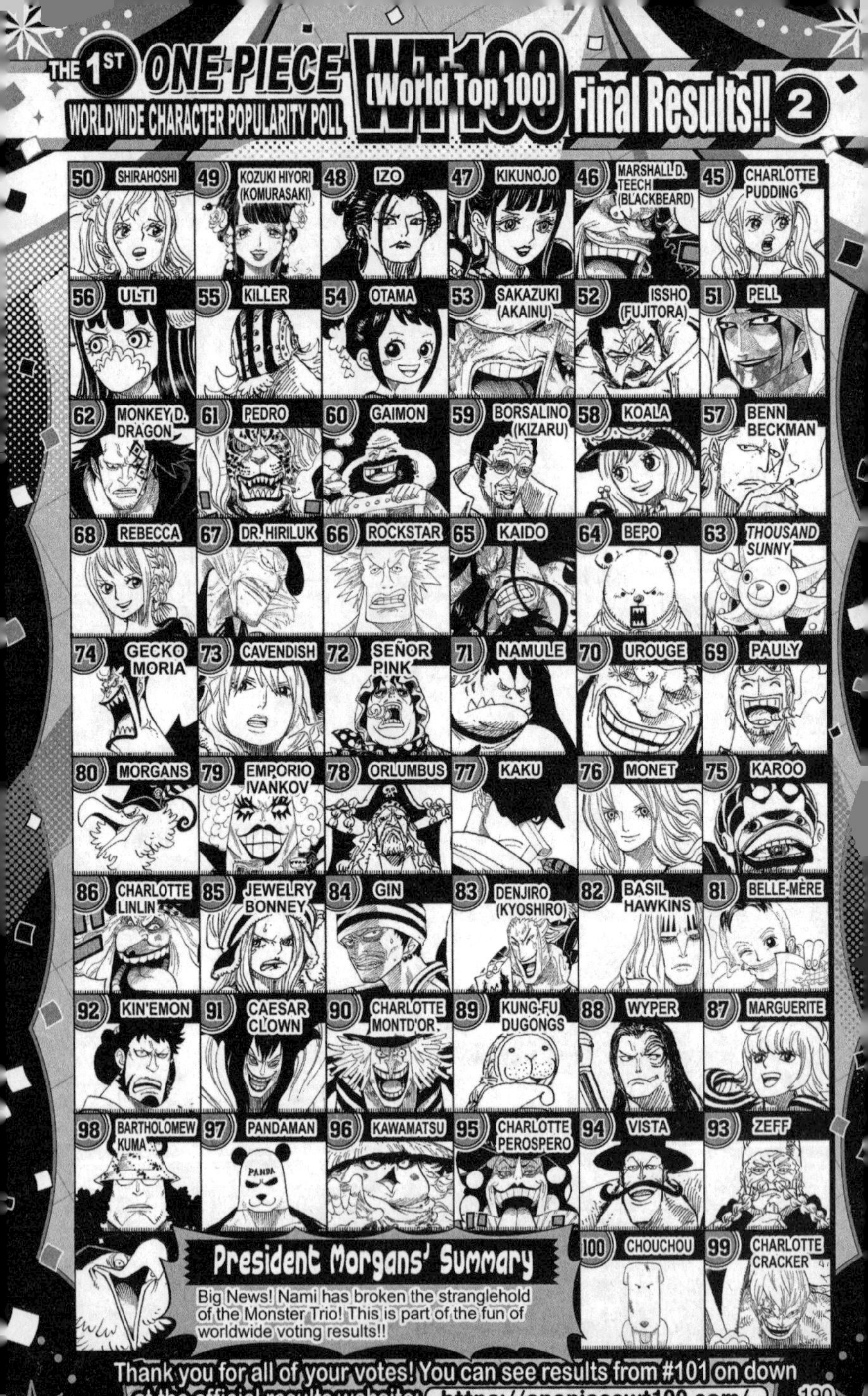
THE 1ST ONE PIECE WORLDWIDE CHARACTER POPULARITY POLL
WT100 (World Top 100)
Final Results!! 2
45 CHARLOTTE PUDDING
46 MARSHALL D. TEECH (BLACKBEARD)
47 KIKUNOJO
48 IZO
49 KOZUKI HIYORI (KOMURASAKI)
50 SHIRAHOSHI
51 PELL
52 ISSHO (FUJITORA)
53 SAKAZUKI (AKAINU)
54 OTAMA
55 KILLER
56 ULTI
57 BENN BECKMAN
58 KOALA
59 BORSALINO (KIZARU)
60 GAIMON
61 PEDRO
62 MONKEY D. DRAGON
63 THOUSAND SUNNY
64 BEPO
65 KAIDO
66 ROCKSTAR
67 DR. HIRILUK
68 REBECCA
69 PAULY
70 UROUGE
71 NAMULE
72 SEÑOR PINK
73 CAVENDISH
74 GECKO MORIA
75 KAROO
76 MONET
77 KAKU
78 ORLUMBUS
79 EMPORIO IVANKOV
80 MORGANS
81 BELLE-MÈRE
82 BASIL HAWKINS
83 DENJIRO (KYOSHIRO)
84 GIN
85 JEWELRY BONNEY
86 CHARLOTTE LINLIN
87 MARGUERITE
88 WYPER
89 KUNG-FU DUGONGS
90 CHARLOTTE MONTD'OR
91 CAESAR CLOWN
92 KIN'EMON
93 ZEFF
94 VISTA
95 CHARLOTTE PEROSPERO
96 KAWAMATSU
97 PANDAMAN
98 BARTHOLOMEW KUMA
99 CHARLOTTE CRACKER
100 CHOUCHOU
PANDA
President Morgans' Summary
Big News! Nami has broken the stranglehold of the Monster Trio! This is part of the fun of worldwide voting results!!
Thank you for all of your votes! You can see results from #101 on down at the official results website: https://onepiecewt100.com/

COMING NEXT VOLUME:

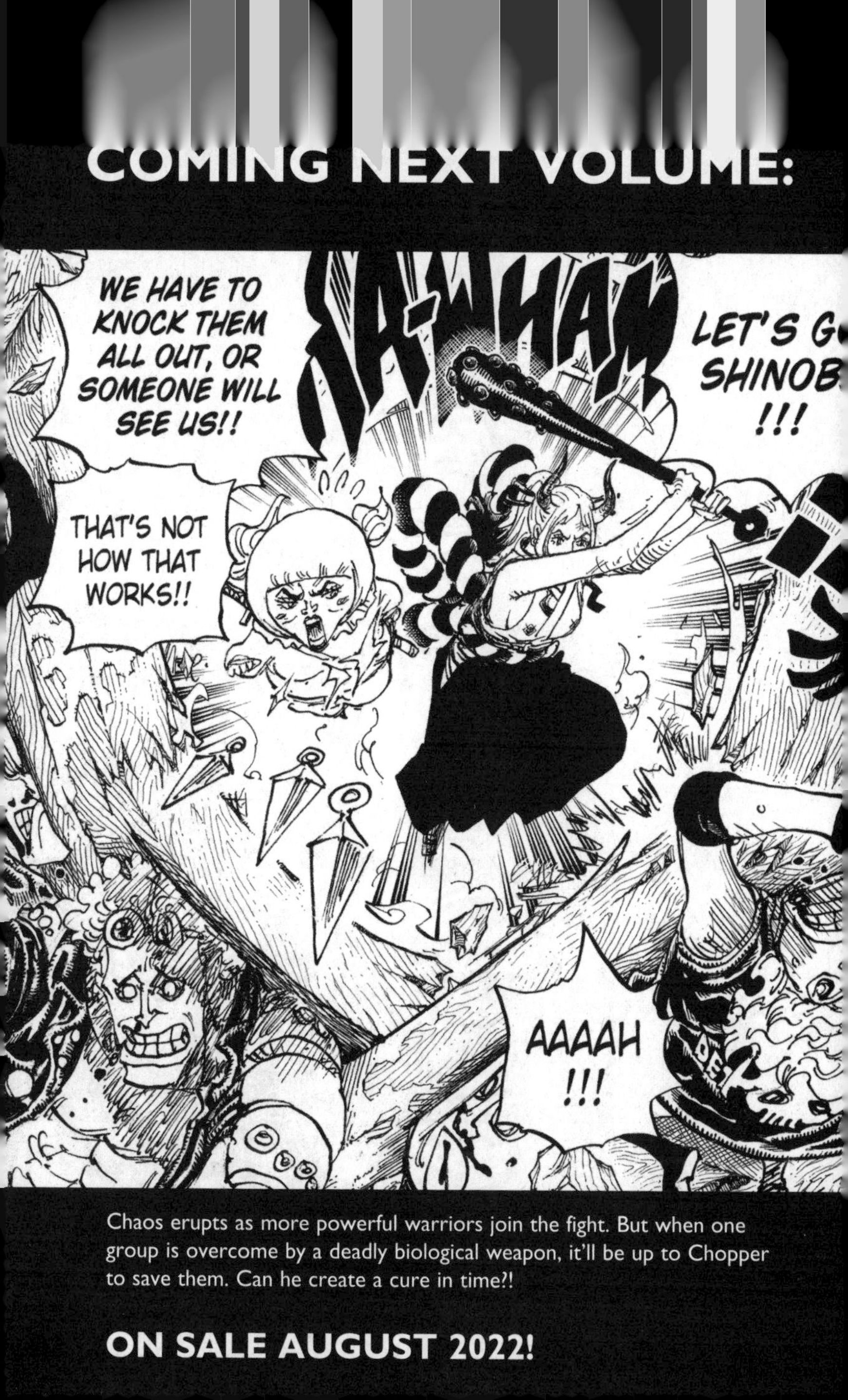
LET'S G
SHINOB
!!!
WE HAVE TO KNOCK THEM ALL OUT, OR SOMEONE WILL SEE US!!
THAT'S NOT HOW THAT WORKS!!
AAAAH !!!

Chaos erupts as more powerful warriors join the fight. But when one group is overcome by a deadly biological weapon, it'll be up to Chopper to save them. Can he create a cure in time?!

ON SALE AUGUST 2022!

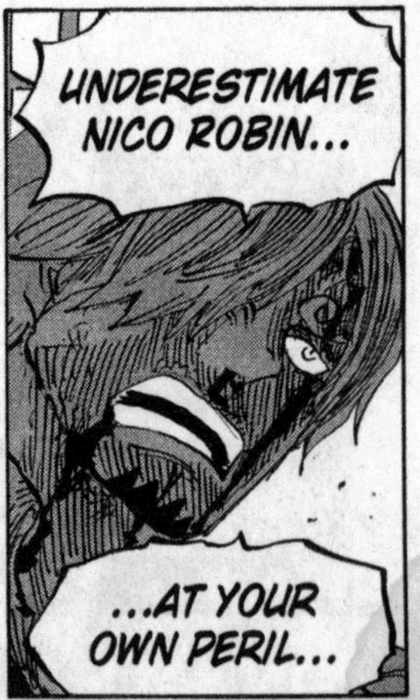
UNDERESTIMATE NICO ROBIN...
...AT YOUR OWN PERIL...

尾田栄一郎

Did you press it?
Be honest, you pressed it! Didn't you?
Well, it's not a video!!! Aha ha ha ha ha!! Gotcha!!
You just can't help but click on that triangle, huh? I saw a
triangle earlier and thought it was a video. Turned out it was
just a sandwich.
Oh, things on paper don't move? Well, that's where you're
wrong. This story is moving, and it's not gonna stop.
Hope you enjoy the connecting covers!!
Here's volume 99, with 100 in sight!!
Let's gooooo!!!

-Eiichiro Oda, 2021

Eiichiro Oda began his manga career at the age of
17, when his one-shot cowboy manga **Wanted!**
won second place in the coveted Tezuka manga
awards. Oda went on to work as an assistant to
some of the biggest manga artists in the industry,
including Nobuhiro Watsuki, before winning the
Hop Step Award for new artists. His pirate
adventure **One Piece**, which debuted in
Weekly Shonen Jump in 1997, quickly became
one of the most popular manga in Japan.

ONE PIECE VOL. 99
WANO PART 10

SHONEN JUMP Manga Edition

STORY AND ART BY EIICHIRO ODA

Translation/Stephen Paul
Touch-Up Art & Lettering/Vanessa Satone
Design/Yukiko Whitley
Editor/Alexis Kirsch

Printed in the U.S.A.

Published by VIZ Media, LLC
P.O. Box 77010
San Francisco, CA 94107

10 9 8 7 6 5 4 3 2 1
First printing, May 2022

viz.com

PARENTAL ADVISORY
ONE PIECE is rated T for Teen and is recommended for ages 13 and up. This volume contains fantasy violence and tobacco usage.

ratings.viz.com

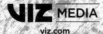

DEMON SLAYER
KIMETSU NO YAIBA

Story and Art by
KOYOHARU GOTOUGE

In Taisho-era Japan, kindhearted Tanjiro Kamado makes a living selling charcoal. But his peaceful life is shattered when a demon slaughters his entire family. His little sister Nezuko is the only survivor, but she has been transformed into a demon herself! Tanjiro sets out on a dangerous journey to find a way to return his sister to normal and destroy the demon who ruined his life.

RATED TEEN

VIZ

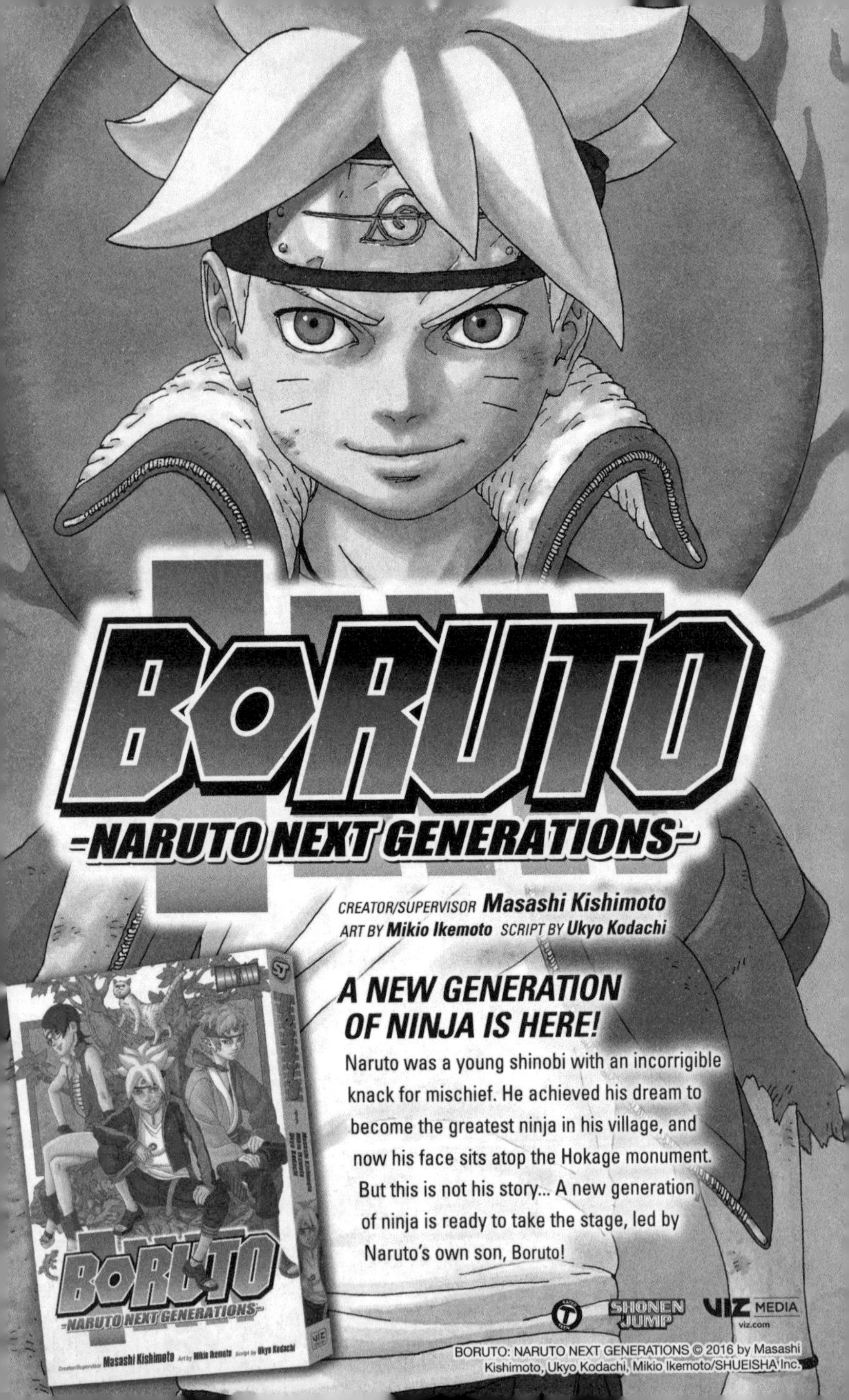
BORUTO
-NARUTO NEXT GENERATIONS-
CREATOR/SUPERVISOR Masashi Kishimoto
ART BY Mikio Ikemoto SCRIPT BY Ukyo Kodachi
A NEW GENERATION OF NINJA IS HERE!
Naruto was a young shinobi with an incorrigible knack for mischief. He achieved his dream to become the greatest ninja in his village, and now his face sits atop the Hokage monument. But this is not his story... A new generation of ninja is ready to take the stage, led by Naruto's own son, Boruto!
BORUTO
-NARUTO NEXT GENERATIONS-
Masashi Kishimoto
SHONEN JUMP
VIZ MEDIA
viz.com
BORUTO: NARUTO NEXT GENERATIONS © 2016 by Masashi Kishimoto, Ukyo Kodachi, Mikio Ikemoto/SHUEISHA Inc.

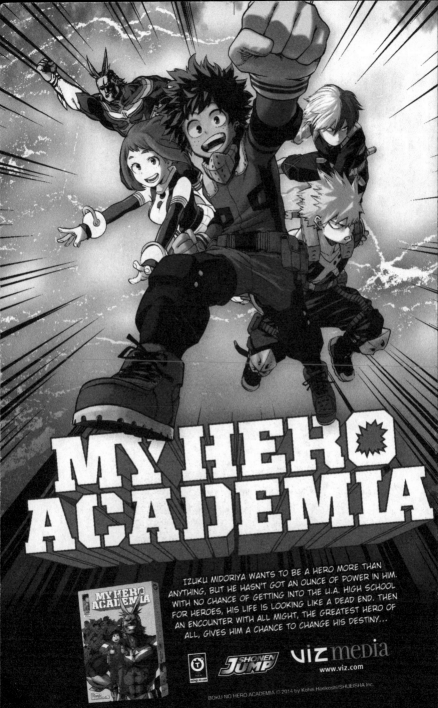

THE ACTION-PACKED SUPERHERO COMEDY ABOUT
ONE MAN'S AMBITION TO BE A HERO FOR FUN!
ONE-PUNCH MAN
STORY BY
ONE
ART BY
YUSUKE MURATA
ONE-PUNCH MAN
01
ONE
YUSUKE MURATA
SHONEN JUMP MANGA
Nothing about Saitama passes the eyeball test when it comes to superheroes, from his lifeless expression to his bald head to his unimpressive physique. However, this average-looking guy has a not-so-average problem—he just can't seem to find an opponent strong enough to take on!
Can he finally find an opponent who can go toe-to-toe with him and give his life some meaning? Or is he doomed to a life of superpowered boredom?
RATED T FOR TEEN
ratings.viz.com
SHONEN JUMP
viz media
www.viz.com
ONE-PUNCH MAN © 2012 by ONE, Yusuke Murata/SHUEISHA Inc.

THE PROMISED NEVERLAND

STORY BY KAIU SHIRAI
ART BY POSUKA DEMIZU

Emma, Norman and Ray are the brightest kids at the Grace Field House orphanage. And under the care of the woman they refer to as "Mom," all the kids have enjoyed a comfortable life. Good food, clean clothes and the perfect environment to learn—what more could an orphan ask for? One day, though, Emma and Norman uncover the dark truth of the outside world they are forbidden from seeing.

You're Reading in the Wrong Direction!!

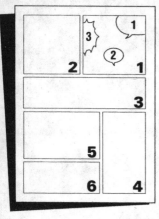

Whoops! Guess what? You're starting at the wrong end of the comic!

…It's true! In keeping with the original Japanese format, **One Piece** is meant to be read from right to left, starting in the upper-right corner.

Unlike English, which is read from left to right, Japanese is read from right to left, meaning that action, sound effects, and word-balloon order are completely reversed…something which can make readers unfamiliar with Japanese feel pretty backwards themselves. For this reason, manga or Japanese comics published in the U.S. in English have sometimes been published "flopped"— that is, printed in exact reverse order, as though seen from the other side of a mirror.

By flopping pages, U.S. publishers can avoid confusing readers, but the compromise is not without its downside. For one thing, a character in a flopped manga series who once wore in the original Japanese version a T-shirt emblazoned with "M A Y" (as in "the merry month of") now wears one which reads "Y A M"! Additionally, many manga creators in Japan are themselves unhappy with the process, as some feel the mirror-imaging of their art skews their original intentions.

We are proud to bring you Eiichiro Oda's **One Piece** in the original unflopped format. For now, though, turn to the other side of the book and let the journey begin…!

—Editor